THE LAST ENGLISH
REVOLUTIONARY

THE LAST ENGLISH REVOLUTIONARY

TOM WINTRINGHAM
1898–1949

Hugh Purcell

SUTTON PUBLISHING

First published in the United Kingdom in 2004 by
Sutton Publishing Limited · Phoenix Mill
Thrupp · Stroud · Gloucestershire · GL5 2BU

British Library Cataloguing in Publication Data
A catalogue record for this book is available from the British Library.

ISBN 0-7509-3080-2

Typeset in 11/14.5pt Sabon.
Typesetting and origination by
Sutton Publishing Limited.
Printed and bound in England by
J.H. Haynes & Co. Ltd, Sparkford.

Contents

List of Illustrations

Acknowledgements

I am grateful to the Director of Archives, Patricia Methven, and her staff at the Liddell Hart Centre for Military Archives (LHCMA) for sorting through the Wintringham papers and for being so helpful to me; and to The Trustees for giving permission to me to quote from them. I have researched in ten other libraries with source material by or about Tom: in London the National Archives (NA), the Marx Memorial Library (MM Lib), the British Library (BL) and the Imperial War Museum Sound Archives (IWM); in Manchester the National Museum of Labour History (NMLH), which contains files on the history of the Communist Party of Great Britain (CPGB); in Salford the Working Class Movement Library (WCML); in Oxford the Bodleian Library; in Leeds the Liddle Collection in the University Library; in Holt, Norfolk, the Library of Gresham's School; and finally the Russian Centre for the Preservation and Study of Contemporary Historical Documents in Moscow (RGASPI). My thanks to them.

I must acknowledge two publishers: Faber for permission to quote from Jason Gurney's *Crusade in Spain* and also to quote from the poem 'The Road these Times Must Take' by C. Day Lewis, printed in Julian Symon's book *The Thirties*; and Penguin Books for permission to quote John Cornford's poem 'Full Moon at Tierz' published in *Spanish Civil War Verse*. All Tom Wintringham's poems, published or not, come from his papers in LHCMA.

I thank Anne Swingler, Norman Mackenzie and the Right Hon. Michael Foot PC, the only three people I found outside Tom Wintringham's family who still remember him; Laura Rodriguez, who interpreted for me at Jarama; the late Martin Lancaster, whose student thesis on Tom contained interesting material on his family background in Grimsby; Professor Kevin Morgan of Manchester University (the biographer of Harry Pollitt), who was most helpful in suggesting where to research and in answering my queries; Professor Paul Preston of the London School of Economics, who guided me towards Moscow and answered queries about Spain; Professor

Alon Kadish of the Hebrew University, Jerusalem, who told me surprising things about Wintringham and the Jewish resistance movement in the 1940s; Professor Cedric Cullingford, who assessed Tom's poetry for me; Monty Johnstone, who must be an early port of call for anyone writing about the CPGB; and Shaun Spiers, who very generously gave me his research notes on Wintringham and in particular his paper 'Tom Wintringham and the Socialist Way of War', which he delivered to the Institute of Historical Research in 1988; and finally Adam Sisman, who made the inventory of the Wintringham Archive.

I thank most sincerely David Fernbach, my predecessor in the Wintringham Archive and the only person who has written about Tom's life in detail before. I found indispensable his unpublished manuscript 'Tom Wintringham and the People's Army', as also his long article 'Tom Wintringham and the Socialist Defence Strategy' published in the *History Workshop Journal*. David gave me letters about Tom written in the late 1970s by those who had known him at different stages of his life; without these this biography, literally, would not have been possible. Finally, David read through this manuscript and came up with corrections and suggestions.

I am grateful to my literary agent, Mandy Little, who went beyond the call of duty and made helpful remarks about my manuscript, more than once; and to my knowledgeable and sympathetic editor, Christopher Feeney.

Above all I must thank Tom's three children, Oliver, Lesley and Ben. They have all been helpful in their different ways and I only hope they think now that this biography of their father is true and was worth writing. I must single out Oliver, or O.J. as he is known in the family. Years ago he asked me to write about Tom's life. From first to last he has been encouraging, tactful, always ready to help and supply me with family material; always supportive of what I wanted to say about his father and mother, which can't have been easy. He made this biographer's task a most enjoyable one.

Introduction

You probably have not heard of Tom Wintringham; but by the time you have finished this book I hope you will agree that you should have.

At present he exists as a footnote to standard histories of the first half of the last century. In *English History 1914–1945* A.J.P. Taylor says that Wintringham was the only middle-class communist revolutionary sent to prison before the General Strike of 1926 – and he was pulled in by mistake. I do not agree with the second of these statements. There was every reason to gaol him for sedition if you thought the Incitement to Mutiny Act of 1797 was worth enforcing. Then Hugh Thomas in *The Spanish Civil War* writes that it is at least possible that Wintringham should be given credit for the idea of the International Brigades. I more than agree with that. Wintringham was a seminal figure, particularly in the formation of the British Battalion which he led in its first and costliest engagement, the battle of Jarama. Finally, Angus Calder attributes to Wintringham the title of his own book *The People's War*, and goes on to call him the best known 'populariser' of war in 1940 and the inspirer of the Home Guard. All that is true. No one person founded the Home Guard but it was Wintringham more than anybody else who devised do-it-yourself defence. He called his best-selling manual *New Ways of War* and its tactics were adopted by people's armies in different wars, in different parts of the world.

He was a most versatile writer. As the foremost, in fact the only, British Marxist expert on warfare during the 1930s and 1940s he wrote several books and many pamphlets to propagate his views. During the Second World War he became a household name as a result of his regular articles about home defence and the war abroad in *Picture Post* and the *Daily Mirror*, and for his many talks on the BBC. He was the author, it may now be revealed, of *Your M.P.*, the anonymously written, 'scurrilous and muck-spreading tract', in the words of one of its targets, that sold a quarter of a million copies and helped sink the Tories in the 1945 general election. His memoir of the Spanish Civil War, *English Captain*, is considered one of the few autobiographies of that war in English to rate as war literature and his poems, particularly of the Spanish war, are in published anthologies.

Wintringham's main achievement, however, was to explore a distinctively English way to revolution. He was expelled from the Communist Party in 1938 for refusing to end a notorious affair with an alleged Trotskyite spy, but his political views were already diverging. Three years before he had written a seminal article 'Who is for Liberty?' that called for an English revolution. At the start of the Second World War, when the Communist Party, always a branch of the Comintern or Communist International, took its orders from Moscow and suddenly decided that fascism was not worth fighting, Wintringham moved towards the mainstream of British politics and joined with George Orwell, J.B. Priestley and others to form a group of so-called 'revolutionary patriots'. They believed that Hitler could only be beaten if Britain was a country worth dying for, and that meant a socialist Britain. After the threat of invasion had receded, Wintringham and Richard Acland founded a new political party 'on the revolutionary side of socialism', so Tom said, to criticise war policy and prepare for a new Britain of 'vital democracy' and 'moral socialism'. It was called Common Wealth and it won over 100,000 votes in the 1945 election, a rare achievement for a minor party in British politics.

Wintringham was 'a uniquely English revolutionary', which is how he is described in the latest edition of the *Dictionary of National Biography*, and it is my intention to elevate him from a footnote of British history to the main text.

Why has recognition of Wintringham come so late? In part it is because he was written out of history by the Communist Party; but because he had been a Communist, the so-called 'Red Revolutionary' was also denied his due by the official historian of the Home Guard. Also it is because he died prematurely, in 1949. Partly it is because his papers have only recently been placed in the Liddell Hart Centre at King's College, London University.

I first saw Wintringham's extraordinary archive soon after his daughter Lesley and I viewed the Ken Loach film about the Spanish Civil War *Land and Freedom*. The film spoke to us. It opens with the granddaughter of a veteran of the old International Brigade, who has just died, clearing up his few effects. She pulls down a suitcase from the top of a cupboard and out spill the memorabilia of Spain: medals, photographs, love letters, political speeches, even a knotted bandana holding the red soil of Spain. Lesley and I left the cinema subdued, but I had a mission. I caught the Eurostar to

Brussels and there, in the house of Wintringham's elder son, were his father's suitcases. I gave them names which later appeared in the inventory. Cunard White Star Line Suitcase had written on it, in the hand of Tom's second wife Kitty, 'Common Wealth'. Larger Black Suitcase was labelled 'World War One and Prison'. Small Black Suitcase was called 'Spain', and in it were encapsulated the idealism, the romance, the pain and tragedy of Tom's war, everything except the bandana. There were other cases too, each containing over twenty numbered files. Kitty obviously intended that one day Tom's story would be written.

So I began, and travelled to Moscow. There I saw Wintringham's file, once held by the Comintern, which includes reports about his relationship in Spain with Kitty Bowler and her interrogation for spying. I read original letters between them which gave me the uneasy feeling that I was the first person to do so. Would Tom have handed over his private correspondence to a Comintern agent? No, they had obviously been intercepted, and read by me in their virgin state over sixty years later. Such is the intrusion of a biographer. In the Wintringham suitcases, too, are love letters to and from several other women, for Tom was a notorious womaniser. Kitty knew this was an essential part of his character for posterity to judge.

The first requirement of a biographer is to know your subject and this is very difficult when he has been dead for over half a century. I have been helped by a surprising amount of written memories of him as well as by contemporary material, all of which I acknowledge below and, of course, by the recollections of his children. But the subject who emerged from two years of research was, essentially, a man who defined himself intentionally and unintentionally through his own writing: his poetry, his fictional prose, his personal correspondence, his political journalism and his books. Few biographers can have such a range of writing to assist them.

Tom Wintringham is to me a very likeable man, worthy of respect. With historical hindsight he was right about many things but wrong about some of the things that really mattered. How could he have misjudged Stalin so badly? How could he have believed that Britain was on the brink of revolution in the 1930s? He was a man of action as well as ideas, and placing him in the forefront of some of the most dramatic events of the first half of the twentieth century has been the other challenge of this book.

Whether he merits the title of 'The Last English Revolutionary' I leave you to judge.

ONE

The Rebel

With Tom Wintringham I share the view that the battles of old should
have an epic quality that leaves an atmosphere behind. So when I
approached the River Jarama, just beyond the final urban sprawl and
industrial detritus of south Madrid, my heart began to sink. I was in a
bleak no-man's-land. Cold wind gusted through the sandy scrub and blew
paper rubbish from the nearby dump on to the high wire fence that
protected the nearest farm. The farmhouse was a trailer, lived in by an
Ecuadorian who had not heard of the battle of Jarama in 1937, and it was
guarded by a barking mastiff. A 'Beware of the Dog' poster was suitably
worded for this wild place: *No Pago El Entervio!* (We Do Not Want To
Bury You!). After driving north a further kilometre over a slight hill and
then west off the unmade track I came to a farm on the site of the *casa
blanca*, the white house shown on the map in Wintringham's book about
Jarama called *English Captain*. A wall plaque unveiled by General Gomez
Zamalloa in 1952, dedicated to the Nationalist (Francoist) 'heroes' who
had defeated the International Brigades fighting for the Spanish Republic,
showed that I was at the right place. Incredibly, the old farmer Rafael
who now owned the property had been one of these so-called heroes.
I recognised his Moorish features and challenged him with the excuse that
I was writing about the 'English Captain', the leader of the British Battalion
which he had fought against. His suspicious look changed to a smug smile.
'Why did he lose when he occupied the high ground?' he asked. I said it
was hard to recognise the lie of the land now. 'That's what General
Zamalloa said when he came back to give us the monument; but it's
because he spent most of the battle on his knees!'

Old Rafael walked me to the ridge of Suicide Hill that sloped down to
the River Jarama. It was here that many of the British Battalion under
Wintringham's command had perished. After only two days' fighting,
nearly two-thirds of the four hundred or so men who had advanced to
Suicide Hill had been killed, wounded or captured; one of them was

Wintringham, shot in the thigh. 'It was very fierce. Soldiers scrabbled in the earth with their bare hands to find cover from the bullets,' said Rafael. His grandson gave me rusty machine-gun clips and a bullet sharpened to a point still in its cartridge:

> Death stalked the olive trees
> Picking his men
> His leaden finger beckoned
> Again and again.[1]

Now I could see it, almost feel it; the confusion and ignorance, the fear and bravery of young British volunteers in their first battle up against Franco's professional Army of Africa, supported by German artillery. In fact they surrendered Suicide Hill but then the survivors regrouped and held the line. The Nationalist advance was halted. A victory? A defeat? What does it matter after all these years? But the undoubted heroism of the International Brigades, volunteer defenders of democracy holding fascism at bay in Spain, remains one of the few noble episodes of the 1930s.

It was the battle of Jarama that first brought Tom Wintringham to people's attention. Then, in the Second World War, he became a household name, particularly to the millions of readers of the *Daily Mirror* and *Picture Post* and listeners to the BBC. He is still remembered as the 'Red Revolutionary' who taught guerrilla warfare to the Home Guard and spoke of his dreams of a socialist Britain to anybody who would listen. In the 1920s he had played a seminal role in the growth of the Communist Party and served a prison sentence for doing so. In all he deserves to be remembered as a uniquely English revolutionary, a title that would have given him much satisfaction. For near that very spot where I now stood with Rafael, the old soldier from the Army of Africa, Tom Wintringham had lain over sixty years before, in dusty earth under the olive trees, and recalled his revolutionary forefathers.

It was dawn. Above him on Suicide Hill a wounded man cried out. A cigarette glowed momentarily and in the frail moonlight he could make out stragglers, perhaps some whose nerve had broken, returning to the front. Tom shivered. Once more his mind turned to the nagging question: why?

Why was I here? Eight or nine generations back before my birth one of my ancestors, a Nonconformist hedge preacher, had his tongue torn out for 'carrying on subversive propaganda'. Something of that man's attitude to life had come through to me from my parents, the most really liberal people I know. That hedge preacher had sent me here. So had the sickly child Tom, who had started to read war stories at the age of ten, had learnt before he was fourteen all the battles, sieges and skirmishes of Wellington's war in Spain. So had the poet who had no time for poems because the miseries of the world shadowed by war 'were miseries and would not let him rest'. So had the lad in prison for incitement to mutiny and sedition; waiting for mutiny and a General Strike. I was here because of all I was and would be.[2]

Wintringham wrote *English Captain*, his account of the war in Spain, when he was back home in Grimsby in 1938 recovering from his wounds. He was still, just, a member of the Communist Party. Forty years old, his life had reached a watershed; but whatever the future would bring, he would see it in the context of his past. He held an heroic view of history, especially when the heroes were revolutionaries, and he was proud that his part of Britain, the East Midlands, had a continuous history of uprising and dissent. The men of Cleethorpes and Grimsby had resisted the Vikings. Not far south, at Ely, Hereward the Wake had held the Normans at bay. Lincolnshire men had marched on London in a so-called Pilgrimage of Grace to oppose Henry VIII's Reformation. Above all, in the English Civil War the Levellers had been particularly strong in the Eastern Command of Cromwell's New Model Army.

Just before going to Spain in 1936 Wintringham wrote *Mutiny – a Survey of Mutinies from Spartacus to Invergordon*. He clearly identified with the Leveller leader John Lilburne, who had dared to oppose Cromwell for betraying the English Revolution. Like Lilburne, Wintringham was a political pamphleteer imprisoned for his writing and a soldier shortly to be wounded in the cause. Wintringham called this chapter 'In Arms, in Judgement and Conscience' and it is a title that could serve as his own epitaph, for as his nephew wrote: 'the adventures of Tom's life sprang from his belief that a good cause deserves action and if necessary sacrifice'.[3]

Wintringham's own genealogy speaks to the liberal and Nonconformist conscience. The hedge preacher who had his tongue torn out by order of a royal court of justice in about 1680 was called Workman and that was Tom's mother's maiden name. In the fifth and sixth recorded generations of the Wintringham family before Tom there were a blacksmith, a cloth worker and a rope maker, all self-educated artisans who quite possibly adopted Nonconformism. As for later generations, Tom wrote:

> They did not join the Church of England, or the Conservative party, or even support wholeheartedly the Liberal Imperialism of Asquith and Lloyd George, in those years before the Great War when the full development of imperialism in Britain was moulding almost all the middle-class into narrow-minded conformity. They were tolerant. I could read anything and everything. I even read about Socialism, in William Morris and H.G. Wells, Bellamy and Jack London, before 1914.[4]

So politics in the Wintringham family meant Gladstone's great Liberal Party. Tom's paternal grandfather was a Liberal agent and his uncle, after whom Tom was named, was elected Independent (anti-Lloyd George) Liberal MP for Louth, Lincolnshire in 1918. After his death, from a heart attack literally on the floor of the House of Commons, his widow Margaret Wintringham took over his seat. Thus she became the first ever English woman MP, for her colleague Nancy Astor was American born.

The overriding image of the Wintringham men at this time is that conveyed by an 1881 election poster titled 'Four True Citizens', and pillars of the Grimsby establishment they look, too. Led by Alderman John Wintringham 'the Old General', who was five times mayor in the mid-nineteenth century, the bewhiskered, mostly balding gentlemen look down from the poster with patrician authority. 'Vote for Wintringham!' Tom's father, John Fildes Wintringham, the brother of the candidate standing for office, was a partner in the most important solicitors' practice in town, Grange and Wintringham. In fact they had Grimsby under their thumbs. 'They were joint secretaries to the Waterworks Company and solicitors to the Anglo-French Steamship Company; and John Wintringham was Chairman of the Gas Company.'[5] Tom's birth certificate was signed by the town registrar who happened to be another uncle, W.H. Wintringham. Grange and Wintringham were known in Grimsby as 'the office' and resented for their power. Today the Wintringham legacy is a street and school bearing the family name; and the solicitors' practice still thrives. Much of the practice's work used to be maritime law, dealing with the collision of shipping in Grimsby harbour for instance. John Fildes used to recite for his grandchildren the Rules of the Road at Sea:

Green to Green or Red to Red; Perfect Safety–Go Ahead!
In Danger with No Room to Turn; Ease Her, Stop Her, Go Astern!

What is remarkable about Tom's upbringing is how different it was from that of nearly all the other early British Communists. In fact he represented the bourgeois world which they were out to destroy. When Tom grew up he was very aware of this. Perhaps taking comfort from the fact that his hero John Lilburne was also a gentleman born, he distanced himself from Grimsby by writing disapprovingly of 'the thriving, pushful fishing town where the half-democracy of getting rich quick reigned'.[6] A Communist friend writing many years later put it more kindly, but nevertheless with an edge of disapproval, when he wrote: 'Tom was brought up in the untroubled hubris of the upper middle class before the first world war.'[7] Tom could never escape the perception of many of his future comrades that he did not truly belong. It marked his life in the Party. When he arrived at Albacete in Spain in 1936 to join the International Brigades he identified his background as petit bourgeois,[8] as if to belittle his middle-class origins. There was nothing petit about Tom's upbringing.

Thomas Henry Wintringham was born on 15 May 1898 and his address was registered as Danesbury in the Bargate area of Grimsby. Soon the family moved out of town to the then salubrious village of Humberston. At The Garden House, built for his timber merchant grandfather 'The Old General' and now a residential home for the elderly, Tom spent his early years. He called himself a sickly child for he suffered from a heart murmur, but sepia photographs show a sturdy, round-faced boy looking confidently at the camera. He has glossy hair that comes as a surprise since all photographs from his late teens reveal first a pronounced receding hairline and later a bald head. It is easy to picture him with his seven brothers and sisters, of whom he was the third, playing in the ten-acre garden or reading his father's large collection of military history in the high-ceilinged library of the Victorian manse. In the background are servants and a governess.

Tom's favourite early reading was of battles; he became 'ecstatic over Fitchett's *Fights for the Flag* and *How England Saved Europe*'.[9] Eventually he made a living out of this 'fierce interest in fighting' as he put it and he retained from his childhood reading the 'ripping yarn' style of writing about it:

Cornered, he fought single-handedly over a hundred men. Bleeding from many wounds he would not surrender alive. . . . When the seventh bullet struck him, he fell. With him fell the hopes of the Levellers, and of the yeomen, the free farmers and peasants of this country.[10]

George Orwell said that Wintringham's stories of past glories were 'most spiritedly retold, much as A.G. Henty would have told them if he had a Marxist training'.[11]

Tom was very close to his mother, who was called Muv by everyone. He wrote in one of his semi-autobiographical stories: 'he was safe from everything while he kept his eyes shut, Muv had taught him when he was a small boy. He had been frightened not of the dark but of the fire-lit corners where things moved.'[12] Muv was born Eliza Workman and she is remembered as an imposing presence, a woman of good works who supported the suffragettes, hosted garden parties for the Red Cross and later worked for the welfare of soldiers' dependants. She held strong democratic convictions and one of her local victories was to insist that the village carpenter should read the lesson in church. Religion, according to Muv, was first and foremost a matter of morality and in the years ahead her moral disapproval of Tom's behaviour would be decisive. Quite possibly she was the one dominant woman in his life.

Furnished with this picture of serene middle-class Edwardian England, it is salutary to compare Harry Pollitt's early years. Pollitt was the leading figure in the British Communist Party throughout most of its existence and he was wholly representative of its solid proletarian membership. He was born eight years before Tom into what Engels described as the 'classic soil' of industrial capitalism, the textile village of Droylsden in south Lancashire. In the 1890s a *Clarion* journalist provided a telling description of the landscape:

Under smoky skies are dirty huddled towns, linked together by clanking chains of hideous railway. . . . Everywhere you will find steam hissing and smoke scowling: factories, forges, chimneys, furnaces, coalpit heads, streams fouled by chemical works.[13]

Pollitt described the themes of his early life as poverty, sickness and death. Three of his five brothers and sisters died in infancy and his mother, Mary Louisa Pollitt, ground out her life in the local mill where Harry joined her when he was twelve. She died in 1940 just as he was completing his autobiography *Serving My Time*:

> My mind is crowded with memories of her as I write these lines – memories of watching for her to come home from the mill, tired out, the once rosy cheeks faded by ten-hour day after ten-hour day in the hot, noisy weaving shed, by frequent confinements and by never ending poverty. . . . Every time she put her shawl round me before going to the mill on wet or very cold mornings, I swore that when I grew up I would pay the bosses out for the hardships she suffered. . . . I was unconsciously voicing the wrongs of my class, wrongs that one day the working class in Britain will pay out as surely as they have done in Russia.[14]

For Pollitt's twenty-first birthday his mother saved up to buy him the first volume of Marx's *Das Capital*. Such was the bitter inheritance of many early Communists and such their faith in communism's founding fathers. Wintringham would have much to prove.

After three years at Arnold House Preparatory School in St John's Wood, London, Tom aged thirteen was sent to school at Holt near the Norfolk coast. Why was it that Gresham's, a small school owned by the Fishmongers Company and founded some three hundred and fifty years earlier by Sir Thomas Gresham, produced so many boys who became notorious Communists, of whom Wintringham was the first? He was followed by Cedric Belfrage, exposed as a KGB agent in 1945, then James Klugmann the spy master and official historian of the CPGB, who recruited as spy another former Gresham's pupil, Donald Maclean; and he was a friend of another life-long Communist educated at Gresham's, Roger Simon. Then there were the two outstanding Gresham's poets, W.H. Auden who was a so-called fellow traveller or communist sympathiser in the 1930s and his friend Stephen Spender, a paid-up but somewhat reluctant Communist during the same period. Perhaps a fairer question would be why Gresham's produced so many outstanding intellectuals – the musicians Lennox Berkeley and Benjamin Britten, artist Ben Nicholson, broadcaster Lord Reith, scientists Sir Christopher Cockerill and Sir Alan Hodgkin, another poet John Pudney, and the President of Ireland Erskine Childers. One answer lies in the reforming principles of the two headmasters during this period, G.W.S. Howson and J.R. Eccles, founders of the modern Gresham's. They rescued it from near oblivion and turned it into the first progressive school of the twentieth century.

Howson's controversial legacy was the honours system which he set up in place of school rules. There were only three rules, otherwise Howson made it clear what he wanted and left the boys to police themselves, and these were the 'unholy trinity' of no smoking, no swearing and no 'impurity'. Presumably this last rule referred to the temptations to which teenagers in an all-male community are susceptible, from the heinous crime that 'dares not speak its name' to the lesser offence that later generations of public schoolboys were told would make hair grow on the palms of their hands, namely masturbation. Why else would only prefects be allowed to wear trousers with pockets? The point was that under the honours system the offender was required to confess and if he did not, then his peers were expected to inform on him. This was all very well in theory as a system intended to give morals a real meaning based on trust, but in practice it led to a fearful and furtive atmosphere, according to W.H. Auden writing in 1934. He went on to say: 'The best reason I have for opposing Fascism is that at school I lived in a Fascist state.'[15]

Howson hated the traditional public school ethos of competitive sport and muscular Christianity; instead he encouraged free debate and a more holistic attitude to learning. He established a modern curriculum that, for example, no longer divided the staff between gentlemen and scientists and gave equal weight to the teaching of modern and classical languages. A look at the motions proposed in the debating society during Tom's years at the school show how open-minded, indeed radical, was the intellectual atmosphere: 'This House considers that the Labour unrest of the past few years has been mainly due to the policy of the present Government' (1913); 'This House deplores the popular attitude of the nation towards reports of German atrocities' (1914). The latter proposal, that won by a landslide, was put forward when anti-German feeling on the home front was at its height. Statues of Prince Albert were being tarred and feathered.

In 1915, T.H. Wintringham proposed 'That this House would regret the adoption in England of compulsory military service'.[16] So, in a long forgotten debate, we see the genesis of Wintringham's military thinking, though his arguments in the debate were economic whereas later they became political. In 1939, just before the outbreak of the Second World War, he wrote: 'instead of turning towards conscription we ought to be turning, in the interests of efficiency, towards making the Army more voluntary. Over two thousand years of warfare the more successful armies had been created by communities relatively freer and more democratic than their opponents.'[17] This was the basis of Wintringham's belief in a people's army, first argued for at Gresham's school when he was sixteen.

Tom took away from Gresham's the encouragement to think for himself across a range of disciplines and to value equally highly the arts and the sciences, the poetic and the practical. Later, he would take the same pleasure in writing a poem as in dismantling his motorbike on the kitchen floor, a versatility that the women in his life were to find very attractive.

In 1937 Wintringham wrote in his 'Short Autobiography':

When the Great War came I was torn between a half-understood idealist socialism and this fierce interest in fighting. But I was also not quite so interested in war as I used to be, because I had begun to write poetry. I was sixteen. The world was a muddle.

He edited an alternative school magazine called the *Merman* (a male mermaid, presumably a play on the Fishmongers Company) and in it he described himself as one of '*genus veritabile vatum* or the veritable race of poets'.[18] One of Tom's first poems is 'The Funeral of Lord Roberts' (Field Marshal Lord Roberts of Kandahar VC had visited Gresham's a few years before his death in November 1914) and it expresses the romantic view of chivalry so admired, indeed reinvented, by the Victorians:

> Stillness and shaded lights
> And the low muffled murmur of the drums
> So the most perfect of an Empire's knights
> To his last vigil comes.
> All war shall cease, but may there never cease
> Warriors, as he was warrior, for the right.
> Peerless in war, he gave an Empire peace
> A captain, too, of courtesy, a very gentle knight.[19]

Two years later the teenage Tom has taken the sword out of the scabbard in a bloodthirsty, doom-laden poem 'Mine-Sweepers' (obviously inspired by John Masefield's 'Cargoes'). It was published in *The Gresham*, alongside obituaries of Old Boys killed at the front and sad letters of comfort:

Out beyond the shallows where are white waves racing,
Leaping up and laughing, swinging in to shore,
Far upon the deeper seas a darker storm is pacing
Darker than all tempests that have burst on us before. . . .

Proudly come the ships through the whipped seas swinging,
Cleaving through the combers that rasp along the side,
Silent in their strength until the battle-bolts are singing,
And they go in flame and fury down the reddened reeking tide.

Proudly come the ships yet they must follow after us;
We sweep their paths to battle – hold they well the paths we've made
For the seeds of death and terror are in flower, and we, the harvesters
Must reap and pay for reaping, as the English ever payed.

An exercise book of W.H. Auden's schoolboy poetry entitled 'A Third Garland of Poesy', dated November 1923, was found in Wintringham's archive in 1997. Its presence was a puzzle because although Auden and Wintringham met in the 1930s they did not overlap at Gresham's. However, Tom's brother Charles who was killed in a flying accident in 1931, was in Farfield House at Gresham's at the same time as the young Auden. Did Wintringham meet Auden to discuss poetry when he visited the school to see his brother in 1923/4? Did Auden give the exercise book to Charles? We will never know. Nor will we know the relationship between Auden and T.O. Garland who was also a boy in Farfield at this time; for surely 'garland' has a double meaning.

Tom was a success at Gresham's. He won his rugby football colours (so much for his sickly childhood) and became a school prefect. In the autumn of 1915 he took the history exam for Brasenose College, Oxford and answered the following question, no doubt with relish: 'Is it true that the epic belongs to the past?' He was awarded the Brackenbury Scholarship. The Liberal MP Wilfred Roberts was a near contemporary of Tom's at school and he also won a History Exhibition to Oxford. He put their mutual achievement down to 'our history tutor who was a little cripple only about four feet high, C.H.C. Osborne by name. He had advanced ideas and believed in self-government in school.' Roberts remembered Tom's untidiness: 'he wore odd socks, saying that "symmetry was the soul of vulgarity"'.[20] Instead of going straight up to Oxford,

Wintringham enlisted on his eighteenth birthday and on 5 June 1916 he joined the Royal Flying Corps. Romantic that he was, he said he was inspired to join up by the poetry of Rupert Brooke.

Wintringham joined the RFC intending to fly but his eyesight was too poor. His elder brother John, who was then serving in Egypt with the Lincolnshire Yeomanry and later won the Military Cross, advised him to 'try machine gunning. There is quite a lot of science and some mechanics about the job; and there is no greater demand for competent officers in any branch of the army.'[21] Twenty years later Tom was to follow his advice when he became machine-gun instructor to the British Battalion of the International Brigades. However, in 1916 he became a mechanic and dispatch rider attached to a balloon corps. His job was to pick up and deliver to base information about enemy artillery placements and trench lines contained in pouches that had been thrown out of the balloons.

Tom was fortunate not to have been a so-called 'balloonatic'. They floated hazardously over the trenches at a height of a thousand feet, tethered to the ground by a long, long cable. Susceptible to the wind that spun or yanked the balloon at the end of its cable, a sitting target for enemy gunners shooting off 'flaming onions' (balls of fire connected by rope), it is not surprising they became pioneers of the parachute. These were attached to the outside of the basket and packed into an elongated wicker container shaped like a candle snuffer. The balloonatic kept his harness on at all times. Training was minimal: 'When you go, just jump out, and keep your feet together when you land.'[22]

The Second Kite Balloon Corps distinguished itself in April 1917 at Vimy Ridge. The balloonatics were sent up in advance of the attack to photograph the land and observe enemy artillery in order for maps to be drawn. The *Official History of the War* stated: 'It is probable that without such assistance from the air the Vimy bastion would have remained impregnable to a frontal assault'.[23] Tom saw action here:

'Dawn near Vimy'

Mutter and thud and shudder, pulse and pause
The guns are waking and warring over the hill.
Swings a falcon, some small beast in his claws,
The air is still.

The ridge that was pulp in April, bare in May
Is caught in a net of delicate green and gold,
Over our dead the children's flowers sway.
Daisies and gallant buttercups carpet the way
And the broken trenches hold.
While ever incessant, crescent and clamorous
runs,
On the breath of the summer morning, the
curse of the crowded guns.[24]

In his riding jacket Tom carried a little notebook with the identification: 'Second Class Air Mechanic T.H. Wintringham, 13 Squadron, 24 K. B. Section' (kite balloon). It is what was known as a commonplace book, popular at the time, and it contains a hundred pages of pencil-written poetry. On the fly leaf Tom wrote: 'almost all these were written out from memory. . . . They were written to pass the time away, waiting in canvas shelters and forty foot dug outs, in Nissen huts and in bivvies of sandbags. This book has been with me in . . .'[25] There follows a list of thirty-five places that ring ominous bells down the years – Le Hamel, Bethune, Vieille Chapelle, Vimy Ridge, Arras. . . . Tom's favourite poets are here: W.B. Yeats, Rupert Brooke, James Elroy Flecker. Understandably they wrote of doomed youth:

Is it so small a thing
To have enjoyed the sun
To have lived live [*recte* light] in the spring
To have felt [*recte* loved], to have thought, to have done,
To have advanced true friends, and beat down baffling foes;
That we must feign a bliss
Of doubtful future date,
And while we dream on this,
Lose all our present state,
And relegate to worlds yet distant our repose?
(Matthew Arnold, 'From the Hymn of Empedocles')

Some poems are set down in French, Thomas à Kempis is in Latin, and some poems are Tom's own. The notebook is a prodigious feat of memory as much as anything else, showing how deeply Tom needed poetry to escape from boredom and fear. Several of his poems, including this sonnet, are dedicated to F.J.T. (Frederick Taylor), a boy with whom he obviously had a special relationship at Gresham's:

> When Death's swift fingers close about my throat,
> And I forget cloud-shadows on the corn
> Wind in the elm trees, silver of the dawn,
> And scent of the dream flowers that round me float:–
> When through the robing purple of the night,
> or through the great white gateways of the morn,
> I pass and wait, without you and forlorn,
> At some far glimmering limit of the light –
>
> I think that if just then you thought of me,
> If even in your dreams a memory came
> Of the strong bonds that held us, of the flame
> Your eyes knew, and the quiver of your hand
> Gainst mine – I think that God would understand
> And for your sake allow me to go free.[26]

Tom's letters home to Muv ('Dearest old Muv', 'Dearest little old lady') show that his Rupert Brooke image of a romantic but doomed patriot soon wore thin. He became strained – 'the tension of affairs is pretty intolerable', and increasingly disillusioned – 'I have found after eighteen months of utter disgust and discontent . . .'. In one letter dated July 1918 he wrote that he agreed with H.G. Wells: 'more than half of human misery and madness, disaster and despair, crumbling rottenness is due to satisfied stupidity'. He blamed the politicians for 'these dirty and degrading businesses of grabbing wars and half baked strained squabbles' and admitted that he had little faith in democracy. Perhaps fearing the censor, or his own mood, he ended: 'Got to stop. Aren't you glad! Cigarettes, bon. May I have some Ovaltine?'[27] Tom was already interested in socialism. In fact he said years later that he turned down an officer's commission because he was a socialist, although there is no other evidence of this. But he had no time for the sort of postwar revolution that was consuming Russia. He wrote in another letter that it posed a threat to Britain 'greater than anything since Napoleon'.

Tom's hope for the world, he said, was the knowledge of God and the potential of the human spirit. In these letters he wrote as a vulnerable, homesick young man. He was cheered up by a lady at the YMCA who 'took me into a private room, gave me tea, talked a little lightly and gave me a Rupert Brooke book'. He was distressed when on leave he witnessed the death of 'Ezz', most probably his younger sister Lesley. 'I remember her face is worth treasuring most carefully for its beauty, there is no other word for it.' Pathetically, he could not get over the gauche formality of their last meeting:

> I remember we had perhaps an hour and a half and were shy of each other. I remember so vividly that I wanted to kiss her goodbye, and saw she thought so too – and shook hands. We Wintringhams are so left handed, so clumsy in dealing with anyone.[28]

Tom would come out of the war with a great respect for the men who spend their lives with machines. As a public schoolboy he cannot have had much contact with working men, certainly not on equal terms, and now he was working with them with the fellow rank of private. 'The men I meet here are open hearted, strong, capable of carrying the intolerable burden of industrial life in manhood without servility or blind obedience. But they have not the development of brain of choice by reason, of rational vision.'[29] This may sound patronising today, but his respect is clear and also his belief in reason; a belief that was soon to motivate him to plough through the collected works of Marx, Engels and Lenin. Tom reported to Muv a conversation he had with a Tommy who in peacetime was the foreman sugar-boiler at Huntley & Palmer's in Reading. His view on the war was the same as Harry Pollitt's and other anti-war protesters back home: 'He put things this way. "They" are making their millions now. In twenty years time their sons will be at Oxford and they will have got the social places they want. Only when they have got enough to make this certain will this war end. . . .' Tom believed too that the war was about greed. In the same letter, written in September 1916, he told Muv that unless 'the nouveau riche and the business men are controlled then the upper class will fall to the guillotine'. Two years later he might have substituted Bolsheviks for guillotine. He ended circumspectly: 'I can't tell you too much about things. I am not an officer who can censor his own letters.'

In the early summer of 1918 Wintringham was arrested for mutiny. In his book *Mutiny* (1936) he defined the term as 'a revolt by men under discipline of life and death, which does not happen lightly'.[30] This explains why he does not even mention his own mutiny, for it was more of a practical joke that misfired, without political implications. Nevertheless it came at a time when discipline behind the lines was shaky. In Arras Canadian troops held the town for two days against military police. At Etaples troops in hospital broke out and chased away the military police who blocked their way into town. On the face of it, Wintringham's mutiny, as he later described it in an article for *Left Review* in 1935, came in the same category. He was recovering in hospital from a serious bout of flu when some of the walking wounded decided to break out of camp by distracting the guards with a bogus pass placed on top of and enticingly revealing a pornographic pack of cards. They intended to walk into the local town, eat egg and chips and meet 'that ordinary, necessary thing, a woman'. Tom was chosen as the fall guy because he looked young and innocent. The plan worked, though Tom was so unnerved that he spent his freedom simply walking along the sands. He returned quietly to camp but was charged two days later with mutiny. Fortunately the charge was reduced to 'absent without a pass' and the sentence was a fine of six days' pay. '"Dismiss" said the Colonel. It wasn't a mutiny then, but these things happen in mutinies. We were just tired of the war.'[31]

In later years Wintringham's war record of over two years' service as a private on the Western Front and being charged with mutiny were to boost his revolutionary reputation. Probably what would have boosted it more was the label 'Conchie' (conscientious objector) because for most of those who would soon become Communists the war was an imperialist confrontation in which the workers were sacrificed either as cannon fodder or as slaves of the munitions conveyor belt. Pollitt was beaten up more than once for 'opposing the warmongers and their lying jingo propaganda and calling upon the workers to use the opportunity to make war on capitalism'.[32] Undoubtedly, Tom's war experience turned him into a rebel if not yet a revolutionary. He was deeply disillusioned:

'Acceptance'

I would turn traitor if I could
And beauty-monger to the bourgeoisie;
But the eyes of men who died in the dark
Do not forget me.

> I would go back to a fair land,
> And believe in the things I see,
> But these were my friends. They believed, and died;
> They will not let me.[33]

Wintringham was not wounded in the war but, ironically, he was nearly killed as an indirect result of the Armistice on 11 November. He was riding his motorbike near Mons at night when he was dazzled by oncoming headlights, forbidden in previous blackout conditions, and crashed onto a railway line. He suffered severe concussion and spent several weeks in hospital.

He was sent to convalesce at an army hospital at Newton Abbot, Devon. In a letter to his father he worried about politics on the home front. He hated Lloyd George for 'making the Huns pay' and agreed with the 'labour people' that a General Strike might be necessary, 'but it may easily fail and send them over to Bolshevism – the dictatorship of the proletariat'. However, he wrote, he had more important things to worry about such as 'the fitting of a word and the weighting of a line'. He set to with this little epitaph on the war:

> A fat man with false teeth, who tells lies for a living
> Told youth that war was making a man of him;
> Youth smiled, well remembering.[34]

By this time Tom had discovered girls. The Wintringham archive contains love letters to and from at least seven women, the first amour having taken place in Flanders as early as 1916. 'Cher ami . . . je vous embrace, attendante de vous voir . . . Marcelle XXX [sic]'. In fact, revolution and women seemed to dominate Tom's life in equal measure. Generally speaking he behaved, in the words of his younger sister Meg writing in 1938, 'perfectly bloodily'. One of his first girlfriends, a nurse named Gwyneth whom he met at Newton Abbot, put it rather sweetly in a letter that spelt his name WintRingham and continued, 'R stands for Rogue and Rotter and Rancid'. She then added, sounding like the silly flapper she probably was, 'I want that futtograf, quick I do!'[35]

In early 1919 Wintringham discharged himself from the RAF. The actual date of Transfer to the Reserve was 6 March but he seems to have walked out before then, impatient at the 'imbecilities of demobilisation from hospital and the business of winning a pension from the medicos'. He set off to Balliol College (not Brasenose which was in the same group) to take up the scholarship in Modern History he had won four years before. He had rebellion in his blood but he was still a rebel without a cause. 'Fed up with the world', as he put it, and dismissive of any conventional political solution, he 'was trying everything: guild socialism, young liberalism, a little mysticism among Indians, even a little religion: none of it satisfied'.[36] This discontented dabbling was about to change.

TWO

The Bolshevik

Oxford University in 1918 was flooded with eighteen hundred ex-service men, many of them like Tom studying a shortened five-term BA course because they could set their war service against the residential requirement for a degree. The returning warriors found the university an unworldly backwater and became impatient with the 'dreaming spires'. Tom was no exception:

'Balliol College, Oxford'

I have seen a dynamo working
And I have smelt a gasometer
That is why I cannot accept your
    comparison
    of city lamps
    To stars—
Possibly also I have heard too many
of the gasometers of God,
felt too few of his dynamos.[1]

He had little time for his officer and gentlemen fellow students. Early on he and other rebels at Balliol objected to the habit of ex-officers walking round in smart army uniforms underneath their gowns so the rebels, most of whom formed the intellectual elite, appeared in Hall wearing their humble khaki under their scholars' gowns. The point was made and 'after much ribaldry, sober flannels or dark suits were mostly in evidence'. This memory comes from Andrew Rothstein, the first of several life-long Communists to influence the young Wintringham at Oxford and after.

Rothstein was already highly politicised. He claimed to be the only paid-up socialist at Balliol because he had joined the British Socialist Party in April 1917 just after he had arrived from army service to take a full three-year degree. 'Tom and others were inclined to ask my opinions on all sorts of things, especially when the facts about what was going on in Soviet Russia began filtering through the thick veil of newspaper lies.'[2] Rothstein's father, Theodore, was one of the very few men in Britain who knew Lenin personally. He was a Lithuanian-born Jewish revolutionary who had fled tsarist persecution and settled in Britain in 1891. When the Bolsheviks started their daily paper *Pravda* in 1912 he was appointed its London correspondent and after the November 1917 revolution he became Lenin's chief agent in London. His task was to publish Lenin's works, send information to Moscow and secretly distribute Bolshevik money to British socialist groups. Tom could have no better tutor in Bolshevism, as Russian communism was called, than Andrew Rothstein.

Tom had, of course, followed its dramatic beginnings. He noted that in October 1917 *The Times* had dismissed the Bolshevik revolution as 'a mere public meeting called a Soviet. Ever since I felt myself on the side of this "mere public meeting".'[3] He must have been enthused, indeed amazed, that workers had actually taken over a state; that they had extricated Russia from a needless war, cut through all the socialist blather and seized power. For Wintringham, always a man of action as well as ideas, it must have been an inspiration.

As soon as he arrived at Oxford Tom steeped himself in the political ideology of the day, socialism. British socialism had been reinvigorated by the writings of Marx and Engels and then found expression in Fabianism and in the Scottish Labour Party; the first a society of middle-class intellectuals led by Sidney Webb and George Bernard Shaw and the second a gritty working-class movement founded by an Ayrshire miner, Keir Hardie. They came together in 1893 to found the Independent Labour Party, which adopted a definitely reformist, evolutionary approach to the coming of socialism. In the somewhat unfortunate metaphor of G.D.H. Cole and Raymond Postgate, both of whom were leading socialists at Oxford in Wintringham's time, they envisaged socialism 'as a heap of reforms to be built by the droppings of a host of successive swallows who would in the end make a Socialist summer'.[4] Their aim was to coax into socialism workers who, mostly through their trade unions, were members of the new Labour Party that had come into being in 1900. (The Independent Labour Party (ILP) became affiliated to the Labour Party as an increasingly rebellious, socialist grouping of non-trade unionists.)

The difficulty was that most British workers, unlike their counterparts in Germany, France and Italy, were lukewarm socialists, this despite the holy writ of Clause Four of the new Labour Party constitution of 1918: 'to secure for the workers by hand and brain the full fruits of their industry . . . upon the basis of the common ownership of the means of production'. This was brought home to Harry Pollitt during his time in the Boilermakers Union during the war. On one occasion a riveter came up to him after a meeting and said: '"Look here, Brother Pollitt. You put our case better than anyone, but just keep the politics out. We're trade unionists, not Socialists!" This attitude was a great obstacle.'[5] And so it would remain throughout the history of the British Communist Party.

The Labour Party and trade unions were keener to fight for welfare improvements than for a socialist Britain which was why, in 1911, the British Socialist Party was founded. Some Fabians and ILP members joined it speculatively and others, such as Harry Pollitt and Andrew Rothstein who from the start believed in revolution rather than reform, joined with single-minded determination. Rothstein, Wintringham and a few others used to gather at a health food shop on Magdalen Bridge to discuss socialism and read BSP pamphlets.

Initially Tom joined the Oxford University Labour Club. He said he became 'sub-editor of a pink magazine', which must have been the *New Oxford*, the periodical of the Labour Party. In November 1920 it carried a review of *A History of British Socialism* by M. Beer, a book that traced the revolutionary lineage of socialism from the Peasants' Revolt, through the Levellers and the rise and fall of Chartism, to modern socialism. The reviewer, Ralph Fox, was fired with a Marxist sense of historical inevitability: 'The author expresses something that is alive and growing from age to age; it grows and fills in before our eyes and we are able to trace step by step in a wonderful way, the evolution of a movement and idea.'[6] Ralph Fox and Tom Wintringham were embarked upon the same political odyssey, one that would end in a peculiar tragedy, for Fox was killed in the Spanish Civil War and his death was reported as Wintringham's own; such was the similarity of their lives.

Wintringham, of course, knew this socialist history. He would have recalled the Putney Debates of 1647 in the English Civil War when Colonel Rainsborough made the declaration that has rung down the years: 'I think the poorest he in England has a life to lead as the greatest he'. Exactly two hundred years later the Chartists collected mass support for their six-point Charter demanding universal suffrage for men and annual Parliaments. Tom knew this too. He must have viewed these events as stages in a class war, the culmination of which, he supposed, would be Bolshevik-style 'soviets'.

Tom read the communist classics and found that they appealed to his rational, deductive mind. Increasingly hostile to capitalist Britain and now convinced that the First World War had been 'an imperialist continuation of the fundamental properties of capitalism' (cf. Lenin's *Imperialism, the Highest Stage of Capitalism*), he felt that Marxism-Leninism provided both explanation and answer: 'the world ceased to be a muddle; it could be understood by those who understand in order to change. That satisfied me.'[7] Elsewhere he talked about 'the development of choice by reason; of rational vision'. Years later one of his friends endorsed this view of Wintringham's beliefs at that time: 'Tom believed that sweet reason and communism were synonymous; that Socialist Britain was just around the corner.'[8] Not that Tom believed the revolution would just happen. He quoted approvingly the saying of Freud: 'When we can see the anvil of fact, then we can use the hammer of will.'

Tom had another life outside student politics. Riding around Oxford on a motorbike wearing a long leather coat, cap and goggles, he enjoyed shocking people with his rough appearance. He acted in a student production of *The Dynasts* and began his first long-standing affair, with Christina Roberts who sent him her gloomy First World War poems: 'and o'er the land, and o'er the sky/ lies the great black wing of death'. He kept up his own poetry too. In June 1920 he obtained his BA in Modern History, though he did not distinguish himself. (The shortened course was not graded so it is impossible to say how badly he did.) The Master of Balliol, A.L. Smith, wrote consolingly and revealingly:

I hope you don't mind about the Schools; we don't, especially in your case and the abnormal conditions. We all recognise your extraordinary abilities and it seems to me you have about two thirds recovered from the War (you yourself agreed with this fraction). I feel you are right that you cannot do a settled job . . . but don't take up rolling stoneship as a profession. This is the dangerous side of your temperament.[9]

Probably Wintringham attributed his bad results less to postwar nerves than to the weighty distractions of the world outside. For in the spring and summer of 1920, just when Tom was taking his finals, it seemed likely that the British Government would declare war on the newly constituted Soviet Union. It was already waging an illicit war against Bolshevism in northern

Russia and now it supported the Polish army when it launched an attack to reclaim its old empire in the Ukraine. The Russia of the Soviets, the hope of the British working man whether socialist or no, was under threat. In the London docks Harry Pollitt distributed Lenin's *Appeal to the Toiling Masses* and, in May, the dockers refused to coal up the SS *Jolly George* because it was carrying munitions to Poland. In Oxford, Rothstein, Wintringham and Fox formed a local Hands Off Russia committee and leafleted the university and town.

Then the tide turned. The Poles were routed and the Russian Red Army advanced towards Warsaw. Its commander, General Tukhachevsky, launched the offensive with the order: 'To the West! Over the corpse of White Poland lies the road to world-wide conflagration.' Would the Red Army reach an unstable Germany? Would Bolshevism spread west? After all, only a year before a short-lived Soviet had been established in Munich of all places and the German Communist Party was the largest outside Russia. Western Governments were suddenly alarmed. The French were eager to intervene militarily on the Polish side and Lloyd George, supported by Winston Churchill, appeared ready to go along with them.

In the midst of this the Oxford Hands Off Russia committee heard that a Unity Conference was being held in London to form a British Communist Party. According to Rothstein, 'Tom was perhaps the quickest to realise that this was an urgent necessity. When I suggested that we might form a "unity group" for representation he was enthusiastic. I have his letter suggesting I should be the delegate.'[10] Did Tom go himself? And if he did, was he therefore a founder member of the British Communist Party? In old age, Rothstein had no doubts that Wintringham was certainly a Communist in 1920, while a press profile of Wintringham from the 1940s states that he did attend the Unity Conference but only as a spectator. Tom himself was careful to disclaim founder status. He asserted that he looked at Russia, which he visited immediately after the conference, 'through the eyes of a non-Party sympathiser', later writing that he joined the Party in 1923.

The 160 revolutionary socialists of the BSP and members of other fringe parties who met at the Cannon Street Hotel near St Paul's, London, on 31 July 1920, may well have read an article in the *Evening News* three days earlier. Winston Churchill had written:

Eastward of Poland lies the huge mass of Russia – an infected Russia, a plague bearing Russia; a Russia of army hordes smiting not only with bayonet and cannon, but accompanied by swarms of typhus-bearing vermin . . . and political doctrines which destroy the health and even the soul of nations.

Looking back from the vantage point of the twenty-first century, it seems remarkable just how widespread was the view in Britain at this time that world revolution threatened. Reporting on the opening day of the conference, the Labour-supporting *Daily Herald* expressed what sounded like conventional wisdom: 'The founders of the new Party believe – as most competent believers are coming to believe – that the capitalist system is collapsing.' To the readers of the *Daily Herald* this was more of a promise than a threat. In the words of the great socialist Nye Bevan in 1951: 'the revolution of 1917 came to the working class of Great Britain not as a social disaster but as one of the most emancipating events in the history of mankind'.[11]

Chairman Arthur McManus, a short, sharp-tongued shipworker from Clydeside with a reputation for fiery oratory and heavy drinking, struck the tone for the conference in his opening speech: 'We believe that a social revolution is absolutely essential, and that it is our duty to get it however much we may be soiled in the process.'[12] The first resolution, carried unanimously, was that the conference approved 'the Soviet or Workers' Council system whereby the working class shall achieve power and take control of the forces of production'.

Despite this heady rhetoric, the defence of the Soviet Union was the first concern of the Unity Conference. In fact its very convening was due to Lenin who, aided by Theodore Rothstein, had already paid over £55,000 to bring together the quarrelsome parties of the revolutionary left in Britain. More than money, he had advised and courted them, displaying a shrewd knowledge of British politics. So from the very beginning Russia steered British communism; now Lenin told his comrades to unite and, controversially, to affiliate to the Labour Party.

Lenin believed, rightly, that Labour was the authentic voice of the working class and therefore the organisation from which the foot soldiers of the revolution had to come. His order was acceptable to the BSP though dyed-in-the-wool trade unionists like Harry Pollitt took some persuading. They considered the Labour Party a distraction from the task in hand. In any event the new Communist Party accepted the tenets of Bolshevism and membership of the Communist International. It also committed itself to fight parliamentary elections and to seek affiliation with the Labour Party. Its platform was to be reform and revolution; in other words, the ballot box and, in theory, the bullet. This was what Lenin intended. 'Offer the Labour Party,' he ordered, 'the right hand of friendship while leaving the left hand free for the knockout blow.' A BSP delegate put it only slightly differently: 'First of all we help the Labour Party into office, and then, when they have got into office, our first act is to kick them out.'[13]

The Communist International or Comintern, as it was called, became the organisation that would rule Wintringham's professional life for the next sixteen years. Based in Moscow, paid for and dominated by the Soviet Government, it was dedicated to world revolution. All the world's communist parties, whether legal or illegal, were represented on the Comintern and all signed up to the 21 Conditions. The first of these called for a complete and absolute break with reformism as opposed to revolution. This was a standard line, almost a cliché in communist circles, as was the doctrine of democratic centralism whereby once a decision had been made at the top it became binding on all members: 'all the decisions of the Executive Committee of the Communist International are binding on all parties belonging to the Communist International'. A further condition that would have daily implications for Tom was that the entire communist press outside Russia was subordinate to Comintern wishes. From the outset, then, in theory the British Communist Party was controlled by the Kremlin.

In August Wintringham and Esmond Higgins, who later became a prominent Communist in Australia, set out towards the hopeful dawn, the new Soviet Russia. They did not sail into a full-scale war because on 10 August Ernie Bevin presented the National Council of Labour's ultimatum: they would stage a General Strike if the Government declared war on Russia. Lloyd George drew back, telling the Labour Party that it was kicking against an open door; he had no intention of going to war. On 15 August, the Polish General Pilsudski rallied his troops and annihilated three Red Armies at the 'miracle of the Vistula'. Shortly afterwards, Lenin sued for peace and the remaining British troops in northern Russia came home. Was it the urge to save the new Russia that had united the British working class? As A.J.P. Taylor put it: '"Hands off Soviet Russia" counted for something; "No More War" was irresistible'.[14] It was the war-weariness of the British that really counted in the end.

Wintringham and Higgins travelled from Norway to Archangel on 'a little yacht-shaped steamer that pitched badly'[15] in order to avoid the

Polish blockade. It was an illegal journey because Russia was still considered an enemy power, so pilgrims had to expect obstacles along the way. The following year Pollitt and his group were stripped naked on the German border despite the fact, or perhaps because, one of them was disguised as a clergyman with a load of bibles on top of his communist literature. Tom carried a letter of introduction from L.B. Kamenev, a Russian member of the Comintern who had attended the Unity Conference, and he was given the code name of VINT. They arrived in Moscow in September. He wrote at the time:

> There is only one red flag high up over the Kremlin to be seen in all Moscow if you look down from the little hills. There are not many in the streets, and this one stands alone to answer the eagles and crosses of gold, and the great gold domes of the high churches that elbow you off into the gutter as you walk in the streets. And in the same way there is but one set of bells to answer these splendid ruffians of the church. With deliberation and delicacy, like a little Swiss toy, it goes through the melody of the 'Internationale' at midnight, or a few moments after when the other bells have stopped.[16]

Fifteen years later Tom recalled his visit in an article for *Left Review*. There was 'a good deal' of ballet, theatre and circus and heady discussions about 'Futurism and seven other-isms, each less comprehensible than the first. On the other hand there were soldiers without underclothing, hunger, typhus, broken bridges, empty factories, an immense, overwhelming effort to keep things going, to get things straight. Into that effort went all the best living beings in Russia, Communist or not.'[17]

His diary entries for the time are prosaic; there are no expressions of joy or awe. Pollitt, on the other hand, was so overwhelmed he could say only: 'My feelings at seeing Moscow for the first time no words can describe.' Tom got a night job checking English and French language scripts for Russian radio. 'My work is immensely instructive – so many things go through my hands that are contemporary history.' He was amused by Trotsky's invective and copied a speech into his diary: 'The present rulers of France are provincial, shyster lawyers in the service of banking interests who now, after the victory, regard themselves as rulers of the world; petit bourgeois upstarts!' Tom annotated in the margin: 'Good specimen of L. Trotsky's style when he gets a bit peeved!' He also described visiting the opera house with Andrew Rothstein, who had joined him in Moscow, and hearing Trotsky speak. 'We stood on tiptoes at the back of the tzar's box. The enormous place was packed. The stir through the audience when T. got up was extraordinary. He spoke very simply; there was no striving for effect. He looks more solid and less theatrical than his photographs make out. . . . A good deal of clapping.'[18]

They may well have stayed in the Hotel Lux, a meeting point for foreign visitors. H.G. Wells was there. Clare Sheridan, a cousin of Winston Churchill and a sculptress, arrived to sculpt the Russian leaders. 'I think she is a bit soft,' wrote Tom. They met several British Communists who had attended the Second Congress of the Communist International rather than the Unity Conference. The famous American journalist John Reed, author of the best-seller on the Russian Revolution, *Ten Days That Shook the World*, was also in town, dying of typhus. Wintringham visited him in his final days. One of Reed's last public acts had been to try and lift Lenin onto his shoulders at the culmination of the Second Congress, a celebratory piece of horseplay that misfired as Lenin disapproved and kicked himself down.

Moscow 1920 remained in Tom's mind as the practical affirmation of his faith in socialism. This was not the Moscow of the 1930s with its paranoia, purges and misery. The mood was youthful, idealistic and free. It was still the revolution of the Soviets rather than the dictatorship of the Communist Party. Tom became convinced.

As always, his poetry and fictional prose reveal a deeper dimension than his journalism. This is the private world of Wintringham, more individual and emotional than the Party approved. In December 1920 he wrote a difficult poem, 'Against the Determinate World', that he and his future wife Elizabeth liked the best from this period. It seems to reveal a man pulled one way by the certainty of knowledge (the laws of physics and of Marx?) and the other by the wildness of nature, but concluding that they are both part of the determinism of life. What a statement of Wintringham's own nature!

It begins:

> The shadows lift, and the silver tree
> That stands by Trinity Gate
> In the breath of the dawn is dancing free,
> Dancing smoothly and beckoning me:

An old book's weight
(Solemn, dusty) slips from my knee.

Folly man, folly! Let it go and get away!
Shout to the sunrise that the whipping winds are loose;
Run through the shadows, long and cool and clover-crisp,
Out to the great hills, clean with the day.

Urgency – and impotence –
of atoms wheeling on their way
Mock you, with their thought-pretence;
While hooded forces bind and bend
brain and body to an end
That is empty and ultimate – and yet lures you to believe!

This you know, this you feel, this you dream – they all are one;
Tenseness of the stooping hawk and sleekness of the lissom earth,
Pain and striving of man's sense to give the clamant Beauty birth,
And yon white cloud's wide immanence –[19]

I asked a professor of poetry, Cedric Cullingford, to evaluate Tom's work. He chose this poem, in its entirety, to make the general point that Tom's love of nature and the lyricism this induces are forcefully conveyed, but that they are secondary to a political message expressed in abstract and somewhat pedagogic language. The result, he considers, is a lack of clarity in which political ideas struggle with a natural love of images. Later, in Spain, Tom acquired the reputation among his men of a genuinely decent fellow who spoilt this impression by spouting Marxist jargon. I see him as a man of his age who believed in scientific reason, as he put it, and constantly tried to impose it on reality; particularly the Marxist laws of dialectic.

When Wintringham was in prison in 1925, he completed a short story based on his Russian experience and he used 'Against the Determinate World' to introduce it. It is a strange and sensual story called, enigmatically, *White Paper: Dedicated to All Unwise Politicians*. It tells the story of young Philip Martinside, alias Tom, and his relationship with a Russian village girl, Olya. Out in the snow-bound steppes Philip's sledge overturns and he is injured. He is rescued by villagers and nursed back to health by Olya, the two of them living with others in a wooden dacha. When Philip has recovered he and Olya go to a torch-dance, a ritualistic mating event that Tom describes vividly. While the short story is fiction, this climax must surely be based on an actual event which he witnessed:

> There was something new and unknown inside Philip, something of which he was uncertain. The touch of her hand in the dance was tantalising; when he found it, he thought of the first chill of moonlit water, bathing. He tingled when her body brushed on his. For a moment she was in his arms, then she spun away again and he lost her. He was clumsy, but all of them were that. The dance hurried, and suddenly he felt that he was away and outside it all, the thread of all his sensations lost, whatever he had been thinking about forgotten. He thought: 'this is how a man feels who is thoroughly fed up about something that he can't tell other people of'. And it was true: he was like a man stunned by the thought of a hidden crime he had committed, who can join in whatever is happening, but cannot understand it. Months afterwards he realised that Olya had felt immediately his change in mood; at the moment he only felt relief, as she swung with him to the side. With their defection the dance broke up; the dancers stood panting or flung themselves down on the ground. The wind came once again, across the shadows that the torches cast. The colours that had swayed were still; the breadth of the dark resumed its power over his mind. Before the talk started again it was possible to catch the whispering of leaves, and notice the trees moving . . . 'I shall have to go back to England soon', he spoke at random.[20]

What is Tom really saying? The title suggests he is warning British politicians about getting involved in something they don't understand (Hands Off Russia), but perhaps there is something more personal, too. Elsewhere he writes of Philip's homesickness. Added in black ink to the typescript on the last page are the words: 'England, it was a promise of something far off and lovely that he must seek'; earlier there was a similar addition: 'England, a place he desired'. If Tom is saying that he (Philip) felt like an impostor, someone who did not really understand Russia, and that his thoughts turned with yearning to England, then that was true of Wintringham the revolutionary. Future events were to prove that he belonged in the English tradition of revolution and he never did comprehend what communism was doing to Russia. He did not go back.

Tom's first stop after his return to England, still with the proverbial snow on his boots or, as photographs show, wearing a Russian fur hat, was a visit to his uncle at the House of Commons. As his old friend Wilfred Roberts wrote over fifty years later, there was much common ground then between Liberalism and Bolshevism as far as progressive politics was concerned: ideas about education, equality of women, and criminal reform among others. Wintringham the communist enthusiast was by no means disowned by his family.

It was difficult, nevertheless, for Tom to join the family firm of solicitors in Grimsby as had once been his intention and in any event he relished the metropolitan life of London. He chose instead to study for the Bar as other Communists would do over the years. In 1921 he joined the Inner Temple and began a somewhat contradictory existence, mixing the practice of bourgeois law with revolutionary politics. Lodging in 1 Dr Johnson's Buildings, a nineteenth-century block of classical design situated directly opposite the Inner Temple Church, he might well have thought he was back at Oxford. A contemporary photograph of Tom fits the image of left-wing barrister. An idealistic-looking young man, informally dressed in a tweed jacket rather than suit, he looks directly at the camera; at ease with it and himself, clear features above a firm jaw and below a receding hair-line.

Wintringham was now a communist in all but name. His radical background was allied to a cause. This cause appealed to his rigorous, rational mind and to his sense of history, for he saw communism in Britain as the culmination of earlier socialist revolutions. He shared the widespread view that capitalism was collapsing and his own experience of an imperialist war made him want to hasten the process. He had seen the Soviet Union and it seemed to work. But he still lacked that intensity of purpose to be one of Lenin's professional revolutionaries. Joining the Party meant dedicating a life and initially that commitment was missing. That it developed over the next two years was due to a most extraordinary couple, Rajani Palme Dutt and his partner (later his wife) Salme Murrik.

Palme Dutt and Wintringham may well have met first at Oxford University, for they were both at Balliol College, though not at the same time. We know that they got to know each other through the Labour Research Department (LRD) because a Wintringham photograph shows them together at the Summer School in Scarborough in 1922. Presumably Tom was a visitor – and not just for study purposes. There was a bevy of young bourgeois women there who worked for the LRD and their smiles for the camera shine through the years: Rose Cohen, Eva Reckitt, Olive Budden and her friend from Oxford University, Elizabeth Arkwright. Extraordinary to realise that when these innocent pictures were taken, MI5 detectives were tailing Cohen and Reckitt, bugging their phones and intercepting their mail. For files newly released at the National Archives reveal that they were considered not just Communists but spies. Whether true or not, they did act as couriers and secretaries for the Communist Party, though what role Elizabeth Arkwright played is not clear; except that she became Tom's wife. Also at Scarborough were Robin Page Arnot and Hugo Rathbone, both prominent members of the Party in later years. They formed an intellectual elite who had in effect hijacked the LRD the previous year and turned it into a communist front. Their leader was Raji Palme Dutt. At Scarborough he gave a lecture that, according to the *Manchester Guardian*, 'was impressive in its effect despite the lecturer's undisguised contempt for his audience and all other points of view'.

Raji Palme Dutt provoked strong reactions, many of them hostile. Within the Party he was dubbed R. Pontifical Dutt for his intellectual arrogance, and that was one of the kinder epithets. He was the most Stalinist of communists; cold and manipulative, totally dedicated to the dictum that the end justified the means. In 1949 the defector Douglas Hyde called Palme Dutt 'utterly inhuman' and the next year a British newspaper described him with some justice 'as one of the few who had reached Communism by the purely intellectual path, with neither emotions, idealism, nor even a real humanism playing any part in his evolution'.[21] Perhaps Dutt himself did not disagree with this judgement. In a most revealing anecdote he told towards the end of his life (he died in 1974), he recalled an international students' meeting he had attended in Vienna in his youth. His companion had been Ellen Wilkinson, who was later to leave the Communist Party and become a Labour cabinet minister:

As so often in international conferences there arose an 'English problem': in this case whether to accept us in the proposed socialist organisation or not. . . . Our organisation and line was analysed relentlessly like a body being dissected on a mortuary slab; at the end the decision went against us. . . . As we came away into the cold winter's night air Ellen Wilkinson said to me: 'This is the most ghastly, callous, inhuman machine I have ever witnessed.' I said to her: 'At last I have found what I have been looking for: socialists who mean business.'[22]

Rajani Palme Dutt was born in Cambridge in 1896, the son of a very poor but brilliant Indian doctor and a poetry-writing Swedish mother, one of whose relatives would become Prime Minister of Sweden, Olaf Palme. Palme Dutt was tall, shy, ascetic and enormously clever, with a long face and earnest features that showed his Indian ancestry. At Oxford he was a member of the ILP and his lanky figure could be seen striding across the countryside to preach socialism in village halls. Like Tom he won a scholarship to Balliol College but, unlike Tom, in communist terms, he had a good war by being imprisoned for refusing conscription and rusticated for supporting the Bolshevik revolution. Allowed back to take his finals, he scored fourteen alphas and won several prizes. He was dismissive of this extraordinary achievement: 'I am sorry to see a mere tedious recital of commonplace examinations without reference to the highest honour Oxford can bestow on an honest democrat.' He was referring, of course, to his rustication.

Palme Dutt became a founder member of the British Communist Party and began with an uncompromising statement: 'Communists declare firmly that their ends can only be obtained by the forcible overthrow of every order of society.' He took for granted the need for socialism and no doubt paid lip service to the eventual withering away of the State and its replacement by, as Marx had put it in 1875, 'the higher phase of communism where society inscribed on its banners "from each according to his ability, to each according to his need"'. But what focused Dutt's cold intellect were Leninist theories of revolution, foremost among which was the need for a minority party of revolutionaries, like the Bolsheviks in Russia, to seize dictatorial power.

Palme Dutt had no trouble with this absolutism, nor its application to Comintern membership. He accepted without reservation that the Communist Party in Britain would not be able to bring about revolution 'unless it is organised in a most centralised manner, unless an iron discipline, bordering on military discipline, is admitted, and unless its central body is armed with extensive powers and enjoys the unanimous confidence of the militants'.[23] Nor, despite his own background, did he have any trouble accepting that the vanguard of the revolution was the industrial working class. He probably wrote this chilling warning that applied to Wintringham as much as anybody:

To the bourgeois socialist who would join the Communist Party we say frankly: it has nothing whatever to offer you; it asks for absolutely everything. It can tolerate neither conscience, cowardice, nor compassion. You must be prepared for the ruthless sacrifice of self, then of others, and if required, of so called moral scruples also. Then there is room for you in the world as workers in your own sphere. But if you attempt to enter the arena of the struggle armed with your particular ideas, you will be mercilessly crushed between the millstones of Revolution and Reaction.[24]

For fifteen years Wintringham maintained this discipline. Why did he do so? After all, it was outside the British socialist tradition that owed so much to Nonconformism; it used to be said that the Labour Party owed more to Methodism than to Marx. Tom did not possess a personality open to extremism; he certainly did not crave authority. Probably his loyalty stemmed from an intellectual belief in Leninism, Duttism too for that matter, and behind this was the gut feeling that socialism, in his view the fairest way to order society, would not come about of its own accord. The end had to justify the means.

In 1920 Rajani Palme Dutt met Salme Murrik, a 32-year-old veteran revolutionary from Estonia, who was in England on Lenin's orders because she had asked him to send her 'where the struggle was toughest'. She was staying illegally and incognito in a flat near Regents Park, London, living off the proceeds of the sale of four diamonds she had brought with her to cover expenses. Venturing outside only after dark, the clandestine existence badly affected her health, an unhappy state of affairs about which 'Ra' (Palme Dutt) in his letters to her was surprisingly tender. Her job was to assist in the formation of the British Communist Party and her high-ranking contacts in the Comintern were an inspiration as well as a help to her lover. When Lenin died in 1924 Ra wrote to her: 'And now has come the hardest blow of all . . . leaving the world so sad and empty and the International somehow not meaning the same. I feel that through you, Sa [Salme], we understood so much about what he meant.'[25] Salme Murrik was an experienced revolutionary who became an authority figure for young Communists working in the London office. Tom referred to her as 'the Governess' and over the years he accepted her criticisms of his manner (cocksure), his poetry (too intellectual) and his love-life (reprehensible).

When Andrew Rothstein had been in Moscow with Wintringham in 1920 he had recommended to the Comintern that Palme Dutt and Page Arnot should edit a magazine to infiltrate the Labour left with communist ideas. This appeared as *Labour Monthly*, a supposedly independent journal of Marxist and Labour unity. Palme Dutt was its editor for the next fifty years and around 1922 he asked Wintringham to assist in its publication. This was probably Tom's first job for the Party although he was not yet a member. But rougher revolutionary tasks were at hand.

If Wintringham wanted more proof that the capitalist state was rotten then it was staring him in the face. In December 1921 over two million British workers were unemployed, 18 per cent of the workforce. Ex-service men wearing their medals were begging in the streets or marching aggressively four abreast down the pavements. Christmas was bleak. Many factories were closed down for an extended holiday. In the iron and steel industry more than one in three men was out of work; in the docks, more than one in five. Unemployment benefit amounted to 23s a week for a family with three children and, according to a contemporary survey, the same amount of money was required for food alone; so nothing was left over for fuel, rent, clothing, cigarettes or alcohol. To the benefit might be added a poor law allowance of a few shillings per child and vouchers for shopping; but this was regarded by the poor with disgust because it was strictly means tested, a requirement that carried with it the implication of blame. The Government had no answer and nor had the Labour Party which, fearful of revolution, was unwilling to encourage extra-parliamentary pressure. It confined itself to official expressions of regret.

For the new Communist Party, on the contrary, the slump was an opportunity for 'struggle', as direct action was called. Much of this was organised by the National Unemployed Workers' Committee Movement (NUWCM) set up in April 1921 by communist Wal Harrington. In July 1921 Wandsworth Workhouse was occupied by the unemployed with their families, the red flag flying from the roof. In the autumn Labour and Communist councillors of Poplar in East London were imprisoned for refusing to levy rates. In Shoreditch Communist-led protesters refused to pay rent unless work was offered. In many industrial areas of the country the unemployed picketed and raided factories where work was undertaken below trade union rates or by blacklegs. In November 1921 a vast demonstration of 25,000 unemployed soldiers marched on the Cenotaph to place a wreath inscribed: 'From the living victims – the unemployed – to our dead comrades who died in vain.' The banners were covered with the medals of those who wore pawn tickets instead on their lapels. Britain was no land fit for heroes.

A year later the first hunger marches converged on London. The reaction of the press showed how imminent and how Moscow-inspired a revolution was supposed to be. On 17 November, while crowds in Hyde Park awaited the arrival of the first marchers, newspaper placards shouted warnings of 'The Great Red Plot' and 'Secret Communist Meetings'. The *Daily Express* reported that 100,000 armed men were about to storm Downing Street with telegrams ready to dispatch to Moscow announcing the capture of Government offices. In fact the demonstrations, the largest since the days of Chartism, passed off peacefully.

Wintringham must have been heavily involved, if not on the streets then behind a typewriter covering events for the weekly *Communist* or a new fortnightly paper *Out of Work*. It was time well spent. In February 1923 the Comintern told Palme Dutt to edit a new publication, the *Workers' Weekly*, a far more vigorous and proselytising paper than its predecessor, the *Communist*, and he asked Wintringham to be Assistant Editor. Tom formally joined the Party. At once he found himself not only at the sharp end of Communist agitprop, for the *Workers' Weekly* was seen as the weapon to spearhead entry into the trade unions and Labour Party, but also at the centre of Communist politics. Raji Palme Dutt and Harry Pollitt were conducting a struggle of their own to modernise the Party and Wintringham was now one of its Young Turks, a committed revolutionary.

THREE

Code Name 'Lincoln'

Elizabeth's first letter to Tom, written on 30 January 1923, ends rather tartly: 'Yrs, Elizabeth Arkwright (with a 'z' please)'. She soon sent him a photograph: 'If the enclosed photograph is any good you may keep it. Esther Tabrisky took it and thinks it's good, but really I was putting on a face as the sun was in my eyes.'[1] It shows a thin young woman, her dark hair cut in the fashionable gamin style, wearing an elegant tea dress and squinting at the camera. Four years older than Tom, she was a member of the Labour Research Department and a medical student at St Mary's Paddington, having left Oxford University without a degree in 1915. She was a founder member of the Party too, most probably the only one with the impeccable private education of Roedean followed by Lady Margaret Hall, Oxford. Her father was the distinguished bacteriologist Sir Joseph Arkwright, who had made his reputation with a book called *The Louse*. Despite her non-political and upper-middle-class background (she once told her son Oliver, 'I suppose we are upper working class'), she was a loyal though unassuming member of the Holborn branch of the Communist Party.

Love was in the air as well as revolution. Tom's companion in Russia Esmond Higgins (Hig), an Australian, was hopelessly, obsessively in love with the beautiful Rose Cohen, a Jewish girl from the East End and former suffragette who had joined the Party with her sister Nellie. Harry Pollitt was also smitten by Rose and confessed to having proposed to her on many occasions, although he soon married Communist school teacher Marjorie Brewer, who, incidentally, had been introduced to communism by Tom Wintringham. Olive Budden, Elizabeth's friend from Oxford and a strong influence on her, was partnered with the Scottish Communist academic Robin Page Arnot, and Raji Palme Dutt had just married in secret the Comintern adviser Salme Murrik. Reading their letters of that time I am struck by their happiness and innocence, an impression reinforced by photographs of the 1922 Labour Research Department group outing to Germany. Here they are hiking and swimming, the women ostentatiously smoking cigarettes. And there is a group photograph at Scarborough taken the same year; conspicuous is a tall man with a sandy beard and quizzical expression standing in the middle, George Bernard Shaw. This was a halcyon summer with no hint of the darkness to come. The Bolshevik revolution was still an inspiration; British socialists and Communists were certain that capitalism was collapsing. They were young and in love and on the brink of a new dawn.

But melancholy questions come to mind. How many of them left the Communist Party shortly afterwards, disillusioned by the lack of democracy? How many suffered when the Communists turned on the other socialist parties in the 1930s? How many remained members of the Party into old age just because loyalty was all that mattered? Probably only Tom Wintringham suffered the fate of expulsion from the Party, in 1938. Certainly, only Rose Cohen was killed at Stalin's orders; either by execution in the Lubyanka prison or sometime later through exhaustion in a Gulag camp by the River Ussuri in Siberia.

They do not look like revolutionaries, but that is how they were perceived. In these early years of the Party the press often referred to 'Red Plots'. Police trailed members, opened their mail and tapped their phones. They raided the CPGB headquarters in Covent Garden, London, and took notes at public meetings. At one meeting in a Midlands hotel the police were told to clear off after they had been discovered disguised as waiters; this incident was amusingly misreported by a journalist who wrote that the meeting was chaired by a Colonel Buggeroff. But victimisation was no laughing matter. In 1921/2 over a hundred Communists were arrested for sedition or breaches of the peace and many were sentenced to prison with hard labour. Nearly all the Party leaders spent time in gaol. Not that every arrest was victimisation, of course. In September 1922, for instance, two Liverpool Communists were gaoled for possessing guns and ammunition. And one can understand the Government's suspicions of a party whose recruitment leaflet began: 'The Communist Party honestly and frankly stands for the abolition of the capitalist State and all its machinery, such as Parliament and the British Constitution.' In fact Communists suspected that the Party might be declared illegal altogether, which it might well have been if the Government had known the true extent of its dependence on a foreign power committed to world revolution.

This is why leading Communists went under assumed names. Wintringham was known as T. Lincoln, Rothstein as C.M. Roebuck. This is why, too, correspondence to Comintern representatives hiding in Britain was written in code. For instance: 'Have fixed with 3/2, 3/3, 5/1 to pick up and deliver 7/3, 5/4, 4/4 sharp on 1/9, 1/6, 3/4 morning' as Palme Dutt wrote to Salme Murrik in January 1924.[2] And this is why the official history of the early years of the CPGB, written in 1969 by Party member James Klugmann, made no mention at all in four hundred pages of the 'Red Gold' or Comintern subsidy that kept the Party going. (The omission provoked Communist historian Eric Hobsbawm to write: 'Unfortunately he [Klugmann] is paralysed by the impossibility of being both a good historian and a loyal functionary.')[3] In fact, the CPGB could not have existed without Comintern backing: between August 1920 and March 1922 around £60,000 was donated by Moscow and only £1,699 1s 10d received in membership dues. Some of the Comintern money was collected by couriers Rose Cohen and Eva Reckitt, who went over to Paris and returned with bundles of used dollar bills. These they gave to Andrew Rothstein.

The fear, even hatred, that British capitalists felt about Communists in particular shows how grave a threat they considered them. It also shows why members of the Party kept themselves to themselves. They were members of a semi-secret and conspiratorial organisation with its own code and language. The bourgeois intellectuals from the Labour Research Department, for instance, some of whom worked at Communist headquarters at 16 King Street (paid for with Comintern money and now, irony of ironies, a boutique called TZAR) tended to live in a North London colony in Highgate. They were a somewhat delicate, cosmopolitan breed that is difficult to associate with the roughness of revolution.

The four thousand or so rank-and-file Communists, indeed most of the leadership too, were different. Many were Irish with revolution and the Troubles in their blood: McManus was the son of a Fenian; Willie Gallagher, later a prominent Communist MP for Clydeside, had an Irish father. He and many others came from the Scottish or Welsh Celtic fringe where the Party membership was strongest. It was in the turbulent, aggressively political coalfields of South Wales and Fifeshire and the shipyards of the Clyde that the seeds of the Party's gospel landed on fertile soil. Here the workers' bloody-minded determination to beat the bosses and control the industries they slaved in day and night was a fact of life. Indeed, it is notable how few of the Communist leaders were of English origin; Harry Pollitt, of course, and the up and coming young journalist Tom Wintringham, alias *Lincoln*.

Did Wintringham actually think he would be fighting bloody street battles? And did he really have the motivation to do this? If these questions were put to the hundreds of rank-and-file Communists who came from the

Red Clyde, for instance, then they would surely have answered 'yes'. Take Willie Gallagher, as different from Wintringham as chalk from cheese, who would eventually confront him in a Spanish hospital when their differences of background and lifestyle would surface.

Gallagher was born, bred and died near the Clyde. In 1918 Lenin called Glasgow 'The Petrograd of the West', but to locals who knew its squalor and destitution it was the 'city of the dreadful night'. Fully two-thirds of the population lived in dwellings below the minimum standards stipulated by the Board of Health. To the teeming thousands crammed round the Clyde and dependent on the shipbuilding industry for any kind of living, socialism was the only answer. In the general election of November 1922, when the new Labour Party doubled its MPs to 142, 10 of these came from Glasgow. When the massive crowd saw them off to Parliament on the night train from St Enoch station they sang with intensity and triumphalism their version of Psalm 124:

> Now Israel may say and that truly
> If that the Lord had not our cause maintained
> If that the Lord had not our right sustained
> When cruel men against us furiously
> Rose up in wrath to make us their prey.

And when the new Labour MPs arrived in the House of Commons they found waiting for them a telegram calculated to stiffen their resolve: 'Thousands of Glasgow children attending school suffering from hunger. Many absent because they have neither boots nor clothes. Only 1,500 being fed. Probably 14,000 in need.' It was a matter, then, of life-saving urgency that socialism should be implemented. To Communists such as Gallagher, who had stood unsuccessfully at Dundee, socialism could not be achieved without violence and the dictatorship of the proletariat; therein lay the difference between the parties.

Gallagher had grown up surrounded by the violence caused by poverty: pub brawls, street fighting between Catholics and Protestants, hooliganism. He had fought with the police over strike action and with soldiers over his soap-box pacifism in the First World War. He had been incarcerated in Calton gaol, the worst in the country. Not that he was a man of violence despite a hot temper; in fact, like many from a Nonconformist background, he knew his Bible and he was teetotal. But he was committed to revolution and a meeting in Moscow with Lenin himself in 1920 had been an almost religious experience. A photograph of him at this time taken in 16 King Street shows a thick-set man, shirt sleeves rolled up, pipe clenched between teeth. A man with a mission.

At this time Tom's Communist activities were sheltered from the reality of class struggle. He lived in an Inn of Court; he wrote in a back office, either weekly journalism or more educational articles for Palme Dutt's *Labour Monthly* and *Plebs*, a magazine for the Plebs League, a Communist off-shoot of the Workers' Educational Association. He taught Marxism-Leninism at evening classes. But Tom had seen violence too in the trenches and he had served in the ranks. Moreover, although he always said he hated war, he was fascinated by it. In years to come he would make his reputation as an expert in do-it-yourself warfare; he would actually devise new ways of killing people, specifically tailored to the kind of guerrilla action needed for revolt. In this sense he was a revolutionary before his time and, to my mind, a man who would not shrink from violence. For the present, he restricted himself to poetry:

'Revolution'

The steel of their wills pointed by bitterness
And all their longing to master earth, to make,
(Now caught and constrained in a network of weariness,
Stifled by monotony, sameness, littleness)
These shall be strong in them, these shall awake
To a light, to a fire, to a bright fire's restlessness,
To a crackling anger.

There will be a stirring, like a trembling of the earth
And men will remember, singing in the streets
Where machine-guns rattle or a cracked drum beats,
That beyond the battle, the mourning, the slain,
The numb crouched agony of wounded in the rain,
There is power for them, freedom, security, friendliness,
Loveliness and laughter made sane and sweet and clean again
And beginning of a new world's birth. (Verse 2)[4]

When Wintringham became assistant editor of *Workers' Weekly* he found himself at the centre of a feud about the future of the CPGB. The previous autumn Raji Palme Dutt and Harry Pollitt had taken the initiative to set up a working party to reform the Party organisation. They had proposed that the semi-autonomous local branches which seemed to do little except recommend speakers for street-corner meetings should be reorganised into tight nuclei groups with orders to infiltrate Labour constituencies and trade union branches in factories. Their tactics, closely controlled by King Street according to the dictat of democratic centralism, would be to elect their own comrades and push through the Party line. Palme Dutt wanted a tight 'Orgbureau, leading and directing members' activities the whole time'. Thus, wrote Dutt, the CPGB 'would become an efficient machine of the class struggle'.[5] Palme Dutt and Pollitt were tightening the screw. No longer would Party officials return from Moscow with money stuffed into their trousers and spend a good deal of it on booze and cigars, complacently expecting that revolution would just happen. But these reforms were resisted by some founding fathers.

That spring, Palme Dutt and Wintringham scandalised the old guard by running in *Workers' Weekly* a fictional serial about a Manchester metalworker (alias Pollitt) passionately committed to socialism who moves down to London to give his all to the revolution. Here he confronts the worthlessness of the 'old revolutionary chiefs with their deep-lying petty sectionalism'. One of them, clearly Tom Bell the Party Secretary, is dismissed as 'an old ass stubborn in everything'.[6] These slurs were not forgotten.

Tom was in no mood to worry. His courtship of Elizabeth was succeeding despite initial resistance. On 27 May she wrote: 'I shall begin right away by telling you one reason why I so much want to wait a little. It's such a short time since I was in love with another comrade, who did not love me. I determined I would fall out of love with him quickly and, as a matter of fact, I have. But an emotional crisis leaves one dazed.' Then, only a week later, 'I do love you dear Tom, my self-doubt and hesitation are melting away so fast. The poem I like best is Against the Determinate World. . . .'[7]

Dutiful Communist that she was, Elizabeth tried some Party correctness: 'We must cut ourselves off from bourgeois ways of thinking. Our minds were made up in a middle class ideology. . . . Tonight I am going to a Central Distribution Committee.' But her mind was really on the hedonistic and *haut* bourgeois matter of a ball at the Inner Temple and what she was going to wear afterwards: 'Do I have to bring a nightdress? I look much better in pyjamas!' The pyjamas become a minor theme: 'I am making some silk pyjamas. I'm going to make them without any buttons because it's so much easier; but that wouldn't do for you would it!?'[8]

Family legend has it that the day after the ball, Christina Roberts's brother called at Tom's flat, 1 Dr Johnson's Buildings, and found Elizabeth in her celebrated pyjamas. So ended Tom's amorous relationship with Christina, though they continued to meet and she said after his death that she had loved him all his life. Elizabeth, who was described by a friend as 'a woman of unimpeachable Marxist propriety', responded in character: 'She [Christina] thinks love and happiness are ends in themselves, whereas I think we should take them by the way, if we can do so without prejudice to what's really important [i.e. the revolution]'.[9]

In June 1923 almost the entire executive of the CPGB was summoned to Moscow to thrash out the future of the Party, an unprecedented order. This left 'Lincoln' in charge not only of the *Workers' Weekly* but of Dutt's *Labour Monthly*; and in receipt of Pollitt's confidential commentaries from Moscow. These he passed on to Salme Murrik, 'the Governess', whom he addressed discreetly as 'Dear Friend'. Excitement was in his voice:

> The whole attitude was 'when is D [Dutt] coming'. Harry says that all the rest of them were 'treated with cold contempt'. The paper is considered by far the best thing in the Party – almost the only thing.
>
> Harry was asked: 'how serious is the position?' He replied: 'so serious that D and I will be forced to resign if it (the feud) goes on and go back to the provinces to work in the local movements'. This was said not as a threat but because Harry feels that this really is likely to be necessary.
>
> Then they asked: 'What are your practical proposals?' Harry replied: 'Remove Bell, give D. his job and make T.L. editor of the paper [T.L. is Tom].
>
> Harry's conclusions. They will not adopt our full demands, or act against the old gang to any great extent; they fear the accusation of dictation (!?) and hope to carry on without splitting the Party. But D. will be listened to with the greatest possible attention.[10]

In the same letter 'Lincoln' turned to more personal matters:

> Elizabeth tells me you are doing well considering all things. She has been staying here [at the Inner Temple], an arrangement we hope to make permanent soon. It will not be allowed to reduce our work for the

nucleus or her local work (of which she does a great deal, very seriously). I think that if you and the job are going to make anything out of me, then Elizabeth will be a great help.

By the way. You seemed to say when we were discussing the paper that I am too cock sure of myself to receive instruction. 'Tisn't true, but I have got to say what I think, because only the nucleus can put it right.

Ever yours, T.L.

On 1 July Pollitt returned home leaving Dutt in Moscow to fight their corner. Soon after he wrote to Salme from King Street:

Dear Comrade. No sign of the Prodigal Son [Dutt]. T.L. is getting fagged on the paper but he has done wonders with me unable to help him [Pollitt was organising a dock strike] and you ill. Above all he is head over heels in love. Yesterday he turned up at the office in a brand new light suit. The last time I saw Elsie [Elizabeth] she was arrayed in some kind of summer dress that made me sit up and take notice. They say that music is the food of love but love seems a recipe for getting new clothes. But in that case why don't I have a wonderful wardrobe?[11]

Weightier correspondence was in the post. Dutt wrote to Pollitt on 21 July:

[Gregori] Zinoviev [the Comintern President] criticises the C.P.G.B. for lack of opportunism; too much preaching of doctrines and not enough struggle. We must proletarianise our group and dip it closer in the immediate issues. We must involve Lincoln and me in some rough and tumble work compelling us to exist in the Labour movement and not simply inside the Party. . . . We have got to fix T.L. as Ass. Ed. He would give his notice straight away [from his law studies] if there was money from the budget.[12]

The divided delegation returned with a compromise agreed. But a new full-time Politburo was established with Pollitt a member and with a new responsibility for industrial activity. Above all the factory nuclei or cell structure of infiltration went ahead and the Party did become more disciplined and centralised. Importantly for Tom the *Workers' Weekly* was confirmed as a six page broadsheet with 'Lincoln' as assistant editor.

On 31 August Tom and Elizabeth were married in a City of London registry office. This was preceded by the familiar bride/mother argument about a church service. 'Dearest Mother, I am very sorry but I can't be married in church. I feel it would be quite wrong! Religion means very little to me.'[13] It was followed by a honeymoon in Ireland where they visited Tom's parents, who were also on holiday there. Muv wrote: 'It was all rather a surprise. My most heartfelt wish is that you and Tom are happy together.' Thus began a close friendship between Elizabeth and the Wintringham family that would outlast her marriage by many years. They called her Lizbeth while to her own family, and the Party, she was Elsie.

The day before the wedding Harry Pollitt had sent his blessing:

Dear Young and Innocent comrades,

Tomorrow you will be off on the long eventful journey. For better or worse you are both fixed up. . . . Poor Higgins and I are thinking of marrying each other and sharing our common sorrow. We both thought of you last night and it caused Hig to drop three glasses of stout without stopping. I hope when you return from your holidays you will either organise a damn good feed (including boiled ham) for the nucleus, or else a charabanc outing from King Street to Southend.

Then Pollitt struck a more serious note on the vexatious subject of the role of the bourgeois (in this case, Tom and Elizabeth) in the proletarian revolution. Obviously, some of the Highgate toffs were offending comrades such as Gallagher:

Don't get downhearted in your work for the Party, or because you meet rebuffs from other people. I know this little Party inside out and up and down the country are working some of the best comrades in the world. These are the people who make the struggle worthwhile, and they are the people to think of when things in King Street don't seem too pleasant, or when a lot of bloody fools are blathering about 'the intelligentsia', because none of you are any better than us poor workers.

But Elsie and Tom are exceptions, that is why I write to them like a father and if your marriage doesn't result in increased work for the Party I shall be frightfully disappointed.[14]

Harry Pollitt was a kind and loyal man with a sense of humour too. Short, heavily built and with a Lancashire accent, he relished a fiery speech to the comrades as much as several whiskies afterwards. He was an old-style class warrior who hated the hair-splitting and infighting of the Highgate intellectuals. His preference was for dogged work with the trade unions in the docks and factories to bring about the revolution in which he passionately believed. He was, however, a dyed-in-the-wool Stalinist and his tragedy would be his inability to come to terms with the revelations by Khrushchev in 1956 of Stalin's regime of terror. He resigned as General Secretary though he stayed in the Party until his death four years later.

From now on Tom's life was dominated by the Communist Party. Although he and Elizabeth continued to live in the Inner Temple and he gave his occupation as law student he never referred to his studies in correspondence. Some of the time he spent travelling round the country as a public speaker, unpaid and uncomfortable work: 'We slept, or did not sleep, poor Gaymann and I, in a bed that caved right down the middle, and each of us had to lie half on the iron bar at either side. That was in Leeds.'[15] Gaymann was a French Communist on a speaking tour with Tom acting as interpreter. They would meet again in Spain thirteen years later when Gaymann, then known as Vidal, was the notorious Chief of Staff for the International Brigade.

Most of the time Tom was in King Street assembling the *Workers' Weekly*. The paper was an instant success, its circulation increasing from 19,000 to 55,000 in a matter of months. Much of this was due to the slog of foot soldiers like Elizabeth who sold it door to door. Palme Dutt and Wintringham were proud that so much of the content came from the workers themselves. In one of his few signed articles, dated 15 February 1924, Tom described how the paper was put together:

The old style of Labour journal consists of long articles and a few notes from branches and committees, with unconnected propaganda notes filling up the odd spaces . . . I only spend one twentieth of my time writing. The rest is reading, sorting, combining and condensing the letters we get . . . I reckon in the first year we used a total of 1,149 letters, news reports and cuttings sent to us by workers.

A good idea of the appeal of British communism at this time may be had by looking at a typical edition. On the sixth anniversary of the Bolshevik revolution, 9 November 1923, the *Workers' Weekly* (banner headline 'Workers of the World, Unite!') stated proudly: 'The biggest thing is that the workers *rule* in Russia. They say that the first charge on what is produced and the supplies that are available shall be to provide the needs of the workers, of the women and children – *and this is done.* In no other country is this the case.' This, no doubt, was an article of faith to British Communists, but the reality of what was happening under British capitalism, described in accompanying articles, was incontrovertible. The front page leader: 'Miners' Call to Action – Fight or Starve!' analysed how miners' pay had been forced below the basic cost of living. On the back page were the 'Workers' Life' columns edited by Tom that gave first-hand accounts of working-class suffering: 'A Hero's Reward – Eviction of Ex-Service Man, Wife and Six Children' and 'Hell in the Dark, men suffering from miners' nystagmus are being treated like dogs. . . .' Reading these letters week after week must have fortified his social conscience. Interspersed were articles with a surprisingly international reach by modern standards, like one on the overthrow of the Workers' Government in Saxony, but also including the amusingly homely: 'Wake Up, Mrs Worker'.

The overall tone was militant, but there was a lack of communist dogma because the paper was designed for political activists across the left. Above all, it was as Dutt had promised: 'A paper for the workers, by the workers'. Twenty years later Wintringham might well have dubbed it with great satisfaction: 'The People's Paper'. It obviously succeeded because in terms of numbers the readership was far higher than the membership of the Party.

In March 1924 the management committee agreed that Palme Dutt and 'Wint' (Wintringham) should be paid £15 a week between them. Palme Dutt noted that such a move would establish Wint but he added that the finances of the Party were a mess: 'I am worried that Harry has had no pay for seven weeks and is piling up debt. I feel we ought to establish a communal system, six or eight of us – not some drawing pay, some not and left to their own helplessness.'[16] Wintringham's future was secure, but not his promotion. The previous Christmas Eve Palme Dutt had been left alone to run King Street and been forced to sleep on the floor. In this lonely state he had written to Salme complaining about his work load and asking, among many other things, whether 'Wint' should succeed him as editor. 'I am afraid he has not the knowledge and judgement yet and would not be acceptable [surely another reference to Tom's background?]. A possibility is Campbell . . . I should like to bring him to London.'[17]

So J.R. Campbell, a small, rugged Scot who had lost his toes in the trenches of Flanders but not his sharp mind, for he was admired as a worker-intellectual, came south from the Clydeside shipyards. This coincided with a fall in the Palme Dutt/Pollitt powerbase, from which we must conclude that Wintringham lost out too. The atmosphere in King Street between modernisers and traditionalists was thick with invective. Rothstein was 'venomously hostile'[18] towards Dutt for favouring Pollitt in the pages of *Workers' Weekly*. Pollitt nearly bashed J.T. Murphy (another Irishman and wartime industrial agitator) on the nose during a meeting for calling him 'sheepish'. The nucleus even discussed gloomily with Salme whether there was much point in continuing with the present Party. In the summer of 1924, Palme Dutt surprised everybody when he complained of stress, announced he suffered from tuberculosis of the spine and moved with Salme to Brussels. Here they lived until 1936. Although he retained influence with the leadership, Dutt was no longer in touch with day-to-day communism in Britain.

Pollitt was on the move too. He was summoned to Moscow and asked to take full responsibility for the industrial policy of the Party. That summer he opened an office in Great Ormond Street, London, and started the National Minority Movement with the aim of taking control of the Labour trade unions from within. By 1926 over five hundred secret nuclei had been set up, most of them in the transport, mining and engineering unions. To Pollitt's relief he was out of King Street, back with the trade unions and being paid. But Wintringham had lost his support.

In January 1924 the Labour Party formed its first national Government, though it held fewer seats in Parliament than the Conservatives and depended on Liberal support. Behind Labour was the working man of Great Britain, the wage earner with the hobnail boots and cloth cap. In 1921 fully 7 million men and women, one in six of the entire population, worked in the heavy industries or on the land, 85 per cent of them members of trade unions. Numerically in the lead were more than 2 million coal miners and farm labourers and following on behind came the railway workers, the iron and steel foundry workers, the dockers, the builders, the textile workers, the transport workers and engineers. The working class was on the march:

'Revolution'

Can you not feel it? The long tide stirring,
The people passing, pausing, returning,
Swaying and surging in the cold wet streets?
And the fear in the faces of the fat? And the burning

Hope in the eyes where, terrible in hopelessness,
Lonely and cold a ghost of hunger sat?

Men will remember the past and its defeats;
Men will remember their dreams trodden underfoot
When they went into the mills, to the docks, to the deep sea,
To the mines where the black dust gleams,
Or scarred the coloured hills with a grey plough—
Man's work,
And boy's hopes, boy's dreams.
Men will remember! (Verse 1)[19]

But the establishment need not have feared. As a commentator said at the time: '[Prime Minister] MacDonald came, saw, and was conquered.' King George V's mind was soon set at rest by Ramsay MacDonald: 'I had an hour's talk with him, he impressed me very much; he wishes to do the right thing. Today twenty three years ago, dear Grandmama [Queen Victoria] died. I wonder what she would have thought of a Labour Government?'[20] To the Labour cabinet 'doing the right thing' meant aiming at socialism through gradual parliamentary reform within the framework of a capitalist state and an imperialist empire. MacDonald rejected the slightest notion of class struggle: 'It cannot be overemphasised that popularism [direct action politics], strikes for increased wages or limitations of output, not only are not socialism but mislead the spirit of the socialist movement.'[21] Railwayman and cabinet minister J.H. Thomas was even more hostile: 'For as long as I can remember I have never disguised my antipathy to class conflict. It must inevitably lead to disaster.'[22]

What, then, should be the revolutionary strategy of the Communist Party? In the short term it decided to continue demands for affiliation to the Labour Party (a united front) but, as usual, with an ulterior motive. Its intention now was to press for radical reforms such as the nationalisation of the mines and full pay for the unemployed in the knowledge that the Labour Government could not fulfil them; its failure would provide the Communists with the pretext for accusing the Labour Government of betraying the working class. But this was not enough for Zinoviev, Lenin's closest friend for many years, long-time Old Bolshevik and now President of the Comintern. In May 1924 he sent an excoriating, confidential memorandum on 'The Immediate Tasks of the British Communist Party':

At present, the task of the C.P.G.B. is not to repeat stereotyped phrases about the united front, but at every step to expose the milk and water and treacherous character of MacDonald's so-called 'Labour Government'. It must raise the tone of its agitation to the stage of lashing and branding that party in proportion as its treachery unrolls itself before the eyes of the working masses. . . . It must pursue revolutionary Parliamentarism.

Finally, it must learn to conduct *revolutionary agitation* among the masses. . . . It must compel the Labour Government to resort to acts of repression, to the arrests of communists for becoming the pioneers of the masses of the working class.[23]

Palme Dutt was stung by this hysterical invective, for he himself was heavily criticised: 'the editorship of the weekly organ is far from satisfactory,' wrote Zinoviev. Perhaps for the first and last time in his life he argued with the Comintern, but he had good reason to do so. Marxism, he said, had never taken hold among the British working class. The workers' 'awakening to the struggle for power' was finding expression within the Labour Party, despite Labour's bourgeois policy and leadership. It was the Labour Party, through the trade unions, that was developing 'the first primitive form of working class solidarity. The Labour Government is "their government" and the workers are strongly hostile to any attacks on it, not on the ground of disagreement with the issues but because they feel their class solidarity is being attacked.'[24] Therefore, continued Dutt, simply ridiculing and lashing out at Labour could be counterproductive. The Communists' agitation and propaganda should be more subtle. It should point out that Labour was not going far or fast enough to bring about socialism; that only a revolutionary approach could overthrow capitalism.

Nevertheless, in obedience to Zinoviev's command to provoke the Labour Government, in July 1924 the *Workers' Weekly* carried 'An Open Letter to the Fighting Forces'. It was written anonymously but it was the work of the new Editor J.R. Campbell, with whom Wintringham worked closely as Assistant Editor. The 'Open Letter' must have exceeded expectations, for it led to the Campbell case and, dramatically, to the downfall of the Labour Government. The offending paragraph exhorted the armed forces:

Form committees (nuclei) in every barracks, aerodrome and ship. . . . Go forward in a common attack upon the capitalists. Smash capitalism for

ever and institute the reign of the working class.
Refuse to shoot strikers in industrial disputes!
Refuse to fight for profits!
Turn your weapons on your oppressors![25]

Was this an incitement to mutiny? The legal meaning of the words would soon be put to the test in relation to a similar but more extreme pamphlet written by Wintringham himself. But the Campbell letter must have rung hollow even then because there was no pretext for it. The army was not confronting the workers anywhere so it is hard not to see the 'Open Letter' as anything more than gratuitous provocation. Nevertheless, the Attorney-General charged Campbell under the Incitement to Mutiny Act. Then, fearing that Campbell would use the dock as a platform and become a martyr of free speech, the Labour Government withdrew the case. The Conservatives were outraged and so was the press: 'A Licence for Sedition' screamed the *Morning Post*. Eventually MacDonald wilted under the criticism and on 8 October 1924 Labour lost a vote of confidence. So the first Government of the working class was brought down by the Communists, the self-appointed champions of the working class.

Wintringham must have felt himself a revolutionary of importance. In an age without radio or television the *Workers' Weekly* was taken very seriously as the main weapon of agitation. Editorial statements were the voice of the Party, a voice articulated by the small team working in the King Street office. First this voice had been singled out by the great Zinoviev himself, a cause of indignation, and then it had led to the fall of the British Government, a cause of understandable hubris. For a man of twenty-six, a Communist for only one year, these were heady times. And so they continued.

An even greater Communist sensation followed hard on the heels of the Campbell case. Two weeks later, in the middle of the general election campaign, the *Daily Mail* published the notorious 'Zinoviev Letter'. This purported to be a letter to the CPGB from Zinoviev and McManus, now its representative in Moscow, encouraging the formation of nuclei in the British armed forces and munitions factories so that, in the event of war, these cells could paralyse military preparations and turn an imperialist war into a revolution. The CPGB, Zinoviev, the Russian Government, all protested that the letter was a forgery, but the British Government took it seriously and the press had, literally, a red-letter day. *The Times* ran the headlines: 'Soviet Plot – Red Propaganda in Great Britain – Revolution Urged by Zinoviev!' Whether or not the Zinoviev letter was a forgery has never been proved conclusively but proof is beside the point because its contents were in line with Comintern policy. It was a straightforward revolutionary tactic. In any event, the Conservative Party won the general election by a large majority and Labour blamed the Communists for their defeat.

That same month a bitter debate raged at the Labour Party Conference over the CPGB's application to affiliate. The case for rejection was argued succinctly by Labour MP G.A. Spencer:

> It was a well-known fact that the line of demarcation between the Communist Party and the Labour Party today was simply that the Labour Party believed in Parliamentary action coupled with the activities of the trade union movement, whereas the Communist Party believed the moment would come when they would be able to use the organised force of Labour to force a revolution.[26]

The Communists did not explicitly deny this charge. They replied that such was the power of the capitalist state that parliamentary action alone would not achieve socialism. Further, the dictatorship of the proletariat was more democratic than the parliamentary system because it meant real democracy for the vast majority of workers. As for the charge that they took orders from Moscow, they were proud to belong to the Communist International: 'Workers of the World Unite!'

The result was a foregone conclusion. By overwhelming majorities the Party's application was rejected. Individual Communists were banned from Labour Party membership and therefore Communists were barred from standing as Labour MPs. (In the recent general election the Communists had put up eight candidates, six of whom had been supported by local Labour Parties; they had polled just over 50,000 votes and returned one MP, the veteran Shapurji Saklatvala in North Battersea.) Fearing that they were now left out in the cold, cut off from the Labour Party that was the instinctive home of the British working class, the Communists vowed to fight on.

Despite this setback the moment when, as G.A. Spencer had predicted, the Communists would be able to use the organised force of labour to force a revolution, seemed to be approaching fast. Through 1925 a growing industrial crisis focusing on the coal industry was leading towards a confrontation between the new Conservative Government and the trade unions. Looming over it was the threat of a General Strike. Would this industrial weapon be exploited by the CPGB for political ends? Would the Communists force a revolution?

In this lull before the storm, Tom experienced a crisis of his own. He tarnished his political career by a private scandal, thus setting a precedent he was to follow more than once in the years ahead. Although he had only been married for two years, he separated from Elizabeth and carried on a passionate but short-lived affair with another member of the Party. At this stage in the Party's history, unlike in the Stalin era, sexual freedom was a matter at least of lively debate but it caused embarrassment in the closed society which Communists inhabited. In August Tom went off to Sweden to think things over and consult his mentors the Palme Dutts who were, presumably, staying with his relations. In a long letter to Muv written on the boat train back to Harwich from the Hook of Holland on 2 September, he said he had been thinking of 'living alone, close to Elizabeth, for a bit', but Raji had cut through this male propensity to have your cake and eat it with his familiar incisiveness: '"Usual thing is", says Raji slowly, "selfishness balanced and excused to oneself by kindness".'[27] Tom returned to a forgiving Elizabeth.

It is possible that Elizabeth had been away too; for in her photograph album are pictures of scruffy children of the Steppe. Underneath is the intriguing caption: '1924, Russia. Taken by Rose Cohen with my camera'. There are no photographs of Elizabeth in Russia; no clues as to whether she was with Rose or not. But in later years she spoke to her son as if she had been.

FOUR

Revolution?

On 14 October 1925, in the late afternoon, Tom Wintringham and J.R. Campbell were arrested at 1 Dr Johnson's Building and charged under the Incitement to Mutiny Act of 1797. The police took away cases of documents relating to the *Workers' Weekly* (which Wintringham had removed from the office anticipating his arrest) and Tom's love letters from Elizabeth. At the same time thirty police raided CPGB headquarters at 16 King Street and stripped it bare. Busts of Lenin and Zinoviev were 'arrested' and carted away along with furnishings, the lavatory ball cock and almost every scrap of paper. Tom wrote an amusing article about it, seeing the raid as a typical example of police overreaction:

> Each room had its plainclothes guard – there are twelve rooms counting cellars and attics. Not a stamp, not a matchbox, could escape. Every visitor to shop or office was detained. A solemn stillness reigned and over all loomed the Chief Inspector Parker like the spirit of God moving upon the face of the waters.[1]

Within a few days almost the entire leadership of the Party was arrested and charged under the same Act, eight out of ten of the Politburo. In Brussels Palme Dutt and a mysterious Miss Mary Moorhouse (Salme Murrik?), were arrested but after two weeks released for lack of evidence. Ironically, arch-conspirator Andrew Rothstein remained at liberty. A photograph taken outside Bow Street Magistrates' shows the twelve 'seditious mutineers' arriving at their trial looking like a group of commercial travellers up to London for the day. Wintringham stands modestly in the back row, his baldness now pronounced, making him appear older than his twenty-seven years. He is smiling shyly, as well he might. Although not a member of the Politburo, he was considered by the State to be a leader of the Party. (In his *English History 1914–1945* A.J.P. Taylor maintained that Wintringham was pulled in by mistake, but I do not think so. His 'Open Letter to the Armed Forces' was more extreme than Campbell's, as we shall see.) He knew that the prosecution would portray him as a threat to the State and the defence as its victim; good publicity in either event. Then he would be sent to prison, thereby satisfying Zinoviev and the Comintern.

A letter to Tom from the loyal Christina Roberts written one week later shows this was his state of mind: 'Good luck to you – I know you have wanted this for a long time. I am torn between a desire that you should not be shut up for a long time and that you should be out of harm's way over the May preparations' (even the expected date of the General Strike was common knowledge). 'Remember your intention long ago to write a novel? It's a good scheme. I expect I can find some money for bail if you want it.'[2] In fact the Labour MP John Scurr stood bail for Tom.

Elizabeth's response was more political. Her local Communist branch was one of the few to hold joint meetings with Labour constituency members 'in the spirit of unity in the class struggle'. So at a meeting of the Holborn Labour Party on 11 November she moved that 'We emphatically protest against the actions of the Government in arresting Communists for their political opinions. The Party stigmatises such action as part of a general attack on British workers. The Party calls on the Executive Committee of the Labour Party and the General Council of the T.U.C. to marshal all the forces of Labour to resist this capitalist onslaught.'[3] The motion was carried unanimously.

Wintringham and the others were sure they had been arrested in order to put them behind bars during a General Strike. The timing of the trial was certainly significant for it could have taken place at any point since the foundation of the Party. It was communism in Britain that was in the dock or, more importantly, Soviet-controlled communism. As Sir William Joynson-Hicks the Home Secretary said: 'while we have to put up with British Communists we are not prepared to put up with foreign Communists'. Counsel for one of the defendants put it more polemically: 'This case has been tried already – not in this court. It has been tried on a thousand platforms. It has been tried in ten thousand newspapers. We know now what it is we have all been seeking to try. We know now the full dimensions of the great Plot. The "Red Conspiracy" is in the dock.'[4] Communist suspicions about the timing of the trial were well founded. Years later a member of that Conservative Government wrote: 'We were at that time particularly worried about the revolutionary activity of the

Communist Party. . . . It was small but dangerous, particularly in the trade unions. . . .'[5] So the cabinet decided to act.

'Possibly the Greatest Political Trial in Modern British History' (*Workers' Weekly*) began at the Old Bailey on 16 November. The Attorney-General, Sir Douglas Hogg, opened for the prosecution. The defence of Wintringham and eight others was led by Sir Henry Slessor using legal arguments while Campbell, Gallagher and Pollitt defended themselves with political statements. The Twelve Apostles, as the *Workers' Weekly* dubbed them, crowded into the dock and were congratulated later by the police for their quiet and studious behaviour. The wives were in the back of the court 'behaving like ladies', according to a policeman, and the *Workers' Weekly* did not dissent from this classist view: 'they behaved with dignity and restraint, carefully following every detail, consistently smiling and cheerful'. The paper carried photographs of the wives; Elizabeth looks fiercely proletarian with a cigarette jammed straight between her lips and a hat pulled down to her eyes.

The Crown's charge was similar to that presented at the Bow Street committal proceedings earlier when Sir Travers Humphrey had outlined it succinctly; this is how it appeared in the issue of the *Workers' Weekly* for 30 October 1925:

All persons disseminating Communism are liable to be prosecuted for sedition. Communism hails from Moscow and Communists receive orders from Moscow. It is illegal because, first, it seeks to overthrow the constituted Government of this country and establish forms of Government by force; second, it involves the creation of antagonism between different classes of His Majesty's subjects; and third, it involves the seducing from their allegiance of the armed forces of the crown.

As evidence of the third charge Sir Travers produced a pamphlet written by Wintringham that was even more provocative than Campbell's 'Open Letter to the Armed Forces'. Wintringham's appeal read: 'Soldiers, sailors, airmen, definitely let it be known that neither in the class war nor the military war will you turn your guns on your fellow workers, *but use your arms on the side of your own class* [my emphasis]. Turn your weapons on your oppressors!' This document was also produced at the Old Bailey.[6]

The most candid political defence of the Twelve at the Old Bailey was offered by J.R. Campbell. In refutation of the alleged revolutionary threat he pointed out that the Party had carried on its work openly for five years. Despite this, he admitted that, so far anyway 'revolution was a hypothetical contingency'. Britain was not yet in a revolutionary situation, defined as one where 'the ruling class was disorganised, where the masses were in a state of revolutionary excitement and where intermediate strata (the middle class or bourgeoisie) might go over to the workers' side'.[7] This was undeniably true and the reason for the Party's impotence, however much the Comintern might refuse to accept it. But the Government's fear was that a General Strike might alter this reality.

When Campbell turned to a defence of 'seducing the armed forces' he repeated what he had said the previous year. Wintringham's document and his own were fair comment; they were not meant to cause offence. Sir Henry Slessor in his more legalistic defence put it differently. The Army Acts and Incitement to Mutiny Act, he said, did not apply to a trade dispute and anyway the notorious 'Don't Shoot the Workers' plea was 'entirely conjectural'. It really meant 'don't shoot a class of persons who are rightly entitled not to be shot'.[8]

On 25 November the judge, Mr Justice Rigby Swift, summed up and put pertinent questions to the jury. Concerning the Campbell and Wintringham pamphlets: 'Look at the quotation, "If you must shoot do not shoot the workers", Did not that mean "Shoot your officers"?' Concerning a sum of £14,000 which the police had discovered on the premises of 16 King Street and the prosecution alleged came from Moscow: 'Why would Moscow supply money if it did not want to encourage a similar revolution to their own?'

The gravamen of the summing up that must have weighed most heavily on the jury and shows clearly how a General Strike and a revolution came together as a real fear, was paraphrased thus by *Workers' Weekly*:

In the documents before them the jury would find passage after passage which referred to putting a nucleus into the Army for the purpose of inculcating communism among soldiers [cf. the Zinoviev Letter]. It was not uninteresting to note that the revolution in Russia had begun in the Army.

The revolution which the prosecution suggested was hinted at in this country was to begin with a General Strike, and the Army was to come in to maintain order. Once a revolution of that kind was started only the armed forces of the Crown could stop it. If strikes led to rioting and the police could not cope then the armed forces would be used.[9]

It was the imminence of a General Strike, then, that was preoccupying the Government and the worry that in the event the Communist Party might subvert the loyalty of the army. This is where the Campbell and Wintringham letters became highly significant, perhaps the most damning evidence that the prosecution had. Could the jury visualise a scenario in which the armed forces, required to restore order, instead obeyed the exhortations of Campbell and Wintringham and turned their guns on the officers?

After only twenty-two minutes' deliberation the jury returned to court and their foreman, an elderly man with a sharp voice, pronounced all the defendants guilty. The Twelve Apostles, wearing red roses in their jacket lapels for the occasion, heard the verdicts in silence. Mrs Rust, one of the wives, fainted and was removed from a packed court. Then the judge sentenced the five with previous convictions to one year in prison. He offered the other seven, including Wintringham, the choice of promising to leave the Party or six months' imprisonment. 'Thomas Henry Wintringham, will you be bound over?' 'No', was the answer given in a steady voice. 'I will not.'

Ever after Wintringham said he was proud to have gone to prison for exhorting army officers not to fire on their own men. A rational reading of what he actually wrote – and Tom always approved of being rational – suggests this statement was highly disingenuous. Wintringham was clearly guilty. In the context of an expected General Strike and the fear that the Communists might use this to provoke a revolution, his pamphlet was highly seditious.

The last word on the trial belonged to Wintringham. As soon as he arrived at Brixton prison he made all twelve Communist leaders sign a press statement that appeared prominently in the *Workers' Weekly* under the heading: 'To our Fellow-Workers. A Warning'. They had heard Sir Douglas Hogg let slip in court the phrase 'if troops are ordered to suppress a strike', whereas when Campbell challenged him he said he had meant suppress *riots*. There was more than a semantic difference, of course, as the judge himself had indicated in the key passage of his summing up. The 'Warning' continued: 'they do mean to suppress strikes and they are resolved to make strikes inevitable. Workers of Britain: Stand Fast and Be Prepared'.[10] From prison Tom wrote to Elizabeth: 'Hogg has this God-Almighty complex. It was a slip but it showed what was inside his mind.'[11]

The Twelve were moved to Wandsworth gaol where, by order of the judge, they were made Second Division prisoners. The intention, apart from subjecting them to a less severe regime, was to keep them separate from regular gaolbirds for fear of mutual contamination. Nevertheless, they were only allowed one visit and one letter a month. They sewed mailbags (one per day in order to earn full remission), scrubbed floors and washed up with cold, greasy water. Their uniform was a brown suit with their number on a pocket, and a cumbersome cap known as a bonnet.

Tom wrote to Elizabeth that he found prison tolerable; living conditions were better than in East Ham or Bethnal Green and at least the building was designed for the job. His routine improved after he got work in the library, always the sanctuary for intellectual revolutionaries serving their time. Nevertheless, he found being 'banged up' alone for fourteen hours every day very trying. He revealed this in an unfinished novel he wrote inside called simply 'Jim':

> They turned Jim into his cell at four in the afternoon, and he knew he must stay there alone until half-past six the next morning. . . . As soon as he got to his cell he always had to take a decision. That was the worst moment in the day – worse even than the half hour after waking. He had to force himself, pledge himself, to think seriously about this or that thing. If he did not do this, if he let his thoughts scatter and 'go bad', he could not sleep. Over and over again would come the injustices and grievances. . . . Worst enemy of all, self pity would stand at the back of his thoughts – that one defeating weakness, able to rub every sore. . . .[12]

The only political news allowed from outside came from a summary of the weekly newspapers read out by the chaplain. Nevertheless, the Twelve Apostles cannot have failed to take heart from the repercussions of their case. They would have heard the slogan chanting and cheering of 25,000 protesters outside the prison. Word must have got through of the petition demanding their release signed by 300,000 supporters. Although the right-wing press gloated over the prison sentences, the general reaction was that the Government had made heavy weather of the prosecution and that the defendants had gained favourable publicity. The Labour Party made it an issue of free speech. The Communist advice was that the Party had not suddenly become illegal. As the law stood, any active member might get arrested but this was not likely to happen. Carry on as before!

Tom's revenge was an abusive but amusing poem published later in *Left Review*:

'Contempt of Court'

Contempt, my Lord? it's not contempt we feel;
We, from the age of science and steel,
Are privileged to view, thus staged, the last
Rite of taboo from our far primitive past.

Your aboriginal innocence forbids
Contempt, your bland blind aspect rids
The enquiring mind of all save anthropology;
Writ, affidavit and apology.

Full-bottomed wig and judge and carefully rounded
Snake-phrases twisting – these will all be confounded
By lazy schoolboys, fifty years from now,
With fetish reverence and the sacred cow.[13]

Tom obviously regarded prison as an opportunity to improve his mind. In his first letter to Elizabeth he gave her a lecture on his favourite theme of historical dialectics:

In the really great things people make you feel the overshadowing fate. In classic times the fates were the terrible blind taboos; rules that were just so because the Gods had made them. At the Renaissance, personal passions loosed from ages of repression, tradition and dullness loomed out as big as fates. There were fevers that seized men (Romeo, Hamlet) or characteristics that dominated them (Lady Macbeth, Falstaff) and the consequences of these were inevitable. The third plan – the future one and ours – will have two forces woven through and the clash of these will be our vision of earth. Sometimes the two will be matter and energy, sometimes past and future, sometimes an older generation and a younger, but the underlying theme will be some process, the reaching of some stage, in the struggle between men and their environment.[14]

Elizabeth's monthly letters to Tom are very different. She writes dutifully and lovingly (sentiments rarely evident in Tom's letters) but always about trivia. She is aware of this: 'Dearest, there seems so little that I can tell you of what you really want to hear and my life is passing so uneventfully. . . . I fear

I am holding you back.' The letters of course were read by prison officers so political content was inadvisable, but nevertheless Elizabeth gives the impression of a young woman who, despite her education, is sensible rather than intellectual, and, despite her best efforts at the trial to dress down, thoroughly bourgeois. She writes about gardening, an article in *Harper's* magazine, a visit to the show *No, No, Nanette*, family chit-chat about using the new wireless: 'Dad will not let it be and twiddles with it the whole time. It is an important but disruptive part of home life.'[15] She seems such an improbable revolutionary.

At Christmas prisoners were allowed cards and *Workers' Weekly* encouraged readers to send them. Tom received a pile from the Communist heartlands of Glasgow Gorbals, Pontypool and London's East End. The typical design was a plastic cover of red and blue flowers stuck on to cardboard. Inside, the sentimental ditty clashed with the political message:

> A spray of blossom fair and sweet
> Oh, take it Dear from me
> For every best wish that I send
> Bears greeting fond of thee.
> – Yours in the fight, Peggy Smyth.

One had more character: 'Dear Comrade, Just a line to let you know a few workers in Woolwich Arsenal will be thinking of you and *the cause* on this anniversary of a half-breed Ghost.'[16] Elizabeth's card must have broken a few rules of Party correctness. It was a picture of Benozzo Gozzoli's *The Rape of Helen* in the National Gallery. A well-timed message arrived from the Inner Temple threatening Tom with eviction from Dr Johnson's Building; a resident Communist was one thing but a convicted criminal was another. Apart from Elizabeth, Tom received visits from Muv, who was loyal but disapproving, and Christina.

He was released at 8.15 a.m. on 11 April 1926, and met at the door of Wandsworth prison by Elizabeth and Rose Cohen. There were 25,000 others too, as described by Palme Dutt writing from Brussels for the *Krasnaya Gazette*:

Workers tramped from districts in every direction from the early hours of the morning, even fifteen miles through the London streets. Banners had been constructed bearing slogans of the fight, demanding the release of the remaining five prisoners and unity behind the miners. Tableaux were drawn on carts; there was a 'Don't Shoot' tableau depicting a soldier in uniform with his rifle fraternising with a worker, there was a tableau of 'Prisoners of Capitalism' depicting a prison cell, a worker in convict dress and a warder.

The drama reached its culmination outside the prison gates. The released Communist leaders shouted greetings through megaphones to those still imprisoned within. The cheers of 25,000 workers and the singing of the Internationale pierced the prison walls. The police took names and addresses of the tableaux actors and issued summons. Mounted police drove into parts of the procession causing injury.[17]

Tom's release was only three weeks before 1 May, the date when a General Strike was expected to begin. As it drew closer its ominous significance seemed to spread wider. Prime Minister Baldwin said in the House of Commons: 'We are nearer to civil war than we have been for centuries.' *The Times* was more specific; it described the prospect of a General Strike as 'the greatest menace which has hung over the nation since the fall of the Stuarts'. Baldwin's Government was sure that the strike was ultimately political. The Home Secretary Sir William Joynson-Hicks remarked: 'Sooner or later this thing has got to be fought out by the people of this land. Is England to be governed by Parliament and the Cabinet, or by a handful of trade union leaders?'[18] This was one occasion when Palme Dutt completely agreed with the Government: 'The greatest strength of the Bourgeoisie [the British establishment] is that they recognise the political character of the conflict. "Either you govern here or we do. There cannot be two dictatorships."'[19] This was not the view, however, of the Labour Party and trade unions. They shied away from the dreadful implication of a General Strike, that if applied ruthlessly it could cause a revolution. To them it was simply an industrial dispute which, they hoped, would not hurt the public, never mind bring the Government to its knees. Their sincere, but in the end half-hearted aim, was better conditions for the miners and therefore a safeguard for all workers.

The coal question, as it was called, was symbolic of the battle between capitalism and labour after the First World War. The coal industry was declining severely as markets shrank and cheaper coal was imported from the Ruhr; the industry lost over 20 per cent of its workforce in the 1920s. But all the traditional heavy industries were suffering as Britain ceased to be the workshop of the world and that is why the miners enjoyed such support. It was widely believed that if they won a good pay and hours deal, others would follow.

What exactly had brought this crisis about? Nine months earlier, the coal mine owners had threatened to reduce the wages and increase the working hours of the miners. The miners, dockers and railway workers had retaliated by threatening to stop all the nation's transport. Baldwin had refused to intervene but then had capitulated by granting a £10 million subsidy to the coal industry provided there was a return to work. The trade unions had celebrated by dubbing the date of victory 'Red Friday', in contrast to 'Black Friday' in 1921 when a previous Triple Alliance of miners, railwaymen and transport workers sworn to defend the miners had collapsed in the face of a State of Emergency. That time the mine owners, and many inside Parliament and out, thought that the Government had given in to blackmail. This time there would be no compromise and the subsidy was due to end on 1 May.

There was no chance that the two sides would reach agreement in the interim. The mine owners, represented by the Mining Association, were rigid and without compassion. The miners' leaders were equally obdurate. Herbert Smith, President of the Miners' Federation, was a blunt Yorkshireman who attended meetings with his cloth cap in his pocket. His negotiating style was to take out his dentures, wipe them and then say bluntly, 'Nowt doin'. His secretary, Arthur Cook, supplied the eloquence. His speeches had a revivalist fervour but a violent rhetoric that sent shivers down capitalist spines. He was proud, he said, to be a follower of Lenin (actually he was not a Communist but a member of the ILP) and he looked forward to the end of the British Empire. Neither side gave the voter any confidence in the British skill of compromise. Lord Birkenhead, a former Lord Chancellor, said he thought the miners' leaders the stupidest men he had ever met – until he met the mine owners. The two sides were on collision course with a belligerent Government and an anxious Labour opposition drawn up behind them. All waited for the subsidy to end and the mine owners to impose their draconian response.

Sure enough, on 1 May a million miners were locked out until they accepted to work longer hours for less pay. A General Strike was called in response but this did not begin until Tuesday 4 May when the strike notices first took effect. By breakfast time between 1 and 1½ million workers were on strike – nearly every worker connected with transport, printing, heavy industry and building. Townspeople noticed the huge number of bicycles and private cars as commuters found their own way to work, and then sat around in offices doing little when they got there. Crowds formed round shops that sold wireless sets. There was an atmosphere of urgent excitement.

Where was Tom Wintringham in all this? He had been on a speaking tour, explaining: 'why I went to Quod [prison], as this would leave no loophole for people who had excuses for being out of the Party'.[20] But on 4 May he was most probably in hiding and getting out the daily, crudely typed *Workers' Bulletin*, a mixture of news, exhortation and propaganda printed for the duration of the strike when the *Workers' Weekly* was suspended. The next day detectives raided 16 King Street, carrying crowbars and jemmies. They ransacked the offices, scattered the bookshop literature and carried warrants for the seizure of any material for the publication of a strike paper. Under the 1920 Emergency Powers Act it was an offence to circulate bulletins 'likely to cause despair and despondency in the civil population', so writing, distributing, even carrying a Communist paper was illegal. In fact, the *Workers' Bulletin* did bear Marjorie Pollitt's name as editor (Marjorie Brewer had married Pollitt just four days before he was gaoled) and gave the address as 16 King Street. This was an act of defiance for which she was a willing scapegoat. She was arrested but the *Bulletin* continued to be distributed daily from secret addresses and was copied by Party members in other towns. No doubt Tom would have received a heavy sentence if he had been convicted so soon after his last offence so his low profile is understandable. But it is a best guess that as the only senior Communist journalist left in London (J.R. Campbell was in Scotland, Palme Dutt in Brussels, and most of the leadership still in prison), this is what he was doing. By the end of the strike over a thousand Party members had been arrested, most of them for selling copies of the *Bulletin*, and many were given prison sentences of between two and six months.

The strike has passed into popular history as a peculiarly British affair in which both sides obeyed the rules and were good sports; when carefree undergrads commandeered buses and police played football with striking workers. This is far too rosy a picture. For instance, the ugly scenes that accompanied the passage of the Government food convoy from London Docks to its Emergency Food Depot in Hyde Park over the weekend of 8/9 May showed just how close the strike came to sparking street battles between strikers and the armed forces. During the first week of the strike no more than 40 out of 14,000 dockers showed up for work and the narrow streets round the wharves were packed with strikers. On Friday night, therefore, strike-breaking students were transported down the Thames by boat to the docks. At dawn on Saturday when the strikers awoke they saw that the gates and buildings round the docks were guarded by a battalion of fully armed Grenadier Guards while hundreds of sailors manned the cranes. In East India Docks naval marines pointed a machine-gun directly at the strikers. In this intimidating atmosphere the students unloaded crates of food and the first convoy of 105 lorries moved out to Hyde Park escorted by 20 armoured cars:

the sullen mass of strikers who congregated after dawn were awed by the military and permitted most of the moving on by the mounted police, backed this time by enough artillery to kill every living thing in every street in the neighbourhood of the docks.[21]

Nor was the violence, or threat of violence, by any means all one-sided. There were acts of arson and sabotage by strikers, of which two spectacular incidents were the setting fire to *The Times* printing presses on 5 May and the derailment of the *Flying Scotsman* on 10 May. Pitched battles with the police were not uncommon either. On 6 May over a hundred police baton-charged rioters in Glasgow and arrested sixty-six.

The government, egged on by Chancellor of the Exchequer Winston Churchill, had spent the nine months' truce before 1 May in preparation; and throughout it acted with a determination to crush the strike bordering on the bellicose. The CPGB's report to the Comintern, written shortly afterwards, described in proud Bolshevik-speak but with accuracy just how ruthlessly the Government had made its preparations:

The Government acted with irreproachable firmness, as real generals of the capitalist army. They knew exactly the weakness of their opponent's generals, and struck hard. Using the Emergency Powers Act, they established a complete capitalist dictatorship, Parliament dropping into the background. WHITE GUARDS: they recruited 300,000 middle-class 'volunteers' as technical aid (train drivers, power station operatives), as auxiliary police and as unskilled labour. VIOLENCE: use was made of battleships, armoured cars and troops to overawe the workers. THE LEGAL WEAPON: summary prison sentences were dealt out lavishly and the strike was declared illegal. PROPAGANDA: it published an incredibly lying propaganda organ under Churchill's editorship, *The British Gazette*, and commandeered all stocks of paper to issue it.[22]

A ruthless Government was up against an irresolute Opposition. The TUC General Council that organised the strike discouraged anything but limited picketing. In fact it ran a selective strike on a national level, not a General Strike, because it kept essential services like electricity and gas going so as not to cause suffering. Its advice to strikers: 'Keep smiling. . . . Refuse to be provoked. Get out into your garden. Look after the wife and kiddies. Get out into the country, there is no more heartfelt occupation than walking.'[23] It discouraged the very term 'General Strike' and from 7 May onwards its paper, the *British Worker*, printed a daily disclaimer, 'like a ghastly chorus', according to the official Communist Party history: 'The General Council does not challenge the Constitution. It is not desirous of undermining Parliamentary institutions. The sole aim of the Council is to secure for the miners a decent standard of living. The Council is engaged in an industrial dispute.'[24]

From the start the Communist Party was a driving force behind the strike. For months it had urged workers to form Councils of Action to administer the strike in each locality: to organise picketing, distribute food, even hand out passes to 'legitimate' transport. Tom had written an instructional article about this in the last edition of *Workers' Weekly* before it was suspended. He had also urged workers to form defence corps. Elizabeth's corps at the Holborn branch was somewhat genteel, more suited to marshalling a meeting in Hampstead than wading in to a street fight. The branch organised voluntary physical training, a cycling corps and a women's section provided all members attended meetings and showed special membership cards. The CPGB poured effort into agitation and propaganda, taking up Arthur Cook's watchword 'All Together behind the Miners; Not a Penny off the Pay. Not a Second on the Day'. During the strike comrades handed out an estimated sixty thousand pamphlets, at great risk to themselves.

The *Bulletin* carried a clear political agenda. It called for the 'Nationalisation of the Mines, without Compensation for the Coal Owners, under Workers' Control through Pit Committees' (cf. *Workers' Bulletin*, 6 May, 'The Political Meaning of the General Strike') and it demanded the election of a Labour Government. But was it a revolutionary agenda? At the very least the Party saw the strike as raising the level of revolutionary consciousness, but it went further than that. It stated openly that it wished to bring down the Government, thereby causing a constitutional crisis out of which Labour would come to power. Wintringham wrote in the *Communist Review* just after the strike:

> The aim of the C.P.G.B. – in the face of the lock-out of the miners and the identification of the Government with the mineowners – was to hold tight until the Government admitted it was beaten, resigned and made way for a Labour Government.

Now that Russian files are no longer secret we can see that the Comintern, as always intending to pull the strings from Moscow, actually hoped for a revolution. At a meeting on 7 May attended by Stalin, Zinoviev said that the situation in Britain was 'the most important since the Russian revolution' and could lead to 'a mass Communist Party'.[25] In a confidential letter to the CPGB the Comintern recommended that if the strike continued to intensify, then the Party should call for Labour militias and widespread nationalisation; the next stage would be a call for workers' Soviets. Undoubtedly, some British Communists and members of the Independent Labour Party saw it the same way: 'We thought the Government would collapse and there would be chaos, and the Councils of Action would move in, form Soviets and run industry. We really thought this. We thought the General Council of the T.U.C. would become the Worker's Government.'[26]

But given the determination of the Government not to back down and the fearful, half-hearted organisation of the TUC there could be only one outcome. Although official reports of the Ministry of Labour to the Government showed that the strikers were holding firm, on 12 May the TUC General Council called off the strike – a 'sell-out' workers called it.

The result was catastrophic for the strikers. Many were victimised when they tried to return to work, just as they had been during the strike:

> At Gateshead Police Court at the end of May a miner was summoned under the Emergency Regulations Act for distributing a local Council of Action pamphlet called Northern Light. This contained the light hearted passage: 'the lowest aim in life is to be a policeman. When a policeman dies he goes so low he has to climb a ladder to get into hell!' (Laughter in Court). The Magistrate asked the accused if he was a Bolshevik? No, replied the Defence, he was a member of the Labour Party. The Magistrate sentenced him to three months hard labour in prison and

added that he would like to fine him £100 as well: 'Why you and those who are associated with you don't go off to Russia I don't know. You are making a mistake living in this country. We don't want you or anyone like you!'[27]

The criminal, who may have spent most of his working life toiling on his knees underground, was striking for a living wage. He may well have been an ex-soldier who had fought for King and Country in the First World War for Civilisation. Wintringham came across hundreds of similar examples of 'class war' as he compiled the 'Workers' Life' columns in the weekly paper. 'Men will Remember!' he wrote in 'Revolution'.

The miners hung on until November 1926 supported financially by the Russian trade unions, a fact that old miners recall with gratitude to this day. In the end they were forced to capitulate through hunger and desperation and so they returned to work for less pay and longer hours. For years a widespread feeling of betrayal separated trade unionists from their leaders. Many members voted with their feet. In 1927 total membership of trade unions fell below 5 million for the first time in over a decade. That year the passage of the hated Trade Disputes Act made another General Strike impossible, even if there was an appetite for one, by imposing restrictive strike laws. Many years later a former Deputy Leader of the Labour Party, J.R. Clynes, provided a postscript:

Early in the strike J.H. Thomas (the railwayman's leader and then a prominent member of the General Council) found that his duties took him to Buckingham Palace. King George V, who was gravely disturbed, remarked 'Well, Thomas, if the worst happens, I suppose all this (with a gesture indicating his surroundings) will vanish?'

Fortunately for Britain and the world it did not come to the worst. The Trade Unions saw to that.[28]

What was Wintringham's verdict on the strike? This we do know, although his archive contains no information about what part he actually played. Did he purposefully not commit pen to paper? Was he too busy to do so? Did Elizabeth much later remove this material because of its sensitivity? In any event, letters suggest that they went off to France immediately after the strike for a brief holiday, for Tom had had no respite since prison and Elizabeth had just finished her medical exams. Tom had been kicked out of the Inner Temple so when they returned they needed to find new lodgings and then he was back in the *Workers' Weekly* office by the end of May. For the 6 June edition he wrote an important article, 'The Party that Foresees and Fights'.

Tom wrote that the Party had got the strike right. 'We told you so!' he begins. From the outset the Party had seen the strike as political; it had warned the TUC to make preparations; it had convened Councils of Action and had been the driving force for maintaining solidarity during the strike; and the workers had stayed out. He ends the article: 'Who is coming in to the Party that foresees as well as fights, whose policy and outlook was right and is right now?'[29] Many did, for Party membership doubled during the summer and sales of the *Workers' Weekly* rose to 80,000. Tom thought, and continued to think, that revolution was only a matter of time. This was the official view of the Comintern too. Its report *Lessons of the British Strike* pronounced that it had brought revolution nearer:

The mass movement developed with unprecedented force. The growing enthusiasm of the masses, in some places spontaneously coming out on to the streets and resorting to methods of revolutionary violence (e.g. destruction of 'blackleg' motor-buses, the calling upon soldiers not to obey orders, the closing down of bourgeois papers), and the organisation of Councils of Action from below that seized socially important functions (like the distribution of food) showed that the strike was moving towards higher forms of the movement.[30]

The next decade would show that this assessment was fundamentally wrong, as Tom admitted in the last year of his life. Nearly all workers regarded the General Strike as an industrial dispute and its failure only provided Communist gains in the very short term. Fabian Beatrice Webb wrote in her diary at the time that the failure of the strike would be 'one of the most significant landmarks in the history of the British working class because it would be the end of the pernicious doctrine of workers' control'.[31] In retrospect we can see that the strike marked the end of the last great period of working-class militancy and showed that the British worker, whatever the poverty of his life or pusillanimity of the Labour Party, did not see a Communist revolution as the answer.

FIVE

'Class Against Class'

After the General Strike a young Communist miner, Abe Moffat (later President of the Miners' Union), was consoled by an old Party comrade: 'Never mind, Abe, we've sown the seeds!' Today, with neither British mining industry nor Communist Party to speak of, we can see that they were completely wrong; but Tom felt the same way. More particularly, taking stock in June 1926 with that historical perspective he was so fond of applying, he must have rejoiced at his own life. Exactly ten years earlier he had joined the Royal Flying Corps and since then he had experienced war and revolution. He had committed himself to a life-shaping ideology and become one of the 'young Turks' of the Communist Party. He had helped plan its strategy in a General Strike which, he believed, was the beginning of the end of capitalism. He had found love and married. He had improved his poetry and ridden his motorbike 'very fast'. Six years later that optimism had evaporated:

'Before Prison'

I have known pride and power,
Seen under leaning wings
Village and city flower –
Queer, tiny, petalled things! –
I know the lilt of the tune
That a great car sings.

And I have lain with my love.

I have known fear, defeat,
Found dead my first-born son,
Found changeling love a cheat,
Lost youth, lost health, let run
Lust's snake across my brain;
And I've known pain.

These you can shut from me
By the prison gate;
But my love's loyalty
And comrades' fellowship
And my hate
Of your wars and your lies and your laws –
These I keep![1]

Tom's sentiments applied to the whole decade until he left for Spain in 1936. It was a depressing decade when hopes became illusions even though the underlying faith remained. It was a drab period when Tom commuted from suburbia to work he disliked and was short of money. It was a humbling time, for he was reduced to the role of Party functionary, as he put it and, later, found that some of his notable work had been whitewashed over by the Party history. For much of this time his private life was in a mess and the Communist Party, riven with feuds and uncertainties caused by the notorious 'class against class' policy, was in a bigger mess. Tom, who admitted that he was not sufficiently interested in nor confident about Party politics, kept his head down. But towards the end of this period he looked up again and regained his pride. He said that two things interested him more than politics: 'war, which I hate, and literature, which I love and where I was given freedom'.[2] By 1936 Wintringham, now a founder editor of *Left Review* and military correspondent of the *Daily Worker*, was beginning to make a reputation which would extend far beyond the Communist Party and eventually establish him in the *Dictionary of National Biography* as 'a uniquely English revolutionary' and the foremost, if not the only, British Marxist expert on warfare.

After the General Strike Tom and Elizabeth moved to 51 Wilson Road in Camberwell Green, south-east London. He never qualified at the Bar but she heard soon after the move that she had passed the LRCP and MRCS exams and could now practise as a doctor. In fact she did not work at all until the Second World War when she joined the Blood Transfusion Service and then the Family Planning Association. So they depended for income on Tom's very modest salary as a journalist on *Workers' Weekly*, perhaps supplemented by the Party the same year when they appointed him manager of Comintern publications in the UK; books like *The Theory and Practice of Leninism* by Stalin and Reid's *Ten Days that Shook the World*.

On 13 November 1927 their first son was born, Robin, named after their friend Robin Page Arnot. He died in his cot six months later:

'For Robin, Aged Six Months'

So sweet the blossom in so short an hour,
So gay, so perfect, and so quickly stilled –
Spring's poignancy, all gathered to this flower,
Knows not the summer's richer ways fulfilled.[3]

Probably in the following year, they moved to 20 Warren Avenue in the conservative London suburb of East Sheen – an unlikely environment for a revolutionary. Elizabeth must have loved the Arts and Crafts style cottage in a terrace of four, with its English lawn and garden, presumably paid for with Arkwright money. No doubt to the disapproval of his neighbours behind their privet hedges, Tom commuted by bus or motorbike to Communist offices in Gray's Inn Road. Here he worked first as Editor of the *Worker*, the 'official organ of the National Minority Movement', and then for a short while in 1929 as Editor of *Workers' Life*, the successor to *Workers' Weekly*, which had been forced to close after a libel action two years earlier.

On 18 March 1929, their second son, Oliver Joseph, was born. A photograph taken two years later shows him sitting mischievously on Tom's motorbike outside 20 Warren Avenue, Tom himself looking raffish and indulgent. Tom was good with his children, when he was at home. He had an easy, friendly manner and the ability to communicate at the right level. He and Elizabeth sang O.J. (as he has always been called) communist ditties instead of nursery rhymes. One favourite was 'Hallelujah, I'm a Bum', then popular among the Wobblies (the International Workers of the World) riding the railroads west to California:

Oh, I like my boss, he's a good friend of mine,
That's why I'm starving out on the breadline,
[Chorus]
Hallelujah, I'm a bum,
Hallelujah, bum again,
Hallelujah, give us a handout
To revive us again.

One of O.J.'s earliest memories is of his father squatting by a motorbike engine stripped down on the kitchen floor and explaining the mysterious actions of piston rings and connecting rods. In 1934 Tom wrote a children's story for *Martin's Christmas Annual* about motorbikes in which the one human character, Joey, is obviously intended to be O.J. There is a political storyline, of course. The mechanics are overworked and as a result the motorbikes are badly made and unsafe; so they go on strike and the bikes decide to help them. In the end lorries and cars and motorbikes charge the factory in a united front and the police run for it. The boss gives in. What is so effective is that the bikes come alive and speak:

> When they were well on the old North Road he heard the spokes in the wheel talking. At first they seemed to have a queer language; they said 'Ennery, dennery, rin, tan, lintidan' and other words like that. Young Joey asked what they meant. The spokes explained: 'It's the old way of counting. We count the times that the wheel goes round.' (They were telling the truth: these counting words are older than Julius Caesar. You can hear a Lincolnshire shepherd count his sheep that way, as they huddle at a gate. . . . But you'll never hear a banker or a millionaire use them. They are part of the old things that some ordinary people keep: the rich, who think they own everything and can know everything, have never learnt them and never will.) 'We count the rods, poles, perches, furlongs and miles,' said the spokes.

Within the family Tom was compared to an absent-minded professor; lazy, bookish, shy. By now his appearance invited that comparison, for he wore small, round wire-rimmed glasses ('granny glasses' his daughter called them later) on his large bald head that seemed to dwarf his other facial features. He walked with a slight stoop, his hands in his pockets. Yet even nursery rhymes and children's books showed where his sympathies lay. The working man, undervalued and exploited through history, may have been down-trodden but he was not beaten. Now he was about to rise and claim his due.

The new Comintern strategy, called 'class against class', was dictated by Stalin himself and imposed on the British by their Comintern representative Max Petrovsky who, incidentally, had married Rose Cohen and set up house in Moscow. Stalin believed that 'the irreconcilable contradictions of contemporary capitalism' were leading the world into a new crisis and war.

The other parties of the left, he added, were 'capitalist lackeys' who would fight against workers in this war. He pointed out that in Britain the Labour Party and trade unions were moving to the right while the masses were moving to the left. The only way forward, then, was to declare that Lenin's advice of 1920 to collaborate with the Labour Party no longer applied. In future the Communist Party must not only advance alone as the only revolutionary party but regard as class enemies, as social fascists, the social democrats or other parties of the left.

For hardened working-class revolutionaries such as Harry Pollitt, who had always been equivocal about affiliation to the Labour Party and viewed its role in the General Strike with disgust, this was a welcome change. The new line was hammered out at a meeting of the Central Committee in January 1928 when one of its supporters, Helen Crawford, made a memorable speech:

> We have done our best to work through the constitutional machinery of the Labour movement . . . and we have been deprived of rights. We have been derided, suppressed, spat upon and kicked. . . . In the eyes of the workers the Party is neither fish, flesh nor decent red herring.[4]

The next year Harry Pollitt became General Secretary of the Party. Raji Palme Dutt, ever the hardliner apart from his wobble in 1924, also came back to prominence with a seat on both the Central Committee and Politburo, though until 1936 he continued to live in Brussels. The Party's first General Secretary, Bill McManus, the hard-drinking Scot from the Red Clyde, had died in 1927, his ashes interred in the Kremlin wall where 'old drinking companions could pay their respects every day'.

In June 1929 Ramsay MacDonald formed his second Labour Government, but once again dependent on Liberal votes. Five months later Wall Street crashed and within a few months 2 million British workers were out of work.

With this as the background we may see from the statement issued by the London and District Committee of the Communist Party, in February 1930, how grassroots members such as Elizabeth Wintringham viewed 'class against class' and argued the imminence of revolution. Communism, the statement noted, had entered its Third Period, a period of war and revolution. As evidence it pointed to 'the growing weakness of British capitalism and the rising wave of working class revolt. The large number of strikes and their political character are evidence of a great revolutionary wave in Britain.'[5] It then surveyed the world for further revolutionary indicators. It said with confidence that in India British imperialism faced the biggest crisis in its history. (At Meerut, Indian trade unionists supported by two British Communists were on trial for conspiracy 'to deprive the King-Emperor of Sovereignty over British India'.) It expressed the profound conviction that the German Communist Party would bring about a proletarian dictatorship. It suspected that the British Government was making 'cunningly hidden' preparations for war on the Soviet Union which, of course, 'was growing stronger under the banner of the CPSU'.

We now know, and much was obvious then, that this survey was wrong in almost every respect. In Germany the 'class against class' policy was to put Hitler in power by fatally splitting the left-wing vote. There was no British war against the Soviet Union. Crucially, at home, there were no real signs of working-class revolt or anything like another General Strike. As communist Dai Davies, a miner from South Wales, had admitted at the Party Congress held two months earlier: 'When comrades speak of the radicalisation of the masses and the great wave of insurrection, I want to tell you that in my experience – which is not small – I have not seen a ripple of it.'[6] To which engineer Bill Stokes from Coventry added: 'Anyone speaking of a revolt of the workers is living in a fool's paradise.'

The London District Committee then moved to a resolution (February 1930). It declared that in order to combat the forces of social fascism and to intensify class struggle the Party had to act exclusively from below. It had to recruit far more among the ranks of the Minority Movement and the National Unemployed Workers' Movement, both Communist fronts. It needed to be resolutely proletarian. Comrades used to reading between the lines of such resolutions probably saw what was coming:

The poor social composition of the party in London, a primary cause of its weakness, is one of the consequences of the social democratic tradition. . . . The sectarianism and exclusiveness manifested by many elements within the party is a most serious political weakness.

A purge was necessary. The Marxist-Leninist vocabulary became more strident:

The more decisively the C.P.G.B. eradicates all remnants of Right opportunist deviations in its ranks and carries out a correct Bolshevik policy, sharpening the struggle of the workers against the so-called Labour Government, the more rapidly will the working class realise its policy of 'class against class'.

Then it named names:

Comrade Rothstein has been guilty of a series of Right wing errors. Comrade Inkpin has shown an absolute lack of understanding of leadership and of self-criticism.

Of course, the doctrine of democratic centralism meant that the London District Committee was not acting on its own. It must have been put up to its resolution by the leadership in 16 King Street. Now the Politburo acted, using the opportunity to settle old scores. Rothstein, in particular, was disliked for his elitist, arrogant manner and his lack of contact with the rank and file. He was banished to Moscow, leaving behind a wife and two children without means of support. The eponymous Albert Inkpin was a clear scapegoat. Thin, pale and hardworking, the chief administrator of the Party since its inception, he had served two prison terms on its behalf. Now he was accused, maliciously and completely falsely, of running a pub on the side and helping himself to some of the 'Moscow Gold' that he had husbanded for many years on the Party's behalf. Despite Pollitt's protests he was sacked.

What was Wintringham's role? He added his voice to the purge of his oldest comrade. Rothstein had introduced him to communism but now Tom pushed him aside. As he put it in an autobiographical outline:

1929. During inter-party struggle opposed opportunistic leadership of Party (Rothstein and Inkpin) who were driven out by end of year: took sectarian ultra-left line. Worked with Pollitt on Trade Union work, editing Minority Movement's paper (The Worker) and later edited Party's weekly paper (Workers' Life) for four months, a successful manoeuvre to discredit critics of leadership.[7]

Why did he do it? Ideologically he had no problem with 'class against class' though he saw the error of his ways earlier than most. He used an analogy from British history close to his heart: the Party was a New Model Army, a revolutionary force with ideological purity, strict internal discipline and ruthless opportunism. However, he probably admitted in private that he was not suited to the personal and social antagonisms of the time. Unlike Rothstein and others, he had no taste for denunciations, recriminations, vehement outbursts and so on. Nor did Pollitt, and he became ill under the strain of it all. Tom was later described as a warm-hearted Marxist and everyone, inside the family and out, attests to his friendliness. He was not by nature sectarian nor was he ambitious politically. Not surprisingly, he said he was dissatisfied with politics at this time.

This period saw the CPGB at its lowest ebb. Membership was down to 3,500, a pathetic figure considering the Depression. The bitterness caused by 'class against class' wrecked the Party. Communist factory workers in Pollitt's National Minority Movement, who had been setting up cells among the trade union branches, now found they had to establish rival unions as an 'independent leadership of the working class'. They were not only ostracised by the Labour Party but now had to regard their old work mates as social fascists. No wonder Pollitt admitted in 1930, when his National Minority Movement was down to only seven hundred members, that 'the transmission belts were turning no wheels' and that 'the bridge to the masses has become only the same faithful few going over in every case'.[8]

The worst indignity, the nadir, must have been the 1931 general election. This brought into power a National Government under Ramsay MacDonald that consisted largely of Conservatives, Labour having resigned office and then split over the policy of imposing a 10 per cent cut in unemployment pay in order to save the pound. Not only did all twenty-six Communist candidates lose but not a single one polled more than his Labour opponent. Even Pollitt lost his deposit. Worse still, most working-class voters who deserted Labour either abstained or voted, in effect, for the Conservatives. This was a dismal Communist failure. Palme Dutt wrote a paper, stuck in his 'class against class' groove, entitled 'The Debacle of the Labour Party'.

During this time Wintringham penned his share of 'class against class' agitprop. In 1928 his *Facing Both Ways* pithily mocked Labour and the Independent Labour Party for their fair-weather socialism: 'The Labour Party's only pretence to Socialism consists of a top dressing of flatulent phrases. These refer to plans for the far future. This year – Toryism; Next year – Liberalism; Some time – Radicalism; Never – Socialism.'[9] He expanded on this in another pamphlet, *War! and the Way to Fight Against It* published in 1932. He mocked Professor Joad of the ILP for saying that socialism was good but it could not be achieved without a violent struggle and this must be avoided at all costs. On the contrary wrote Tom, with a neat piece of double think, capitalism meant an imperialist war and the way to fight against it meant organised resistance to capitalism. This would lead to revolution 'which only implies killing and destruction to the extent that capitalists have the strength to fight it'.[10]

The sheer vindictiveness of 'class against class', bordering even on hysteria, is conveyed in a note Palme Dutt wrote to Pollitt at this time. Pollitt was about to debate with Fenner Brockway, a gentle and principled politician. His ILP was cutting loose from Labour and moving further left towards Communist territory:

> NO POLITENESS! No mere 'difference of opinion'. No parliamentary debate. No handshakes. Treatment is CLASS ENEMIES throughout. You speak for holy anger of whole international working class against the foulness that is Brockway. Make the whole audience HATE him.[11]

Not surprisingly in this poisonous atmosphere, Wintringham kept his head down. The copious files of the CPGB kept in Moscow, with their thousands of pages maintained in neat chronological order, each page numbered in pencil on the top right-hand corner, contain no reference to Wintringham on any leading committee; not the Politburo, nor the Central Committee, nor any visiting delegation to the Comintern in Moscow. This is odd considering Tom's role in the Party during its early years. Now another group of 'young Turks' had succeeded him, working-class Londoners such as William Rust, the first editor of the *Daily Worker* and Dave Springhill, leader of the Young Communist League. Why? Tom was not really a party-political apparatchik. Further, like Rothstein, he had neither working-class credentials nor support. Other so-called bourgeois intellectuals kept out of the way, too. Palme Dutt continued to live in Brussels and Robin Page Arnot was the Party's representative in Moscow for much of this time. The CPGB was overwhelmingly working class, deeply rooted in the Labour movement, and now this background had become almost a badge of membership. For the adherents of 'class against class' anyone with a bourgeois taint could be the legitimate target for a witch-hunt. Residence in East Sheen was not the kind of address that one admitted to.

At the height of this Third Period, as it was called, Tom wrote 'The Immortal Tractor' (1932):

I have heard Lenin speaking. And I know
This Tractor we are building – it will grow. . . .
We are moulding, forging, shaping the steel of our iron wills
Into pinions, into pistons, crankshaft-web and crankshaft-throw,
We are building Lenin's Tractor. It will grow!

He sent it to Raji and Salme for their approval. They replied briefly: 'from *both of us*. Change the Lenin and I touch.'[12] Was it the poetic licence they did not like, the presumptuous name-dropping, or was it simply the first line of an unconvincing attempt at political correctness?

From the inception of 'class against class' a daily paper was considered an important weapon and in 1929 Pollitt asked Wintringham to work full time in preparation for its launch on 1 January 1930. It is hard to uncover precisely what Wintringham did because he was completely airbrushed out of *The Story of the Daily Worker* written in 1949. Wintringham does not help matters because in various autobiographical outlines he calls himself Founder Editor, which he was not. He used this title when he spoke at the Cambridge Union on 11 March 1930 in a debate, 'This House has no confidence in His Majesty's Government', but as he was described in the order paper as 'an honorary colonel in the Russian army' we know not to take him seriously. Elsewhere he wrote that he was asked 'to prepare the technical and business side of the paper'.[13]

Tom found premises for the *Daily Worker* at 41 Tabernacle Street, London EC2, in offices rented from the Ecclesiastical Commissioners. The Commissioners were difficult from the start, holding up arrangements for obtaining possession so that the handful of staff could only move in a few days before the launch and had to work without heat, light, telephones or tape machines. The pre-1914 German printing presses were two hundred yards away at Utopia Press Ltd in Worship Street. At first the problems seemed insurmountable. Tom asked Pollitt to delay the launch but 1 January 1930 had a symbolic appeal: new decade, new revolutionary era. Tom wrote: 'So we got it out [on time] with antiquated machinery, makeshift organisation, candles lighting the grim warehouse that was our office, the newspaper trains closed to us.'[14]

Publishing Britain's daily Communist newspaper was a difficult business. The owner of Utopia Press, William Wilkinson, 'an old, nervous gentleman',[15] was uncooperative, frequently refusing to print potentially troublesome articles, which was not surprising as policemen actually stood by the presses censoring on the spot. Editions were run off with some pages blank apart from the words 'censored by police' written over them. These teething problems were slight compared to the boycott by the Provincial Wholesalers Federation, which refused to distribute the paper. This meant that teams of loyal comrades had to be organised to get up in the early hours of the morning, pick up parcels of the *Daily Worker* at local railway stations, deliver them to retailers and collect cash in return. In London a network of dumps was arranged for a similar system. Fortunately, the Retail Newsagents Federation stood out against the boycott so that the paper was available at the point of sale. To add to Tom's problems, there was little chance of collecting advertising revenue nor enough subsidy from King Street.

The *Daily Worker* in its early days was not so much a newspaper as an organ of agitation and propaganda, and proud to be so. The first edition carried the following quotation from Lenin: 'without a political organ, a movement deserving to be called a political movement is impossible in modern Europe'. *The Times* was right when it called it a flagrant piece of Bolshevik propaganda. So it is not surprising that the police and the law courts were active. The first business manager, Frank Priestley, was sentenced to nine months' gaol for an article that described Judge Swift as a 'bewigged puppet' for sentencing three Communists to a most severe eight to eighteen months in prison for distributing 'revolutionary pamphlets' to soldiers; the same judge and the same offence as in Tom's trial five years before. It must have touched a raw nerve. From the start the name of the Chief Political Editor of the *Daily Worker* was never made public so as to make arrest more difficult. In 1931 the printer himself, poor William Wilkinson, was charged under the Incitement to Mutiny Act of 1797. For him this was the last straw; he was too afraid to go on printing.

The CPGB found money to take over Utopia Press and in 1933 Wintringham became its Chairman. His archive has the signed menu of the Third Anniversary Dinner of the *Daily Worker* held at the Three Nuns Hotel in Aldgate on 13 April 1933; the main course was roast beef and Yorkshire pudding and there was dancing to the Yovas Dance Band. As he wrote, his business experience was as important as his knowledge of the law: 'I had to pay printers with I.O.U.s, stave off landlord and business, keep the paper going in spite of a mountain of debts for paper and machinery.'[16]

Whether the intended reader of the *Daily Worker* wanted to spend a penny to buy six pages of agitation and propaganda was another matter.

Tabloid newspaper editors have always worked on the principle that workers want the essential news and after that entertaining reading, in order to escape from the dreariness of work. There was little news in the *Worker* in the early days, unless you wanted to read very politically slanted articles about unemployment, strikes and the Soviet Union, or absurd sectarian propaganda. Sporting items were removed after a scarcely believable article appeared on 25 January 1930, written by the joyless, austere Palme Dutt, whose knowledge of the subject must have been non-existent. Was it a parody written by one of his many enemies?

> In Sport There Can Be No Peace Between The Classes.
> Shall the Daily Boost the Thing that Dopes the Workers?

> Capitalist sport is subordinate to bourgeois politics, run under bourgeois patronage and breathing the spirit of patriotism and class unity; and often of militarism, fascism and strike breaking. Sport is a hotbed of propaganda and recruiting for the enemy. Spectator sports [horse racing and football] are profit run professional spectacles thick with corruption. They are dope; to distract the workers from the bad conditions of their lives, to stop thinking, to make passive wage slaves. You cannot reconcile revolutionary politics with capitalist sport!

So the racing tipster *Nilats* (Stalin spelt backwards) lost his job.

Almost immediately the *Daily Worker* was heavily criticised by the leadership. Even the Comintern threatened to remove its subsidy. After only a few weeks the circulation had dropped from 45,000 to 39,000 and the paper was losing £500 a week. By the end of 1932 sales were down to 20,000 copies a day but more at the weekend. Nevertheless, despite criticism and opposition it survived. By 1939, in very different circumstances but still with a wholesalers' boycott, its circulation had more than doubled.

In August 1932 Wintringham contributed one of his few signed articles: 'Allies Are Needed for the Revolution'. It was certainly provocative. He wrote it soon after the Japanese army had occupied Chinese Manchuria, an invasion he saw as the inevitable act of aggression of a declining capitalist state that needed to increase its markets by the acquisition of colonies. This was communist orthodoxy but Wintringham then pointed out that, like it or not, movements of resistance and national liberation were being led by members of the bourgeoisie: Chiang Kai-shek in China, Mahatma Gandhi in India (who had practised law in South Africa) and Eamon de Valera in Ireland. The 'petit bourgeois and peasant alliance' was to be welcomed wrote Tom because, as Lenin himself had written, 'every possibility, however small, of gaining an ally must be used'. Wintringham then offered his own red rag to the 'class against class' bull by writing that Chiang Kai-shek and the others were allies of the British working class because colonial revolt was a precursor to revolution at home. He went further. In Britain the petite bourgeoisie, whether trade union officials, shopkeepers or smallholders, should be allies too. 'We must attack their ideas but bring them with us.' This was heresy.

The article blew up a storm of protest that the *Daily Worker* aired in the weeks ahead; the usual vocabulary of communist invective rained down on Tom such as 'serious errors', 'dangerous nonsense', 'distorting', 'opportunistic' (this last criticism from the editor, William Rust). Tom collected all the cuttings and stuck them on the left-hand pages of an exercise book; on the right he wrote his reply. This ran to thirty-two pages, written in increasingly excitable style, before it ended abruptly with the succeeding pages torn out. I believe it is a most important statement of his views at this time; a personal testament that shows him to have been more free-thinking and far-sighted than was safe in those pernicious times. Not surprisingly, the *Daily Worker* did not publish it and nor did the high-brow *Communist Review*, to which he sent a version entitled 'To Hit the Target We Must Learn to Aim'.

Wintringham's unpublished reply to his critics began: 'The question of possible allies for the working class in a time of revolution is one of the most important and immediate practical problems.'[17] It was no use the *Daily Worker* claiming that the colonial debate was a side issue. Tom then surveyed the state of communism in Britain. He approved of the new leadership and considered the *Daily Worker* an invaluable weapon, but the gap between the potential strength of the Party and its actual strength remained as wide as ever. 'Progress is slower than the rate the crisis has developed.' What was wrong? The Party was too opportunistic, he said, and too sectarian. Here he gave an example of his own behaviour in 1929: 'I believed the I.L.P. leaders were the most dangerous opponents of working class action.' But his main criticism was of the 'English aversion to theory. This is at the root of the Secretariat's exclusion from discussion of the question of allies for the revolution.' In particular, wrote Tom agitatedly and for him almost illegibly, the theories of Lenin were not read and therefore not taught on Party training courses. He quoted a text from Lenin's 'The Discussion on Self-Determination Summed Up':

To think that a social revolution is conceivable without risings on the part of the small nations in the colonies and in Europe, without revolutionary outbursts on the part of the petty-bourgeoisie, with all its prejudices, without movements of the unconscious proletarian and semi-proletarian masses against landlord, clerical, monarchical, national and other oppression – means to deny the social revolution.

What Tom meant, surely, when he criticised the English 'aversion to theory' was that the Party had got the theory wrong. He was really attacking the 'class against class' doctrine. And here, expressed for the first time and much earlier than is supposed, were two of the beliefs on which his later reputation was based. The first was his belief, which would become passionate after his experiences in Spain, that a united front of all left-wing parties was necessary for revolution. The second was his belief, which owed much to his theories on guerrilla warfare also developed in Spain, that revolutions of national liberation were not only connected to revolution in the industrial West but were the future of Marxist struggle.

One of the signatories on Tom's menu at the dinner to celebrate the third anniversary of the *Daily Worker* in April 1933 was Millie Wintringham. She was the mother of Tom's third child. Millie was a member of the Party who probably worked either at 16 King Street or in the City for the Soviet Trade Mission. She was also a personal friend of Harry Pollitt. Tom and Millie began an affair in 1929 and the next year he deserted Elizabeth and O.J. to live with her in Surbiton. They remained together for eighteen months and in September 1931 Lesley was born. Tom was cited as co-respondent in Millie's divorce which became absolute in January the next year. In May 1932 Tom returned to Elizabeth because, said Lesley, 'Muv wagged her finger', but later that year Millie changed her name to Wintringham by deed poll. This was a painful period for all concerned. Perhaps Elizabeth saw it coming:

'The Game'

Now the sweet game begins afresh;
The wild blood leaps again, and cries

> Upon delay; the urgent flesh
> Forecounts its sharpest ecstasies.
>
> But when I pause, the voice is there;
> 'You knew love once; what game is this?'
> The flame is quenched in chill despair
> And bitter tastes each foolish kiss.[18]

It is easy to account for the promiscuous behaviour of communists by saying that they regarded marriage as a bourgeois convention, but that was not the orthodoxy, at least in Russia. Unlike in the 1920s, Soviet Communist society disapproved of adultery and divorce. In order to de-individualise the individual, love and sex were downplayed and nonconformity frowned upon. Freud's work was banned and criminal sanctions against homosexuality were reintroduced. Certainly, Tom's growing reputation for 'liking a bit of skirt', as one of the comrades put it, undermined him in the Party and, later, Harry Pollitt's disapproval of Tom definitely owed something to his bad treatment of women. After all, Pollitt knew the women concerned and that was part of the trouble. Elizabeth wrote bleakly:

> 'Only Wait'
>
> Time will fall like snow
> On all our woe;
> Like resting snow, like rain,
> On all our pain
> To soften and assuage
> Our trouble and our rage.
>
> Like an autumn leaf
> The days drift over grief.
> Let me be quiet; I know
> That time will fall like snow
> Like soft and softening rain
> On all our pain.[19]

Tom wrote to Raji Palme Dutt on '31' (*sic*) June 1932 when he was back in Warren Avenue, East Sheen: 'I have had a very difficult 18 months –

since M decided that she was going to have a babe, and no opposition mattered.'[20] If this was true it still shows how weak Tom was in his dealings with women. In 1923, after his first love Christina had discovered his affair with Elizabeth, he had wanted to tell Christina that he still loved her. Elizabeth had written to him: 'Dear Polygamist, don't persuade yourself that telling her will make things easier, it won't.'

Elizabeth displayed her usual tolerance when Tom was living with Millie, although her attempted detachment, in conformity with her principles, was unsuccessful: 'I know you are having a mouldy time [she wrote to him]. Don't think of me as someone you have hurt, but I am so utterly sure that M. cannot give you more than passing happiness that it terrifies me to think of you tying yourself up only to have this sort of experience again.'[21] She was also brave in another way. Early in 1932 she was admitted to Bexhill hospital suffering from pleurisy and pneumonia; the treatment required one lung to be drained through a tube. Tom went to visit her, himself recovering from ill health. He had just had fifteen teeth removed as a result, he told Palme Dutt, of his crash at the end of the war which blocked the antrum's (a cavity in the jaw bone) normal ventilation passage. He assumed, however, that this lingering complaint was brought on by his personal crisis. He continued: 'Elsie is immensely plucky. I didn't know how strong she could be when I lived with her.' His return was only four months away.

When Tom went back to Elizabeth and O.J. he did not atone for his sins. He continued to see Millie brazenly, even to the extent – if family stories are true – of spending nights with her and then boasting about his experiences over breakfast with Elizabeth. Moreover, by leaving Millie and Lesley to fend for themselves he caused them hardship and much suffering. Soon economic circumstances forced Millie to put Lesley into a children's home where she spent her childhood. For a man of progressive ideas, a poet's sensitivity and a kind heart, Tom behaved brutishly. Looking back from today's perspective Lesley considers that he was a rotten father and that his views about half the human race were not revolutionary at all.[22] It was Elizabeth who considered adopting Lesley and made sure that O.J. and Lesley met and played together as small children. Tom may have excused his behaviour as belonging to a political period when relationships were coarsened, friendships broken. But this would have been wrong, for more brutish behaviour was to come.

SIX

Wintringham on War

Wintringham said that he became Military Correspondent of the *Daily Worker* in early 1936 when, without warning, he was required to write a succession of articles about Mussolini's invasion of Abyssinia. The truth was that since 1930 he had written two party pamphlets (*War! – and the Way to Fight Against It* (1932) and *Air Raid Warning, Why the RAF is to be Doubled* (1934)) plus several analytical articles for Dutt's *Labour Monthly* ('Modern Aeroplanes and the Next War' (August 1930); 'War and the Social Democrats' (May 1932); 'Modern Weapons and War' (August 1932); and 'Modern Weapons and Revolution' (January 1933)). To this specialised journalism he added his first full-length book, *The Coming World War*, published in 1935 and reprinted the next year. So by the time the book came out he had already earned the reputation given him in the Introduction as 'the leading Marxist expert on military affairs at present writing in English'. In the copy he gave to Elizabeth he wrote coyly in the margin, 'I'm a little against using this, but don't mind much.'

Tom had grown up with a fierce interest in fighting. Later, of course, he gained practical experience in the trench warfare of Flanders. Now he saw himself as a modern man of the machine age who firmly believed that Michael Faraday, the inventor of the first electric motor, had more influence on the fighting of war than his contemporary Karl von Clausewitz, the acknowledged expert on warfare. One of Tom's favourite subjects was the growing mechanisation of war and its potential for revolution. In 'Speaking Concretely' (*Left Review*, 1934) he saw himself as a construction engineer building the road to revolution and welding the masses:

> Marx for your map, Lenin's theodolite –
> This is a thing Smolny's October showed –
> Crag-contour pioneered, valley and peak's height
> Known: all is ready? No, steel wire must be
> Inseparable from concrete, you from me,
> We from the durable millions. Then there's a road!

The Coming World War, a title that Wintringham had used as far back as 1929 in a talk he gave to a Communist Party discussion circle, was the culmination of his writing on war up to 1935. Its essential premise? War between capitalism and communism was inevitable, and capitalism would be its sole cause. The first edition of his book, written in the 'class against class' period, quoted from the Sixth World Congress of the Communist International (1928) and therefore expressed this in class terms:

> The cause of war as an historic phenomenon is not the 'evil nature' of mankind, nor the 'bad' policies of Governments, but the division of society into classes, into exploiters and exploited. Capitalism is the cause of the wars in modern history. Imperialism, the monopolist stage of capitalism, sharpens all the contradictions to such an extent that peace becomes but a breathing spell for new wars.[1]

Wintringham predicted that the Second World War would break out in the Far East with an attack by Japan on the Soviet Union. In fact, when Japan occupied Manchuria in the spring of 1932, the CPGB considered that this was the beginning. Tom wrote a letter to Elizabeth that unintentionally reduced this dreadful discovery to the level of a domestic inconvenience:

> I was trying to get tomorrow morning (Friday) clear to come down to Hastings. But it can't be did. The war pamphlet I wrote (*War! and the way to fight against it*) is n.b.g. [no bloody good] and is having to be redone. We have just decided that the second world war has really begun; it may remain in its present preliminary stage for some time. But it has really started. That needs a recasting of all our propaganda. Shall be too busy with this over the weekend.[2]

According to Wintringham, Japan would be joined in its attack on the Soviet Union by Nazi Germany. Hitler had made this clear in his statement of intent, *Mein Kampf*; Nazi Germany coveted Russia's raw materials and hated Russia's implacable opposition to fascism (which Tom termed derisively 'capitalism in a panic'). What would be the position of Great Britain? Early on Wintringham thought that Britain might attack the Soviet Union too, but by 1935 he considered it more likely that Britain would 'support and shield' Nazi Germany's own attack. In his more optimistic moods he thought the result would be an uprising of German Communists and the consequent Soviet occupation of Germany, a situation that would bring Britain even closer to war – and revolution.

Wintringham took for granted that the October Revolution was a success and that the first duty of all Communists was to defend it; any war in support of the world's only communist state was a just war. 'When Soviet Russia is attacked,' he wrote in 1932, 'we fight for the Soviets' victory – the victory of the international working class. The Red Army can never be for us an enemy army. It is our own.'[3] For as long as he was in the Party and for several years afterwards Tom made no public criticism of the Soviet Union. As late as 1941 he wrote that 'the Soviet Union proves itself clearly a success from every point of view'.[4] In *The Coming World War* he unwisely stuck his neck out: 'any unprejudiced visitor to the Soviet Union would confirm the fact that the Soviets are the most democratic and therefore the most influential mass organisations'.[5] He completely ignored the fact that they were dominated by the Communist Party with its policy of democratic centralism. Nor did Wintringham seem aware of the huge costs of the Five Year plans; the failure of collectivisation, famine, forced labour, the movement of entire populations.

Interestingly, the same edition of the *New Statesman* that reviewed *The Coming World War* ('it has considerable merit as a work of vulgarisation and restatement', wrote the reviewer) also reviewed *I Speak for the Silent* by Vladimir Tchernavin. This was the remarkable story of a Soviet scientist who was interrogated on seventeen occasions to make him confess that he was a wrecker, out to destroy the new communist state. Although there was absolutely no evidence of this, he was sentenced to five years' hard labour in the Siberian Gulag, from where he escaped with his family to tell the tale. In the opinion of the reviewer, A.J. Cummings, 'the Soviet Union is a merciless and relentless police state that casts its sinister shadow over the Russian people'. If Wintringham believed this, he would still have retorted that any price was worth paying to prevent counter-revolution. All his life Wintringham just could not bring himself to criticise Stalin.

So far *The Coming World War* was a good Party book, notable for its wide range and technical detail more than its originality. However, in two ways it broke new ground and became both controversial and subversive. The first was in its historical survey of the revolutionary potential of the armed forces, particularly during war, and the second was an extension of this: a Marxist analysis of how economics and class determined the way wars were fought. The novelty of this approach was recognised by reviewers. Air Commodore

Charlton, for instance, writing in *The Listener* called it 'vastly interesting'. The next year Wintringham amplified his theme in his second book, *Mutiny – a Survey of Mutinies from Spartacus to Invergordon.*

Wintringham's aim in both books was to show that either an imperialist war or a war against the Soviet Union, both of which were, in his view, 'likely if not certain', offered the best chance for revolution. His major precedent was the October Revolution in the Russian army and navy that brought the Bolsheviks to power in 1917 during the First World War. He went so far as to spell out his belief that: 'big wars can only be ended by working class revolution. That revolution ended the war of 1914; it will end the present war' (he wrote this in *War! and the Way to Fight Against It*, when the official Communist line was that the Second World War had already begun).

Then he surveyed English history. Tom began with the mutinous Levellers who, inspired by their text, *The Light Shining in Buckinghamshire*, took on Cromwell as well as Charles I during the English Civil War:

> This was the first document of the modern revolutionary movement with its claim that all existing property rights are the product of the Norman conquest and therefore no rights at all because 'the outlandish bastard William came to be king by conquest and murther'. . . . They were the first Communists.[6]

Warming to his theme that war could bring about revolution, Tom pointed out that the war against revolutionary France had triggered the naval mutinies at Spithead and the Nore in 1797 and the consequent Incitement to Mutiny Act, the Act that had sent him to prison. Forty years later, the Chartist movement had showed that the army was on the side of revolution. Soldiers had joined the mob thrashing the police in Hull with the shout, 'Damn your eyes, we are all Chartists'. The Chartists, said Wintringham, always thought the army would support them because 'they would not serve corruption's cause', which was why Prime Minister Peel had formed the armed police. He then pointed out with 'impressive and surprising facts' (cf. the *New Statesman*'s review of *Mutiny*) the extent of insubordination in both the British Army and Navy at the end of the First World War. 'Mutinies . . . might have ended the war on our side in 1919 if similar movements had not ended it in 1918 on the German side.'[7] Moreover, continued Wintringham, sympathies in the British armed forces for the Bolshevik revolution strangled the Government's attempts to invade Russia and led to several minor revolts in the Royal Navy before the Invergordon Mutiny of 1931. The trouble was, said Wintringham, that mutinies jumped the gun: 'The danger from the revolutionaries' point of view is that they break out before the revolutionary movement is strong enough and ready enough to work with them.'[8]

Wintringham then introduced his Marxist analysis of warfare. His aim was to prove that the working class now held the power in the waging of war. First, he illustrated the concept of economic determinism as applied to warfare by quoting from Friedrich Engels' *Anti-Dühring*, the seminal Marxist text on war written in 1877–8:

Gunpowder and firearms completely revolutionised methods of warfare. They required industry and money and both of these were in the hands of the burghers of the towns. From the outset, therefore, firearms were the weapons of the towns. The feudal lords' supremacy of the castles was broken. With the development of the bourgeoisie, infantry and guns became more and more the decisive types of weapons.[9]

So, wrote Wintringham, 'technique develops; warfare changes; class power is shifted'. Whether the weapon was now the tank, the aeroplane or the battleship, it relied on the skilled working class to make it and man it. In fact,

these weapons are never actually in the hands of the imperialists; they are always, in action, controlled by members of the working class or petty bourgeoisie. Ships have changed into vast and intricate machines; the seamen have become a leading section of the industrial working class, the most modern revolutionary force in modern society. This is, in widest outline, the reason why navies have taken the lead in modern mutinies.[10]

Mutinies, he continued, were always likely in the armed forces because formal hierarchies sharpened confrontation between the officer class and the rank and file. Moreover, they were more likely in modern forces because, he claimed, increasing specialisation 'makes arbitrary discipline, the only sort that can exist in a capitalist force, more difficult'. And it showed up the incompetence of officers: 'the inability of the command to handle new weapons will be one of the biggest revolutionising factors at work among the troops'.[11] Mutiny could easily spread to the civilian workforce because of the growing dependence of armies on industry. In support of his argument, Wintringham quoted the military expert Captain Liddell Hart who had written in his *History of the Great War* that whereas in the past one spoke of the 'nation at arms' now one had to speak of the 'nation at war'. Whether it was the manufacture and maintenance of an aeroplane in the factory or its skilled operation in the air, there was now a network of dependency that 'makes more certain that any working class resistance to war will rapidly cripple the forces of imperialism'.[12]

So Wintringham enlisted English history, Engels and Marx to show that the best hope of a communist revolution in Britain would come through war. He then turned to the Abyssinian conflict of 1935–6, Mussolini's conquest of modern-day Ethiopia, to predict a new kind of modern guerrilla war that communists would make their own. He planned a 40,000-word book on the Abyssinian War and wrote much of it at the same time as he updated *The Coming World War* for the second edition. Only two of the chapters were published, both as articles in *Left Review*: 'The Road to Caporetto' in November 1935 and 'War is also an Art', four months later. These, together with several journalistic pieces he wrote for the *Daily Worker* that May under his new byline 'Our Military Correspondent', are his first writings about the subject on which he was to become an acknowledged expert – guerrilla warfare.

Tom began by criticising the form of warfare that was the antithesis of guerrilla war: trench warfare followed by attack in rigid lines against an enemy at his strongest point. He called this 'a general contradiction in the development of modern war', an elevation to a 'mystical insistence' of Clausewitz's doctrine that the chief concern of a commander should be the principal armed force of his opponent. This was an error, Wintringham wrote scathingly, that had resulted in what he termed 'the futile massacres of Verdun and the Somme'. Wintringham had read the British General Staff's textbook of 1932, *Modern Formations*, and saw that it too advocated attacking the enemy where it was strongest by a furious onslaught of tanks and infantry. Now he saw the fascist adventure in Abyssinia as

a caricature of the worst phase of this decadent theory. Any idea of movement, of manoeuvre, of surprise and deception has been abandoned, for a cumbersome and over-equipped advance on a main front moving slowly forward and unable to retreat, like the armed dinosaurs of the Mesozoic past.[13]

Wintringham saw in the guerrilla resistance of the Ethiopian army the opposite tactics, the tactics that Chinese Communists were developing at about the same time in order to resist the Japanese invaders. Mao Tse-tung urged:

> Select the tactic of seeming to come from the east and attacking from the west; avoid the solid, attack the hollow; attack, withdraw, deliver a lightning blow, seek a lightning decision.[14]

Wintringham claimed:

> Today the only examples of the real art of war will be found in the campaigns of primitive peoples, revolutionary-nationalist alliances of classes, and the armies of the working class.[15]

This was more than a pious cliché. Although Ethiopian resistance was broken by mustard gas and aerial bombardment, a few years later the guerrilla warfare guided by Orde Wingate, Wilfred Thesiger and others did drive out the Italians. Subsequent wars of liberation against imperialism in many parts of the Third World, from China to Yugoslavia to Cuba, would show how the Marxist science of war would be developed in a new way.

Tom was building a reputation as a military expert, aided at last by the small advertisements carried by the *Daily Worker*: 'JIM. Wintringham's war articles are great. Please get me a copy of his book, THE COMING WORLD WAR. It's five shillings – MOLLY'. Nevertheless he was still short of money so he took a part-time job with Russian Oil Products, a company that was ostensibly selling Russian oil to the UK. He disliked the job, he told his son, because he was a lousy salesman and a teetotaller in a firm with a strong culture of drink. In fact, Russian Oil Products was a Communist front organisation that existed to spread communist propaganda and to subsidise British Party members; they numbered over 600 in a hugely over-manned workforce of 1,300. This much is known, and was known then.

However, the files at the Public Record Office kept out of the public domain until 1983 reveal that the company also planned acts of sabotage. In fact they tell an extraordinary story that, as far as I know, has not been told before, and the plot relates exactly to the time that Tom worked for the company. It was exposed by the doughty Duchess of Atholl, Chairman of the Government's Russian Trade Subcommittee, who was so concerned that she sent her committee's report to the Prime Minister, the Home

Secretary and the Foreign Secretary. Her committee took evidence from, among others, former Russian Oil Products employee Harry Jones, a so-called 'loyal English engineer'. He had been in charge of the construction of the company's depots in the West of England, so he knew what he was talking about. At Avonmouth he had found that

> the underground system of drainage had been installed which entirely destroyed the value of an 8 foot fire wall. These drains would allow the whole of the contents of the tanks to flow into the Severn, or the Bristol Channel, or the docks, merely through ordinary gravitation. These drains were entirely contrary to Home Office regulations.[16]

He had also discovered that the telephone connecting the tank compound to the main office had been removed, as had steam fire extinguishers. Jones said he had been asked by Naginsky, a director of the company, how long it would take for the incoming tide to reach the City Docks from Avonmouth; 18 minutes, he had answered.

At Grangemouth, Jones reported further, similar sabotage had been carried out. A system of land drainage had been dug that could drain the entire contents of the tanks into the Firth of Forth. The ports of Avonmouth and Grangemouth, he continued, were practically under Communist control. Similar illegal drainage had been dug from the company's depots into rivers or harbours at York, Hull and Warwick. Jones had reported his findings to the Chief Constable of Bristol, after which he had been sacked.

The Duchess of Atholl summed up her committee's findings:

> It is clear from Mr Jones' evidence and others that in R.O.P. we have an enemy organisation pressing a plan of action and apparently preparing to cripple the country in the case of a General Strike or similar national danger. Through their drainage system, in time of crisis, they can drain their petrol tanks into the docks or harbours and set fire to, or explode, the petrol and so block the traffic. This calls for immediate investigation by the Home Office and The Admiralty.[17]

Her committee had a more general concern too. Russian Oil Products heavily subsidised its petrol so that it sold into about 12 per cent of the British market. 'Should a foreign government,' her committee asked the Home Secretary, 'be allowed to operate inside a utility industry of national importance?'

The Home Secretary, Sir Herbert Samuel, ordered a watching brief to be kept. In the margin of the report are suggestions by civil servants that licences should be restricted by local authorities and that the Ministry of Labour should refuse to renew harbour permits. But nothing else. The Foreign Office brought down the curtain: 'We have nothing more to say.' Perhaps the Government dealt with the matter discreetly to avoid provoking a diplomatic incident. Perhaps the plot, though real enough, was never meant to be hatched. The CPGB often whistled in the dark, hoping that revolution was just around the corner; but it never was. Probably Tom did not know about this criminal sabotage, but presumably he would have approved.

In 1934 he was still bed-hopping between Elizabeth and Millie. Both were Party members, but Millie was the more active and argumentative:

'We Quarrel So About Politics'

When she changes, from your lover,
To harvest-headed lioness,
The days of lazy love are over.
Is that loss?
Sure, there was kettle-comfort then,
And beauty in soft heelless shoes.
Now beauty battles lash-tail. . . . When
– Win, lose –

There's ever-human need to feel,
Grow, see, do, sleeplessly enduring
New tempering and new edge to steel.
The true ring
Of the metal's lacking if we lack
Love dialectical with anger:
Love hammer-matrix, parry-attack,
As strangers stronger.[18]

At about this time Tom began to complain of the lack of culture among his comrades. He had just been to hear Beethoven's *Eroica* at a Prom in the Queen's Hall and wondered why so few of his friends had gone with him. Some preferred to listen to Grace Moore singing 'Our Night of Love', he wrote, others to go on a pub crawl, while a third group used the excuse of doing extra Party work. To them all Beethoven was highbrow, far from the struggle, of no immediate importance. This was where they were wrong, Tom believed, because the community of the arts was a new recruiting ground:

> All over the world a considerable number of artists and scientists are looking to us, to the revolutionary movement, to Communism, for a lead. They are hesitant, unsure, but they want to find out, they want to know if they can help. Names that occur to me almost at random are Augustus John, Naomi Mitchison, W.H. Auden (the best of the postwar generation of poets who already calls himself a Communist).
>
> They are ready to listen. Are they of use to us, as allies? Of course they are. Any work of art that is of importance is a thing that really moves, convinces, builds itself into numbers of people; a really good poster or pamphlet cover, a song, even a short story, may have immediate and immense effect on everyday revolutionary work.[19]

Tom had spotted the revolutionary optimism of many young British intellectuals; the antithesis of the cynicism and despair of others who thought that the rotten society they lived in would never change, unless for the worst. In Britain the National Government had come to power with a huge majority of over 500 seats and, although the economy was near to collapse with high unemployment and widespread poverty, it seemed set to stay in the saddle for years. The Labour Party was hopelessly weak while Mosley's British Union of Fascists was holding huge rallies. Both optimists and pessimists were attracted to communism because they feared a democratic Government was ineffectual in managing the economy and resisting fascism. Only the Soviet Union with its Five Year plans seemed able to manage its national economy and only Russia was standing up to the rapidly increasing fascist menace from Germany, Japan and Italy. Moreover, Russia was casting off its isolationism and welcoming new allies. Stalin was saying that a new direction was needed; one that presented a united clenched fist against the swastika and fasces, the symbols of fascism in Germany and Italy. His first step in this new direction was for Russia to join the League of Nations.

The next year, in July 1935, at the Seventh World Congress of the Communist International in Moscow, General Secretary Georgi Dimitrov declared that to confront the fascist menace a new united people's front was required that embraced all social democratic parties. 'Class against class' was officially over, regarded by many – though not publicly admitted – as a mistake. According to *Labour Monthly*, edited by Palme Dutt, the new line 'was received amid scenes of enormous enthusiasm'. As he was present in the Moscow conference hall he no doubt joined in the applause, but took his cue from Stalin. For him it was just another manoeuvre in Party strategy; but for Wintringham it was a reality that he had been urging since he had written 'Allies Are Needed for the Revolution' three years earlier.

The road to revolution was now open to all who wished to march along it. So-called Popular Front organisations sprang up to unite the left. Already the Soviet Union had set up a Writers' International and in February 1934 its British Section was formed at a meeting in the Conway Hall, London. On the Executive Committee was John Strachey, whose recent political allegiances showed the search for a modern ideology that worked; first Labour, then Oswald Mosley's New Party (the precursor of the British Union of Fascists) and now virtually a card-carrying Communist. He was joined by Ralph Fox and Tom Wintringham who was the Secretary. It called itself 'an association of revolutionary socialist writers who are working for the end of the capitalist order and a new order based on co-operative effort.' It was open to all who saw fascism as 'a final expression of capitalism and a menace to the best achievements of human culture'.[20] Nevertheless, despite its catch-all membership, it was increasingly run by the CPGB and Wintringham was instrumental in this.

He had been working behind the scenes for some time, writing to Palme Dutt that he had said at a meeting, typically, 'we needed not proletarian ethics but dialectical materialism as the foundation of our work'.[21] In February 1936 he wrote a paper for discussion by the Central Committee of the CPGB about the Party's role entitled 'Among the Intellectual and Professional Sections of the Middle Class':

Our whole work must bear a positive character. We must appear as a Party with a programme and outlook of Socialist humanism, fighting for the social and economic emancipation of the people, and the re-fashioning and developing of the great traditions of past struggles for freedom.[22]

No doubt he was sincere in this, but he had an ulterior motive. He proposed a Party strategy for a national fraction to infiltrate professional organisations such as the British Medical Association and the Law Society, similar to the nuclei that had been set up by the National Minorities Movement in the 1920s to infiltrate the trade unions. A Popular Front was all very well but it had to be controlled by the Party.

In October 1934 the first issue of *Left Review* was published under the umbrella of the Writers' International and at first it was edited by a committee of three, Montague Slater, Annabel Williams-Ellis and Tom Wintringham. Although it was ostensibly a non-communist magazine, it took as axiomatic that all literature was political. As Montague Slater put it: 'One of the strongest arguments for a Writers' International is that it brings writers into touch with life. Life, in this context, equals the class struggle.' The trouble with *Left Review* was that political correctness seemed more important than literary merit. In one article, for instance, called 'Electricity Comes to Husler Street':

> Old Mr Myers finds this new fangled electricity is wonderful, but simply hasn't enough shillings for the meter. He goes back sadly to dimness and a pennyworth of candles. A group of young people come down the street selling Russia Today, and give him a copy. His eye falls on the headline: 'Electrification plus Soviet Power equals Socialism'. He began muttering, meditatively, as he sat down to read.[23]

Nevertheless, intellectuals were back in favour with the Communists after years of having to pretend they wore a cloth cap. As Editor, Tom must have conducted a literary love affair, wooing Stephen Spender and the leading Communist poet Cecil Day Lewis:

> Yes, why do we all, seeing a communist, feel small? That small
> Catspaw ruffles our calm – how comes it?
> Mark him, workers, and all who wish the world aright –
> He is what your sons will be, the road these times must take.[24]

Tom relished the comparative freedom from agitprop journalism. At last he had a job for which he was suited, as poet, lover of the arts and firm believer in the new Party line of the Popular Front. Between October 1934 and August 1936 when he left for Spain, he published in *Left Review* four poems, two autobiographical essays, book reviews, editorials and three political articles.

The most important of these contributions was 'Who is for Liberty?' (September 1935). Tom began by quoting the patriotic boast made by the French Communist leader Marcel Thorez at the recent Seventh World Congress: 'We claim as our own, for the working class, the revolutionary heritage of the Jacobins, of our revolution, and of the Paris Commune. We do not hand over to the enemy the tricolour flag and the Marseillaise.' What, Tom asked rhetorically, was the British revolutionary heritage? His answer was that although revolutionaries always believed that socialism was the political goal, now this had to be merged into a wider tradition:

There is a tradition of freedom and the struggle for freedom that is fundamental in the development of this country, built into our lives and minds. This tradition has at times been neglected, avoided, rejected by revolutionaries. But it is our heritage. Roundhead, Whig, Radical – there have been many versions of the idea. . . . Freedom can only be made real to the extent that socialism is made real but there must be change and growth among revolutionaries. . . . We must follow the French example, make our own, win from the enemies of peace and the working class those symbols and that 'heritage' that are the British equivalents of 'Liberty, Equality, Fraternity', and the Marseillaise.

He argued that unless Communists embraced this tradition the intellectual left would remain suspicious. 'The reason why non-revolutionaries work with us only on some issues, guardedly and with reservations, is that they feel our talk of liberty is a ruse, a manoeuvre – since they believe, we aim at a rigid, restrictive dictatorship.' He then tried to disprove, unconvincingly, that the Soviet Union was a dictatorship; that freedom did exist in Russia – except the freedom to attack communism. But that was not the point. The point was that Wintringham's own English, Nonconformist background shone out in this essay bright and clear. He saw the radical left, those who had always acted to increase or protect the liberties of England, now joining forces with Communists on the road to socialism.

Wintringham embraced the Popular Front with relief for, he hoped, it was inclusive of all that was best in his English heritage. 'Who is for Liberty?' was a seminal article in Wintringham's search for an English way to revolution. He was, however, still a loyal Communist and he would follow for a while yet the Comintern policy that was to dominate the popular front in the interests of the Soviet Union.

A year later, in September 1936, Tom was in Spain and writing 'Barcelona Nerves' for his new-found love, Kitty Bowler:

> Neither fools nor children any longer:
> Those ways, traits, gone and away
> That once made life a luck-game, death a stranger:
> We're going on!
>
> Neither fools nor children we who are joining
> (Twenty years ago I knew war's face)
> We make what can wreck others into our gaining,
> Into our choice.[25]

In a personal sense Spain made Wintringham and in retrospect the period that preceded his time there was a preparation for it. His new authority on warfare, his professional interest in poetry, above all his growing belief in a non-sectarian, national revolution, were all to find fulfilment in Spain. And he made his choice.

SEVEN

The English Captain

They say that when men are drowning their past lives go by them. There under the olive trees I remembered my own history and many other men's. What was happening to me and through me was not strange or unlikely; I was doing what men of my sort and my blood had often done before. I realised this because in the battle I answered to a new name that had not previously been given me. They called me 'the English Captain'.

The commander of the English battalion [here Tom uses the third person about himself] was partly the creation of two Officers' Training Corps in England and more than two years spent with the B.E.F. in France. He was partly – very little I fear – the product of Clausewitz and Liddell Hart and other philosophers of war; his views were based more on the theories of Friedrich Engels, and on the general Marxist idea of the connection between war and politics. But more than any of these things he was the re-embodiment, for a new cause and in the newest army in the world, of that traditional well-known thing, the English captain.

There was something useful in the idea.[1]

Wintringham's book *English Captain*, published in 1939, is considered one of the best autobiographies by a British fighter in the International Brigades, an introspective but vivid account of how a Commander tried to lead his men in the savage battle of Jarama. In a typically self-conscious and romantic way he saw himself not only as an English Captain but as an English revolutionary, for much of the rest of the book is an account of the techniques of revolutionary war – how a people's army should wage guerrilla warfare in the town and countryside against a professional army. These techniques would become the basis of his teaching at the Home Guard Guerrilla Training School in 1940 and 1941, and of his wartime book *New Ways of War*, the famous 'do-it-yourself guide to killing people', as it was dubbed. This was not a bad achievement for a soldier who by his own estimate fought in Spain for only four days in months of war; 'not much to boast about,' he admitted.

Yet *English Captain* is also conspicuous for how much Wintringham omitted. When he wrote it he was still influenced by the Party and therefore he did not refer to the extraordinarily equivocal role that the Comintern was still playing in Spain. Only later did he express his disgust at the political tightrope on which he and other Communists had been forced to balance, and he never blamed – openly at least – the cynical and self-serving foreign policy of the Soviet Union that had required these acrobatics. Nevertheless, for Wintringham Spain was a watershed; the experience which terminated his faith in the sectarianism of the Communist Party but awakened his belief, so he said, in genuine democracy.

The Spanish Civil War aroused stronger feelings in Britain than any other foreign event since the French Revolution; so much so that over two thousand young men and women went there illegally to fight, and over five hundred to die. It is not hard to see why. The red soil of Spain, cut off from the rest of Europe because its people had depended for centuries on their empire in the New World, was a battleground for the European ideologies of fascism and communism. The Spanish people, fighting a civil war to establish their role in the twentieth century, were at the mercy of the monster ideologies of that century. And it looked as if this confrontation on foreign soil would soon engulf the European mainland.

In 1931, after generations of monarchical rule latterly assisted by a military dictatorship had left Spain a century behind the rest of Europe, King Alfonso XIII abdicated and a general election returned to power a Republican Government. But this new democracy was not enough adequately to address years of subjugation, ignorance and poverty. Many Spaniards wanted a full-blown revolution that would destroy their oppressors, the establishment of Church, army and aristocracy. The strongest political group to make up the Republican Government was the Socialist Party led by the self-styled Spanish Lenin, Largo Caballero. He made his objective clear from the start. While defending the Republic his aim was also to replace it with 'revolutionary Socialism. Our aspiration is the conquest of political power. The present regime cannot continue.'[2] In alliance with but also in opposition to the Socialists were other revolutionary parties of the left, particularly in Catalonia, the most industrialised and powerful of the provinces. First among these parties were the Anarchists.

Tom Wintringham had a soft spot for members of the FAI (the Iberian Anarchist Federation formed as a secret society in 1927) saying that their error was naïvety: 'the anarchist thinks he can step right from today into the paradise of freedom when every village or street will run its own affairs by simple agreement, without external Government'.[3] Nor was this assessment far from the truth. The FAI seemed to believe in the so-called 'miracle of holy revolution'. It advocated sudden uprisings when the Anarchists would march into town, take over the civic offices, run up the black and red diagonal flag and declare libertarian communism. All property deeds would then be set alight, land declared communal and money abolished.

In Catalonia there was the POUM (the Workers' Party of Marxist Unification), which in its attitude to revolution was halfway between the Anarchists and Socialists. In 1936 it was only five years old, having been formed by Andres Nin, a Spanish Communist who had returned after ten years in Russia in disgust at Stalin's treatment of Trotsky. His new party supported Trotsky's views on permanent revolution and was considered anti-Stalinist. POUM disagreed with parliamentary democracy, preferring to replace it with a constituent assembly to which the militias, factories and peasant assemblies sent delegates. The party shared with the Anarchists an abhorrence of an organised state army; true to their revolutionary beliefs they insisted instead on local and political militias, often run by trade union branches, in which leaders were elected, commands discussed and individual freedom considered more important than discipline. Tom considered this 'all sheer silliness and disaster'. Nevertheless, committees of workers did begin to take power into their hands and Barcelona in 1936 must have resembled Paris in 1792. The effect on George Orwell, who arrived there in December 1936 to join a POUM militia, was 'startling and overwhelming':

> It was the first time I had ever been to a town where the working class was in the saddle. Practically any building of any size had been seized by the workers and was draped with red flags or with the red and black of the Anarchists; every wall was scrawled with the hammer and sickle and with the initials of revolutionary parties; almost every church had been gutted and its images burned.[4]

Where did the Spanish Communist Party (the PCE) stand on this alignment of the revolutionary left? Paradoxically, indeed cynically, it hardly figured at all. It was positioned firmly under the control of the Comintern, which had been ordered by Moscow to oppose a revolution in Spain. For Stalin had less provincial considerations on his mind than a mere civil war; he was manoeuvring in a global battle against fascism in which Spain was simply the front line in this ideological conflict.

When, on 17 July 1936, senior officers of the Spanish army led by General Franco raised the banner of military revolt against the Republican Government, a full-scale civil war was detonated that also became a dual revolution. The sizeable extremes on both sides sought not only to destroy each other, but to replace the bourgeois democracy of the Republic with their own ideological regimes – either some sort of dictatorship of the proletariat of the left or a fascist regime of the right. For Franco wished to restore more than military dictatorship; he intended, and eventually succeeded, in turning Spain into a quasi-fascist state. Right from the beginning Franco was aided by the fascist dictators Hitler and Mussolini who sent arms, men and munitions and gave diplomatic support. They wished to crush communism and, it was confidently supposed, try out their weaponry for the European, perhaps global, confrontation that was to come.

This blatant intervention by fascist dictators in a civil war put Stalin in a quandary. On the one hand his highest priority was to make allies of the democracies of Europe in order to enlist their help in the defence of the Soviet Union against fascist attack, which the example of Spain seemed to show was imminent. This is what his Popular Front policy was all about. He did not want to frighten off Britain and France by exporting communism to Spain. On the other hand he could not stand by and watch the forces of fascism crush a communist-inspired revolution. So he eventually decided on a dual policy. The Soviet Union joined Britain and France on a Non-Intervention Committee while surreptitiously supplying arms and advisers to the Republic. Moreover, the Soviet surrogate, the Comintern, assembled, organised and commanded an international brigade of volunteer soldiers to fight with the Republican forces. This, of course, made nonsense of non-intervention, but Germans and Italians sat on the Committee too and their countries supplied Franco with an air force (German) and an army (Italian), not to mention every kind of weapon. The international policy of non-intervention was a complete farce.

So the International Brigades run by the Comintern came into existence, their aim to help defend the Republic and defeat fascism. As early as July 1936, Harry Pollitt declared at a rally in Trafalgar Square, London: 'We must compel the national Government [of Britain] to render every assistance to the Spanish peoples' front Government. Let us organise a mighty united movement of solidarity.'[5] But it was not to help a revolution. As the leader of the Spanish Communist Party Jose Diaz said in February 1936: 'The immediate task now is not the struggle for the dictatorship of the proletariat but the development of the anti-fascist struggle.'[6] The International Brigades were forbidden to carry revolutionary slogans on their banners or 'make irresponsible statements about the future "reorganisation of society"'.[7] Paradoxically, the Communists aligned themselves on the right wing of the Popular Front and were considered by the Anarchists and POUMistas as counter-revolutionaries. In turn the Communists hated their allies in POUM for being anti-Stalin. Since its inception the main aim of the Comintern had been to encourage and foment world revolution – but not now, not in Spain.

At the time Wintringham accepted this self-denying restraint and, anyway, there was a practical justification for it. With fascist troops not just over the horizon but frequently on the next hill, the priority had to be resistance not revolution; hence the Communist slogan, 'Everything and Everybody for the Winning of the War'. Nonetheless, a most revealing observation comes from Jason Gurney, a Chelsea artist who joined the British Battalion of the International Brigade and was Tom's runner at Jarama. He arrived in Spain a Marxist, he said, but became genuinely and sincerely shocked when his idealism was considered anathema by his Communist comrades in the British Battalion:

I now learned about the doctrine of 'revolutionary expediency' propounded by Lenin. In its simplest form it is that the end justifies the means, as long as the end is advancing the revolution. Its application produces a complete reversal of any kind of morality to which I had been accustomed. Apparently I was a Marxist without being able to become a Leninist, and this, in the Communist mind, put me perilously close to being a Trotskyist which is quite literally a capital offence in any Communist organisation.[8]

Tom's other omission from his book *English Captain* is any mention of his affair with Kitty Bowler, the American journalist who was accused of being a Trotskyite spy. This is understandable because he was writing about his experiences in the International Brigades and she was a controversial figure at the time, about to be responsible for his expulsion from the Party. Yet it is a pity, for no writer of romantic fiction could want a better scenario than their love and war in Spain. Their true story, the story of how they fell in love, of how he sent her to London to persuade Pollitt to send out recruits for a British Battalion, of how she was arrested and interrogated as a spy, of how she nursed him back to health after Jarama, of how she was suddenly expelled from Spain and nearly suffered a nervous breakdown in America, and of how they battled with the Communist Party – and lost – would surely have made *English Captain* a best-seller. Moreover, much of it had already been written by them before they left Spain. For instance, Kitty described at the time their first meeting in Barcelona in early September 1936; she was homeless, having given up her hotel room to a family of exhausted refugees:

> I wandered over to the cafe Rambla feeling desolate and forlorn. Like the story book waif, who peeks through frosted panes at the happy families gathered round the fireside, I eyed the little group at a corner table. I saw a 'moving forest of bare knees'. Only England could produce anything so incredibly tall and fresh as those boys. Shy but desperate I approached. All conversation stopped. Blankly and coldly they looked at me as only the English can. Then a soft-voiced bald man touched my arm: 'You must join us.'
>
> Relaxing gradually I realised I was talking to a gifted conversationalist, cultured, intelligent, witty. I liked this man's mind and the amusing twist he would give a phrase. But I was puzzled. This quiet literary individual wasn't my idea of a military man. 'That's Tom Wintringham', I was told, 'the author of a book on Marxist military strategy. He's a big shot in the English Communist Party, but he's an old sweetie.'[9]

Tom took up the story a few days later after Kitty had returned from Madrid. He called it 'An Improbable Chapter: such as no publisher will let me put in a serious book' (he was right because it certainly did not appear in *English Captain*):

> It went quickly then, though not very quickly: some meals together, coffee and cognac at the cafe Rambla where friendly waiters knew what was happening at least as soon as the pair did, and indicated with a nod or a lifted hand to the latecomer where to find the other. After that there

was the going home to her hotel, 'hell and gone' down the tram lines in the dark. He walked with her three times before he kissed her goodnight. Then he had to go to the Front for a couple of days and was nervous, hating war; he knew it too well from 1916–1918. It was just before going that he proposed to her, curtly, nervously, without prejudice to any other interest either might have in other people a thousand or three thousand miles away.

The hotel at which he stayed that night was noisy and he couldn't sleep. He wrote 'Barcelona Nerves' and arranged to send it to her:

> Neither fools nor children any longer
> Those ways, traits, gone and away
> That once made life a luck game, death a stranger,
> We're going on. . . .

Next morning these scribbled verses were brought to her before she woke: he was already a hundred miles off, breakfasting on raw onions and cold fish and red bitter wine at a bare-roomed village inn half way to the front. . . . A day before she expected he was back, to find her compact of tenderness, a warmth and reassurance of humanity. And someone in the room below hers snored like a grass-cutter mowing, all night long. They laughed, but not because of this; they laughed because a loneliness and strain was ended, with release and happiness.[10]

To start at the beginning. Any account of Wintringham in Spain must try and answer the unexpected question: did Wintringham have the original idea for the International Brigades? Even without access to the Wintringham archives the authoritative historian of the Spanish Civil War, Hugh Thomas wrote in 1961: 'It is at least possible that Wintringham should be given the credit for the International Brigades.'[11] Now I believe we can go further and say that he was more than a pioneer, he was a seminal figure. What happened was this.

While he was attending an anti-fascist peace camp in Wales in mid-August 1936 Tom was telephoned by Harry Pollitt and told to pack his bags. Pollitt asked him to go to Spain as the 'responsable' or representative of the CPGB in Barcelona. But from the outset Wintringham had his own agenda, which went against the wishes of the Party. He intended to prepare the ground for a British contingent to an international legion that he hoped would be formed by the Comintern to fight for the Republic. He was already arguing in private the political and propaganda case for creating an international force and as he was military correspondent of the *Daily Worker* his views carried weight:

> I believed in the idea of an international legion. Militias can do a lot. But a larger-scale example of military knowledge and discipline, and larger-scale results, are needed too. You have to treat the building of an army as a political problem, a question of propaganda, of ideas soaking in. You need things big enough to be worth putting in the newspapers. . . . Surely a big-scale, well-placarded example was necessary?[12]

The evidence that Wintringham was acting on his own initiative comes, initially, from two letters. The first he wrote a year later to Kitty: 'I was starting out on the line I had been told to avoid, mid-August when I left London, but which proved to be correct by November.'[13] The second comes from a letter he wrote Elizabeth just before he set out on 21 August, five weeks after the start of the war in Spain. Somewhat secretively he gave his reasons for going: 'Aim a) to represent the paper in a part not covered. b) to organise reception in Paris and there for others following me. c) to prepare there a further development of which you will read in the papers. . . .'[14] He dropped similar hints in a letter to his mother. We know that Tom stayed in Paris for several days visiting contacts before moving off to Perpignan. He was indeed followed by others because the rendezvous in Paris and then the train journey down to the Pyrenees became the established route into northern Spain for recruits to the International Brigades.

Wintringham went out to Spain with the first ambulance unit paid for by the Spanish Medical Aid Committee, a Popular Front organisation supported then by the Labour Party. According to the *Daily Worker*, it left Victoria Station on 24 August to the cheers of 3,000 supporters who had marched from Hyde Park to see them off led by the Labour mayors from East London boroughs wearing their full regalia. In Paris they caught the train to Perpignan and so did Tom. He made himself known to the leader, Dr Kenneth Sinclair Loutit:

> Tom was carrying a knap-sack and wore a trench coat; the sort of stuff that Millets sold in their army surplus stores. He looked battered but had a good smile and a small subaltern moustache below his bald head. His

approach to me was characteristic, direct, friendly, pragmatic, constructive. 'How can your presence be explained?' I asked. 'Look,' said Tom, 'the Party as you saw in Paris is the brain, heart and guts of the Popular Front and it's even more so in Spain. Unless the unit is right with the Party you'll be lost.' He went on to suggest that his party affiliations should be neither concealed nor advertised.[15]

What Sinclair Loutit gleaned at this stage was simply that Wintringham was exerting, albeit discreetly, the Party's authority; but more was to come. Presumably the ambulance unit, because it was non-combatant, did not have to cross the Pyrenees clandestinely on foot, like the volunteers who followed. When they reached Barcelona, Tom was immediately intoxicated by the atmosphere:

Barcelona, largest city in Spain and capital of Catalonia, is colour, noise, heat, dust, violent traffic and quick-moving people. Many of the men carry rifles slung on their backs, slung all ways; they wear cotton sandals, rope-soled, workmen's overalls of blue, brown and khaki. They march in groups of ten and sections of thirty, in centurias and columns, shuffling a little because of their sandals, in light smooth quick-step. They sing a little, salute often, with a raised clenched fist. Men and women crowd and climb to see them, cheer, clap. Banners are carried in front of each unit: the red and black, diagonally divided, of the Anarchists, the red with white letters of the Socialists and Communists, the hammers and sickles of the P.O.U.M; and there are also orange-striped flags, sometimes with a white star inset on blue, Catalan nationalism, and the red-yellow-purple of the republic of Spain.[16]

'Already,' observed Sinclair-Loutit, 'Tom was formulating the concept of the International Brigades. The foreign sympathisers of the Republic gathering in Barcelona were capable of being a real military force but Tom saw the need for a much more military approach.' Tom's thinking was influenced strongly by a couple whom he met as soon as he arrived in Barcelona and with whom he became lifelong friends. Nat Cohen was a tough Jewish clothing worker from Stepney who had cycled out to Barcelona for the Workers' Olympiad in July and joined a local militia to try, unsuccessfully, to recapture Mallorca from Franco's forces. Now, together with his Spanish girlfriend Ramona, he was recruiting for another *centuria* (a group of 100 men to fight with a people's militia). Tom wrote to Pollitt on 10 September, already lobbying for his volunteer brigade:

> He [Cohen] is now busy raising a Tom Mann centuria which will include 10 or 12 English and can accommodate as many likely lads as you can send out. I propose to join it, provided I can still write for the D.W. [Daily Worker]. I believe that full political value can only be got from it (and that's a lot) if its English contingent becomes stronger. 50 is not too many.[17]

Tom joined the Tom Mann *centuria* but his participation did not amount to much more than an iconic photograph. Instead, he went off with Sinclair Loutit to observe the fighting on the Aragon front north-west of Barcelona, stopping for a while at Granien where there was a hospital staffed by the British Medical Unit. Along the road to the front near Huesca Wintringham saw the ground from the point of view of a soldier who had survived trench warfare. He was shocked at what he felt was the 'amateur-anarchist' way the militias fought, even the Thaelmann *centuria* fighting with them. This was a force of German volunteers, the first to arrive. Wintringham thought they were hopelessly, even fatalistically, brave but without much discipline or even interest in the basic necessities of staying alive: camouflage, trench digging, sandbag filling, repair of broken weaponry, organisation of strong points:

> An army that consists of troops who are willing to do nothing much except at intervals find graves and glory – such an army needs an example and training of exactly the opposite sort to that given by the Thaelmann centuria. It allowed itself to be used in very gallant, almost futile, repeated attacks on an impossible position. It attacked an enemy hill as if it was Verdun.
>
> How could these incredibly gallant Spaniards get hold of the art, the science, the discipline of war? By example and by training, given them by foreigners, but not in this hopelessly slipshod, casual, unscientific way.[18]

Wintringham returned to Barcelona all the more convinced about the need for an international force. He continued to lobby Pollitt, writing about the exact route volunteers should take to get to Barcelona and the clothing they should wear. By this time he had been reconnoitring the terrain, planning the organisation and persuading Pollitt for about a month – not to mention the time he spent developing the idea of an international legion before he set out for Spain. Shortly afterwards, on 18 September, the Comintern met in Moscow, undecided what to do. Its former General Secretary, Grigorii Zinoviev, was at that moment on trial for treason and delegates were fearful of Stalin. What line would he take on Spain? A brave, impassioned speech by Zinoviev's successor, the Bulgarian Georgi Dimitrov, stiffened resolve. The Comintern agreed to send in International Brigades. Whether Wintringham's advocacy was enlisted we do not know because no written record of the meeting survives. The British Battalion was formed a few months later.

This was the only occasion in the twentieth century when a British political party sustained a significant military contingent in a foreign war. It added hugely to the Party's new reputation as custodian of Britain's finest radical traditions (despite its underlying duplicity). As Pollitt wrote in his eulogy for Tom's old friend Ralph Fox, who was killed in December 1936:

> The British Battalion has upheld the fine democratic traditions that have characterised the fight on behalf of liberty. The great poet Byron went to Greece to fight for liberty; this is the example that our British comrades are following today in the conditions of our time.[19]

The comparison must have appealed to Tom. His own favourite analogy was predictable: 'It's the first battalion put together by English speaking people – the first since Cromwell's day – to be part of a people's army. It's as important as the New Model Army.'[20] Fighting in Spain to resist fascism was called the 'Last Great Cause' and Tom was undoubtedly one of the pioneers who turned this cause into effect. A pity the Party never gave him credit for it.

Why, then, did the CPGB warn Wintringham off when he had argued for an international legion back in the summer of 1936? His plan, of course, was a highly exposed initiative that might well have failed, so the CPGB needed the endorsement of the Comintern and this did not come until the autumn. Moreover, as Wintringham's continued badgering of Pollitt makes clear, the CPGB's response to the call was comparatively slow and small scale compared to that of the Communist Parties of Germany, Italy and France. It was not until October, when the Soviet Union decided to intervene in the war, that the CPGB plucked up its courage to send out volunteers; only in January 1937 was it confident enough to form a British Battalion.

Pollitt, as we know, had other jobs for Wintringham to do in Barcelona. The first of these was to act as the Party's representative, setting up an office, coordinating the activities of the British Communists who were converging there to help the Republic, liaising with the many Catalan and Spanish political committees. It was a job Tom disliked almost from the start. He wrote in exasperation to Pollitt:

> We must have a Comrade to act as the representative here. This is a bloody political town – militias, unions, the parties are running everything. It's a mixture of war and proletarian revolution. I can't do the job without spending full time on it. I am a much better journalist than committee man.[21]

Wintringham had other tasks, too. Towards the end of August the Red Army general Walter Krivitsky was ordered by Moscow 'to mobilise all available agents and facilities for the prompt creation of a system to purchase and transport arms to Spain'. Meanwhile, in Barcelona the Hispano-Suiza aircraft factory was busy reconditioning aeroplanes to make up the Republic's air force and we know that Wintringham was supervising British mechanics who worked there. He was also trying to help implement a report by General Motors in Barcelona to increase massively its production of cars and lorries. All this accounts for the following entry which he made in the outline autobiography he wrote in November when he joined up to fight with the International Brigades: '1936; Sept 1, Barcelona. Worked as "responsable" for British C.P.; also on aircraft production questions and with comrades in the General Motors group; and at journalism.'[22] He wrote to Muv: 'The things I can do are useful. "I am also a man under authority." I feel certain that this tragedy will be spreading to swallow us if this war is not ended quickly.'[23]

By this time Sinclair Loutit had got to know Wintringham. He described himself as 'a non-party, radical intellectual aged 23, frightened and disgusted by the inhumanity of the depression'. In this tender state he must have found Tom a father figure. They had been under fire together at Huesca, for Sinclair Loutit a baptism of fire, 'when those funny zinging wasps of death passed so it seemed right by my ear':

> He [Wintringham] was helpful and kind in great things and small. To be with a warmly human Marxist who was also a cool soldier made it

possible for me to find the beginning of the path and I count him one of the best friends I ever had. I understood exactly what Kitty saw in him. He still carried some of the hubris of that gallant generation that bore the weight of 1914–18.[24]

Others were less impressed. The writers and fellow Communists Sylvia Townsend Warner and her female companion Valentine Ackland were in Barcelona that September, initially keen to aid the cause but growing increasingly disapproving of the CPGB office. They wrote a report of unmitigated complaint to Pollitt in which they compared the British Communists in Barcelona to members of the Raj in India: cliquey, isolated and racist. They alleged that Comrade Loutit had said that 'the best way to speak to Spaniards is with a whip'. (This criticism could not apply to Wintringham, who always referred to the Spanish people with admiration and affection; later he would complain to George Orwell that it was the Russians who sometimes behaved like racists in Spain.) Moreover, the women claimed that the Party organisation was virtually non-existent and that this was Comrade Wintringham's fault as he was the political leader. Although they were old friends of Tom, they concluded bluntly: 'He is unequal to the responsibility. He is largely occupied with personal affairs and side issues of journalism.'[25] It is clear that warfare, journalism (he was still sending dispatches to the *Daily Worker*) and Kitty Bowler were all, in the Party's eyes, making Wintringham an 'ir-responsable'.

There was something about Barcelona that infected everybody: a sense of freedom, of a daydream that could come true. Everybody, it was said, was ready for the unexpected, and it happened. Tom's life would never be the same again after he met Kitty Bowler that evening in very early September 1936 at the Café Rambla while he was drinking with the ambulance unit.

'Kitty Bowler is an arresting young woman of twenty-eight,' wrote a journalist in Kitty's home-town newspaper in Plymouth, Massachusetts, 'of less than medium height, slender, with large brown eyes and a short tousled bob, not unlike Amelia Earhart.'[26] She spoke excitedly and volubly which, in the conspiratorial atmosphere of Spanish politics, was not a wise thing to do. Her petite and mischievous appearance make it easy to understand why Tom called her 'shrimp', a nickname that evolved into 'Schwimp' because, Kitty claimed, he spoke with a slight lisp. Sinclair

Loutit adds his own impressions: 'Kitty was a neat, active, progressive, American girl who had nipped across from France to see what was going on and maybe to make a name for herself. It was before drip-dry cottons but Kitty, though often dusty, always looked pretty good and smelt nice.'27 Kitty was not a Communist nor at this time an accredited journalist, facts that became crucial later. She was a young adventurer (in fact she was born on 10 February 1908), out for excitement and a shameless flirt, perhaps in reaction to her wealthy, overbearing and conservative mother. She had reached Spain from the Soviet Union where she had spent the previous few weeks as a tourist. She had, literally, danced her way on board ship up the Baltic to Leningrad and there continued in the same style. This twenty-four hours she described to her closest friend, the New York playwright Leslie Reade:

> July 29. As for bed, it just doesn't exist. Yesterday a great time, went to a steel lathe factory. Later, I acquired me a French boy from Egypt who told me all about French writers of the Left and took me to a Park of Rest and Culture for the evening. Had a grand time; saw a circus and I was going in a parachute but didn't have time. Afterwards this Miller person [?Henry] the writer I told you about, took me out to dinner and we stayed up until after 3. Today I'm going to a carnival unless the honourable Durante is free as I haven't seen him for several days. Just made up my mind to go to Yalta!28

Breathless, impressionable and naïve (her description of visiting a forced labour camp would have made her blush with embarrassment had she been alive today) but also determined and courageous, Kitty duly embarked on a whirlwind affair with the *New York Times* correspondent Walter Durante and arrived in Barcelona eager for more adventure. Tom found her irresistible! He also found her politically sympathetic. She had pronounced left-wing views that, Tom said proudly, she inherited from an ancestor who had helped to abolish slavery. He had in mind Edward Everett who had been President of Harvard and Abraham Lincoln's Secretary of State, from whom Kitty was directly descended. Her parents belonged to dynasties that both rated on the Social Register: her father was Robert Bonner Bowler and her mother Charlotte Everett Miller. She had majored at Bryn Mawr College in economics and politics and then volunteered to work with the League Against War and Fascism and the International Labour Defence. In

August 1936 when she was with Durante in Paris, both of them trying to get into Spain, she told him about her heightened political consciousness:

> My whole generation is being drawn into politics, whether they will or no. I prefer to be conscious about it. I don't like Fascism. Liberalism is as seductive and untrustworthy as a mistress. In these tumultuous days I prefer a good trustworthy companion, who'll stick by me thick and thin. I want something that works. So it will have to be one of the brands of socialism – the one that works best and gives the greatest good to the greatest number.[29]

According to Kitty, who wrote an unpublished memoir about her first months in Spain 'Just Try and Get In', Durante took a frivolous view of the risks she was taking:

> I have to admit women don't get raped in Spain. On the contrary, they get away with murder. Young women like you ought to be forbidden. You're perfectly capable of looking after yourselves but the male animal likes to forget it and be chivalrous!

She obviously showed this to Tom because he wrote in the margin like a jealous lover: 'Particularly vicious! With so much hair you have no right to look like a wide-eyed child of eighteen.'[30]

Kitty Bowler probably knew Martha Gelhorn, who later became a famous war correspondent. They had much in common. They were born the same year into wealthy American families and went to the same women's university, Bryn Mawr. Both took up left-wing causes and aspired to journalism. Both wanted 'to be with the boys in Spain' as Gelhorn put it, and both found a mentor and lover as soon as they got there; at first to make life easier as much as anything else. Ernest Hemingway, Gelhorn's lover, was just one year younger than Tom and arrived in Spain towards the end of 1936, four months before Gelhorn whom he had already met in New York. Did they all meet up in Spain? It is highly likely, for we know that Hemingway visited Tom in hospital in April 1937 and Martha and Kitty were probably with them. Lovers became marriage partners but whereas 'Schwimp' stuck to Tom like a limpet, Martha could not wait to disentangle herself from Hemingway. They divorced in 1945.

In October Tom took Kitty to the British hospital at Granien where she helped as a nurse and wrote one of her first articles, published by the *People's*

Press of New York. On the same occasion Tom wrote a strong poetic statement of his philosophy that goes beyond ideology and sentimentality:

'British Medical Unit – Granien'

Too many people are in love with Death
And he struts thigh proud, never sleeps alone:
Acknowledge him, neighbour and enemy, both
Hated and usual, best avoided when
Best known.

'Weep, weep, weep!' say machine gun bullets, stating
Mosquito like, a different note close by;
Hold steady the lamp; the black, the torn flesh lighting
And the glinting probe; carry the stretcher; wait
Eyes dry.

Our enemies can praise death and adore death;
For us endurance, the sun; and now in the night
This electric torch, feeble, waning, yet close-set,
Follows the surgeon's fingers. We are allied with
This light.[31]

While Tom and Kitty were falling in love they were also exploiting each other. She used him to guide her apprentice journalism; he used her as unofficial secretary and messenger. Perhaps it was the heady atmosphere of Barcelona that caused Tom to forget his usual tact in relations with the Party; perhaps he no longer cared. Anyway, he gave her a political prominence he never should have done in such an exclusive, secretive Party. In December the novelist Ralph Bates, who had lived in Barcelona for many years and was a veteran Party member, sent Pollitt a very rude report about Tom and his relationship with Kitty:

Everyone here was very disappointed with Comrade Wintringham. He showed levity in taking a non-Party woman in whom neither the P.S.U.C. [the Communist Party of Catalonia] nor the C.P.G.B. comrades have any confidence to the Aragon front. We understand this person was entrusted with verbal messages to the Party in London. We are asked to send messages to Wintringham through this person rather than the Party headquarters here. The Party has punished members for far less serious examples of levity than this.[32]

In many eyes Tom's behaviour amounted not only to levity but also to heresy, for Kitty was not even a member of the Party. No wonder Pollitt was exasperated with Wintringham and his affairs! It is clear from correspondence that Pollitt had doubted from the beginning whether Wintringham had the sense of responsibility necessary for the job, and now he was proved right. The London incident to which Bates referred took place early in November when Kitty was in town partly to pick up commissions from the *Manchester Guardian* – 'my line is "little girl wide-eyed in Spain"', she wrote to her mother – and partly to give Pollitt another of Tom's written arguments for a British Battalion.

Sinclair Loutit's description of Kitty's visit to the proletarian comrades of King Street, while third-hand and written forty years after the event, nevertheless shows how she must have confirmed their every prejudice about Tom as a frivolous, bourgeois womaniser:

> She bounced in as fresh as the dawn, looking as bright as a new dollar and bringing an unaccustomed waft of Elizabeth Arden fragrance through the dusty entrance. She asked for Harry Pollitt. He was out at the time but she was received by Jack [J.R.] Campbell and by (what was that Indian called who spent his life as a Party theoretician?) [Palme-Dutt, of course]. She saw Pollitt later but the damage was done. Tom had sent back a bourgeois tart – a great talker, some said she clearly had Trotskyite leanings – Ernie Brown [does he mean George Brown, member of the Central Committee who later joined the Brigade?] whom I met a year later said 'Eeh lad, what d'y expect; smelling like a whorehouse and dressed like for the races!' It must not be forgotten that Tom had a wife of deadly respectability and unimpeachable Marxist propriety who went about with the refrain 'I hesitate to believe appearance and I do not wish to believe that Tom has sold-out'.[33]

It was on this occasion, according to Kitty, that Pollitt became exasperated with her no doubt voluble exposition of Tom's case. 'Tell him to go up to the front and get killed,' Pollitt retorted, 'the movement needs a Byronic hero.' Others, who knew Pollitt, doubted he ever said such a thing.

The first International Brigades were formed in October 1936 base, Albacete, a small town in the plain of La Mancha on the between Valencia and Madrid. Wintringham joined up at the end month and wrote to Kitty that the medical commission had marked him fit for service and that he would probably go to the Officers' Training School as an instructor; then the front 'as soon as possible'. As one of the prime instigators of an international force he could hardly not join, particularly as there was a chronic shortage of officers with war experience. Hanging over his head, he said, was Pollitt's insult. He had called him 'a coward' for refusing to join a militia (not strictly accurate for Tom had joined the Tom Mann *centuria*), although how this fitted in with Pollitt's appointed task for him as 'responsable' is not clear. In any event, Tom was enthusiastic. He wanted to be a participant in the war and not, as he put it, 'an inefficient string-puller trying to straighten it out'.[34]

Between 1936 and 1938, over thirty thousand volunteers came from over sixty countries but most from France and Belgium, Germany, Austria and Italy to fight in the International Brigades. They were regarded as the elite of the Republican People's Army although they formed only 5 out of the 225 brigades. Of the volunteers, 2,300 came from Great Britain, of whom 526 were killed. Initially, the CPGB denied it was responsible for the British Battalion as it wanted to hedge its bets; the enterprise could end in disaster. *Daily Worker* editor William Rust wrote ambiguously in *Britons In Spain*: 'The International Brigades arose spontaneously in the minds of men . . . from the spontaneous movement of volunteers there naturally arose the decision to form the International Brigades.'[35]

Most recruits did indeed make the conscious political decision to go and fight fascism, but as the predominantly working-class and urban composition of the British recruits show, many joined also because they were unemployed, footloose and persuaded by Communist propaganda. From the start the International Brigades were run by the Comintern. Political commissars were attached to each battalion to ensure correct political thinking (among other duties) and Albacete was a Comintern town.

In charge there was Andre Marty, described by Tom as 'an incredibly expansive old sea-lion in the biggest beret ever worn by man', and by Jason Gurney as 'a sinister and ludicrous figure . . . quite literally mad at this time'. The two descriptions are not incompatible. The truth is that Marty, a founder member of the French Communist Party and folk hero ever since as a sailor he had mutinied rather than attack the Bolsheviks in 1919, was now a rigid Stalinist. Moreover, he was one of the few non-Russian Communists in whom Stalin had confidence. He had the classic symptoms of a bully in that he fawned before Soviet advisers but tyrannised subordinates. Paranoid about his position and sensitive to any perceived political dissidence, he ordered the execution of several hundred men for cowardice or Trotskyism. Not for nothing was he known as Le Boucher de Albacete. To paranoia, incompetence and cruelty may be added misogyny; all of which traits were to have a bearing on the future of Tom and Kitty.

Marty's chief of staff and crony was known as Vidal, the French Communist with whom Tom had shared a bed many years ago while on a speaking tour in South Wales. In *English Captain* Wintringham writes highly of him as 'a soldier of real war'; he had fought at Verdun and carried in his desk-drawer small range finders made from a compass and a distance measurer. Typically, this gadget appealed to Tom as much as Vidal's supposedly heroic past. Gurney took a more critical view, accusing Vidal and those whom he termed his 'villainous henchmen' of robbery, laziness and indiscipline. In any event, in November 1936 Tom waited to see him for several days, sitting outside the dining room of the Gran Hotel,

> listening to all the languages of Europe and drinking anis that tastes of liquorice or bad cognac that tastes of petrol; the Germans card-indexed each other and everyone else and the French darted from table to table with expressions of 'formidable' and 'bougre' and when the doors of the dining room opened a tidal wave of leather-faced men jammed through them, racing for seats.[36]

And then Vidal gave him a job, as machine-gun instructor to the XI and XII Battalions. He wrote to Kitty:

> I believe I can write war like no-one else; now I think I can fight it too, this time like anyone else. I'm blooming with uppishness at having vicious little guns to learn and handle. . . . Think of me with my devil-guns. There's a certain exact, free of frills sensible beauty about a good piece of engineering. I can get in a daze and thrill writing, sometimes, that is more exciting but much less satisfying than discovering the timing of an ejector or the way a barrel is released. Some poems are better than any machine guns; but men have been making poems for a much longer time.[37]

So Wintringham, the lover of deadly machines and the poet who hated war, got to work with his Colts, Chauchats, Maxims and Lewises, old guns from different countries with different ammunition. Vidal gave him ten days at each training camp and told him the instructional language was French. In early December he narrowly avoided being sent back to Barcelona by Marty to organise munitions production. 'This is not my choice, I wanted to be a soldier', he wrote to Kitty, and then, displaying his liking for innovation and gadgetry, 'in particular I wanted to organise anti-gas defences and develop smoke. But if this is the job they want me to do, I'll do it.'[38] Luckily for Tom it came to nothing.

Meanwhile, Kitty had joined the PSUC English-speaking radio service in Barcelona and in early December she also joined the UGT (the Socialist General Workers' Union), the better to obtain contacts for her budding writing career. She was given an assignment from the *Toronto Star* and wrote to her mother: 'I've gotten in with the editor of a Spanish newspaper and am getting all sorts of inside news and rushed around in cars etc. and am working even more than before, no time to breathe.'[39] Importantly, she still did not possess a formal press card because she did not formally represent a paper; she was a freelance. She obtained a *laissez passer* to visit Madrid or Valencia by having typed in, or writing in herself, 'Kitty Bowler of the People's Press'. About this time she and Tom spent a brief leave together in Valencia, after which she wrote to him from the Hotel Espagna:

I love:
  * your funny childish lisp
  * the soft spot on the back of your head
  * the way you throw your chin back in the morning.

What had begun as infatuation was growing into something much deeper. Tom wrote to Millie Wintringham and told her, in brutal terms, that their affair was over.

In November the first thirty British volunteers were already in action assisting the Republican militias in their successful defence of Madrid. Some, including the poet John Cornford, fought with the Commune de Paris Battalion of the XI Brigade while the remainder, including Esmond Romilly, nephew of Winston Churchill and husband of Jessica Mitford, fought with the Thaelmann Battalion, now part of the XII Brigade (confusingly, the Brigades started their numbering at XI). Only five survived, of whom one was Esmond Romilly, who wrote about his experiences in *Boadilla*, and another Cornford. This small remnant returned to Madrigueras, a small village some 20 miles from Albacete.

This was now the British base because in November and December nearly five hundred recruits came out from Britain, the result in part of Wintringham's urging. They were attached to the new XV Brigade. Tom transferred to them and added to his duties that of Capitaine adjoint-majeur or assistant to Wilfred McCartney, the Commander of the British contingent. On Christmas Eve the first British company, No. 1 Company, was formed and immediately entrained to fight with the XIV Brigade on the Cordoba front. Fortunately for Tom he did not go with them.

The survivors returned a few weeks later. They were without Ralph Fox, John Cornford and seventy-five others who had been killed or wounded in bungled action at Lopera. Some months before, at Huesca, Cornford had written one of the most poignant poems of the International Brigades, 'Full Moon at Tierz'.

> Then let my private battle with my nerves,
> The fear of pain whose pain survives,
> The love that tears me by the roots,
> The loneliness that claws my guts,
> Fuse in the welded front our fight preserves.
>
> Freedom is an easily spoken word
> But facts are stubborn things. Here, too, in Spain
> Our fight's not won till the workers of all the world
> Stand by our guard on Huesca's plain,
> Swear that our dead fought not in vain,
> Raise the red flag triumphantly
> For Communism and for liberty.[40]

Rupert John Cornford had been conceived the month of Rupert Brooke's death and named after him; he died only days before his twenty-first birthday. After Lopera the commander of the Marseillaise Battalion, Major Lasalle, was shot as a spy on Marty's orders although he had been a lifelong Communist. Tom actually approved: 'he was given a fair court martial', he wrote. The *News Chronicle* mistook Ralph Fox for Tom

Wintringham and rang Pollitt with the news that Wintringham had been killed. He went round to tell Millie.

Tom and Millie had remained intimate correspondents. She wrote as often as five times a week with political news and views: what Mosley and his Fascists were up to, her idea for a women's battalion. She supported him financially too, athough hard up herself, and acted as both editor and agent in his dealings with publishers. On 23 January 1937 she wrote to Tom telling him how she had heard of his death:

> When I saw Harry come up these stairs I was immediately uneasy as you can imagine. I saw at once that he looked terribly worn. I said 'What have you come to tell me?' He just looked at me and said 'Take a cigarette and sit down'. And I knew. He told me that the *News Chronicle* London office had received a report that you had been killed in action near Madrid. He had begged them not to publish until confirmation was received. He then came to me.
>
> He had been very torn about giving me the news but thought it best. He moved heaven and earth to find out what had happened and even phoned the Spanish Ambassador, from the flat. But nothing doing, we just had to wait until we could get word from our own friends in Albacate. I didn't cry much. But I did feel lost.

There was no news the next day so Millie decided to go and stay with their friends, Sylvia Townsend Warner and Valentine Ackland:

> I was greeted on arrival by a jubilant Valentine shouting 'Have you heard the good news?' as I came across the garden to the house, and we all stood in a terrific downpour of rain and hail trying to get used to having you 'alive' again, so don't die another time . . . or if you do, let it be as skilful an 'exit' as the first. It was all so much like sleep-walking . . . you were dead . . . for two and a half days. R [Raji Palme Dutt] told me yesterday that it had shaken more people even than the news of Ralph. He mentioned Emile [Burns, Pollitt's deputy in King Street], himself and Harry.[41]

What was it about Tom that however much he let people down they continued to regard him with such love?

The British survivors of Lopera became the nucleus of the British Battalion. This was formed just before the end of January 1937 when 600 men were grouped into three infantry companies and one machine-gun company, with headquarters staff and political commissar. It was called the Saklatvala Battalion after Shapurji Saklatvala, the British Indian who became the first Communist MP. The name had been kicked around for some time since King Street had proposed it. Ralph Fox had had his doubts. He had written to Pollitt: 'Would the name have enough appeal to non-Communists at home to help the growth of the People's Front?' Presumably the answer was no, because the name was eventually changed to the Clement Attlee Battalion, though this went down equally badly with many of the Communist volunteers, who regarded Attlee as an enemy of the working class. Not that it mattered. It was always known as the British Battalion or *el batallon Ingles* because the Spanish did not distinguish between English and British.

29/1/37. Dear Muv,

I carry now a silver-handled walking stick. I'm appointed to the English speaking battalion as 'Capitaine adjoint-majeur'. In a few days I get a real officer's uniform, Sam Browne belt and all. But the real pleasure I get is teaching and learning from men I like and respect, and who like me – comrades who have got 'real faith and fire within us'.

Good, too, to make real the game of manoeuvre I used to play – do you remember? – with counters or with matches, books for hills and pencils for rivers, all over the floors and desks of the Garden House. I can do this job.[42]

Tom made a favourable impression on Jason Gurney:

He [Tom] was a slim man of medium height, with large, round, steel-framed spectacles, a high-domed bald head and an academic stoop. He always wore a khaki beret, a shiny black mackintosh coat of vaguely military cut, riding breeches and high laced boots. The total effect suggested a motor-cyclist rather than a soldier. [This was true as Elizabeth had sent out his motor-bike coat.] He was invariably pleasant, informal and unpretentious. He was a completely sincere radical who did his best to be useful to the cause without any idea of personal aggrandizement.

His only apparent vice was a weakness for delivering long and tedious lectures on the Marxist theory of warfare, heavily larded with texts from Marx and Engels which were supposed to re-inforce the argument.[43]

Madrigueras in January was a miserable place. Out in the bare, featureless plain of Murcia, with hardly a tree to break up the horizon, the dwellings huddled together under a chill rain. The unpaved streets churned up into a grey-green mud and there was little fuel for heating. The people were desperately poor, depending for their livelihood on the annual harvest of saffron from the crocus fields. The social centre was the Casa del Pueblo set up by the UGT but, according to Jason Gurney,

> Few people used the place – three or four groups of silent men in shabby clothes with black hats and black scarves wrapped round their faces. The women walked round with black shawls. All the life seemed to have gone out of them. It was now winter in a despoiled and empty world. There was neither warmth nor heat nor light nor food nor health nor love. When we arrived the Church had already been converted into a Battalion mess hall but the people seemed to avoid even looking at the place, as if they had a sense of guilt about it. It left me with an uneasy feeling.[44]

Other British recruits had a less unhappy experience. George Leeson remembered the relentless rain, but also that his group of friends was adopted by village families who cooked them eggs and sometimes *curiscos* (sausages) for supper, though they could barely afford to eat themselves. When they left for the front the villagers assembled to cheer them off and refused any payment. Many volunteers developed a deep admiration for the Spanish people. One wrote home: 'the poor class of Spain are 500 years behind time . . . they have been kept under like dogs but the people have risen now, by George'. Another wrote, forgetting the Comintern veto on revolutionary talk, 'Spain is going to be a wonderful Socialist country in a few short years.'[45]

After he returned from Spain Wintringham boasted to the military expert Basil Liddell Hart that at Madrigueras in only six weeks he had created, in his words, 'second-rate but useful infantry' out of volunteers of whom 'only about 30 per cent had fought before'. The equipment was extremely poor, partly a result of the non-intervention policy that prevented the importing of arms. At first there were hardly any rifles and decent Russian ones arrived so late that the British Battalion had only time to fire off five rounds in practice before they marched off to fight. Apart from the old Maxims, the machine-guns were extremely erratic; Tom considered the French Chauchats, known as 'shossers', the worst light machine-guns ever devised.

The Communist scientist Professor J.B.S. Haldane arrived to lecture on the Mills bomb, but there were none to practise with and very few grenades. Then a consignment did arrive, but without any instructions so Tom took one apart, reassembled and threw it, with the desired result; he sent the pin home as a souvenir.

Wintringham and McCartney took the Battalion on field exercises. 'I've been haring across country organising manoeuvres and deployments', wrote Tom. But, complained Gurney, these exercises did not include practice in how to fortify a position or beat an organised retreat. This seems unlikely, but the behaviour of the British at Jarama bore out this criticism. Tom taught lessons in compass reading, though they possessed hardly any compasses, and map reading, though at Jarama they possessed no maps. A Scottish recruit, Donald Renton, remembered Tom teaching them how to use the Lewis machine-gun against aircraft and added praise that probably meant more to Wintringham than any other:

Wintringham had an absolute genius not only in his ability to inspire but in his capacity to invent weapons. He established for us that even in the worst of conditions it became possible for ordinary men and women who were fighting for proper causes to find the means through which, in one way or another, they could improvise arms against the enemy.[46]

During the evening the old cinema at Madrigueras was used for lectures. Tom gave one on street fighting, based on the urban warfare he had witnessed or heard about in Barcelona and Madrid. Peter Kerrigan, the Political Commissar, spoke on the political situation.

Tom's 'devil-guns' were the cause of Kitty's arrest as a spy. This was an extraordinary incident that was to tarnish her political reputation ever after, and by implication Tom's too. Only now may the story be pieced together.

The wretched Colt machine-guns kept jamming and, at Tom's request, Kitty consulted two experts in Valencia who knew why and how to prevent it. She was unable to phone through to Albacete with her information and reluctant to visit because she knew it was off-bounds to non-Party members, particularly to female journalists. However, she was reassured in Valencia by a senior German Communist Jorge S., who gave her a pass. So on 20 January she hitched a lift on a lorry from Albacete and arrived at Madrigueras with this technical information.

Here Kitty takes up the story.

McCartney, susceptible to my charms, enrolled me as a Colt Machine Gun Instructor carried on the strength of the Saklatvala Battalion. [A copy of this order is still in the Wintringham archive.] At midnight there was a great banging at the door of the cubby hole where I was trying to sleep. There was Mac tousled and distraught. I was under arrest! I'd better return to him my lovely paper making me temporary machine-gun instructor. Then he was off to keep them (two guards) quiet while I dressed.

She was taken by lorry to Albacete where, after questions in German from a 'lean and hard faced individual', she was ordered into the next room. Andre Marty was waiting:

Behind a rolltop desk sat an old man with a first class walrus moustache. He was sleepy and irritable and had pulled a coat on over his pyjamas. He reminded me of a petty French bureaucrat. [Perhaps that was just as well.] To my surprise my mass of Spanish papers did not interest him in the least. Even my U.G.T. card and pass were thrown back in my face, contemptuously. My past was all that interested him, but I was sure it would all be cleared up in the morning when Mac and Tom came over. . . . At the end of an hour he read out the charges and they shocked me out of my certainty. 1) Travelled from Albacete to Madrigueras by truck without a pass. 2) Penetrated (literal transl. of the French) into a military establishment. 3) Interested yourself into the functioning (bad) of machine guns. 4) Visited Italy and Germany in 1933. THEREFORE YOU ARE A SPY.[47]

Then, Tom wrote afterwards, she was carted off for interrogation for three days and nights, in French, by relays of investigators, the main interrogations taking place each night at 2 a.m. after she had been woken from sleep.[48] One of the grounds of suspicion, ironically, was Tom's poem 'Contempt of Court' which she carried with her. Apparently, it was a secret code. More significant causes for suspicion were admitted by Tom in a report he wrote for the Comintern the following July when he was trying to clear her name. She had a camera with her, which at first she denied, and she did not have an official press card. At the time Tom was worried about her 'fever-talk' too. Kitty just could not help talking too much. He was distraught, unable to see her and writing off streams of notes to her instead:

Monday. 2.30. Oh, my dear, I hate to think of you under strain at this time. You impressed Marty as 'very, very strong, very clever, very intelligent'. Although this was said as a suspicious point against you – women journalists should be weak and stupid – I got a jump of pride from the words.

6.30. I am still waiting. What the future holds I know not – anyhow, immediately, some hours with you. I know the time will be too short; the time apart, later, will be too long. But we're going on! Yes. T.[49]

When Kitty was released she was sentenced without her knowledge to be expelled from Spain. This order was not handed to her until the following July, possibly because of the lack of evidence against her but, more likely, because she was at the time a member of the foreign press corps, however tenuously. Why was she condemned as a spy when clearly she was, at worst, a foolhardy and gabby young woman? Albacete was in a state of spy fever. Marty was a paranoid psychopath and a misogynist for whom, according to Tom, a young woman travelling without her husband was *ipso facto* up to no good. Marty neither trusted the character assessments of Spaniards or Germans (Jorge S.) when it came to issuing passes, nor did he follow the concept of presumed innocence until found guilty. But what made it harder for both Marty and, indeed, Wintringham was that neither Wilfred McCartney nor Peter Kerrigan was prepared to intervene. McCartney was particularly unsympathetic, judging pithily that Tom's problems were 'skirt not line'.

It was only years later that Tom gave his version of what happened, having kept quiet about it, he said, out of deference to the Party. But in 1941 a manuscript written by McCartney that referred to the incident, coupled with an off-hand remark McCartney made at a dinner in Kitty's presence – 'I would not have minded if she had been shot' – so incensed Tom that he gave his side of the story. In fact, he threatened the publisher Victor Gollancz he would sue for libel if he turned McCartney's manuscript into a book. It was withdrawn.

Tom and Kitty went to Madrid for rest and recuperation. She wrote afterwards from the Hotel Inglesi in Valencia:

My own T. Just those few hours with you were enough to wash all bitterness out of me. You made me strong again. You need not worry.

I will go on and on. Now 'Neither fools, nor Children' applies to both of us. You took a somewhat undirected little lost girl and made a person of her. I love you, love you, all of you, your long tall body, your sweet steadying voice, your brains and good sense mixed with good emotion. Salut y republica! Your Schwimp.[50]

He wrote from Albacete: 'Good gallant Schwimp. You know a good deal about giving a man a good time, and then some! The total effect on morale of my 24 hours leave was A1 Magnificent. I'm on top of the world!'[51]

When Wintringham returned to Madrigueras he found that Pollitt had been complaining about him to Kerrigan, presumably after a wire from Marty. But McCartney put up a stout defence of Tom's military ability. He wrote to Pollitt: 'Don't get any silly ideas into your head that Wintringham is not pulling his weight. He is the best man in Spain at his work; an ideal staff-officer and machine-gunner.'[52] The truth was that the Battalion was chronically short of experienced officers and other ranks too. McCartney continued his letter: 'The method of selecting [volunteers] is the worst muddle I've experienced. I've commanded the Battalion for nearly a month by kicking, yelling, nagging, swearing, and I've nearly killed myself. But I've made something of them.' Kerrigan sounded equally stressed in his letter to Pollitt:

Some lads have no desire to serve in the army. *All recruits must understand they are expected to serve. Tell them; this is a war and many will be killed.* This should be put brutally, with a close examination of their hatred of fascism. A much greater discipline is needed. Recruits must be told there is no guarantee of mail and the allowance is only three pesetas a day.[53]

Tom added his anxieties: 'About ten percent of the men are drunks and flunkers. I can't understand why you've [Pollitt] sent out such useless material. We call them "Harry's anarchists".'[54] This little joke can have done nothing to improve their relationship.

The desperate complaints from Madrigueras give the lie to the Communist line that all recruits joined up spontaneously to fight fascism; and that the volunteers went into battle well armed and well disciplined. Some of the Battalion at this time disapproved ideologically of obeying orders, demanding to call a fraction (group meeting) to discuss the command. After all, this was a people's army and all ranks were addressed as 'comrade'. Others, several of whom had mutinied in the official armed forces, were just bloody-minded. The Irish contingent insisted at a drunken Burns Night supper that they would not fight with the British and left to join the (American) Lincoln Battalion, also in XV Brigade. All this was bad for morale and everything was exacerbated by the weather, the hanging around and the lack of sanitation.

McCartney was unpopular. A former British Army officer recently released from prison for spying for the Soviet Union, he was not a Communist. He frequently lost his temper and he held hierarchical views about his status that were out of place in a people's army, however disciplined. When news came through from London that he had to return to England because his ticket of leave after prison parole had expired, no tears were shed. Then an extraordinary accident occurred. On 6 February, Kerrigan entertained McCartney to a farewell dinner in Albacete during which he persuaded him to leave behind his big Mauser pistol in exchange for Kerrigan's Belgian .22. The Mauser was loaded and accidently Kerrigan touched the trigger, shooting McCartney in the arm and instantly rendering him unfit for combat. By such an improbable accident – for it was an accident, despite suspicions to the contrary – did Tom Wintringham become Commander of the British Battalion on the eve of its first battle.

The next day, 7 February, Tom wrote a typically generous letter to Pollitt and Palme Dutt: 'I'm very proud and hope I can carry the job well. It will be tragic if Mac does not come back *to this Battalion*. I am the least ambitious person imaginable, really fond of Mac, v. willing to keep the place warm for him.'[55] But the Party did not allow McCartney to return. The same day Tom wrote to Kitty:

Going at last, temporarily in command. All in the game and I love it: beautiful new uniform and field glasses.

I love you, and much more than that I don't need to tell you. If you had seen my quietest comrade smile as he handed over your violets, you would know how my man's world likes the sight of you and is pleased with the idea you are my 'young lady'.[56]

That very day the Battalion marched off to fight its bloodiest battle of the war. It was only while waiting to entrain at Albacete that most of the Battalion realised Wintringham was in command. George Leeson recalled:

This was a tremendous shock! Nobody liked McCartney with his 1914 ideas but to find your battalion commander is not there when you are about to go into battle and a kind of instructor is in command! Well, it's a very demoralising thing, particularly in these mysterious circumstances. All sorts of rumours started to go round: 'McCartney's deserted!' 'McCartney's committed suicide!' 'Pete Kerrigan's shot McCartney!' This turned out to be true.[57]

Kerrigan was contrite, in fact he offered to resign, but at that moment he was also inspired. He wrote a heartfelt letter to Pollitt:

The boys looked splendid when we left them. They are keen and, I think, v. efficient. They know what is expected of them and will do their best to carry out the job. They are anti-fascist, they understand it's got to be fought here and they are prepared to take all the risks implied in this fight. They are too close to it to see that history is being made here and this generation and the one that follows will be filled with a great pride. After all it is no little thing to hold back International Fascism and help save the peace of the world a little longer.[58]

EIGHT

The Battle of Jarama

On 11 February 1937, when Tom was on his way to the front, his sister Margaret wrote to 'Darling Muv' with photographs of him sent by 'that American woman journalist'. Kitty had enclosed a note to Margaret, already sounding a little proprietorial: 'he is adored and respected by his men. So think of him as happy and don't worry much about him, he has a way of looking after himself.' So had Kitty, of course. She wrote to her mother at the same time with the news that she was now the *Manchester Guardian*'s stringer in Valencia and known by the press as 'Kitty with the red ribbons in her hair'.[1] Before the week was out Tom was lying wounded in hospital at Elda-Petral, among the orange groves of Alicante province, and Kitty was on her way to join him.

February had begun badly for the Republic. On the 6th, a Nationalist offensive had begun to encircle Madrid from the south, aiming to capture the capital's lifeline road to Valencia in the area of the River Jarama. On the 11th, the Nationalist army (or fascist army as the British Battalion invariably called it) crossed the Jarama by three bridges along a 10-kilometre front; but there on the heights of the east bank of the river the Republican line held, still protecting the Madrid–Valencia road. The Nationalist army consisted of 40,000 men, mostly Moors from the Army of Africa, supported by German machine-guns, tanks and artillery. Against them the Republic threw its best Spanish brigades, now under unified command, aided by the XI, XII, XIV and XV International Brigades.

The XV Brigade, made up of the Dimitrov Battalion (volunteers from the Balkans), the Franco-Belge Battalion and the British Battalion, was ordered to the southern end of the line where the Nationalists had crossed the Jarama on the bridge carrying a dirt road between San Martin de la Vega and Morata de Tajuna. The British were to hold and, it was hoped, counter-attack, along the extreme southern flank. There were no Republican troops on their left nor after a short while on their right, the other side of this dirt road, for the remainder of the XV Brigade was soon forced to retreat. In other words, when Wintringham and his 600 men took up position on the morning of 12 February and watched as thousands of Moorish troops – 'ferocious brown bundles appearing out of the ground at one's feet' is how Gurney described them – advanced up the hill towards them, they were exposed to the enemy along their front and both their flanks were unprotected.

None of this was known to the men of the British Battalion until it was too late. According to George Leeson: 'We did not know what position we were going into; we didn't know that there had been a heavy enemy breakthrough across the river; we didn't know whether we were going into an offensive or defensive position. We just knew we were going in to the front line.'[2] The British Battalion advanced to the front line at about nine in the morning of 12 February, from a farm about three kilometres back that served as cookhouse and headquarters. The men scrambled up a rock escarpment and then fanned out across a wide plateau covered with olive trees. Then they dipped down to a sunken road, crossed it and climbed again to a ridge at nearly 700 metres. Here the olive trees ended and the ground fell away before rising to a secondary ridge with a small, white house built on it, the Casa Blanca. Beyond that the land fell away again, in broken terrain covered with short grass, and ended at the River Jarama. Walking it recently at the same time of year, a cold wind gusting across the dusty plateau now stripped of olive trees, I was reminded of the sights Gurney saw when Wintringham ordered him back from the sunken road to the farm headquarters during that first day:

> The signs of indiscipline and of a totally unrealistic optimism lay on every side. Most men had apparently decided it would all be over in a few hours and had left their greatcoats, blankets and personal possessions stowed away behind olive trees. There was an extraordinary variety of books littering the ground. Marxist textbooks, being heavy, lay near the bottom of the hill; then there was pornography, copies of Nietzsche and Spanish textbooks, Rhys David's Early Buddhism and every kind of poetry. But [as now] the rubbish consisted mainly of dirty paper, broken food and defecation.[3]

During the advance Wintringham said he felt anger and fear because the Battalion was pushing on into an impossible position. Brigade headquarters had given the original order: 'Square-faced, gruff, grim-faced, Colonel Gal said nothing except you will advance at once in this direction. A thick-tipped finger pointed to a heavy blue pencil line on the map.'[4] When the three infantry companies moving ahead of Wintringham reached the highest point of the ridge, a reasonable defensive position, they should have obeyed Wintringham's orders and halted. But they saw the Jarama in the distance 'as clear as can be' and took Colonel Gal's order to override those of the 'English Captain'. In an excess of enthusiasm but indiscipline 400 men, 'a collection of city-bred young men with no experience of war up against professionals', as Gurney called them, continued down the slope towards the smaller ridge round the Casa Blanca, and then beyond until they saw Franco's Army of Africa advancing towards them. Here they stopped, under fire, without any idea of the overall strategy or enemy strength, without entrenching tools, provisions or maps. They were on exposed ground shielded only by shortish grass, some at first standing and firing their new rifles from the hip in a show of bravado. Jason Gurney watched the tragedy unfold:

> Casa Blanca hill became completely obscured by clouds of smoke and dust. When it lifted I could see the chaos; some of the men were working away with bayonets and tin helmets in an attempt to produce some sort of fox-hole in which to hide. None of the Colts or shossers were firing, and very few rifles. Our men seemed to be fascinated by the little white house which was already in ruins. They kept moving towards it, presumably because it was the only solid cover, undeterred by the fact that the enemy were using it as a ranging mark, and it was here the shelling was heaviest.[5]

Throughout the day the three forward companies were bombarded by German artillery, and shot at by the Army of Africa who were using their knowledge of camouflage and cover to advance up the hill towards them. So the British dubbed their front line Suicide Hill. That first day, over 250 men out of the 400 stuck on it were either killed, wounded or captured. Around midday Tom sent Gurney down Casa Blanca hill to get a report:

> The survivors were in good heart but very angry. Some were still trying to scratch cover and cursing the lack of tools; others were trying to unjam the wretched shossers jammed with earth; everyone was asking for water. We were all frightened by the sheer din of battle, so intense it

seemed to have an inescapably destructive force of its own, and the number of casualties. The horror of seeing close friends being killed and broken did not really penetrate my mind until later. It was all too fantastic, like something seen in a nightmare.[6]

It was a catastrophic beginning for the British Battalion. Over 150 of its men were killed at Jarama, nearly one-third of its fatalities for the entire war, and most of them died as a result of the first two days fighting when Wintringham was in charge. From his command post in the sunken road, which gave him protection but only a poor view of the battle, he coped as best he could, aware that he was a victim of other men's failings. He could only watch the impetuosity of his men as they charged ill-equipped into an untenable position. He had to endure the 'at all costs mentality' (as he put it) of Brigade Headquarters who, often shouting down the telephone in Russian, ordered him under threat of arrest to advance or hold his ground. After that first morning he refused to advance, a defiance that in the First World War would have resulted in a court martial; but he did order his men to hold their ground longer than was feasible because, as we shall see, he felt he had no option. Tom hated the 'at all costs mentality'. He wrote in *English Captain*:

They are not soldier's words, but propagandists'. They represent the romantic, unreal view of war, boastful, blindly gallant, that makes courage more important than brains. They are words for battles such as Verdun and the Somme. They should be used with the utmost caution.[7]

It is difficult to know what Wintringham was thinking when men were dying 'at all costs'. In *English Captain* he distances himself from the tragedy by referring to himself in the third person:

He was something of a stranger. I am self-conscious, and he had been, through pressure of things to do, unconscious of himself. I am untidy and he had been, in new uniform and clear giving of orders, fairly neat and precise. I am afraid of bullets and he had been too busy to notice them. Yet he was not wholly a stranger; he was what I had wanted to be for the sake of this raw battalion entrusted to me, these excellent men. . . .[8]

The reason for Tom's alter ego, this casting of himself in the third person, was surely because he was experiencing a crisis of confidence:

What on earth was Tom doing among these olive-trees, dusty earth, cold February hills, with hundreds of men to lead in unequal battle? He belonged to a quiet writing-desk or the clatter of a print shop, little rooms where committees met. . . .

Tom's way of coping, at least in *English Captain*, was to transform himself in his mind from an armchair revolutionary to an English Captain:

Ah! of course! Before me there had been so many English captains, through centuries of invasion, civil war, piracy and adventure. The last great war fought on Spanish soil had seen many of them marching, under Wellington and Sir John Moore, across half the peninsula. . . . And not only in Spain, but over half the world people like myself had taken the sturdy English riflemen, musketeers, archers. . . . There was something useful in the idea.

Tom is 'Fighting for the Flag'. The daydreams in his father's study at Grimsby become the fantasies of the Spanish olive grove. But they give Tom the confidence to fight on. At dawn on the second day Wintringham briefly lost his grip and Gurney, a shrewd observer, remarked: 'anxious to succeed in the role of English Captain, in which he had cast himself, the realities failed to live up to his imagination and he could no longer recognize himself'.[9]

The next muddle inflicted on Tom was over his precious machine-guns. His attempts to prevent the Colts and 'shossers' from jamming had proved ineffective; few worked and most were discarded within an hour of the enemy's advance. But Sergeant Harry Fry and his No. 2 Machine Gun Company put their reliance in eight old Maxim machine-guns. They dragged them up to the high ridge with a clear field of fire towards the advancing enemy – and then discovered they had been given the wrong ammunition. A hapless Sergeant H. in charge of the lorry that had brought the ammunition was sent off to Morata to collect the right cartridge belts. In Morata he drank several brandies to calm his nerves. On the way back he crashed the lorry. It was the lack of covering fire from Harry Fry's machine-guns that prevented Tom from ordering his front line to retreat.

This is where Fred Copeman entered the story. Gurney described him at this moment as 'a great bull of a man, who was by this time more or less insane, giving completely inconsequential orders to everybody in sight and offering to bash their faces in if they did not comply'.[10] He had been wounded twice already but was totally without fear; the bloodlust of battle was in his veins. Now, staggering back into action from the advance casualty station, he came across the crashed lorry with the correct ammunition. Wintringham continued: 'Fred came up the sunken road swearing and blinding, dragging a Maxim with his uninjured paw. I asked him if there was any ammo. and was glad to hear: "Of course there's f—ing bu—ing, so—ing ammo; but we'll have to fill the belts.".'[11]

The Maxims were dragged into place again on the high ridge and primed with the right ammunition. Late in the day, much too late, Wintringham ordered a retreat from Suicide Hill to the ridge, up past the machine-guns, and down towards the sunken road where his command post was based. When the jubilant Moors chased the British up the hill they were mown down by Fry's machine-guns. The fascists retreated back towards the Casa Blanca. It was a redeeming end to a dreadful day.

During the afternoon Jason Gurney had been ordered by Wintringham to reconnoitre to the south of the sunken road:

I had only gone about 700 yards when I came across one of the most ghastly sights I have ever seen. I found a group of wounded (British) men who had been carried to a non-existent field dressing station and then forgotten. There were about fifty stretchers, but many men had already died and most of the others would be dead by morning. They had appalling wounds, mostly from artillery. One little Jewish kid of about eighteen lay on his back with his bowels exposed from his navel to his genitals and his intestines lying in a ghastly pinkish brown heap, twitching slightly as the flies searched over them. He was perfectly conscious. Another man had nine bullet holes across his chest. I held his hand until it went limp and he was dead. I went from one to the other but was absolutely powerless. Nobody cried out or screamed except they all called for water and I had none to give. I was filled with such horror at their suffering and my inability to help them that I felt I had suffered some permanent injury to my spirit.[12]

Wintringham said he hated war but there is nothing in *English Captain*, nor in his war poems, to show that he experienced any such trauma as this.

'Spanish dawn comes almost as quickly as a theatre curtain opens', wrote Tom. The second act or day of the tragedy began with the remains of the British Battalion too weak and shell-shocked to do more than hold their position on the sunken road. They were shielded to an extent by Fry's Maxims dug in on the ridge above but not from fire coming in from the flanks. Tom admitted to an early panic attack when he was rooted to the ground in the orange grove above the sunken road, afraid to move:

> Trees twitched and rustled in the still air as bullets cut into their lower branches. A gap in the wall of the sunken road was sprayed patiently and continually. Moving in the olive grove was like wading into breakers: crack-phht of bullets came in a regular rhythm as the guns traversed, interweaving, shaping a swinging net of lead over us. This probing fire gave me a sinking of the guts such as I had felt as a small boy when told that God was everywhere and could see everything. . . . I could hear three or four shots for each step I took, and three or four pac noises as the bullets hit olives near me on the hard soil. A bullet twitched the front edge of my tunic, cutting a half-round hole just in front of my trouser buttons. Too near I thought, and dropped behind an olive-tree root.[13]

And there he stuck 'until I no longer felt an omnipotent eye looking firmly at me. I put aside foolishness and ran, fast, back to my headquarters'. Then he had enough presence of mind to order a small counter-attack along the left, southern flank to take the pressure off Fry.

When Tom wrote *New Ways of War* three years later, in 1940, he emphasised how important it was to teach people not to be afraid of being afraid. Every soldier is afraid of battle the first time, he wrote, and in a candid admission that must have given heart to Local Defence Volunteers expecting a German invasion, he told how at Jarama he had repeated a mantra over and over to himself in order to try and take his mind off the fear: 'Why die crying? Why die crying? I remember saying to myself.'[14] Tom was no fire-eating warrior but he did not let the side down.

The end came quickly, confusingly, late in the afternoon. Gurney remembered:

> Suddenly there was a terrific din from the machine gun trench – shouting, cheering, a short fusillade of rifle fire and the dull thud of hand grenades. I started across towards the trench but our own Maxim guns opened fire in our direction and I ran back to the shelter of the sunken road.[15]

It turned out that Bert Overton, in charge of No. 4 Company which was supposed to protect Fry's right flank, had lost his nerve and scrambled down to the sunken road followed by some of his men. This left the Machine-Gun Company exposed and it was quickly overwhelmed by Nationalist soldiers of the Foreign Legion who had replaced the Moors during the night. In the confusion some of Fry's men mistook the Legion soldiers for another contingent of XV Brigade and therefore they held their fire. This did not save them. Three were executed in cold blood and the others, including Fry and Yank Levy, later to become a close friend of Tom and Kitty, were marched off to prison singing the Internationale. Gurney continued:

At this particular moment, we were all a little mad – the sheer weight of noise was tremendous, coupled with a feeling of desperation and excitement. Wintringham ordered us to fix bayonets, which was quite absurd. We all clustered against the bank ready to go over the top, like some totally improbable incident out of the Boys Own Paper. Wintringham stood up to lead the charge, was almost immediately shot through the thigh, and collapsed into the sunken road.

Years later, in an interview for the Imperial War Museum, Fred Copeman recalled that he and George Aitkin (the Political Commissar with the British Battalion) had picked up Wintringham, who was sitting behind an olive tree. 'He had a wound in the eye [*sic*]. Well, we knew he shot himself!'[16] This is refuted by Aitkin, a dour Scot who speaks on the same collection of tapes with a slow, measured voice, and Gurney, who was no lover of heroics – unlike Tom. In fact it was a malicious lie. Why Copeman tried to ruin Wintringham's reputation as Commander at Jarama we do not know, except that he tried to ruin other reputations too in order to advance his own; but such was his notorious lying that few listened. Later in Spain he too became Commander of the British Battalion. Afterwards he swapped communism for catholicism and, improbably, joined Moral Rearmament; an unstable record if ever there was one.

At about 6 p.m. on 13 February 1937 George Aitkin, left in temporary command of only about thirty fit men, was still holding the sunken road. Then two Russian tanks appeared and blasted the fascists in the machine-gun trench above. Night came; the firing died down and the Nationalists withdrew. Gurney, Aitkin and others fell into an exhausted sleep while Tom lay on a stretcher and was carried back through the olive groves to the farmhouse.

At first Tom's wound gave no cause for concern, despite his trip to hospital in a 'nightmare' ambulance. Moreover, the next day other wounded brought news from the British Battalion that was almost miraculously good. Tom was able to write a note to Kerrigan that was passed on to Pollitt: 'I think the battalion did damned well. Morale and effectiveness of fire were still high after four days. There can be few bodies of troops who have experienced anything like it as their first four days of war.'[17] In fact the surviving British, last seen by Tom cowering in the sunken road, had retreated the next day back to the farmhouse. There, however, they were revived by food and encouraged by their new commander, Jock Cunningham, who was an experienced though mutinous soldier who had served with the Argyll and Sutherland Highlanders. He had survived the desperate defence of Madrid in December but missed the earlier action at Jarama through fever. Now he led the British Battalion back into the line.

Others from broken units, Spanish, French and Irish, fell in behind and on the way stragglers swelled the numbers. They picked up the march and sang the Internationale. It must have been an inspiring sight and it took the Nationalists by surprise. They retreated from the land they had gained beyond the sunken road, back over the high ridge and down Casa Blanca hill. During the night the Republican line was strengthened to the left and right. The British had filled the gap: a front line of trenches now held the Nationalist advance around the area of the high ridge where the olive trees ended. The Jarama had been crossed but the Madrid–Valencia Road was not cut.

Tom did not doubt that Jarama was a significant victory:

If the battle had gone against us and the Valencia road had been cut, Madrid could have been surrounded and starved out by June 1937. And those who are reading this book in 1939 might instead be reading of bombers trying to hammer Paris into surrender, might be hoping for a breathing space before London's turn comes.[18]

Accepting Tom's overview but with the hindsight of history, we may say that Jarama afforded just a year's delay; but a more critical judgement on the first days of Jarama came from Jason Gurney:

It was true that we contained an offensive by the finest troops the enemy could muster, but the cost was appalling. One of the slogans in the early days of the war was 'Resister y fortificar es vencer'; to resist and fortify is to conquer. . . . Jarama was the ideal site for a defensive battle. Had we fortified the escarpment before the bridges were lost then the enemy would never have held the valley at all and our casualties would have been low. The whole concept of replying with a counter attack was ridiculous in itself because we had no reserves nor the armament strength to carry it out.[19]

The British Battalion was not withdrawn from the line until 17 June, by which time the savage fighting had long been replaced by the monotony and discomfort of stalemate; of guard duty, stand to and sniping. One of Tom's friends, Alex McDade, wrote a rueful poem about it that was sung at reunion dinners to the tune of 'Red River Valley':

> There's a valley in Spain called Jarama,
> That's a place that we all know so well,
> For 'tis there that we wasted our manhood
> And most of our old age as well.[20]

Read over sixty years after Jarama, *English Captain*'s value is that it provides an honest account of how a Commander tries to lead in battle and of what effect that battle is having on him. This is how it was reviewed in 1939:

The interest of this clearly and brilliantly described action lies in the battalion commander. One can see his mind working under conditions of considerable danger, conjecturing what is happening on his flanks, trying to interpret the orders from brigade in a practical way, timing the exact moment of retreat and how it must be made. Almost every unlooked for misfortune that can assail a C.O. befell him. . . . The story is studded with lessons and warnings for the commander in the field, the correct timing of movements, the unorthodox, but effective handling of machine guns, the evil of conditional messages; and, most of all, the lesson that the other side knows as little as you do. It is the precise detail of what happened and why, that makes this unique account remarkable and valuable.[21]

This is a somewhat clinical legacy. For an emotional impact still, there is in the Wintringham archive the original note which Tom scrawled to Kitty when he arrived in hospital on the night of 13 February 1937. The writing falls down the page, ending illegibly:

Dear Kitty,

Hit in thigh while trying to organise bayonet charge. Damn these out of date sports. Nice wound. 2 days hard fighting: done well, lost all . . .

Love Tom

NINE

'And These Were Ours Who Died'

When Kitty found Tom in hospital she interviewed 'Captain T.H. Wintringham' for the *Manchester Guardian*. Her dispatch was a reply to a scandalous article in the *Daily Mail* on 20 February headlined 'BRITONS LURED TO THEIR DEATH IN SPAIN'. The *Daily Mail* alleged that many so-called volunteers had been press-ganged into the British Battalion and that at Madrigueras those who did not want to fight 'were lined up and shot; the remainder like cattle were then driven to slaughter . . . commanded by an Englishman named Wintringham'. A hero of Kitty's rejoinder was 'Lt Fred Copeman', who exemplified the fighting spirit of the volunteers: 'persuasion, threats, pain, nothing could restrain him. Finally, at the end of 36 hours even his strength failed. He fainted from loss of blood.' Later, when Tom's reputation mattered in the next war, he won a retrospective libel action against the *Daily Mail*.

In fact Copeman was charging about the hospital at Elda-Petral having his wounds dressed and spreading rumours more scandalous than the *Daily Mail*'s. His blood seems to have been replaced by poison:

I found Tom in a private ward with a pretty little Spanish girl [*sic*] and the doctor was playing up like hell because in Spain you don't have little girls in hospital with officers. I said: 'Tom, you've got a bloody cheek! You and I know what you've done [a reference to his apocryphal 'blighty' or self-inflicted wound]. I'm prepared to forget it but get that bloody woman the hell out of here'. So he got rid of the girl.[1]

Did Kitty know her hero was so dismissive of her? The story was an invention, another example of what George Aitkin called Copeman's 'romancing', yet it exists in the Imperial War Museum as oral testimony. On 27 February, Tom and Kitty left the hospital for four days' sick leave in Valencia.

Two days later Elizabeth wrote to Tom, relieved that he was not badly injured: 'When I tell him [O.J.] that he must be proud of his father fighting the fascists he clenches his fists and looks so serious and fierce I could weep.' And she expressed another concern, although with a light touch: 'You are indeed indeed having a lot of varied experience, but shall I know you when you come back? I shall be most anxious to make your acquaintance you may be sure!'[2]

Tom may well not have read the letter because immediately after he and Kitty arrived in Valencia he succumbed to a raging fever with a temperature of 104°C and soaring. He became delirious. Kitty was frantic with worry but when the International Brigades office in Valencia appeared unable to help, she stiffened her resolve. With the help of two British journalists she went directly to the office of Prime Minister Largo Caballero and insisted that his secretary contact a specialist. A Dr Mendez diagnosed typhoid and Tom was rushed into a private room in the public hospital for infectious diseases. It was here that nurse Patricia Darton found him on about 5 March. She had been flown out from Hendon Aerodrome by the Spanish Medical Aid Committee in London in order to try and save Tom's life. At the airport 'Mrs [Elizabeth] Wintringham, in a great state', had pressed into her hand her last three pounds:

> I found poor Tom in a very bad way in this terrible hospital. He was running miles of temperature and the place was so dirty, full of flies, and shit was all the way up the walls of the loo, which was blocked anyway. I took a dim view of that. He was looked after by this American girl who didn't know anything. He was so wretched, dirty and prickly and horrible that I thought first thing I'd give him a tepid sponge bath. A doctor came in furious and made me sign a form that I was responsible for killing him. So I signed the thing. Then I threw poor Kitty out. I said: 'If anyone was going to sleep here which heaven forbid, I think I'd better while Tom is as bad as this. Anyway, I shall want lots of things, fresh fruit and stuff to keep the flies out, and you'll have to go and get them.'[3]

If Tom remained where he was, said Dr Mendez, he would be sure to die as the conditions were exceedingly insanitary. So, according to Kitty, on 8 March he was transferred to a private room in the Pasionaria Military Hospital, Valencia. Together, Kitty, the formidable Nurse Darton and Dr Mendez had saved his life.

After a few days Nurse Darton diagnosed that Tom was not only suffering from typhoid but also from a sort of septicaemia: 'so I poked around with a pair of scissors and found he had a lot of pus in his wounds which had been sewn up too tightly. And that was it; he got better very quickly.' Nor was her ingenuity limited to surgery. She and Kitty managed to get medical provisions from a British hospital ship that was in the harbour, though Tom warned them of political trouble if the British Embassy, applying the policy of non-intervention, got to hear about it. This was also the cause of a row between his two nurses. 'You may hear sounds of conflict', Nurse Darton wrote to Elizabeth: 'she's [Kitty] a good little soul but a bit insensitive.' At the height of Tom's illness Kitty wanted him transferred to the hospital ship but Nurse Darton insisted he was too ill to be moved. Later Tom was ashamed of this attempted string-pulling and insisted that Kitty should write to the CPGB emphasising that had he been conscious 'he would have refused to go on the ship, as a long-standing Communist and Captain in the International Brigade. He would be the last person to set such a precedent over his men.'[4]

Meanwhile, the Wintringham family all wrote thank you letters to Kitty:

Dear Kitty (I hope I may call you that)

How perfectly splendid you have been! Is Tom sensible at all, or rambling all the time? If it's possible please give him my love and Oliver's. If he seems inclined to worry about Millie and Lesley assure him they are being looked after. You may know who they are. I shall hope very much to meet you someday before long. Yours, Elizabeth Wintringham.[5]

His youngest sister Margaret, who had joined the Party and was Tom's closest friend within the family, wrote her brother a teasing letter: 'You seem to be having quite a "Farewell to Arms" experience if you get my meaning!' In fact, Ernest Hemingway was one of Tom's visitors; others were Stephen Spender, whose friend T.A.R. Hyndman was a fellow patient and desperate to leave Spain; Professor Haldane; and Viscount Peter Churchill, the treasurer of the Spanish Medical Aid Committee and Winston's cousin.

Harry Pollitt breezed in. 'Such a dear creature,' said Nurse Darton, 'very Harryish to a nice young girl but only in the nicest possible way.' Probably Tom was rather less pleased to see him because he came with a friendly warning to drop Kitty: 'recommending me with enthusiasm and details the charms of "Spanish dames"'. Willie Gallagher's separate visit was uncomfortable, and ominous. Gallagher himself was a man of the utmost rectitude who was married to Jean, 'a local lassie' as he referred to her, all his life. He simply did not understand a Communist who upset the Comintern because of a woman and he told Tom so, despite Tom's state. Tom wrote in 1941: 'The Party Order that I should leave Kitty was delivered to me by a very embarrassed Bill Gallagher while she was nursing me through typhoid before I was strong enough even to stand.'[6] This confirms that Marty had decided to get rid of Kitty back in January. She was unaware of this, but she certainly knew she was regarded as an untrustworthy outsider and that the sooner she joined the Communist Party the better. The PCE washed its hands of her so she wrote to Leslie Reade on 30 March asking him to suggest contacts among his American Communist friends.

In mid-April Nurse Darton told Tom 'very firmly', she said, that he was now better and she would be of more use elsewhere. They had become friends. He was amused by her very British rebuffs of amorous young Spaniards and tactful about her political ignorance. She obviously admired him: 'He was a very sophisticated, high level creature in all directions. Very intelligent, long standing Communist, central committee I should have thought.' Kitty too was keen to be off. She wrote to her mother on 21 April: 'We will go up the coast to some small village and disappear for a month or so while T. recoups and writes a book. I have taught him chess.' And so they left for Calpe on the Costa Blanca for a convalescence that they remembered afterwards as more of a honeymoon:

Our memories of Calpe; the sun and sea, chess and vermouth, afternoons resting, an occasional rough house. The happiness we shared there was more real than I've known since I first got leave during what I still think of as the real war – nineteen years old and nothing to worry about except would I ever grow up![7]

So Tom would write to her later in nostalgic mood. They were there for six weeks. He also wrote Kitty the most romantic of poems, though tinged with sadness:

'Poem in the Summer of 1937'

Morning across the field a girl in a pink dress,
over the sky white clouds shadowed with pink,

dark on my vision, near to me, your black hair;
While the viola and the voice keep
                         their lovely argument.
In my hand the spray of elder golden pale
                             and sweet with summer.

Hay in the meadow cream-folded lies
to darken in the sun, tomorrow and tomorrow,
richening the scent already heavy
in honey loops on the cream taste of summer.
Feasting goes on all day, all night; all senses
banquet in June, and love uninterrupted
and timeless wakes in morning, sleeps at night,
rises and sets in the clear skies of joy.

Not uninterrupted. Love is not
timeless. Love is over
for thousands who went out this summer weather
and found the feast set, and the feast was death.

And these were ours who died.
Dark on my vision your black hair,
So near to me, it shadows all the sun.[8]

When the two lovers returned to Valencia Tom found an intimidating
letter from Charlotte Everett Bowler, who was in Scotland on holiday:

Your description of your idyll with my daughter is just what I supposed.
A lonely man, probably dissatisfied, possibly rather unhappy, a war,
complete detachment from the rest of the world. . . . And then what? It's
all very charming and delightful for you; you gain almost everything. For
my very dear child it's pretty tragic any way you look at it. I resent her
giving her all – her mind, body and spirit – on such insecure grounds.
Naturally I am distressed.[9]

Tom admitted to Kitty he found this a difficult letter to answer, but he did
his best:

I owe my life to your daughter, and a great deal more than just going on living. . . . But there is very little I can say to reassure you because security does not exist. If I could have married Kitty I would have done so: if I can, I will. But better this might be in the future, rather than tie her to a blind or crippled husband.[10]

In one way marriage was easier. In May Elizabeth visited Spain and found Tom with Kitty in Calpe. She realised that this time her marriage was over in all but name. When she returned to England she continued to write, as helpful as ever, and thanked Tom for 'being frank'; but from now on she wrote with a more formal and distant tone. This did not stop Tom from suggesting that when he returned to England they might adopt two Basque children. Facing the consequences of his love life was not one of Tom's strong points.

Tom was probably ignorant of the nasty little civil war within the civil war that erupted in Barcelona on 3 May 1937. For George Orwell, who took part in it, the clash between the Spanish Communist Party and its rivals, the Anarchists and 'Trotskyists' (POUMistas) was a disillusioning experience: 'I realised "a war for democracy" was plain eye-wash; Spain would be ruled by some kind of dictatorship, either communist or fascist, or be broken up.'[11] The historian Hugh Thomas saw it differently. He wrote that the 'May days' in Barcelona, as they were called, marked the real end of the revolution; from then on the Spanish Civil War was still between the Republicans and Nationalists but no longer a revolution of the left. He meant that the heady months of extremism, of belief that every change was possible, were now replaced by a grim reality in which winning the war was all that mattered.

Barcelona had changed over the last year. The revolutionary consensus had evaporated. Now bread queues formed at four in the morning while black-market restaurants and night clubs were open to the rich. In particular, the working-class camaraderie had gone, replaced by suspicion between the Communists on the one side and the Anarchists and POUMistas on the other. The first clashes between the two broke out on 3 May when the Communist police chief arrived at the telephone exchange with three truck loads of armed police and attempted to wrest it from Anarchist control. He was halted by a machine-gun at an upstairs window. Thus began the violence of the 'May days' when warfare broke out between rival revolutionaries who fired at each other from balconies, sand-bagged doorways and armoured cars.

Behind this fratricidal street war was a struggle at national level over the very nature of the revolution. The majority of the Republican Government, supported by the Spanish Communist Party (PCE), wanted centralised control and discipline. In particular they called for the unification of the Communists with the Socialists and the merging of the Anarchist and POUM militias within the Republican People's Army. Further, they demanded that all private supplies of arms should be confiscated and that industry should be nationalised; not collectivised or socialised because Spain was not ready for that, but run by the Government. 'A United Army and a Unified Command. Nothing is more Revolutionary than Winning the War' ran the slogan.

These demands were rejected by the Anarchists and POUMistas. They claimed that the suppression of the revolutionary spirit negated everything they were fighting for. Moreover they were deeply, and reasonably, suspicious of the Government because they knew it was increasingly influenced by Russia. Soviet influence in Republican Spain had spread enormously over the past year through Russian advisers in the Army, International Brigades and Government. They were backed up by the fearsome weapon of the Russian secret police, the Cheka or NKVD. Hundreds had moved in during the previous autumn with orders to purge the country of alleged enemies within. The Russian aim was not only the centralisation of power under Communist control but also the suppression, indeed liquidation, of Trotskyists. This meant getting rid of POUM, for Spain was now coming to be another execution ground in Stalin's reign of terror.

The Old Bolshevik Leon Trotsky, in exile in Mexico, was still dedicated to permanent revolution. He fiercely opposed Stalin's determination to consolidate the revolution in Russia first – 'Socialism in one country' – and considered that Stalin had reneged on his duty to world revolution. Trotsky may have been the conscience of Bolshevism and he may have tried to wreck Stalinism, but the point was that he was now a marginalised figure, doomed to exile. The purge of Trotskyists that swept through the Soviet Union at this time had a lot more to do with Stalin's extraordinary paranoia and the reign of terror it provoked than to the power of Trotsky.

Trotskyism became a term of abuse allied with fascism, and in Spain Communist propaganda peddled the line that POUM was aiding the fascist forces. For instance *Our Fight*, the paper of the British Battalion, ran an article on 16 May that claimed: 'the plans for an insurrection in Barcelona were worked out in Fribourg, Germany, where a meeting between P.O.U.M., the Gestapo and Italian Fascists took place'.[12] There was absolutely no evidence for this incredible assertion but Wintringham believed it too, such was the power of Communist propaganda. He wrote to Kitty in September: 'the best evidence of all comes from the I.L.P-er Stanford [the British Independent Labour Party sent recruits such as Orwell and Stanford to fight with the POUM militias] who says that shipments of supplies have been sent from Barcelona to the Fascists via P.O.U.M. lines'.[13] Wintringham was on surer ground, however, when he wrote that among the Anarchists and POUMistas were 'uncontrollables' who used the ideals of revolution for their own villainous ends: extortion, racketeering and political power. He wrote a short story with that title about a brigand, Pancho Villa, who controlled the village near the hospital at Granien.

Wintringham approved of the suppression of Anarchism and Trotskyism during the May days. In his archive there is a speech translated into English given on 28 May by the Communist Minister of Education, Jesus Hernandez. It is well thumbed because Tom used it in his political classes pronouncing it 'a masterpiece'. Hernandez fully justified the successful Communist action: the killing of 'uncontrollables' however they might be defined (and many POUMistas were found with bullets in their necks, obviously assassinated), the banning of POUM and the end of its militias, the confiscation of arms and the suppression of collectives. As far as the Communists went 'Everything and Everybody had been united for the Winning of the War.' Remarkably, George Orwell said that he saw the Spanish Republican flag flying over Barcelona for the first time, only at the end of the May days.

Centralisation also meant, of course, more power to the Spanish Communist Party and behind that to the Soviet Union. Of this too Tom thoroughly approved. Russia was the one foreign country to help the Republic and the only communist state in the world; living proof that socialism worked. It had to be defended at all costs. He must have been referring to this when he wrote to Kitty on 17 July; as she had just been expelled from Spain his loyalty to the cause is even more remarkable:

My dear, the party, our party, yours and mine, is sometimes hard on individuals. But look at the job of work it does as a whole and there's nothing like it on earth or ever has been. Quae regio in terris nostri non

Happy Days!

1. Tom in Moscow, 1920. *(Wintringham Archive)*

2. Rose Cohen, later murdered by the NKVD, at the Labour Research Department's summer school at Scarborough, 1922. *(Wintringham Archive)*

3. Elizabeth, known within the CPGB as 'Elsie', and Tom Wintringham with Harry Pollitt, Amersham, 1924. *(Wintringham Archive)*

4. 'Muv', Eliza Wintringham (née Workman),
c. 1930, a few years before her death.
(Wintringham Archive)

5. Elizabeth Arkright in 1923, when she was 29.
'I was putting on a face as the sun was in my eyes.'
(Wintringham Archive)

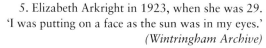

6. Kitty Bowler in 1936, aged 28. 'Schwimp's' press pass. *(Wintringham Archive)*

7. The Communist leadership arrives at Bow Street, 'like a group of commercial travellers up to London for the day'. Tom is hatless in the centre; Harry Pollitt is fourth from left, front row, J.R. Campbell fifth from right and Willie Gallacher extreme right. *(Copyright unknown)*

8. The 'comrades' reception committee waves the red flag outside Bow Street. *(Getty Images)*

9. Food supplies under armed escort are moved up East India Dock Road, London. (*Getty Images*)

10. Retaliation! Strikers attack a volunteer worker at King's Cross, London. (*Getty Images*)

11. A volunteer conductor, down from 'varsity', mans the buses. (*Getty Images*)

12. Tom with 'O.J.', East Sheen, 1934.
(Wintringham Archive)

13. Millie with Lesley, 1932.
(Wintringham Archive)

14. Tom with Ben, 1948. *(Wintringham Archive)*

15. That iconic photograph. The Tom Mann *centuria*. Tom is crouching centre left, with Nat Cohen and Ramona standing together on his right. (*Marx Memorial Library*)

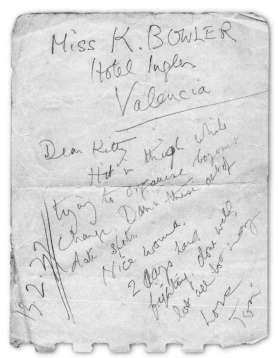

16. The note Tom wrote to Kitty after he had arrived in hospital, evening of the second day. 'Hit in thigh while trying to organise bayonet charge. . . .' It ends illegibly. *(Wintringham Archive)*

17. The Machine-Gun Company captured on the afternoon of the second day. 'Yank' Levy is in front wearing a cap and with his hands behind his back; Harry Fry is fifth from the right in the back row. *(Marx Memorial Library)*

18. Harry Pollitt speaking to the British Battalion on one of his five visits to Spain. (*Marx Memorial Library*)

19. Tom with his new officer's uniform. 'Dearest Muv, here I am all dressed up. I swear the photo has given me a squint I don't possess.' Madrigueras, July 1937. (*Wintringham Archive*)

20. The standard bearer of the British Battalion. (*Marx Memorial Library*)

21. 'As without sound the / Splint bites tighter; there are still / Four hours to dawn: why is it a sin / To moan, to give in? / There is no answer from the bitter pillow.' Tom in hospital at Benicasim after being wounded for the second time, autumn 1937. *(Wintringham Archive)*

22. Recovering with Kitty the next year, London, 1938. *(Wintringham Archive)*

Picture Post, June 29, 1940

THEIR FIRST LESSON IN TAKING COVER

How to use cover, how to load and fire a rifle—these are the basic facts of warfare for a citizen army. Tens of thousands are now learning them. Hundreds of thousands need to learn them.

23. 'Arm the Citizens': the *Picture Post* illustration for Tom's article on 29 June 1940.
(*Getty Images*)

24. Learning to drill, Buckhurst Hill, 1 July 1940. (*Imperial War Museum*)

25. Tom on the platform addresses recruits at the Osterley Park Training School, summer 1940. (*Wintringham Archive*)

26. *Right*: 'The dive bomber is vulnerable – if you know how to tackle it.'
27. *Below*: 'A lesson in dealing with a tank' – in fact an old car towing a trailer.
Both photographs, taken at Osterly Park, illustrated Tom's article in *Picture Post* on 21 September 1940. (*Getty Images*)

28. An enemy agent, disguised as a nanny, holds up a Home Guard . . .

29. . . . and is then ambushed by Dad's Army, 1941.
(*Both photographs from Imperial War Museum*)

30. *Answering You*: a scripted discussion on the BBC's North America Service, London, 1942. Opposite Tom is Tom Harrison, founder of Mass Observation, and next to him is George Strauss MP. (*Getty Images*)

31. 'Win with Wintringham': Tom plans his by-election campaign with Tom Dryberg MP (behind), and Sir Richard Acland MP, President of Common Wealth (front) Edinburgh, 1943. (*Getty Images*)

32. 'I believe in people': the photograph for Tom's election leaflet, 1943. (*Getty Images*)

plena laboris? [Virgil: What region on earth is not full of our labour?] In Spain the 'slogan-shop' has been saying the needed thing, the neat thing, all the time. What we've got to do is prove ourselves on the level with that.[14]

In mid-June Tom was marked fit for light duty by a medical board. He returned to Albacete to prepare lectures on the theory of war as part of a course he was to teach as instructor at the Officers' Training School for English-speaking volunteers. Kitty resumed her journalism and applied to visit Madrid. They planned a gradual return to the war, but suddenly the Comintern police swooped. Alerted to Kitty's existence they arrested her on 2 July and told her that the order expelling her from Spain had been in force since January. She was ordered to leave Spain; presumably behind it lay an implicit threat from Marty that brooked no argument. The details are not known for this was one incident that neither Tom nor Kitty described. They just had time for a final leave taking in Valencia. Afterwards their letters reveal the shock and bitterness that Kitty felt.

To Miss Katherine Bowler c/o American Express, Paris. 6/7/37.
    Dearest Lass,
    The last few hours of my leave in Valencia were better than we could possibly have hoped. You made an effort to make our happiness sing and now you must be tired and empty. . . . Be kind to me by looking after yourself: when you blow up and want to scream let me be there to cool you off: when you are really bitter put our candles on the table. Don't despair of this war! I love you so, my dear; be happy, Tom.

The next day Kitty wrote back:

To T.H. Wintringham, c/o Socorro Rojo, Albacete. 7/7/37. From Hotel Victoria, Valencia.
    Dear Tom,
    I've slept two nights of nervous exhaustion. I have a feeling your people are using me for their own political ends, but if I must be used by someone, I prefer them. Oh, my love, I feel so lonely. People have been sweet but they don't seem to reach more than one layer deep and sometimes I reach out and can't find you.
    Salud y republica. We're Going on! Your Schwimp.[15]

A few days later, still in a state of shock, she met her parents in Paris. By the end of the month she was back in New York.

When Wintringham took over the Officers' Training School at Pozorrubio near Albacete he found that forty out of the fifty young officers under his charge were American. In the summer of 1937 there were so many Americans fighting with the XV Brigade, mostly in the Lincoln Washington Battalion or the Canadian Mack-Paps (after two leaders of the Canadian independence movement, Mackenzie and Papineau), that it was known as the Lincoln Brigade. The Americans were based at Villaneuva de la Jura in a barracks that had inscribed along one of its white walls: 'No Comrade is Worth Living who is Afraid to Die Fighting Fascism'. Next to it was the clenched fist of international solidarity; a red flag flew from the roof.

Tom liked the Americans from the start, pointing out to them that they shared a common name in Lincoln. He told them that like George Washington in their Revolutionary War his job was to turn an intractable militia into a permanent standing army with the necessary order and subordination. Enjoying his forays into American history he tried some controversy. The Republican Army in Spain, he said, could be compared with Grant's Army of the North during the American Civil War. This remark did not go unchallenged. He wrote to Kitty:

> I am liking more and more the Americans, most from Ohio, Detroit and New York. It is very difficult for me to remember they are a different nationality from my own and impossible to forget they are the same as yours. A genius for pure nonsense is almost the only cultural characteristic we have in common along with a respect for cleanliness. The differences between us are pleasant and interesting – like those between men and women – and not the nagging incomprehensiveness that exists sometimes between husbands and wives, or French and Germans![16]

Wintringham wrote in *English Captain* that Americans were ideally suited for the kind of war that the Republican Army had to fight in Spain if it was to contain and then defeat Franco's more professional and better-armed troops. The army needed the paradox of discipline and freedom which, said Wintringham, was part of American life. On the one hand the pace and industrialisation of American life, particularly in the North, brought with it a 'jump-to' obedience and standardisation. On the other hand Americans were conscious of being a free people and with this went argument but also tolerance:

Modern war demands a type of army that feels free; an army in which the corporals, sergeants and lieutenants in particular are men skilled in an art and not drilled robots obeying mechanically the rule book, the blue-print and the boss. . . .

His experiences in Spain convinced Wintringham that free armies could be 'man for man and unit for unit, more efficient in actual battle than the drilled war machines of Fascism'. This belief became fundamental to his views on war and he amplified it later in *How to Reform the Army* (1939) and *Armies of Free Men* (1940). What he observed in Spain was that ordinary men, 'exactly the same sort as you would find in any London bus or tube train', were capable of extraordinary courage and reliance if properly led and motivated.

Tom's belief had a tactical dimension too. In *English Captain* he quoted from Gen Erich Ludendorff's *My War Memories* which showed how he had broken the stalemate of trench warfare in 1918 by drastically reducing the size of the German army's tactical units and allowing them more freedom of movement. The mantra of 'Here I must stand or fall' had been replaced by the right to choose whether and how to retire or counter-attack. The position of the junior officer or NCO thus became more important than that of the senior officer commanding a company. Tom developed this notion:

The Spanish militia had to become an army. That is one side of the paradox. The other side is that this army had to learn how to do its fighting mainly as a mosquito cloud of tiny, almost independent units spontaneously alert to every change in a film of events moving at winged speed. . . . Individual initiative based on understanding and consultation is the central feature of the discipline and tactics that can win modern war. And this sort of initiative can only be produced by a democracy.[17]

It was a belief he reiterated in the Penguin edition of *English Captain* published in 1941: 'the main lesson I learnt in Spain is that modern war calls for all kinds of initiative that arises from democracy'. At Pozorrubio he divided the men he was training into small units of six to eight and required them to take turns in command. Each was expected to learn a specialism which he then taught to the others.

This kind of warfare is close to the guerrilla war with which Wintringham would later be identified. He told Harry Pollitt in 1936 that the way to relieve Madrid was with a 'baby blitz'. What he had in mind was a combination of guerrilla tactics and motorised vehicles which, he said, 'I still hold to be the essence of the highest technique of modern war. The [British] Communists did not understand that in 1936, nor have they to this day', he wrote to his friend Victor Gollancz in 1941. Wintringham was ahead of his time. The experience of most fighting men was still dominated by the First World War twenty years before. Tom was yet to write *New Ways of War* but what he conceived in Spain helped to overturn traditional thinking.

Wintringham preferred the manoeuvrability of light vehicles to tanks which, in 1938, military experts regarded as the most effective weapon on the ground:

> The verdict of Spain is not that the tank is an utter failure but that it has restricted use as a weapon of opportunity. Tanks cannot replace infantry as the basis of an army because they cannot hide, go to ground, become dangerous vermin hard to brush out of the seams of the soil. Tanks are short-sighted, noisy and bad gun platforms; they can be knocked out by handy little weapons.[18]

At Pozorrubio in 1937 Wintringham taught how to knock out tanks, and he taught the basic skills too: formations, fire-control, the handling of weapons and maps. He also taught Spanish commands. All orders had to be given in Spanish because, Tom said, apart from the practical sense of this it required officers to think before they opened their mouths. Above all, he taught the Lincoln Washington Battalion how to stay alive, for very few had experience of combat and many considered that bravery was a compensation for ignorance. There were two orders, said Tom, that he was incapable of teaching: one was the salute and the other was 'Break ranks, lie down' when troops were halted. The first was seen as undemocratic and the second as cowardice.

Although Tom's weight had fallen from 180lb to 130lb, so that he felt 'lazy' much of the time, and in spite of Kitty's absence, he was happy.

He was good at teaching. In the words of Ephraim Lesser who was taught by him before rejoining the British Battalion: 'He was an experienced trainer, comradely, important. He was positive, knew what he was doing and did it well.'[19] Tom wrote to Muv on 31 July:

My general health has improved and I shall be joining the boys in August. But as I'm clearly indestructible you musn't worry. In the autumn we'll clear up this mess [Tom was encouraged by the initial Republican Army advance at Brunete to the south of Madrid] and next spring I'll go to China to settle things there.

It was the Master of Balliol who warned me against being a 'rolling stone': well, I've been stuck in London for years since he said that, and now that I'm unstuck I don't want to resume offices and evening papers and Mr Lyon's nasty restaurants. In a queer way this life suits me.[20]

Kitty, meanwhile, was having a miserable time in New York. Encouraged by Tom she was trying to write about Spain. He even sent her some of his short stories to pass off as her own and give to Leslie Reade for publication; but her muse was missing:

439 East 51st New York. 6 August

My Man,

For the moment I can't seem to write to you the things I want to say. There's something tight and tense deep, deep down. This different world, continent of which you know nothing makes me afraid sometimes it was just a dream and then somehow I know better and that nothing can happen to us after surviving so much. There is so much life in Spain and so much less here. I sit in luxury in a grand cool apartment and think of a funny tiny room with no window that was home. And always, deeper than the tenseness, you, us, exist. Good night, good bye, Your Schwimp.[21]

Tom was soon missing the intensity of the fight too. 'Honey', he wrote to Kitty on 28 July, 'I shall be glad when this is all over! A schoolmaster's life might suit me some day. But not now.' A few days later he told her that he had been encouraged to rejoin the British Battalion by a chance meeting:

An ex-British officer, Cameron, back from the Front called in here a little tight to tell me I must go back to the Battalion 'because the name counts:

even the men who don't remember you know your name and will feel better, the morale will go up!' I wouldn't write it except to you but you know how much I loved the Battalion.[22]

Vidal allowed Tom to leave his training course halfway through and on 18 August he rejoined XV Brigade as a staff officer. Once again he was rushed in – and out – of the front line.

Another Republican Army offensive was under way on the Aragon front with the eventual aim of taking Zaragoza and the immediate aim, for the XV Brigade, of capturing Quinto, a small village on the edge of the lush Ebro valley that now straddles the Zaragoza to Barcelona railway. The attack began on 24 August and the next day the British Battalion, that had been held in reserve, went in to knock down the church and capture the fascists hiding inside. Tom described what happened to his son O.J., aged eight, in a letter he wrote several weeks later:

Our tank straddled a street corner and started firing at the church: whoof BANG clatter, clatter, clatter – the clattering was bits of roof and wall falling down. I walked down the side of the street, scouting. I wanted to find a house we could set on fire so that it would set fire to the church. I was just having a good look round, nipping round corners and doors very quickly so they couldn't shoot me, when WHACK – a bullet hit me on top of the shoulder. It didn't hurt much but my arm went all wibbly-wobbly.[23]

So Tom was wounded a second time on the second day of battle. By the time he left Spain, he would have spent over four months in or around hospital for four days of fighting. This time he felt no elation only deep disappointment and some embarrassment, for he had been teaching his officers how to avoid snipers' bullets. He wrote to Kitty in a shaky hand: 'No luck, my lass. A bullet through the shoulder, cracking a bone or so. Lost a lot of blood. I love you. Being away from you hurts more than silly bullets.' Quinto was soon taken, and the neighbouring town of Belchite too, but then the attack petered out and Zaragoza remained a Nationalist city.

Kitty was going through agonies of her own. Without knowing of Tom's injury she wrote a piteous letter to him on 29 August:

Went to a party last night. It is agony – all they did was talk about drunken exploits, golf and wall paper. That same old life I fled from years ago. . . . My home is with you in Spain; your shoulder, a bit of straw and a tiny tin ash tray. Tell your boys how a mere glance at them – one hour's eager conversation – I'd exchange for all the baths and comforts of this so-called civilisation.[24]

Between 28 and 30 August Tom moved by train, in increasing discomfort, to the base hospital at Benicasim, by the Mediterranean coast north of Valencia. At a low ebb he met a fellow soldier who confirmed his faith in the goodness of the working man. It became a symbolic encounter:

I was nearly all in when there turned up a little brown-eyed Scotsman who had fought in the great War in the 51st Division . . . He let my splint rest on his shoulder, held the nerve-jumpy hand, found me food and wine, protected me in the train.[25]

Despite the Scotsman's humanity, from now on Tom's mood changed. Depression began to set in, weariness and disillusion too, as is clear from his poem 'Hospital in August':

> Only the dust filled wind that drifts and dies
> Gives scent or stir or colour. Lying here
> Cold and stiff shadowed, long and grey and bare,
> Blank walls enclose me. . . .
>
> The long hours lying wounded in the sun –
> The ache and throb and rattle of the train –
> The weariness of waiting and of pain –
> Little are these beside a tortured mind,
> Recalling how to cool streams swift feet run,
> Naked and free and restless in the wind.[26]

One obvious reason for his despondency is that for the next three months Tom was in a lot of pain. He was examined by the British doctor Alex Tudor-Hart, who told him after looking at his X-rays that his shoulder bone had splintered and one particular splinter extended almost down to his elbow; this became infected. Tom underwent at least two operations in Spain and a third in England, between which he was heavily bandaged. He had lost his kit, his passport and his false teeth, and conditions were spartan. He wrote to Kitty:

No kit, no disinfectant, no soap, no comfortable lying down or sitting up. Mosquitoes at night in stifling room. I'm unsociable and spend most of my time waiting for dressing, queuing for the canteen or reading my one book. I try not to sleep in the afternoon, but there's nothing more to do. When do I think of you? All the time![27]

Tom, simply, had had enough of hospitals and there were personal reasons for his misery too. Elizabeth wrote to him that Muv had died on 13 September. 'She was a damned intelligent woman,' wrote Tom to Kitty, 'within the limits of Victorian nonconformist liberalism. Always interested in everything. And a dear.'

Kitty was in a worse mental state than Tom. Apart from her withdrawal symptoms from him she was frightened and hurt to discover that her attempts to join the American Communist Party were being blocked. 'Someone is checking my story in Spain . . . I was informed in so many words that the old man [Pollitt's nickname] was the nigger in the woodpile', she wrote to Tom. The nadir came when her fund-raising event for Republican Spain hosted by rich Uncle Harry was boycotted at the last moment by her Communist contacts. She was being frozen out:

20 September. 349 East 51st. New York
    Oh my darling! I never thought it would be as bad as this. My body and nerves have betrayed me completely. What has really broken my courage is drying up and not being able to do any decent work. Don't deny me the right of one thing – to come to you when you need me – *crashing through everything*. I love you so – no matter what! Schwimp.[28]

Tom was now resolved to return to England at all costs, as he told Elizabeth. 'I have applied for indefinite leave and as I have been in Spain for over a year, may get it.' Kitty was equally determined to join him. There is no more talk in his letters of going off to China to help Mao's revolution, 'swapping paella for chop-suey' as he had jauntily put it to Kitty in the old days. There is no more talk, even, of returning to his former career of working for the Party. In escapist mood he ran through the options to Kitty: 'What to do instead of warring? Live in Shetland with McCartney and write? Become left-wing publisher? Endow London with left-wing holiday camp!? Something peaceful and fruitful!'[29] The Communist Party seemed a long way away. The pain was incessant:

'The Splint'

Hours in the night creep at you like enemy
Patrols, quiet-footed: powers
And pretences that are yourself give way
As without sound the
Splint bites tighter; there are still
Four hours to dawn: why is it a sin
To moan, to give in?
There is no answer from the bitter pillow.

But there's answer, back of your thoughts,
Can keep mind and mouth shut:
Can, if you'll hear it, release you. These men
Count you a man:
In and because of their friendship you can remember
One who's the world's width away: can think
To moan, to give in,
Would waken the curved girl who shares your pillow.

I am tempted to think that something else happened to Tom to disillusion him: a fateful encounter. He wrote to Kitty on 29 September: 'I've had a good talk with Gustav R. who used to be Lukacs' commissar, all about propaganda and heroism and what not.' By then Gustav Regler was an esteemed German writer and revolutionary who had come to Spain after living in Moscow for about a year and been appointed by Marty as Senior Political Commissar to the XII Brigade. Badly wounded, he and Tom found themselves in the same hospital, convalescing in the same group of villas along the sea front, revolutionaries of the same age. What did they talk about, as the wind blew off the sea that autumn, billowing 'the sun-faded window curtains, old and heavy with long watch o'er agonies . . .'?[30] We cannot know for Tom's letters were heavily censored. But Regler had much to tell in whispered conversations that were obviously significant because Tom referred to them more than once. What Regler had seen in Moscow 'revealed to me a world of hypocrisy which left me crippled in spirit', he later wrote. In Spain Regler's experience of Soviet tyranny deepened his disillusion so that he left the Party shortly afterwards. He called his autobiography *The Owl of Minerva* (1959) because, said Hegel, 'it spreads its wings only with the falling of the dusk'; so Regler's account is a requiem for communism.

Did Regler tell Wintringham how, after Jarama, the remnants of the Franco-Belgian Battalion got drunk and how, hearing of this, Marty had ordered Regler to tie the men to trees to sweat it out in the sun and 'shoot a few in the presence of others' if he had any trouble? Did he tell him of the cruelty and cynicism of the NKVD in Spain who tortured Andres Nin so that his face was a shapeless mass of flesh? Did he tell Tom of his experiences in Russia the previous year? How he learned that a decree permitted the police to shoot dead any destitute boys over the age of twelve? How he saw a row of hillocks next to a state farm and was told that it covered a mass grave of peasants who had opposed collectivisation? How he watched the show trials of Gregorii Zinoviev and Leo Kamenev, both of them known to Wintringham personally, who were found guilty and executed, accused of completely fictitious acts of terror against the Soviet Union? How an old, loyal Communist friend whispered to him outside the Kremlin: 'We're beginning to devour ourselves. Everything has the true reek of hell!'?[31]

We will never know. But whereas during their time in Spain Wintringham and many other Communists were loyal to the Comintern, or at least gave it the benefit of their doubt, as a result of Spain and the related purges in Russia they lost their loyalty. It was not that Tom lost his faith in revolutionary socialism or in Marxism but rather in the Comintern's ability to achieve it. In 1941 Tom summed up his year in Spain and expressed the testament that he lived by for the rest of his life:

Spain woke me up. Politically I rediscovered democracy, realising the enormous potentialities in a real alliance of workers and other classes, the power that can come from people working together for things felt and believed, when a popular front is not just a manoeuvre but a reality. I was disgusted by sectarian intrigues and by the hampering suspicions of Marty and co. I got self-confidence from K. and from the fact that some anonymous simple man always bobbed up to see me through tight places. Two bullets and typhoid gave me time to think. I came out of Spain believing, as I still believe, in a more humane humanism, in a more radical democracy, and in a revolution of some sort as necessary to give the ordinary people a chance to beat Fascism. Marxism makes sense to me, but the 'Party Line' doesn't.[32]

This was a testament Wintringham would not have written even in July 1937. Its true significance was that Spain had showed him democracy in action. From now on the democratic centralism of communism was no good; socialism and real democracy had to advance together. The corollary to this, that became increasingly clear to Wintringham, was that the CPGB could no longer remain as it officially called itself 'The British Section of the Third Communist International'. It had to join a genuine popular front free from the cynicism of Russian foreign policy.

There is a coda to Tom's meetings with Regler. In July 1952 the Veterans of the Abraham Lincoln Brigade published a memorial anthology called *The Heart of Spain*. At the last minute, after objections from European Communists who took a Stalinist line, contributions from Gustav Regler, Tom Wintringham, Arthur Koestler and Ernest Hemingway were all taken out. In *For Whom the Bell Tolls* Hemingway calls Marty, by name, 'as crazy as a bed bug; he kills more than the bubonic plague'.

TEN

Expulsion!

Kitty crossed the Atlantic by sea and arrived in London in mid-October 1937 to wait for Tom. She found a flat in York Street, W1 and an unwelcome reception from Margaret, Tom's sister, who had become prominent in the Young Communist League:

> I'm afraid I think it's rather a pity that you have come to London. . . . I have grown to love and admire Elizabeth – I think she is a very good person – and I deprecate the sentimental streak in Tom's nature. I am terriffically [*sic*] proud of the work he is doing and I think this heel of Achilles may interfere with it badly. I know that the Party was pretty annoyed with him some time ago and the Millie–Elizabeth situation has been a source of embarrassment to Harry Pollitt. One or two people back from Spain have spoken of Tom's affairs as a joke, which is intolerable. So you see I must take sides against you.[1]

Tom's application for repatriation was granted – clearly he was no longer fit for 'warring' – and although his departure from Spain was delayed, he eventually travelled overland by train (there is no evidence or reason why, as his family thought, he escaped over the Pyrenees) and was reunited with Kitty on 6 November. Almost immediately he went on to his sister Jim's home at Owmby in north Lincolnshire where his brother John hardly recognised him: 'he looked as if he had been dead and buried for six or seven weeks'.

All Tom seemed good for was sitting in front of the fire, dozing and eating large teas, but he did arrange to be admitted to St Thomas's Hospital in London for a further operation on his shoulder. He also discussed with his brother and sister his intention to divorce Elizabeth and whether or not to tell his ailing father. In the end his father took the news well, though regretfully, for Elizabeth was much liked and respected by the family and in those days divorce carried with it an air of scandal. Tom wrote to Kitty with the news, ending: 'I love you so much my dear. I can see your lovely body re-womanised and alive, your imperious grasping and your kindness of eyes and lips. You are a safety for me and a promise: we'll live fully. Love Tom.'

Tom went up to London at the end of November and found the four women in his life all waiting for him, three calling themselves Mrs Wintringham. This must have confused the nurses. There was Elizabeth, as ever helpful and restrained, with O.J. There was Millie with little Lesley. Then there was Kitty who, although sensitive to Tom, must have exhibited 'imperious grasping' to the others. She was also calling herself Mrs Wintringham. Finally, there was the ever faithful friend Christina Wood (née Roberts) who had exchanged letters with Tom in Spain; indeed, Tom had asked her to tell Kitty in the event of his death. Christina had struck up a pen-friendship with Kitty that was now made real. It was all too much for Tom's sister Margaret:

Dearest Tom,

You simply can't get away with all this irresponsibility. Granted you have to abandon two sets of families, you might at least spare them minor anxieties. You could spare Elizabeth the small humiliation of ringing up the hospital and being asked if she would like to speak to Mrs Wintringham.

You know you have a strong faculty for inspiring affection but I repeat, you can't get away with things like this. When I saw you the other night I went away thinking 'How sweet Tom is!' but after a bit I thought 'But, by God, he's behaving bloodily'.[2]

When Tom came out of hospital in December his shoulder was still not fully mended so he needed another operation the following summer. He had three immediate tasks: to find somewhere to live with Kitty, to write *English Captain* and to work out where he stood with the Party. The first two were accomplished without difficulty for Tom and Kitty moved in to 30 Arundel Square, London N7 and also rented a cottage in Kent. Here the book was written. Tom's first book, *The Coming World War*, had been published by the communist publisher Wishart, but *English Captain* bore the imprint of the progressive but non-sectarian Faber & Faber. Together with Routledge and Kegan Paul and Penguin, publishers with a similar left-wing reputation, they brought out Tom's next nine books over a five-year period. He was a prolific author, much in demand by a general readership and reasonably well paid.

O.J. said that home life in East Sheen was little different after Tom left because his father had spent so much time away or shut in his study. Elizabeth continued her quiet, suburban routine of jam making, gardening and knitting. She made a fuss of breakfast tea, which she always made just so; she drank Indian, Tom had drunk China (out of political sympathy?). O.J. now had a nanny. It was an incredibly bourgeois life for the wife of a revolutionary. The main sign of her intellectual upbringing was her addiction to the tortuously difficult 'Torquemada' crossword puzzle in the *Observer*. 'I was well brought up,' she used to say, 'with a good grounding in the King James Bible – it's marvellous for crosswords!' A sign of her continuing political allegiance were the Geoffrey Trease children's books she bought O.J. They were communist propaganda of breath-taking innocence; *Red Comet*, for instance, was published that year, 1937, at the height of Stalin's reign of terror.

The young adventurers of *Red Comet*, Joy and Peter, are Enid Blyton-type children. They fly off to Leningrad with two workers who have built a small aeroplane to donate to 'the first workers' state in the world':

> The children walked on and leant against the parapet of the long bridge spanning the Neva. Across a great expanse of twinkling blue water dotted now with ice-floes, loomed the grim fortress of Peter and Paul, where political prisoners used to languish for years in the damp unlighted cells.
>
> 'Are there any political prisoners now?' Joy wanted to know.
>
> But the little man (whose name was Ivan Phillipovitch) only laughed and said: 'No, it's a Revolutionary Museum. We use it to remind people what they have escaped from.'
>
> 'It's a lovely city,' Peter murmured to himself. As the youngsters got very hungry Ivan took them into a cafe where they chose from a great tray of the most marvellous cakes they had ever seen. 'I wish Uncle John could see us,' mumbled Joy through a mouthful of chocolate eclair. 'He said that everyone in Russia was starving.' At that Ivan laughed till the tears ran down his cheeks and glistened on his beard.[3]

Elizabeth and O.J. continued to live in East Sheen until the war, when fear of bombing caused Elizabeth to move out of London and send O.J. to boarding school in Derbyshire. During the war she cancelled her Party membership, although in 1941 the CPGB presented her and all other founder members with a drawing of Lenin to celebrate its twenty-first anniversary. Obviously Elizabeth was more a child of her family than she was of the Party, and as the years went by so she reverted to type. She was no match for the passion of Millie nor for the adventurousness of Kitty.

Tom's problems with the Party proved intractable. The Control Commission of the CPGB had to decide what to do with a senior member who intended to marry a 'Trotskyite spy' – so called by no less a figure than the head of the Comintern in Spain, who had the ear of Stalin. It met in March and April 1938 and recommended that Wintringham should be given a choice – either the Party or Kitty. Tom refused to make the choice. According to the Politburo meeting of 18 May: 'He refused to accept discipline in relation to a personal question not considered to be in the interests of the Party.'[4] Comrade Dutt, Tom's long-time mentor and friend, was asked to make a final recommendation. No one who knew Dutt's rigid conformity to the Party line expected that friendship would get in the way of expediency, and it did not. Dutt recommended expulsion unless Tom changed his mind within two weeks. Tom still refused to leave Kitty and still continued to plead his case. The Politburo meeting of 1 June noted his pleas, including his placing on the table of letters of support from Harry Fry and Yank Levy who had been released the previous August from a Nationalist prison. 'I do not know what is your particular job in the Brigade,' wrote Fry, 'but whatever it is I would like to be with you as somehow I work better that way. Salud, Harry.' (Fry's letter was received posthumously because he was killed on 13 October 1937.)[5] The Politburo judged these letters irrelevant. Tom was excluded. The *Daily Worker* of 7 July printed the verdict:

> The Control Commission of the Communist Party has recommended the exclusion of Tom Wintringham for refusal to accept a decision of the Party to break off personal relations with elements considered undesirable by the Party. This exclusion is not a reflection of the services of T.H. Wintringham in Spain, but he has shown himself unable to fulfil the obligations of a Party member.

But Tom still refused to go and the Party, showing that bureaucracy was the reverse side of discipline, allowed him one more committee. This time the Appeals Commission reported to the Central Committee that met on 9 October. Chairman Bob Stewart began the discussion by saying:

I have known no case in my experience of the Party – since 1920 – in which greater pains have been taken by Pollitt and others, but apparently there is an infatuation here or some kind of reasoning that is completely impervious to discipline, to the need of what constitutes marching orders.[6]

The Central Committee upheld unanimously the decision to expel Wintringham. Tom was out.

Why did the CPGB agonise for so long and then take this extreme decision when Kitty was clearly not a Trotskyite spy and Tom was a senior member of the Party who had narrowly escaped death on its behalf in Spain? The answer lies in the reign of terror in Russia. Senior members of the Party were petrified they might lose their jobs or even their lives if they showed the slightest taint of Trotskyism. At the very time that Tom was fighting for his professional life his old friend Rose Cohen was waiting to be shot in Moscow. Her husband, Max Petrovsky, had been arrested the previous year as a wrecker (he had known Trotsky) and all British Communists who knew him had to make statements. Pollitt, who had rallied to Petrovsky's defence, was himself accused by the NKVD of being 'a spy, a secret adviser of British Intelligence Services with a fondness for terrorism'. Unbelievable! This must account for the fawning speech J.R. Campbell made in the Politburo on 5 March 1938, no doubt aware that his Soviet masters would read it and also aware that his stepson Willie Campbell was living in Moscow:

Every weak, corrupt or ambitious enemy of socialism within the Soviet Union has been hired to do dirty, evil work. In the forefront of all the wrecking, sabotage and assassination is Fascist agent Trotsky. But the defences of the Soviet Union are strong. The nest of wreckers and spies has been exposed before the world and brought before the judgement of the Soviet Court. We know that Soviet justice will be fearlessly administered to those who have been guilty of unspeakable crimes against Soviet people. We express full confidence in our Brother Party.

To which Pollitt added: 'Not one of these bastards has ever confessed anything. Not even one!'[7]

After Petrovsky's arrest and before her own, Rose Cohen was ostracised by the very British Communists with whom she had grown up and whom she had entertained in her Moscow home. 'Do please write soon,' she wrote to her sister Nellie on 22 April 1937, 'M is away and I'm feeling very lonely [her husband Max had just been arrested].' Her last letter to her sister was written on 4 July: 'No-one remembered my birthday. . . . I'm sorry this is such a dull letter, but I'm feeling in a dull mood. So I had better stop. Please write oftener.'[8] Soon after this she too was arrested, leaving behind a young son, Alyosha. In March 1938 the British Government tried to intervene on her behalf and when this got out to the press the following month (at exactly the same time that the Control Commission was hearing Tom's case), the *Daily Worker* wrote an indignant editorial telling the Foreign Office to mind its own business; Rose Cohen was no longer a British citizen. So in public at least the Party washed its hands of a loyal member, with whom years ago Pollitt himself had been in love. She was thought to have been shot in the Lubyianka prison as her husband had been before her, though her recently released MI5 file says she perished in the Siberian gulag. Alyosha grew up in grim Soviet orphanages and is alive today.

J.R. Campbell's stepson, Willie, had an extraordinary escape. He had emigrated to Russia in 1932 with his bicycle and ukulele and eventually found a job as a dancing clown with the State Circus. In 1937 his bosses were arrested, as were several of his troupe. They all disappeared or 'went away on a long trip', as the survivors told each other, quaking with fear. Eventually, the dreaded night-time knock on the door by the NKVD came for Willie and his remaining partner, Elena, but luckily they were out of Moscow. The next time the authorities called it was to order them to dance in the Kremlin in front of Stalin; such was the fearful arbitrariness of the terror. 'Although we could not see Stalin we felt his awesome presence. It was an appalling experience,' Willie told me many years later after he and Elena, now his wife, had defected to Britain.[9]

This was a shameful period for the CPGB and no time for a senior comrade to insist on marrying a so-called Trotskyite spy. No one was going to defend Kitty either. She was not a member of the Party nor even British and she was a personal embarrassment to Pollitt. But given Tom's disillusionment with the Party at this time, why did he not simply walk away from it or, at least, accept the initial decision that would have saved everyone's face? There are several answers. In the first place Tom wanted to clear not only Kitty's name but his own, for he was convinced that his conduct was on trial too, particularly his behaviour in Barcelona in 1936: 'There are a long series of accusations that I wasted time and opportunities and did not do my job to the limit of my ability', he wrote to the Politburo.

Obviously this hurt. Tom also believed that 'the decision to exclude [him] from the C.P. had political roots as well as personal; it represented a political decision to treat the Popular Front as a manoeuvre, not as a reality'. He goes on to tell Victor Gollancz (in his letter of 1941) how, as we have seen, he and Pollitt had come increasingly to disagree through the autumn of 1936 over how the Communists should wage the war in Spain. The CPGB had its own reasons for describing Tom's expulsion as personal, but for Tom there were policy issues too.

However, unlike many who left the Party, whose 'God had failed' to use a phrase of the '40s, until his dying day Wintringham remained a Marxist and international socialist; a very English revolutionary who nevertheless believed in the ideals of communism as applied to all humanity. His was a kindred spirit with old-style Communists such as Pollitt and Campbell and this made him loath to leave. No doubt, too, he shared the mind-set of revolutionaries that made it hard for him to leave the sect although he disliked sectarianism. For years the Party had had the real claim on his life. He had accepted its directives, its discipline and its hierarchy. He had seen himself as a professional revolutionary who had made a life-changing decision, a decision that had cost him his freedom and nearly cost him his life. It had determined his friends and his choice of partners; even Kitty had wanted to become a Communist. And now that structure to his life was torn down.

What choice would Tom have made if the Party had fully embraced the Popular Front, had committed itself to the revolution in Spain with ideals rather than expediency, and still asked him to ditch Kitty? Political loyalty or personal love? This little jingle Tom wrote in 1939 may leave a clue:

> I found first love not far from Passchendale
> And true love in the battle of Madrid.
> New war may give power, name and hope yet fail
> To give what the others did.[10]

Frivolous maybe, but it was Tom's favourite poet Virgil who wrote: '*Amor vincit omnia*'.

The years 1938 and 1939 were another low period for Wintringham. He needed to survive as an independent writer but found that the CPGB blocked his ideas. Despite this he felt a residual loyalty. Indeed, he and Kitty still thought of the Party as the only organisation that offered hope for the future. Perhaps what he had in mind was the prescient view, expressed in a letter to Palme Dutt (did he know that Dutt held greater responsibility than anyone else for his expulsion from the Party?), 'that the colonial revolution would become, at some stage further on, as important in world affairs as the spread of fascism'. While rejecting various writing proposals from Tom, Dutt had the generosity to reply that *English Captain* was 'brilliantly written'.[11]

At this time, the end of 1938, the British Battalion returned from Spain. Tom's valediction was true to his romantic, revolutionary view of British history, to the Popular Front image worked up by the Communist Party and to his own persona of English Captain. 'The British battalion now returning from Spain inherits directly from the buff-coated Independents and Levellers who made "liberty and England" words respected in all Europe.'[12]

Elizabeth told Tom that now he was no longer in the Party his life seemed isolated and useless. This seems uncharacteristically hurtful and she took a hard line over the divorce too. In October 1938 she would not proceed towards divorce nor would she allow Tom to see O.J. Tom wrote to her: 'I hate not seeing Oliver, who must necessarily forget me if this goes on.'[13] Kitty was unpopular throughout the family and remained so but no one could have approached the extreme dislike of Salme Dutt, who opined that Tom's big mistake had been to allow Kitty to nurse him through typhoid, even if by doing so she had saved his life!

One of Tom's minor achievements in the autumn of 1938 was the 'Dig or Die' campaign round his house in Arundel Square, north London. In the panic of September, when many people thought that Britain would go to war against Germany over its intended invasion of Czechoslovakia, Mass Observation reported that such was the fear of air raids that a surprising number of Britons even contemplated killing their families if war broke out. A prosaic answer to this anxiety was the air-raid shelter trench. Tom formed a group of ex-service and unemployed men who called themselves the Barnsbury Diggers. Blaming Home Office red tape for procrastination, they went ahead digging trenches in Arundel Square and elsewhere in Islington. According to Tom, the idea of direct action took off and the local Communist branch, which sponsored the initiative, was 'flooded with support' and offers to extend the digging. This seems a bit precipitate, however, for only two days later on 25 September the Air Raid Precaution Service (ARP) was mobilised and all over the country trenches were dug by day and night in the parks of big towns.

The significance lay in the future, for when Britain really did go to war the following year the only important contribution the Communist Party made on the home front was to campaign for air-raid shelters for those living in towns who could not afford them. Professor Haldane chaired an ARP Co-ordinating Committee that advised the Government. During the London Blitz, this initiative developed into a mass movement of direct action when Phil Piratin, a Communist councillor for Stepney, led a storming party of East Enders to occupy the shelter beneath the Savoy Hotel. A month later, in October 1940, the Home Secretary announced that deep stations on the London Underground would be converted into night shelters. It was a significant victory for direct action that could be traced back to the Barnsbury Diggers; but by this time Tom was inspiring a far bigger mass movement, the Home Guard.

Wintringham's dislike of the Party line, of treating the Popular Front as 'a manoeuvre not as a reality', as he put it, turned to disgust in September 1939. On 23 August the Soviet Union, after claiming for a decade that communism and fascism were mortal enemies, signed a non-aggression pact with Nazi Germany. At first British Communists were taken by surprise and Pollitt said 'it left a nasty taste in the mouth'. Then they hailed the pact as a Soviet master-stroke. The Soviet Union, they claimed, had been let down by the Western Powers, Britain and France, because they had appeased Hitler and therefore they could no longer be trusted to oppose fascism; so the Soviet Union needed to keep out of an impending war and strengthen its own defences. The CPGB claimed too, with less conviction, that it did not see the pact as a victory for fascism. On the contrary, Comintern members would still stand up to the fascist dictators. France still had a treaty with the Soviet Union and Britain should continue to work towards one.

So, when Britain and France declared war on Germany on 3 September over its invasion of Poland, the Central Committee of the CPGB put out a *War on Two Fronts* policy statement. It called for a real war against fascism and a political war against the Chamberlain Government. It demanded a new Government of what it termed trusted representatives of the people, the nationalisation of the arms industry, freedom for colonial peoples and greater democracy in the army.[14] As we shall see, this is exactly what Wintringham wanted.

Harry Pollitt went around saying 'Smash the fascist bastards' and dashed off a pamphlet, *How to Win the War*, that sold 50,000 copies:

The Communist Party supports the war, believing it to be a just war. To stand aside from this conflict, to contribute only revolutionary-sounding phrases while the fascist beasts ride roughshod over Europe, would be a betrayal of everything our forebears have fought to achieve in the course of long years of struggle against capitalism.[15]

He might have added that it would be a betrayal of his old comrades in the International Brigades, over five hundred of whom had died fighting fascism. Then, on 14 September, on exactly the same day that this pamphlet was published, Pollitt received a telegram from Moscow. It was deeply shocking. Stalin had decreed that the war changed everything. Before 3 September there had been bourgeois democratic states, with whom Communists could do business, and fascist states, who were the enemy. Now, as in the First World War, they were both imperialist states. The conflict was 'a robber war kindled on all sides by the hands of two imperialist groups of powers' and not an anti-fascist war after all. The working classes should have nothing to do with it. Britain was at war with Nazi Germany and could be conquered; but that was no concern of Communists. Once again Soviet foreign policy made nonsense of the aims of the CPGB.

Over the next three weeks the atmosphere in 16 King Street was thick with anger and insults. Palme Dutt was the first to sniff the air from Moscow and, as ever, he performed an about-turn to march towards it. He proposed a reversal of the Party line that had appeared so correct to comrades, including himself, only a few days before. At the Central Committee Meeting on 2 and 3 October he was opposed by three of the most senior members of the CPGB. Willie Gallagher retorted that Dutt was 'unscrupulous and opportunist'. Pollitt did not mince his words either: 'I was in this movement practically before you were born. If you want to have a political conviction, Dutt, you have to learn how to present a case in a different manner.' He added with emotion: 'I am ashamed that because of what we have heard about the line, we have not been able to treat the Warsaw resistance in the same way that we treated Madrid, Valencia and Barcelona.' J.R. Campbell added a dose of awful reality. By standing aside from the war, he said calmly, they would be unable to defend themselves against a Nazi attack that might well prove a mortal blow.[16]

Their resistance to the new Party line was a bitter failure for they were outvoted by twenty-one votes to three. Probably the newer members of the

Central Committee were more intimidated by the Comintern. Gallagher was persuaded to have his vote changed to an assent because the Party could not afford to lose its one MP. He agreed with 'a real deep-seated disgust'. J.R. Campbell was demoted from editorship of the *Daily Worker* (to be replaced by Rust) and Pollitt, after ten years in charge, was demoted from his post as General Secretary. He was replaced by his former ally but now very personal opponent, Palme Dutt. Pollitt went back to work voluntarily in a Manchester district office, increasingly frustrated and hard-drinking.

However, neither Pollitt nor Campbell resigned from the Party. After years in its service they were imbued with the doctrine of democratic centralism and they were incapable of walking away. Wintringham had had no option. Nevertheless, he saw that the new Party line was 'disastrous, wrong, non-Marxist, contrary to the interests of the working-class and of the revolution',[17] and although he only said this publicly eighteen months later, it seems most likely that he would have resigned in 1939. His disillusionment with sectarianism in Spain, and all his subsequent actions, point to this. In any event, the public disgrace of the CPGB as Britain prepared to withstand a Nazi invasion was Wintringham's opportunity. And he seized it with both hands. For him the war was a continued fight against fascism and the chance for an English kind of revolution.

ELEVEN

The Revolutionary Patriot

In the summer of 1940, after the Low Countries and France had surrendered in the face of the Nazi blitzkrieg and the British Army had been evacuated from Dunkirk, Britons awaited their fate, sure that Hitler would order an invasion across the Channel. Prime Minister Winston Churchill roused the morale of the nation with BBC broadcasts of stirring defiance that were listened to by two out of every three adults. He was followed onto the airwaves by the writer J.B. Priestley, whose homely Yorkshire voice extolling the British way of life was listened to by one in three. Then there was Tom Wintringham with his huge readership of several million from weekly articles in the *Picture Post* and *Daily Mirror*, his BBC talks, his columns in *Tribune* and *New Statesman* and his popular books *New Ways of War* and *Armies of Freemen* that together sold well over a hundred thousand copies in a matter of months. While Churchill's deeply patriotic oratory called to mind an aged Henry V and Priestley was compared to that 'honester and true-hearted man' Falstaff, Wintringham's persona called to mind that of his hero, the Leveller John Lilburne. His slogan in the *Daily Mirror* was: 'An Aroused People, An Angry People, An Armed People', and in *New Ways of War* he pledged an equal sacrifice for a better Britain:

> Knowing that science and the riches of the earth make possible an abundance of material things for all, and trusting our fellows and ourselves to achieve that abundance after we have won, we are willing to throw everything we now possess into the common lot, to win this fight. We will allow no personal considerations of rights, privileges, property, income, family or friendship to stand in our way. Whatever the future may hold we will continue our war for liberty.[1]

Wintringham had found his voice. How was it that this unambitious and mild person became a household name, the inspirer of the Home Guard and, in George Orwell's words, 'a notable voice in stemming the tide of defeatism'?[2] The answer is partly the obvious one that Wintringham's ability to tell people how to defend themselves, how to wage guerrilla war, was heeded by a population expecting a Nazi invasion at any time. But it was more than that. For the first time in his life Wintringham's political convictions answered a public need. Like Orwell, Wintringham believed that war provided the best opportunity for revolution and that a revolution was necessary for fascism to be defeated. What he had learned in Spain was that if people were going to be prepared to die for their country, then it had to be a country worth dying for; and this meant a socialist country. 'We are in a strange period of history, in which a revolutionary has to be a patriot and a patriot has to be a revolutionary', wrote Orwell.[3] Wintringham saw himself as a revolutionary patriot whose time had come. His political beliefs, shorn of their Communist wrappings that had made the package so unacceptable, found a ready audience that summer when the national mood has been described as 'a collective aggression for change'.[4]

This is what made Wintringham a dangerous revolutionary in the eyes of the state. When his knowledge of people's warfare was added to his political agenda it made a suspicious combination, like a home-made grenade in the hands of a civilian. It made the authorities wonder who would be its target. Wintringham's main aim was to fight the Nazis, but could there be another enemy too? Wintringham, again like Orwell, made no secret of his hatred of the British establishment; 'fifth columnists' or 'defeatists' he called them. And there were very many British citizens in the summer of 1940 who not only wanted to fight, and arms to fight with, but shared this hatred.

On 14 May 1940 Anthony Eden, Secretary of State for War, broadcast a call for Local Defence Volunteers – 'now is your opportunity to make assurance [that an invasion would be repelled] doubly sure'. Within twenty-four hours, a quarter of a million men virtually besieged police stations to enrol in what became the Home Guard. This was Wintringham's people's army and from his experience in Spain he knew exactly how it should be trained; not just to patrol, observe and report like a special constabulary armed with shotguns, which appeared to be what the War Office wanted, but as a properly armed irregular army ready to use guerrilla tactics. Wintringham's access to the popular press gave him a powerful platform for his instructional articles on guerrilla warfare; they often mocked military orthodoxy and were always written in a clear and forceful style.

Moreover, very soon he was given the means of practising what he preached. On 10 July *Picture Post* opened a private training school at Osterley Park in London to begin Home Guard training along guerrilla lines; Wintringham was its founder and director. In the first three months he trained five thousand recruits in the rudiments of guerrilla warfare. The Government was in a quandary. Wintringham was a hero of the hour who had inspired a new army in the heart of Britain, but he was not to be trusted. What could be done with him?

It will come as a surprise to many that the summer of Britain's 'finest hour' was, in fact, a summer of seething discontent with the Government. What was the revolutionary temper of the time and how far did Wintringham influence it? In particular what was the real aim of Wintringham's 'quasi-revolutionary' school at Osterley Park, as George Orwell dubbed it? First we need to go back two years and assess two books which Wintringham wrote about warfare. They show his unique combination of modern military thinking and socialist politics that made him so influential during the war.

The British Army that was evacuated from the beaches at Dunkirk in May 1940 had caused anxiety long before. In 1937 Prime Minister Neville Chamberlain had appointed Leslie Hore-Belisha as Minister for War in order to push through army reform and 'stir up the old dry bones [at the War Office] till they fairly rattle'.[5] When Tom returned from Spain he saw this as his opportunity. Determined to bring home to the War Office and a wider public the lessons he had learned in Spain and their implications for the war to come, he wrote a 20,000 word *Fact* pamphlet entitled *How to Reform the Army*. *Fact*, incidentally, was one of many left-wing educational publications of the time. Dubbed a 'monthly monogram for sixpence', it was edited by Raymond Postgate, one of Tom's circle who also edited the socialist weekly *Tribune*. *How to Reform the Army* was a precocious title for a booklet written by a former RFC dispatch rider with only four days' actual battle experience since, but it made an impact. Over ten thousand copies were sold. Tom found himself in the odd position of being consulted by very senior army personnel, although he had been rejected for an army officer commission, whether because of his Communist past or his age and wounds is not clear. In particular he was interviewed at the War Office by Sir Ronald Adam, then Deputy Chief of the Imperial General Staff, Sir John Brown, the Deputy Adjutant-General, and Maj Gen Augustus Thorne who was then Commander of the Brigade of Guards. Tom joked to Kitty that the ruder he was about the British Army – he said he wanted to dynamite the British officer conventions – the more he seemed in demand by its generals.

From the perspective of 1940 the most important chapter in *How to Reform the Army* was 'Security is Possible', Wintringham's argument for creating what became the Home Guard. He wanted twelve divisions, a force of about a hundred thousand volunteers, made up largely of ex- and would-be service men. Tom being Tom, he could not resist prefacing his argument with a Churchillian-style history lesson:

> This army of free men available for service at a few hours notice is part of a tradition of the people of these islands, going back over a thousand years, from the 'fyrd' and 'wapentake' through the 'posse comitatus' and the assizes of arms, to the militia of Queen Elizabeth or the volunteers of the last century.[6]

The purpose of this volunteer force was not only to build trenches and air-raid shelters but to provide a stop-gap fighting militia armed with rifles and machine-guns. Once again, what Wintringham wrote in April 1939 has the ring of prophecy – '100,000 is in fact a far smaller number than the volunteers who would clamour for arms tomorrow if the bombing of our cities began today'[7] – as well as the thud of sound common sense. He sent a more technical paper on this subject, 'Memorandum on Second Line Infantry', to the military expert Basil Liddell Hart, who was unofficially advising Hore-Belisha. Despite his support nothing happened. Once again, as with the International Brigades, Wintringham inspired a movement that overcame official resistance and succeeded.

When *How to Reform the Army* was published what struck home was Wintringham's attack on the 'Colonel Blimps', the army traditionalists who still seemed to believe in the age of cavalry. Invented by David Low in 1934, Colonel Blimp was a cartoon character who figured in the *Evening Standard*. A round, bald figure with a drooping walrus moustache, Blimp became a symbol of military incompetence and political reaction. In 1943 Michael Powell made a film, *The Life and Death of Colonel Blimp*, and, as an extraordinary coincidence, he illustrated Blimp in print by removing Tom's photograph from *Picture Post* and inserting one of the mythical Blimp instead. Tom was amused by this, although for him Blimp represented all that he loathed most about the army: 'spit and polish' meaning mindless drill and 'their's not to reason why' epitomising the even more mindless, robotic obeying of orders. Tom turned to current army pamphlets to pour scorn on the Blimps:

Cavalry Training (Mechanised) Pamphlet No 1 1937: 1. The principles of training in field operations are, in general, applicable to armoured regiments. 2. Mounted Drill (drill in armoured cars) is based on the same principles as that of cavalry. 3. To think quickly and make rapid decisions; with this object officers will be encouraged to hunt and ride across country. . . .

The War office obviously believes [observed Tom] that the Charge of the Light Brigade is still possible. Should armoured cars be given a lump of sugar after a good gallop?[8]

Pamphlet No. 1 1937 was thus a sitting target if a minor one. More significant were the *Field Service Regulations* ordering infantry to close with the enemy, an instruction that called to mind all too vividly for Tom the First World War nightmare scenario of a frontal attack in extended line:

A drawing shows an unfortunate man being poked in the back with a bayonet; he has his mouth wide open and is suffering severely from 'moral effect'. In fact bayonets have not been in use in war except for opening tins, for a long time; they are some of the useless weight that cavalry generals make infantry carry. . . . Here we find, still, the same bluff Colonel Blimp, working up the same scarlet enthusiasm for the classic advice: 'Biff the Bloody Boche in the Belly with a Bayonet'.[9]

Tom was working up to his own advice: only a free army using modern tactics, a New Model Army he called it, could win a war. He had written to Liddell Hart after the publication of *English Captain* describing the book in military terms as 'a frontal attack on many received ideas about war. I hope my ideas will infiltrate as comment, analysis and comparison.'[10] Now in *How to Reform the Army* he expanded on his theme. A democratic army was, in essence, a meritocratic army that practised a voluntary and thinking discipline because it believed in the society for which it was fighting. 'Men who feel free and the equal of their fellows will obey orders because they strengthen their collective actions and achieve their own desires and aims – an army of freemen.'[11] Moreover, only a democratic army was capable of fighting a war with the modern tactics which were based on the initiative and independence of small fighting units. Tom then described again the tactics of infiltration in attack and elasticity in defence that, he first wrote in *English Captain*, were developed by General Ludendorf and broke the trench deadlock in 1918.

Obviously, Wintringham and Liddell Hart were not exactly voices in the wilderness advocating these tactics; modernisers in the army had been employing them in field exercises since the 1920s, but the mind-set of the traditionalists still prevailed. In his next book, *Deadlock War*, published just before Dunkirk, Tom wrote that the very word 'infiltration' had been banned by the French army in 1918 because of its suggestion of cunning, of a treacherous action impossible to avert. Infiltration was not gentlemanly, wrote Tom sarcastically. It reminded him of the snobbery in the British Army at that time when civilian officers were classed as 'temporary gentlemen'. Tom had supporters in high places too. General Wavell, Commander of the British Army in the Middle East, very largely agreed with Wintringham's call, made in *Deadlock War*, for more freedom of initiative and more individual tactics, though he made the strong point that these did not depend on any political system. Tom did not seem aware that the Wehrmacht was a superb fighting army – and the product of a totalitarian society. Indeed, this became clear as soon as the book was published when the reality of the blitzkrieg made nonsense of his central contention that the war would result in a positional stalemate.

In *Deadlock War* Tom expanded on his theme of class. Tom pointed out that Ludendorf himself came not from the traditional Junker class of fighting nobility but from the meritocratic class that 'represented progressive, scientific, modern culture – the culture of the middle and lower middle classes, the skilled and thoughtful workmen'.[12] This class had the right mentality for the new kind of warfare and the new kind of society too. Tom's revolutionary class had expanded from the vanguard of the proletariat to embrace the Popular Front alliance of classes. In 1940 he and George Orwell pinned their hopes on this class to bring about a social revolution. 'They are the great mass of middling people,' wrote Orwell, 'the £6 a week to £2,000 a year class who will defeat Hitler if class privilege is wiped out and socialism brought in.' They would make up the bulk of voters for Tom's new political party, Common Wealth, founded in 1942, and were the bulk of his readers in *Picture Post* and the *Daily Mirror*.

When Britain declared war on Germany in September 1939, Tom and Kitty were living at 41 King Henry's Road, just north of Regents Park in London. Kitty wrote to her mother that neighbours were already leaving or sending away their children, such was the fear of aerial bombardment. This was a rare letter home from Kitty because the Republican Bowlers disapproved of Tom's politics and kept their distance. When Kitty married Tom in 1941 she said with some pride that she had received 'not a cent' from her wealthy parents.

They relied on journalism for their income and Tom's earnings were considerable. He boasted to his children that he received sixpence a word, to which Lesley responded: 'Surely they don't pay you a whole sixpence for EVERY word, even easy words like AND and THE?' In 1939 Kitty wrote on British politics for the left-wing American press such as the *People's Independent* of St Louis County (Michigan) while Tom's paymasters were gratifyingly varied. The War Office paid him for a series of illustrated booklets on *Battle Training* and the Labour newspaper the *Daily Herald* paid him, in effect, to bite the other hand that was feeding him:

If England remains at the mercy of bureaucratic Mr Muddle, a senile Government and a ludicrous censorship we cannot create a military force that will rescue our country. We need to remake and widen democracy, make it a power in men's hearts and minds. There can be no truce with conservatism [26 December 1939].

When Tom landed a job on *Picture Post* in 1939 it was a red letter day. 'Darling Schwimp – Good, big, semi-permanent job on a new periodical. We'll buy a car – we need one!'

O.J. attended Abbotsholme School in Derbyshire, paid for by Elizabeth's parents. When he returned for the holidays Tom took him to the local cinema and bookshops, taking care not to meet Elizabeth on the way. She had petitioned for divorce on 12 February 1940, so in the eyes of the law they must not be seen together as a still-married couple. On one occasion Tom wrote to Elizabeth after an outing with O.J.: 'We walked in the park and the sun came out from behind a cloud. Father and son sneezed in unison.' They both suffered from light-stimulated sneezing which is hereditary in Wintringham males. On another occasion Tom took O.J. to the Unity Theatre in Camden Town just round the corner. This was a left-wing community theatre where the audience were participants and the plays, like *Waiting for Lefty*, were about social action. O.J. sang:

> Sing me a song that has social significance
> There's nothing else that will do!
> It must be packed with social fact
> Or I won't love you!

This song, incidentally, came from the 1937 hit musical *Pins and Needles* and was performed by rank-and-file members of the International Ladies Garment Workers Union.

O.J. recalls that he 'rather enjoyed the experience at boarding school of being the only boy, as far as I know, whose parents had divorced'. He does not remember Elizabeth ever speaking rudely of Tom and it was many years before he realised that divorce was supposed to be an unhappy experience. Elizabeth continued to be good friends with Lesley too. Tom's daughter remained in a children's home until her eleventh birthday in 1942, when she was sent to Hurtwood Boarding School in Surrey, spending the holidays with Millie and her new family. She remembers Tom coming to see her, 'trudging up the long drive with the sun shining off his bald head'.

Tom and Kitty lived on the other side of Regents Park from Fitzrovia, a down-at-heel version of Bloomsbury where writers and artists lived promiscuously, the better to forget the dangers – initially more imagined than real – of a capital at war. Their friends included the socialists Storm Jameson, Naomi Mitchison and Pearl Binder. Then there were renegades from Spain such as Wilfred McCartney and the endearing desperado Yank Levy. They still kept up with some comrades in the Party including Nat and Ramona Cohen and Tom's sister Margaret, now married to fellow communist Edmund Penning-Rowsell; but most of Tom's old Communist friends shunned him.

A frequent visitor to King Henry's Road in the spring of 1940 was Anne Swingler, who came to type out Tom's manuscripts:

Everybody was after Tom because, you see, he had knowledge of street fighting and we all thought that's what we might be doing! He spoke with such authority but he was gentle and charming too. Quite a lady's man! And he thrived on women's company; he was sympathetic and warm. He looked a bit like a professor but he had a military bearing too.

He was an all-rounder. Kitty was different. She certainly didn't like pretty young girls around. She was thin, with wild dark hair and an awkward manner. I thought she was scatty, an endless talker, but bossy too. She was very possessive of Tom. People avoided her. A pity![13]

In particular, Anne Swingler typed out *Armies of Free Men*, a hastily written morale booster by Tom and Anne's husband, Stephen, who was then a WEA lecturer and later a Labour MP. It was a book of unabashed 'Fights for the Flag' stories adapted to the needs of 1940; true tales of battles in which volunteer armies that believed in their cause had defeated conscripted cannon fodder. Washington's victory at Trenton in 1776 and the triumph of the French revolutionary rabble at Hondschoote in 1793 were cases in point. It was obviously a book to match the hour, for in August the BBC commissioned Tom to give a talk on the Home Service with the same title, 'Armies of Free Men'.

The country's finest hour, then, found Tom ready. He was now a popular journalist and broadcaster in the mainstream. A well-known campaigner for army reform, he was consulted, indeed employed, by the War Office. He was one of the very few experts on the kind of fighting that might well be required on the Home Front and he had passionate views, shared by many, on the kind of Britain he wished to fight for. Yet, in April 1940, Tom cannot have foreseen the whirlwind that would engulf him and others that extraordinary summer.

At dawn on 10 May 1940 the German army invaded Belgium and Holland. On 17 June France surrendered. In between, the blitzkrieg smashed everything in its path. It overran the Low Countries. It almost trapped the British Expeditionary Force at Dunkirk. It brushed aside French resistance. It made nonsense of Chamberlain's announcement to Parliament the previous month that 'Hitler has missed the bus', a wrong-headed statement that contributed to his fall from office. On 10 May Churchill became Prime Minister. There then followed a summer and autumn when the tempo of change was so rapid, emotions beneath the surface so overwrought, that Britons thought the unthinkable – surrender? revolution? The world seemed to be coming to an end.

Some had predicted the inevitability of radical change. In November 1939 the Tory MP Robert Boothby wrote: 'Nothing is more certain than this war will mark the transition from monopoly capitalism to socialism. You cannot go through a world convulsion of this magnitude without fundamental changes in the social as well as the economic structure.'[14] The Labour Party thought the same way: 'There can be no going back,' said Herbert Morrison, the Labour MP who would become Home Secretary later in the war. The mood of instability turned to collective aggression when the British Army was fighting its retreat to Dunkirk. The Director of Military Information was outspoken with British journalists at Lille: 'British history has provided many examples of the British Army being asked to operate under appalling handicaps by the politicians but it has never found itself in a graver position than that in which the Government of the last 20 years has placed it.'[15] He repeated this on the BBC during the evacuation (26 May–4 June), after which he was warned off the air. It was not the Blimps who were responsible, then, so much as *The Guilty Men* who made the policy.

This was the title of a book written in four days after the retreat from Dunkirk. The authors were three journalists who gave themselves the pseudonym of 'Cato'. One was Michael Foot, later Leader of the Labour Party, who remembered that it sold like a pornographic classic because after it was banned from bookshops it was sold under the counter and by news vendors on street corners. Some two hundred thousand copies were snapped up. The guilty men, headed by Chamberlain, were the politicians who had first appeased Hitler and then during the phoney war just ended failed to put the British economy on a war footing and fight the war with any determination. *The Guilty Men* savagely, unfairly, listed their errors in turn and in retrospect this was not difficult to do. In fact Chamberlain had thought Hitler was bluffing. He believed that Hitler did not intend to invade Britain or wage a total war, and therefore that there was still the chance of a negotiated peace. His attitude to Hitler was interpreted by Wintringham and the Communists as worse than appeasement – it was pro-fascist. To them Chamberlain, Lord Halifax and others who were still in power after Dunkirk (Chamberlain as Leader of the Conservatives and Halifax as Foreign Secretary) were fifth columnists, traitors.

The voices for transforming British society were several and varied. The call for socialism, if necessary through direct action, came from J.B. Priestley, who broadcast the BBC *Postscripts* throughout that summer. On 21 July he suggested that property was an old-fashioned idea that should be replaced by community. 'We may need houses for billeting. There are hundreds of working men who need ground for allotments. Therefore, I say, that house and garden [lying empty because its owner had fled] ought to be used whether the owner likes it or not.'

The harsh words of revolution came from the typewriter of George Orwell. When Priestley spoke of militant citizens Orwell spoke of revolutionary patriots. In an outburst typical of this distraught period he wrote in his diary on 20 June: 'If we can hold out for a few more months, in a year's time we'll see red militias billeted in the Ritz.'[16] Orwell joined the Home Guard and saw it, as in Spain, as a people's militia. In another emotional outburst he wrote in the *Evening Standard*: 'THAT RIFLE HANGING ON THE WALL OF THE WORKING CLASS FLAT OR LABOURER'S COTTAGE IS THE SYMBOL OF DEMOCRACY. IT IS OUR JOB TO SEE THAT IT STAYS THERE.' In *Tribune* he mocked the Communists as the revolutionary party that was staying out of the war although a revolution was in the offing: 'The Communists and all their kind can parrot "Arm the Workers", but they cannot put a rifle into the workers' hands; the Home Guard can and does.'

A year later he took a more considered view of 'The English Revolution':

What are the politics of *Picture Post*? Of Priestley's broadcasts, of the *Evening Standard*? They merely point to the existence of multitudes of unlabelled people who have grasped within the last year or two that something is wrong. But since a classless, ownerless society is generally spoken of as socialism we can give that name to the society towards which we are now moving. The war and revolution are inseparable. We cannot establish socialism without defeating Hitler; on the other hand we cannot defeat Hitler while we remain economically and politically in the nineteenth century.

There was nothing woolly or liberal in Orwell's approach:

There will be a bitter political struggle. It may be necessary to use violence. But just because the British sense of national unity has never disintegrated, because patriotism is stronger than class hatred, the chances are the will of the majority will prevail.[17]

What of Wintringham? He shared Orwell's political views and added his own, but his priority was different. As soon as Local Defence Volunteers began to queue up at police stations on the evening of 14 May 1940 he saw that his main role was to make sure they became a properly armed, irregular fighting force. He began his own lightning offensive. On 17 May he wrote in *Tribune* 'Now Arm the People'. Three days later he was signed up with exclusive rights by the *Daily Mirror* as Military Correspondent and soon afterwards he met with a group of cross-party, radical thinking MPs including Harold Macmillan, Robert Boothby, Tony Horabin and Leslie Hore-Belisha. They drew up a memorandum for a *levée en masse*, or mass rising to resist invasion, and this filtered through (Tom's words) to *The Times*. On 28 May it carried a first leader that expressed Wintringham's own views of the LDV's role – prepare for home defence and be answerable not to the War Office but directly to Churchill.

The same day Wintringham wrote his famous article in the *Daily Mirror*. It began 'My Proposals for Him [here an arrow pointed to a picture of General Sir Edmund Ironside, Commander-in-Chief of Home Forces] and You' and ended with the slogan:

AN AROUSED PEOPLE
AN ANGRY PEOPLE
AN ARMED PEOPLE

This stirring alliteration caught on. A few days later Wintringham wrote a 'Plan of Action' for the Government. He discussed it with the Ministry of Supply and sent it to Tony Horabin MP on 16 June. His plan called for Churchill to broadcast an appeal for a citizens' army, and to promise 100 million hand-grenades within a fortnight, 2 million rifles as soon as possible and 50,000 Tommy guns from America. 'All weapons issued must be carried at all times', Tom wrote excitedly.[18] He then proceeded to outline a command structure and what to do if invasion took place.

The day before, 15 June, Wintringham wrote the first of two major articles for the *Picture Post*: 'AGAINST INVASION' and, on 29 June, 'ARM THE CITIZENS'. These gave practical instructions for a people's war to resist invasion based on his experience in Spain: how to destroy tanks and bridges, capture or kill German parachutists, fortify a village, make and throw hand grenades, engage in street fighting. The second of these graphically illustrated articles was bought by the War Office which printed off 100,000 copies and distributed them to LDV units.

On 20 June 1940, only two weeks after the last British and French troops had been evacuated from Dunkirk, Wintringham called for a raid on the Belgian coast, thus putting into practice his principle that an elastic defence should include a lightning attack. Finally, on 10 July,

Wintringham became Director of the Guerrilla Warfare Training School in Osterley Park.

The story of Osterley Park and of Wintringham's attempts to turn the Home Guard into an irregular army is told in the next chapter. Here I have sketched his role in the first two traumatic months. This was a time when those in authority were as much engulfed by the whirlwind as anybody. Where home defence was concerned the War Office disagreed about what to do or, indeed, whether anything should be done. It was another case of the modernisers versus the Blimps. In Wintringham's archive there is a document marked 'Secret', written in 1942 and recalling the summer of 1940. It was written by Brig W. Carden Roe who, on the morning after Eden's historic appeal for volunteers, was summoned to a meeting at the War Office:

Sir Frederick Bovenschen said the whole thing was most irregular and a thoroughly slap-dash scheme. Was it realised that it had taken many years of planning and an Act of Parliament to form the Territorial Army? In addition to the financial side that required Treasury sanction, there was also the legal status of the L.D.Vs which would have to be carefully explored. Why all this precipitancy? I lost my temper and said: 'In order to try and avoid losing the war.'[19]

The Blimps continued to stall and dither but, as we shall see, Wintringham's powerful voice calling for an irregular army – the Home Guard – carried the day. Not that his was a lone voice in the wilderness, by any means; as with the formation of the International Brigades, public opinion was wholeheartedly on his side. In fact, the Home Guard came into existence because of pressure from the bottom up, not from the top down. And Wintringham became a hero of the hour. The editor of *Tribune*, Raymond Postgate, wrote effusively on 9 August:

Readers should know Tom Wintringham's work: if they do not, they have missed the foremost military expert in the world. I wonder if that phrase isn't a little gross? Never mind, let it stand. It is because he is the only *socialist* who has paid attention to the theory and practice of war. He is not a pundit: he does not work through the usual channels. His education of his fellow citizens has been carried out strictly democratically and by writings addressed to the public. Major-Generals have had to go out and buy *Picture Post*. Although the political deductions Tom has drawn made scarlet majors turn purple, the technical truth and importance of what he said is so great they had to read on, and in the end their blood pressure went down.

In fact, Tom's political deductions were few. His press articles were meant to inspire and inform rather than criticise or proselytise. But he most certainly did have a political agenda. In *New Ways of War* published in July, a hastily written book largely pulled together from his *Picture Post* articles, he included a Four Point statement of political aims, of which the third asserted: 'Those who are unable to use the forces of the people (red-tape civil servants, the Petain sort of generals) must be removed [Marshal Pétain was the collaborationist ruler of Vichy France]. Mr Chamberlain and those who helped to build up the strength of Fascism must go from the Government.'[20] The other points in Wintringham's statement were more positive – and Marxist. They were, in fact, very similar to the CPGB's aims of 1939 and in some respects they looked back to the Communist policy during the General Strike fourteen years before. Wintringham called for the nationalisation of industry with factory committees on which workers would sit; for the confiscation of private land; and for the setting up of Councils of Action to assume control in each locality of the citizens' army.

Wintringham criticised the Communist Party for telling its members not to fight. Palme Dutt's line was that Hitler had no intention of ordering an invasion and Churchill was scaring the public as a ploy to divert attention from his government's domestic problems. This preposterous idea caused the Party to be more isolated than at any other time in its existence. A year later in a letter to the *New Statesman* Tom summed up his political approach in 1940 with a Leninist slogan and he took a side-swipe at his former comrades:

'Turn the imperialist war into a civil war.' The only form of civil war that a Marxist could aim at in 1940 was anti-fascist war. This meant fighting the friends of fascism here and also those reactionaries who cannot win this war. We must fight against these reactionaries not as war-makers 'spreading the war' but as half hearts who are losing it.

What would have happened if the CPGB had campaigned for these aims in 1940? Orwell for one thought that revolution was waiting to happen.

He wrote in *Partisan Review* on 3 January 1941: 'last summer a revolutionary situation existed in England, though there was no-one to take advantage of it.'

One of Wintringham's proposals was international; it was first outlined in the plan he sent to Horabin on 16 June. Tom wrote that the war should be a fight for freedom everywhere including in the British Empire and, to this end, the King should renounce his title of Emperor. Until the colonies decided by plebiscite what their future should be the King should call himself Head of the British Commonwealth. India should be set free immediately. This seems an obvious suggestion now considering that the colonies were fighting for British freedom, but then it was probably the most controversial of Wintringham's proposals. He wrote to Horabin: 'I suggest that if you are showing this to other people, the above may be deleted as premature.'

Histories of the Home Guard have said there is no evidence that Wintringham taught his political agenda at Osterley. This is not strictly true. Among his private papers on Osterley are notes for a 'Lecture on Popular Theories of War: War as necessary act to liberation (Danton, Lenin, International Brigade); War is politics (the agitators, the delegates, political commissars); Popular Tactics in past history etc.'[21] Wintringham thought that war and politics went together. In *How to Reform the Army* he used the 'agitators' in Cromwell's New Model Army and the political commissars in the Soviet army as precedents for a Corps of Adjutants whose job would be to explain and remind the troops why they were fighting. At Osterley several of the staff were former members of the International Brigades who empathised strongly with the revolutionary values of the Republicans. Orwell said of them: 'Their teaching was purely military, but with its insistence on guerrilla methods it had revolutionary implications which were perfectly well grasped by many of the men who listened to it.'[22]

What did the Government think of Wintringham, whose nickname in the press was the 'red revolutionary'? To the War Office Wintringham was a former Communist who had been expelled for personal reasons and as long as he did not speak out against the Party he remained a Communist in all but name. On 6 July the War Office sent round to LDV Company Commanders a secret memorandum forbidding them to enrol Fascists or Communists. Moreover, the memorandum stated, 'whenever it comes to the knowledge of a L.D.V. Co. Commander that in spite of registration with the police, a Fascist or a Communist has been inadvertently enrolled in his company and consequently discharged, the C.O. should confidentially inform the police of the names and addresses of such men.'[23] In 1940 Wintringham was not enrolled formally into the Home Guard and perhaps this was the reason. He feared he might be rejected. The War Office view in general was perfectly understandable for Communists had signed up to a non-aggression pact with Hitler and therefore should not be fighting against Nazism. For this reason few Communists wanted to enrol anyway. The *Daily Worker* sneered: 'It is pitiable to find a man of Wintringham's record engaged in deceitful propaganda.'

On 10 July 1940 the Security Executive of MI5 suggested to the Home Office that a defence regulation could be drafted making it an offence to 'subvert duly constituted authority'. This catch-all phrase may well have included Wintringham's Four Points in *New Ways of War* published the same month. It was, however, rejected in eloquent terms by Sir Alexander Maxwell of the Home Office:

Our tradition is that while orders must be obeyed, every civilian is at liberty to show, if he can, that such orders are silly and mischievous and the duly constituted authorities fools or rogues. Contempt is not subversive; it is only subversive if it incites to break the law or change the Government by unconstitutional means. This doctrine gives, of course, dangerous liberty to persons who desire revolution, but the readiness to take this risk is the cardinal distinction between democracy and totalitarianism.[24]

This was a brave decision considering the instability of the State, and MI5 continued to take a hard line against Communists. For example, it recommended to the Home Office that the CPGB Central Committee minutes of October 1939 (quoted in the previous chapter) should be published as proof that the Party was subject to foreign control and dedicated to the defeat of Britain. In February 1941 it succeeded in getting the *Daily Worker* banned for seeking to destroy the authority of Government. It claimed that if one hundred leading Communists were imprisoned the Party would be hamstrung, but that was another recommendation that the Government rejected.

The officially approved *Home Guard of Britain*, written in 1943, gives the Government's view of Wintringham: 'Unfortunately, some of Osterley's sponsors, notably Tom Wintringham, seemed inclined to make a political issue of their admirable exercise, and the War Office could scarcely be expected to approve of it in its entirety.'[25] Behind this emollient Civil Service-speak was the determination to dismiss Wintringham and close Osterley down (see Chapter 12). With this in mind the Government commissioned MI5 to investigate Osterley and report on its personnel; a file that is still unobtainable. In November Sir Edward Grigg, who had been asked by the Government to make recommendations on the future of the Home Guard, advised:

> About the desire in some quarters to characterise the Home Guard as a 'people's army' different from the Army as a whole and not coming under the War Office: No, the Army is 'the nation at arms' and should be led by officers holding the King's commission. The creation of private armies or of paramilitary armed formations has often proved fatal to the stability of the state and the liberty of citizens.[26]

Wintringham's maverick summer was over; the red revolutionary was muzzled. The all-important question remains. Was Osterley really a quasi-revolutionary base that could have threatened the stability of the State? Of course, if the German army had invaded and Britain had surrendered, then guerrilla war could well have been waged against whatever occupying Government was in power. There was another possibility, too. Throughout that summer there took place a flurry of peace feelers, culminating in Hitler's offer of a compromise truce with Britain made in a speech to the Reichstag on 19 July. The British left deeply mistrusted the appeasers and not without reason, for during Dunkirk Lord Halifax, the Foreign Secretary, had wanted to open negotiations with Germany. Its main bogey, however, was the former Prime Minister and still charismatic David Lloyd George. He had said, notoriously, that Hitler was the greatest living German and that any peace offer from him must be taken seriously. In fact Churchill had already offered Lloyd George a place in his War Cabinet in case, as he put it, 'he became a focus for regathering discontents'. This suspicion that the British establishment could succumb to Hitler or make a deal with him is clear from Orwell's diary for 1940:

> 27 June: How can these people [the Government] possibly rouse the
> nation against fascism when they themselves are subjectively

pro-Fascist? The British aristocracy is utterly corrupt and lacking in the most ordinary patriotism.

3 July: Everywhere a feeling of something near despair among thinking people because of the continuance of dead minds and pro-Fascists in positions of command.

25 July: There are rumours that Lloyd George is the potential Petain of England. It is easy to imagine him playing this part . . . but less easy to see him collaborating with the Tory clique who would in fact be in favour of such a course.

Wintringham, who saw a lot of George Orwell that summer, thought that an armed Home Guard might be needed to deter those in and out of Government who wanted a deal with fascism. His fellow instructor at Osterley and former comrade in Spain, Hugh Slater, wrote:

From a military point of view the Home Guard, combined with the regular forces, makes a military occupation by German Fascists fantastically improbable. Politically, a fully developed Home Guard provides an absolute guarantee against both the crude fascism of Mosley and the more insidious Fifth Column activities of any would-be British Petains.[27]

The Osterley irregulars at war with their own Government? It may sound unlikely, but that summer very little was unlikely. In fact, this possibility was confirmed sixty-four years later by the veteran *New Statesman* journalist and academic Norman MacKenzie. In June 1940 he was a member of the Independent Labour Party and among the second batch of LDVs to enrol at Osterley:

If the Government had made peace that summer we would have rebelled; abortive, no doubt, but we would have tried. We saw ourselves as the heirs of Spain. We wanted a socialist Government and we were going to fight fascism at home, if needs be, as well as the Nazis.

This promise, or threat, was confirmed by the veteran politician Michael Foot, who was to meet Wintringham the next year. The Left, he said again, saw the war as a continuation of fighting fascism in Spain and any British politician who suggested yielding an inch 'would have been torn limb from limb'. After his crash course in guerrilla warfare MacKenzie joined the real, secret, guerrilla army known blandly as the Auxiliary Units (see Chapter 12). His task was to prepare to take a band of men underground, literally, to resist a German army advancing through Sussex, where he still lives. 'It was the most wonderful summer of my life,' he recalled with excitement.

In 1941, Kitty Wintringham wrote about the events of the previous year: 'Remember, we expected a sell-out or successful invasion any moment. There was just a chance of social upheaval at that point too.'[28] Might the Wintringhams have used Osterley Park as a recruiting ground to fight for the kind of socialism George Orwell described? I think the idea that they might have turned against Churchill's Government for this purpose just when it was struggling for national survival against the Nazis is very far-fetched. As Tom may well have said, recalling the Communist slogan in Spain, 'Everything and Everybody for the Winning of the War'. He wrote that he saw the political value of the Home Guard as that of 'a democratic force capable of aiding the social revolution if fascism is to be defeated'. I take this to mean that he hoped his own political agenda as outlined in *New Ways of War* would be accepted, argued for and insisted on by his 'army of free men', as he sometimes referred to the Home Guard – but not fought for in a way that would threaten the stability of the State.

Calling for the Home Guard to resist a Pétainist, collaborationist Government was one thing; but to force a socialist revolution was quite another, even though Wintringham had believed a decade before that war was the mother of revolution. Yet he suspected that the Government did not believe him. He wrote in May 1941 that the War Office's decision not to enlarge the Home Guard beyond 1½ million and to keep so many Blimps in positions of command was because of its percieved 'social danger'.

If this perception did exist in the minds of the War Office then it was misplaced. By May 1941, despite what Wintringham believed, the public mood had changed. Churchill had gradually shifted the ground from under the feet of the social revolutionaries with his 'New Deal at Dunkirk'. In the very week that France surrendered and the British Army realised that it was virtually incapable of resisting an invasion, the Director General of the Ministry of Information asked: 'Should an all-party Government make some promise as to social reforms after the war?' And Clement Attlee, Leader of the Labour Party and now Lord Privy Seal in a coalition Government, replied: 'We must put forward a positive and revolutionary aim admitting that the old order has collapsed and asking people to fight for the new order.'[29] No doubt this was a shrewd political move to assuage the national mood, but in the circumstances it was also a noble aspiration. Shortly afterwards a War Aims Committee was set up that called, prophetically, for the kind of peaceful revolution that Attlee's Labour Government implemented after the war via the Beveridge Report: social services available to all, a national health service and equality of opportunity in education.

More immediately, in fact the very week of Dunkirk, a 100 per cent tax was imposed on war profits thereby scotching one of the most obvious discontents during the previous world war. In June and then July, Attlee's Food Committee promised, first, subsidised milk to mothers of young children and, second, free school meals. The principle was that as everybody might suffer in the war so the Government should cater for everyone's welfare. The Ministry of Labour became a powerhouse for change under its mighty boss, the former General Secretary of the TGWU (the dockers' union) Ernie Bevin. An enemy of the CPGB since the General Strike, he was nonetheless a tough socialist. As early as 22 May he pushed through the Emergency Powers Act that allowed the Government to confiscate private property and conscript labour. Throughout the war wages rose while salaries and income from property fell; unemployment virtually disappeared. A more equal and communal society was evolving, based on J.B. Priestley's slogan 'We're all in this together'. The changes did not satisfy Wintringham and Orwell, nor Priestley for that matter, but they were enough for the majority of Britons. On 1 June 1940, the *New Statesman* declared: 'the democratic revolution has begun'. This was not obvious at the time. Indeed, very little was clear in that summer of uncertainty, but two years later Mass Observation estimated that there was a definite swing to the left in British politics; two out of five voters had changed their views since the beginning of the war. It was, indeed, a democratic revolution and not a social upheaval with its overtones of violence. As we shall see, it was one to which Wintringham responded.

TWELVE

The People's Army

The photograph shows a bald middle-aged man in a worn suit standing on a platform, hands in pockets, addressing a motley crowd of about a hundred men. They are in a park. It could be Speakers' Corner in Hyde Park were it not for the clothing, for some of the crowd are wearing Scout uniforms, some irregular battle dress and a few are in civvies. A group of Regular Army officers stands at one side. The speaker is Tom Wintringham and he might well be asking: 'What is the Home Guard for? Should we be a body of sentries and observers or should we have a more active function – should we be an armed irregular army?' The audience appears raptly attentive. One of the onlookers recalled later:

> There was an atmosphere of suppressed excitement. Tom spoke quietly but firmly and decisively. His rather anxious face peering through spectacles was misleading, as was the amateurish set up. The course was very businesslike and realistic. Tom had about him the qualities of leadership; he knew what he was talking about and he was extremely able at communicating it. His forcefulness suited his passionate military interest so well.[1]

This is a snapshot from the notorious Osterley Park Training School. Tom, the red revolutionary, is running a guerrilla training course, aided by desperadoes from Spain like knife expert Yank Levy and Philipe, a Basque miner who specialises in gunpowder. Inspired by the militias that held Madrid in 1936 they are training a citizens' army to resist German invasion. 'It is a pioneering place which I hope will be developed all over the country,' wrote a participant at the time, 'for all those who are determined that never will this soil be yielded up without the bitterest struggle.'[2]

The Osterley Park Training School was conceived one evening in late June 1940 when Tom and Kitty were dining with Tom Hopkinson, editor of *Picture Post*, and its young, energetic owner Sir Edward Hulton. Tom was venting his frustration at the lack of training provided for the Local Defence Volunteers. All they did, he said, was practise forming fours and their only equipment was a canvas armband with the letters LDV; all they wanted to do was to learn how to fight. According to Hopkinson:

The question came up, why don't we ourselves provide the training? Between dinner and midnight everything was organised. Hulton's friend, the Earl of Jersey, owned Osterley Park, a mansion with lavish grounds just West of London. Hulton phoned him and he came round at once. Yes, of course we could have his ground for a training course provided we did not blow the house up. 'Could we dig weapon pits? Loose off mines? Throw hand grenades? Set fire to old lorries?' Wintringham asked. 'Of course, anything you think useful', Jersey told him.[3]

The next day Tom left for a War Office lecture tour and it was Kitty who chose the instructors. They were a colourful bunch who must have posed quite a challenge for MI5's vetting procedures later that summer. Apart from the International Brigades members headed by Hugh Slater, once the Head of Operations XV Brigade and an expert in the tactics of modern warfare, Kitty signed up the Surrealist painter Roland Penrose to teach camouflage; the Boy Scouts' chief instructor in field-craft Stanley White; and the former Labour MP Wilfred Vernon who was a 'mixer of Molotov Cocktails, inventor of new bombs and rather mad', as Slater's wife Janelia recollected. The school was heavily promoted in *Picture Post* as a place for learning 'ungentlemanly warfare'; hand-to-hand combat, ambushing of tanks, hit-and-run raids and much else of a guerrilla nature. It opened on 10 July, a private but prestigious guerrilla warfare training school paid for by the Earl of Jersey and *Picture Post*. Kitty was indispensable, according to Hopkinson, acting as everything from secretary to manager.

It was while on this lecture tour that Tom learned that his father had died. The funeral of John Fildes Wintringham was a big Grimsby occasion, as befitted the town's most prominent solicitor. Tom wrote to Kitty fretfully, anxious to get back to London but aware that he needed to represent the family at the sort of formal and religious occasion he so disliked. He does not mention his father in the same personal terms as he had his mother when he had written to Kitty about her death three years before.

Tom had outlined his views on the expected German invasion and the emergency measures to be taken before it occurred in a letter to his brother, written as early as 19 May, just five days after the call for Local Defence Volunteers and a week before Dunkirk. He held to these views for a year because in May 1941, when German airborne troops conquered Crete and their way to the Suez Canal seemed wide open, Tom and others again considered that an invasion of Britain might follow. In their minds the threat was only lifted the following month because of Operation Barbarossa, the Nazi invasion of the Soviet Union. Having observed the blitzkrieg and bearing in mind Ludendorf's tactics in 1918, Tom was convinced that the German invasion of Britain would be a lightning attack in depth that would combine heavy bombing of major cities with the landing of troops by plane or parachute hundreds of miles behind the main coastal offensive. This could take place anywhere along the south and east coasts, which were only four hours by fast vessels from Nazi-occupied northern Europe. To add to this tripartite attack was the danger, in Tom's mind, of sabotage by fifth columnists, which shows once again just how suspicious he was of Mosley's Fascists and the establishment appeasers.

Britain's response, in Tom's view, had to be defence in depth. This could only be achieved by widespread mobilisation and the arming of a citizens' army to support what was left of the Regular Army and Territorials. The role of the citizens' army should be to guard strategic points such as bridges and petrol supplies, a task for which it was ideally suited; recruits knew their locality and could carry on working in essential industries until required. But the LDVs were needed for a more active role too. Working with regular troops they should form mobile striking units 'to hit at any foothold gained by landings from the air'.[4] For these reasons the LDVs should carry rifles at all times and be trained in demolition work with gunpowder. Last-ditch forms of fighting might be needed: street fighting, the hit-and-run tactics of a guerrilla army, even jamming pieces of tram rail into tank tracks or blankets soaked in petrol.

At first, until the end of June 1940, the War Office was reluctant to give the LDV a combat role in the event of invasion. It was much clearer what its role should be before the invasion – to observe, patrol and report to the police or military any suspicious behaviour, rather like a special constabulary. Gen Pereira, the seventy-year-old commander of the London area, said that one function was simply to patrol the streets in units of fifty to reassure the population. For these duties arms were not needed. 'These foolish plans', as Tom described them, were brushed aside after Gen Edmund Ironside became Commander-in-Chief of Home Forces during the

Dunkirk evacuation and made a belligerent speech to senior LDV officers. Referring to German parachutists, he urged his audience to 'shoot them, shoot them, shoot them without reference to taking any kind of care of their future'.[5] This encouraged the LDVs to think they were part of the action! Towards the end of June the Under Secretary of State for War, Sir Edward Grigg, made an important broadcast telling them that they were armed forces of the Crown and therefore their most important right and duty was to bear arms and defend their country, even if their arms were only twelve-bore shotguns. At the same time Churchill insisted that the LDV, disparagingly called the 'Look, Duck and Vanish Army', should be renamed the Home Guard as this gave a more accurate description of its role.

Blimpish obduracy lingered even so. Pereira's successor Brig Whitehead told a Home Guard audience that as far as using a rifle went, their job was simply to sit in a hole and shoot straight. This showed, Tom said sarcastically, that the Maginot Line mentality was still a Blimpish preserve, unchanged by the reality of the blitzkrieg. He coined a new phrase, 'Hit don't sit'. Whitehead disliked the whole notion of amateurs being trained in guerrilla warfare. After the first week of training at Osterley, that is in mid-July, he summoned Hulton and Wintringham and told them to close the school down. It was not needed, he said, and he had circularised Home Guard units telling them not to attend. Furious, Hulton went to see Sir Edward Grigg who told him to carry on while he made enquiries. These resulted in a new War Office Department of Military Training for the Home Guard, and for the time being Osterley continued as before. Tom took Whitehead's rebuff phlegmatically. Perhaps his lack of personal ambition helped, but he must have been hurt to realise that his drive, enthusiasm and expertise were so undervalued or mistrusted; and it was to happen again and again over the next few years. In all probability it was Brig Whitehead who so incensed George Orwell when he heard him speak in August:

> Dilating on the Home Guard being a static defensive force, he said contemptuously that he saw no purpose our training by 'crawling about on our stomachs' etc. etc. evidently as a hit against the Osterley Park school. Our job, he said, was to die at our posts. Was also great on bayonet practice, and hinted that regular army ranks, saluting etc., were to be introduced shortly. . . . These wretched old Blimps, so obviously silly and senile, and so degenerate in everything except physical courage,

are merely pathetic in themselves but they are hanging round our necks like millstones.[6]

Meanwhile, the notoriety of Osterley added to its appeal and from mid-July to mid-September the number of trainees quadrupled to 250 men a week. The Basque miners became celebrities and Wintringham earned a backhanded compliment when the Nazi-controlled Bremen Radio broadcast: 'It is irresponsible of the British censor to allow reckless appeals by Mr Wintringham to the natural fighting spirit of the average British citizen . . . and to encourage them to use shot-guns or cans of explosives to kill Germans.'[7] Tom noted with delight that in August the American press gave more column inches to the school than to the British Cabinet.

Members of the Home Guard came to Osterley from all over the country for a two-day crash course. As its reputation spread that summer contingents from the Regular Army came too. These included soldiers from the elite Brigade of Guards, probably sent along by their Commanding Officer, Gen Augustus Thorne, who had been a supporter of Tom's ever since the publication of his booklet *How to Reform the Army*. The structure of the course was deliberately democratic and informal; no compulsory uniform, no rank, no parades or drill. The exercises were improvised but highly practical. In one a lorry representing a tank was towed behind an old car and blown up with landmines; in another a replica model of a Stuka bomber descended on wires over a dug-out and was, it was hoped, shot down by rifle fire; in a third bombs were improvised – the jam-tin bomb, Molotov cocktails, smoke bombs, mortars. *Picture Post* magazine carried photograph spreads of the exercises, not always to universal approval. 'We Make Our Own Mortar for 38/6d', for example, was disapproved of by the War Office with the quibble that all scrap metal was needed for recycling into proper arms. A reader wrote in: 'Where is this Buffalo Bill mentality supposed to get us? What are these Marxist hooligans doing with their little jampot bombs?'

In another area of the park, away from mad Maj Vernon and his Basque bombers, Stanley White conducted a quieter exercise with a Boy Scout flavour:

In my section there was a general, two colonels, a man about town of the old school and an advertising director. We were taught the use of cover, how to approach silently. One lesson was demonstrated by masking a man completely, seating him on the ground and placing a bunch of keys between his legs. The object was to seize the keys before he could point out your position. The knack is to walk with bent knees, one hand on each, placing the feet carefully in a straight line. . . .[8]

The instructors studied recent experiences of guerrilla war, defined by Yank Levy as 'little war, the method of fighting which is employed by men living in an area occupied or surrounded by the enemy'.[9] Pride of place was given to Liddell Hart's book *Colonel Lawrence*, an assessment of the guerrilla leader T.E. Lawrence who had fought the Turks in the Arabian desert during the First World War. Then there was E.O. Malley's *On Another Man's Wound*, an account of urban guerrilla war against the British in Ireland. Hemingway's *For Whom the Bell Tolls* was studied because of its well-observed description of blowing up a bridge north of Madrid in the Spanish Civil War. Edgar Snow's *Scorched Earth*, an account of Mao Tse-tung's continuing guerrilla war in China against the Japanese, was also in the library. Orde Wingate visited Osterley with tales of his experiences in Palestine and Abyssinia.

Officially, the Regular Army seemed uninterested in guerrilla warfare (quite different from commando raids), although some of its modern pioneers were British and although, too, it was shortly to be waged all over Nazi-occupied Europe by partisan bands. It was similarly uninterested in street fighting, another important form of modern warfare learned in Spain and taught at Osterley. Tom told an anecdote that illustrates the Blimpish suspicions he was up against:

A very great gentleman who had been a cabinet Minister met a friend who said he had just been to Osterley. 'Terrible' said the great gentleman. 'I hear that Anthony Eden is going to take them over and legitimise them. And they're teaching street-fighting – just planning to murder us in our beds!'[10]

The course ended with a discussion in which the most frequent question, said Tom, was 'how to get rid of the Blimps who were stopping things getting done'.

Behind the fun and games was an air of recklessness, perhaps even desperation, as the course notes of one of Tom's colleagues show:

Go out and hunt the invader as well as guard essential points. Get him at his weakest point. Get him resting. Do any dirty trick you like. Knife him. Live for your country, make the enemy die for it. If you carry a gun, carry bullets always. Do anything that destroys enemy's morale e.g. report that Germans hand out poisoned sweets to children.[11]

It was in similar mood that Churchill gave the grim advice that summer: 'If you've got to go you can always take one with you.' In fact the War Office was creating, officially, a clandestine guerrilla organisation. So-called Auxiliary Units of well-armed young men, dressed like the Home Guard to avoid local curiosity, were planting caches of weapons and preparing to go underground. They were totally separate from the Home Guard though they may well have attended Osterley incognito. Tom knew of their existence because his brother showed him one of their underground hide-outs near Grimsby.

On 12 September 1940 Churchill delivered another of his morale-boosting broadcasts. He told the Home Guard:

[You are] as much soldiers of the regular army in status as the Grenadier Guards; determined to fight for every inch of the ground in every village and in every street. It is with devout but sure confidence that I say 'Let God Defend the Right'.

Churchill was expecting Hitler to give the order to invade Britain any day. In fact, we know now that on 15 September Hitler postponed Operation Sealion until further notice, although he wanted the threat of invasion to be maintained. He turned his attention instead to Russia; but the Luftwaffe intensified its bombing of major cities, hoping to hammer Britain into surrender.

Wintringham saw Churchill's broadcast as a victory for his campaign. A year later he wrote: 'the War Office had to accept many of our proposals that the Home Guard should be a fully combatant force. It cancelled earlier instructions that had laid down almost entirely non-combatant duties.'[12] This was indeed a victory for which Tom had given direction to the public mood and with others pressurised the Blimps in the War Office. But no force could be fully combatant unless it was properly armed and this now became Wintringham's priority.

In Tom's eyes the symbol of the Home Guard was the rifle; without the intention of providing a rifle for every guard the Government was not taking a citizens' army seriously. From the outset his call to 'arm the people'

(*Daily Mirror*, 28 May) unnerved some in the Government with its connotations of revolution and from the beginning Tom circumvented officialdom by obtaining arms his own way. Once again his genius for getting things going bore fruit. In July, through Kitty's family connections the Wintringhams helped set up the Committee for American Aid for the Defence of British Homes and persuaded it to accept private requests for second-hand arms from wealthy patriots such as Edward Hulton and another press baron Lord Beaverbrook. Both were active supporters of the Home Guard who did not let bureaucracy or official timidity stand in their way. When the War Office refused to help with shipment, Beaverbrook agreed to import the arms through his Ministry of Aircraft Production. Then they were distributed to factory companies of the Home Guard.

The first shipment of weapons arrived in Liverpool docks in November 1940. Hopkinson was there when it was opened: 'It was a motley collection, varying from long rifles used in the Louisiana Civil War of 1873, plus Teddy Roosevelt's favourite hunting rifle and a number of ancient buffalo guns, to modern pistols, revolvers and gangster's tommy guns.'[13] Tom made his own choice, arming himself with a Colt .45 and fifty rounds of ammunition that had previously belonged to Harold Fowler of Fair Hills, New Jersey. He kept it until 1944 when the police cancelled his licence, 'now that the arms situation has changed for the better'. In June 1941 Tom wrote to Gen Thorne, now General Officer Commanding Home Forces Scotland, and told him that the committee had sent over 10,000 arms of which one-third were rifles with 20–50 rounds of ammunition for each.

This public-spirited gun-running was quite an achievement and one that ought to have been appreciated by the War Office. By 1941 the combat role of the Home Guard was well established although there was still a chronic shortage of weapons; but back in the summer of 1940 there had been hardly any. Tom Hopkinson said of his Turville Heath Home Guard in Buckinghamshire, which was ordered to defend an area where German paratroopers were expected to land: 'We had in the whole unit a single shot gun with one cartridge intended for deer shooting.' As late as June 1941, at Churchill's insistence, the War Office issued the Home Guard with pikes, long metal tubes with surplus bayonets welded to one end. This was a public relations disaster of the most Blimpish kind. 'What about bows and arrows?' mocked Beaverbrook, whose Ministry of Aircraft Production was supposed to make the pikes. 'We can obtain plenty of flint to turn into flintlocks,' he added sarcastically. 'Would these be any use?'[14]

Wintringham had inspired the Home Guard, led the campaign in the media to make it a fighting force, even spirited guns out of America, but he could not save its symbol of do-it-yourself defence, the Osterley Park Training School. Its closure was a lesson in civil service sleight-of-hand.

The War Office had disapproved of Osterley from the start. Were desperadoes from Spain really the chaps to train the Home Guard? Yet it was too successful and Wintringham too high profile for it to be closed down. So the War Office adopted the policy of if you can't beat it, join it – and then take it over. As early as 16 July 1940 the Inspector's Directorate of the Home Guard discussed Osterley. The minutes record: 'While approving of the school in principle, the London District Assistant Commander did not think the Instructors were of a suitable type because of communistic tendencies. MI5 have been asked to vet names of Instructors; matter to be taken up at once.' Referring Osterley to MI5 was the beginning of the end. A bland minute of the same meeting on 10 September said: 'I.G.H.G. [Inspector General of the Home Guard, Gen Pownall] informed meeting that the school at Osterley was gradually being taken over by the War Office and would re-open elsewhere on a smaller scale on 30/9.'[15]

At the same time Osterley was quietly removed from the public eye. In early September the press was discouraged from writing any more feature articles and the BBC was forbidden from making a radio programme. Then, in a cunning civil service move, on 2 September an official in the new War Office Department of Military Training issued an instruction: 'I am to state that in future no private schools for the training of volunteers should be recognised without the direct sanction of C in C Home Forces.'[16] This direct sanction was then granted to Osterley, but with strings attached. Edward Hulton was offered material aid on condition that the military authorities became involved in the running of the school. This, of course, was a first step towards taking it over. Hulton agreed, provided the instructors were kept on. On 12 September there was another bland but deceptive War Office statement that amounted to an announcement of a *coup*: 'An Army School for the instruction of Home Guard personnel is to be instituted. It will be located at Osterley Park until 30 September.'[17] The announcement then outlined the same course of instruction that was, of course, already being taught with great success in Wintringham's own school at the same address!

The school was then transferred to a less conspicuous location. It reopened at Denbeis near Dorking in Surrey under the command of a

Regular Army officer, Lt Col H.A. Pollock. Meanwhile, Wintringham and his eccentric band were naïvely unaware of what was going on behind their backs. On 7 November *The Times* quoted Sir Edward Grigg's speech to Parliament on the future of the Home Guard in which he referred to the 'admirable and invaluable privately run course at Osterley Park'. Janelia Slater remembered that 'at first the staff had all been gratified'. Tom assumed that in accordance with the Grigg recommendations and the promise made to Hulton, he and his instructors would have their positions at the school regularised by being commissioned into the Home Guard and given suitable ranks. In March 1941 he suggested to George Strauss MP that a suitable rank for himself would be lieutenant-colonel, that Slater and Vernon should be majors and Yank Levy a captain; 'we not only formed Osterley but have done almost all the instruction since then at the War Office School', he pointed out.[18] How naïve he was! In fact, as early as 1 October 1940 a War Office memo only made provision for 'Mr Wintringham' at the new school, and even then the Treasury quibbled over his fee. 'Try him for £450 p.a. and go up to £500 if necessary', wrote civil servant Crombie.[19] In the spring of 1941 the War Office got rid of Wintringham and his staff altogether.

Slater was conscripted into the Regular Army. A leading expert on the tactics of modern warfare, he was sent to an anti-aircraft unit with the rank of private. History does not record what happened to the Basque miners but Boy Scout Chief Instructor White, who obviously posed no political threat, was commissioned into the Home Guard and continued at Denbeis. None, including Tom, was offered army rank. These last few months at Denbeis were 'very sad', wrote Janelia Slater, 'the school lost all the versatility, freedom and fairness it once had.' Tom said he was 'seldom asked about anything more important than the sofa cushions for the instructors' mess'.[20]

Wintringham wrote letter after letter of complaint, and not just about lack of recognition and status. He believed that the Home Guard was being held back by the War Office from the role that Churchill himself had given it the previous September. Why were crucial members of the Home Guard not given exemption from conscription like their counterparts in the police and Civil Defence? Why, in April 1941, were 300 senior commissions in the Home Guard out of a total of 319 given to peers, baronets, knights and retired generals? Why were there so few young men in positions of command? Why was the role of the Home Guard still committed to static defence when the whole doctrine of defence in depth depended on mobility? Why was there so little training in guerrilla warfare? Tom answered his rhetorical questions succinctly: 'There is a reactionary clique with power in the War Office.' All this and more he poured out in an article in *Picture Post* on 17 May titled 'TRAIN THE HOME GUARD FOR WAR!' It began with an editor's warning: 'This is a highly critical article. Copies were submitted to the War Office for comment. They had none.' Wintringham was bound by War Office confidentiality so he must have had resignation in mind. He handed in his notice on 6 June and joined the Dorking Company of the Home Guard as an 'ordinary volunteer'.

Tom displayed no anger in his letter of resignation. It was reasoned, polite, formal: 'My letter of appointment calls for a fortnight's notice. I shall be glad if you will forward it to whatever department receives it besides your own. Yours etc.' Although he was a mild man he was essentially a man of action and ideas; and he had been purposefully smothered by Whitehall procedure and broken promises. His departure was as undignified as constructive dismissals usually are, but at least he could look back with pride. Eventually the school which he had founded became the prototype for three other War Office training schools, followed by twenty travelling wings and a system of summer camps.

Tom and Kitty had moved out to West Humble, near Dorking, to live near the school and they missed London. At least they were relatively safe from the bombing. Tom wrote to his brother John that he had lost touch with Elizabeth and his solicitors could not contact her about the divorce. John replied: 'Jim says that E's front door was blown in by a bomb, and back door out, and telephone smashed, so she sleeps with friends nearby. Your solicitors may have rung and got no answer.'[21] Not a couple to be deterred by enemy action, Tom and Kitty moved back to the centre of London early in 1942 and found a flat near London University in WC1.

Now that he had left War Office employment Tom was free to make 'a sharper attack on the Home Guard and Regular Army training', as he put it. Between July 1941 and the end of that year he toured on average one Army Division per month giving ten lectures or more to the units of each division. He received piles of letters of support from the Home Guard and went on civilian lecture tours, on one of which he was compared to Walter Raleigh and T.E. Lawrence. A letter of appreciation came from the Avonmouth Company Home Guard, motto: 'Mobile and Aggressive, hidden like lice in the seams, surprise, attack and kill'! H. Foster, the librarian at the Imperial War Museum and an enthusiastic Home Guard recruit, wrote to Tom with a significant complaint: 'There are far too many elderly men in the Home Guard giving the Corps a bad name. The public sneers, cheap jokes are made about "playing at soldiers". The speed of a convoy is determined by its slowest ship. The moral is obvious.'[22]

The character of the TV series *Dad's Army* was by no means based on fiction. The duffers of Walmington on Sea would have been horrified to learn that the real dad of the Home Guard was a 'red', and not least because he would have got rid of them. If Tom had really had his way, a typical unit would have been a factory company of young men, some of them exempt from conscription because of special skills, led on merit by one of their own, properly armed and trained to defend their locality by street fighting and mobile enough to carry out surprise attacks. The 'red revolutionary' was not against rank or discipline *per se*, but he believed fervently that his model Home Guard should be a model of his new society – classless, meritocratic, consensual in that it managed itself in a democratic way; a socialist army. This, he believed, was the wish of the volunteers themselves. As he expressed it in a new preface to the reprint of *English Captain*: 'Then from the British people itself, from our unformed but real democracy, came the million-fold impulse to make a new sort of army, that which we now call the Home Guard.'[23] The fact that some units did resemble the ideal and a large number of others worked towards it was due to Wintringham and others like him.

On 21 May 1943, Tom presented a BBC radio feature to celebrate the third anniversary of the Home Guard, for a new series *The Voice of Britain*. The announcer, obviously trying to set the tone for what was considered in those days a down-to-earth programme, introduced Tom by describing him as 'a studious tough who was in at the birth of the Home Guard'. And that was about right – as the dad, or a dad, rather than the midwife.

Tom now had an international reputation due in part to his overseas broadcasts but more particularly to his booklet *New Ways of War*. It was advertised as 'a do-it-yourself guide' to killing people when it was published in Britain in July 1940, and then abroad in the United States, Canada, Australia, Sweden, India and the Dutch East Indies. It was a modest publication of only 130 pages that encapsulated the teaching at Osterley and the articles in *Picture Post*, but it became the most successful of all his books. In Britain 75,000 copies were sold in the first few months and, since the shortage of paper meant that books were passed around, the readership was far higher than that. It also had an army edition with the title *The Home Guard Can Fight*, but this was not stocked on the shelves of libraries because it was marked 'Not for Publication'; a dotty War Office ruling considering that it was based on *Picture Post* articles that had already been read by hundreds of thousands. A reprint came out later in 1941 but it did not credit Wintringham as he had left the Home Guard.

The idea of a people's army was now fashionable in the British Empire. Even the British West Indies wanted one, although the Japanese would have to invade through the Panama Canal to get there. In Palestine there were more realistic fears of a German invasion through French Vichy – controlled Syria. The British High Commissioner and the Commander-in-Chief Middle East (still Gen Wavell) suggested a three-tier defence of the Jewish settlements: regular Jewish troops fighting with the British Army, then the Haganah or Jewish Defence Force as a sort of territorial army, and finally a Home Guard operating through the Jewish Settlement Police who had a branch on every kibbutz. This structure was implemented and although it was not needed in 1941 or 1942, it was activated to great effect during the War of Independence six years later. The Haganah kept back numbers of Wintringham's *Picture Post* articles in their Tel Aviv offices and these were translated into Hebrew for use by the Irgun, a semi-clandestine force of freedom fighters. Wintringham, then, was not only a source of instruction for defending settlements against Arab attack but also for terrorising the British Army. Had he known about this – and presumably he did not – he would have faced a moral dilemma!

In December 1941 Tom was invited to Santa Barbara, California to set up the first Home Guard training school in the United States. Lawyer Buell Hammett wrote: 'Inspired by your book *New Ways of War* a group of us a year ago started a Home Guard battalion. . . . .'[24] Tom and Kitty were keen to go because, Tom said, he was tired of being critical and wanted to do something constructive. They arranged to lecture in Australia afterwards and eventually obtained exit permits. On the eve of departure the following April, with the faithful Yank Levy already on his way, the invitation was withdrawn. Buell Hammett had pulled a Colt .45 gun on regular army officer Maj William Wenstrom because he had criticised his command of the Santa Barbara Home Guard; in the shoot-out that followed Hammett had killed both Wenstrom and his wife and he had been badly wounded. In itself this was a farcical though tragic episode of the Wild West, but it played into a far more significant tragedy that in effect changed the course of Indian independence. Tom had a walk-on part in this, as usual acting as a Lilburne-type pamphleteer and soldier.

In early 1942 Wintringham was asked by Sir Stafford Cripps to go to India and 'report on the possibilities of guerrilla fighting'.[25] Cripps, an austere politician and lawyer of whom it was said during his undemonstrative speeches that 'you can just see the home-made lemonade boiling in his veins', knew Wintringham and was sympathetic to his political views on colonial freedom. Cripps was more a leader of the left than Attlee and with a new place in the War Cabinet as Lord Privy Seal he was seen by many in 1942 as the champion of the people to rival, even replace, Churchill. In March, Churchill sent him to India to do a deal with the rebellious Congress Party and Wintringham was part of it.

Churchill admitted that he hated the Indians; he called them 'a beastly people with a beastly religion'. But with the Japanese at the gates, for they had captured Singapore in February and then Rangoon, he reluctantly sent Cripps with an offer – would the ruling Congress Party drop its position of neutrality and join the British Army in resisting the Japanese, in return for Indian independence after the war? Confident that he could obtain an affirmative answer, Cripps sounded out Wintringham.

Initially, on 16 March, Wintringham turned down the Cripps invitation because of his prior engagement to go to California. In his place he recommended to Gen Lockhart of the India Office his friend Orde Wingate. But then the California offer was withdrawn and Wintringham changed his mind. On 1 April he sent Lockhart an essay, 'Guerrilla Warfare in India'. This was at the very least a tactless paper, for it made no reference to the reality that India was still part of the British Empire and that many Indians actively resented this. Tom proposed the formation of a people's army that could just as easily be used against the British as against the Japanese.

Wintringham wrote that Indian civilians should arm themselves immediately by whatever means, including setting up armouries to convert saltpetre into explosives and to manufacture guns. He envisaged a guerrilla army supported by the local population acting on its own initiative. Therefore local units should be answerable to their own provincial Governments and not to the British Army in India. Lockhart might well have been aware that the author of these proposals was the same Wintringham who in June 1940 had insisted that 'India should be set free immediately'; the same Wintringham who had not lost his Marxist belief that the liberation of colonial peoples would aid the cause of communism at home.

In fact, the paper was not only tactless but extraordinarily ill-timed, for it arrived at the India Office exactly when the Cripps mission was stalled over the issue of the defence of India. Cripps was told that the Congress Party wanted its own Minister of Defence on the Executive Council that would govern India, under the Viceroy's authority, until independence was granted after the war. Its leader, Pandit Nehru, said that Indians must feel the war was theirs. With the Japanese rampaging towards the Bengal border (Cripps thought there might well be an invasion while he was in Delhi) and offering Indians independence, only an Indian politician could ask young men to die in defence of their country; and only if he could tell them that India was on the brink of achieving complete freedom. Cripps, on the contrary, maintained that the British Government had to keep overall responsibility for India's defence as part of its global war strategy; that was why Wavell was in Delhi as Commander-in-Chief, India. It was a sticking point.

When Nehru met Wavell on 5 April he determined 'to ask 100 per cent on defence'. Would Wavell step down and accept the subordinate role of Executive Adviser to an Indian minister? Wavell's reply was unequivocal: '"If that is your case there is no more to be said." There was dead silence. After a pause Wavell stood up and the Indian leaders took their leave.'[26] That was really the end of the Cripps mission. Five days later he wired Churchill: 'There is clearly no hope of agreement', and flew home. Mahatma Gandhi, the inspirer of non-violent revolution against the British, had always been against the mission. He wanted independence at once, not in the future, so he announced with satisfaction that India 'refused to accept post-dated cheques upon a bankrupt empire'.

The tragedy was that there existed a large measure of agreement between the British and the Indians, and between the Indians themselves, on the form that independence should take after the war. This was not to be repeated. In fact the failure, or 'fiasco' as Gandhi called it, worsened the atmosphere. Gandhi and Nehru started a Quit India movement and were imprisoned; an uprising of their supporters was suppressed by the British with considerable violence. It looked as if in south Asia Britain was fighting a war on two fronts.

Tom must have been briefed about the failure of the mission for he met Cripps after his return. Was he told how pertinent had been the role of a people's army in its failure? Nehru told the press in late April: 'To the last moment it was not clear whether we could, if we were to join the Government, raise and develop a people's army. The only assurance I could get was that C in C General Wavell would not stand in our way in certain circumstances.'[27] In any event, Tom did not think that the failure of the

Cripps mission meant the failure of his own. A people's army was still needed to resist the Japanese, whatever the future of India, and he was the man for the job. The War Office now thought otherwise.

On 27 April Tom secured an interview with Lord Alanbrooke, Chief of the Imperial General Staff, to push his case. Alanbrooke adroitly passed him sideways by telling him that as he was a civilian he should deal with the India Office. Wintringham then encouraged a letter lobby to get himself to India. He asked the Earl of Jersey to write to the Maharajahs of Jaipur and Jodhpur recommending his case, and he also asked Lt Gen Thorne to write to Wavell himself (16 May). 'I am almost certainly being sent to India,' wrote Tom to Thorne. 'I know Wavell has read one of my books, *Deadlock War*, about the worst book I ever wrote as it was completed before Dunkirk. The C.I.G.S. [Chief of Imperial General Staff] has approved in principal [*sic*] and I am told I should have the status of Brigadier.'

Wintringham was also sent urgent invitations addressed to 'The Pioneer of the Home Guard' from Indian political organisations such as the National Democratic Union, the Indian Federation of Labour and the Radical Democratic Party; how they knew that Wintringham had been asked and whether Wintringham solicited their letters we do not know. We do know, however, that he assured Lockhart of the India Office that an article in the *Daily Herald* on 16 May, 'Mr T. Wintringham has been invited to visit India to train thousands of anti fascists . . .', was not leaked by him. A highly compromising letter in the circumstances was sent by the veteran campaigner for a free India H.N. Brailsford to Pandit Nehru:

> Wintringham has a powerful yet flexible mind. I have seen him in three backgrounds – Moscow, Valencia and London. If ever during his work in India a conflict should arise between his duty to the Indian masses and his inherited instincts as an Englishman, you may trust him to follow his duty as an International Socialist. You may trust him completely. How I wish he might serve under you in training a people's army![28]

This was just the sort of letter to confirm the worst fears of the War Office, had it known. On 18 May Lockhart wrote to Wintringham in no uncertain terms: 'Wavell has Wingate for the job he originally asked you for – and there is nothing else in India in which he can usefully employ you. At present there is no opening for you in India.' Tom appealed to Cripps and tried to be conciliatory:

I agree with Wavell. I should not be any use teaching guerrilla tactics under officers who find it hard to believe in them to men whose feeling for freedom is not enlisted [i.e. regular troops]. I do believe I could help hundreds of thousands of Indians to arm themselves, train themselves, and fight against a Japanese invasion.[29]

The War Office dropped Wintringham like a hot brick. Finally, on 15 June, Lockhart wrote: 'You will recollect you suggested Wingate as a suitable subject yourself. He has been chosen for the post.'

This, in fact, was completely untrue. Wavell had given Wingate his orders as far back as 19 March: 'Proceed to Maymyo to the east of Mandalay and assume control of all guerrilla operations against the Japanese in Burma.' Wingate hardly went to India. His goal was the reconquest of Burma and he died achieving it. Ironically in the circumstances, he said he had no time for the Indian army, which he called 'the largest unemployed relief organisation in the world'; he refused to have any Indian soldiers under his command.[30] The impetus for raising a people's army in India petered out.

At least the collapse of schemes to employ Tom as a teacher of civilian defence and guerrilla warfare allowed him time to write more on the subjects. Apart from *New Ways of War* Tom also wrote a good deal of Yank Levy's *Guerrilla Warfare* (1942), so much so that in his signed Introduction he refers to it unguardedly as 'my' work. At the time, this was the only book specifically on the subject written in English and with particular reference to British conditions. Yank Levy made the cover of *Life Magazine* – 'looks tough, is tough, fights tough, Yank has made a career of the quick, quiet kill' – and in one review the book was hailed as required reading for every soldier in the American army.

At the same time that Tom was collaborating with Levy he was also translating and co-writing F.O. Miksche's *Blitzkrieg*. Miksche was a lieutenant in the Free French Army under General de Gaulle for whom Tom became a somewhat unwilling mentor because Miksche was excessively argumentative and demanding; Kitty said he should not be allowed in the house. *Blitzkrieg*, however, became the classic analysis of the subject and was recognised as such by the *Times Literary Supplement*: 'the best work on modern tactics the present war has produced'. The book formulated an answer to the blitzkrieg, the concept of web defence. This was illustrated in *Picture Post* by an elaborate graphic showing both Regular Army and Home Guard in tank-proof islands of resistance joined by minefields and protecting each other by lines of fire. With observation posts in front and strategic reserve behind, the whole construct seems impregnable if highly elaborate. Web defence was never put to the test, of course, but it did have a topical urgency. Tom's *Picture Post* articles based on the book came out in May 1941, the month that Crete fell and, for the last time, invasion seemed possible.

During this period Tom also wrote three small books under his own name with a wider scope than fighting the current war. For a man who freely admitted that he was lazy – a judgement confirmed by his children – the threat of invasion and the Blitz had awakened energies and qualities that he cannot have suspected; and this must have applied to millions of others. *Freedom is Our Weapon, A Policy for Army Reform*, came out in the summer of 1941. His innovative idea was for army education in politics and current affairs to replace the existing patriotic lessons on the theme of 'The King, God Bless Him!' Most probably he wrote this knowing what his ally Sir Reginald Adam, the new Adjutant-General of the army, was about to do. In August Adam created the Army Bureau of Current Affairs (ABCA) based on the conviction that a soldier in a modern democracy had a right and duty to reason why he was fighting. As Tom put it, paraphrasing Cromwell, 'we can only fight well if we know what we fight for and love what we know'. So adult education in the army became compulsory and its distinctly radical approach helped the Labour Party win the 1945 election. *Freedom is Our Weapon* ends:

> If we are able to achieve the making of a people's army, we can be sure that the men will come back determined to achieve and capable of achieving for themselves their own homes for heroes, their own society linking liberty, agreement and co-operation.[31]

Once again, Wintringham could claim to have played a pioneering role.

In 1943 Tom wrote *Weapons and Tactics* with the aim of placing current warfare on land and in the air in its broad historical context and giving it a theoretical basis. Aimed at 'civilians in a democracy so they can understand the mystery of war', it was updated thirty years later by John Blashford-Snell and reprinted.

Liddell Hart was supportive of Wintringham's prolific output but sceptical about its effect:

You have a background knowledge strangely lacking in military commentators. I hope you are usefully employed in the national interest but can hardly imagine this is so. Your ideas are pure common sense. Therefore they will not be accepted.[32]

To which Tom replied: 'Keep alive, maybe we'll fool them yet!'

Tom's third book, *People's War* (1942), was his most important. He saw it as a sequel to *New Ways of War* and it began similarly with a theory of war and ended with a political prescription. Tom wrote that currently there were three kinds of war: first the German and Japanese blitzkrieg and second the British response to it, 'imperial war':

it is essentially defensive, for the defence of imperial possessions, for the security of this straggling mixture of exploitation and justice, finance and 'white man's burden' that we call an empire. It is opposed to revolution in warfare. It is a conservative war, holding to old ways and shackled by old ideas.[33]

Thirdly, there was a resurgent kind of war, People's War, that was being fought in China, Russia and, increasingly, in occupied Europe. The distinguishing characteristic of a modern people's war, wrote Wintringham, 'is that it plans its offensives or counter offensives as operations combining guerrilla forces behind enemy lines with a blitzkrieg striking force'.[34] Guerrilla forces could not survive unless they were supported by the local population in a common cause of liberation and, to that end, all guerrilla operations were offensives; the antithesis of imperial war. This had huge implications for the opening of a Second Front in Europe which, wrote Tom, should have happened some time ago (before August 1942) in order to take the pressure off Russia. This sounds a foolhardy proposition now and no doubt it did then too, but when Tom and others made it Hitler had not started to build his Atlantic wall of fortifications. Moreover, Tom offered an important proviso: 'A Second Front can only be established if it is thought of and organised as part of a People's War of liberation by the population of Europe against fascism; if it is thought of as an old-style military expedition it will fail.'[35]

Tom was hugely enthusiastic about waging a true people's war. He compared it to 'a forest fire jumping across Europe, spreading through the air when blocked on the ground, and becoming an explosion when it reached the big cities'. He estimated there were a hundred million potential allies, the population of occupied Europe, 'provided we hammer out a policy that will link and lead these peoples'. This sounds a pipe dream but Tom shared it with others, for Kingsley Martin and Richard Crossman wrote a book with the same title: *100,000,000 Allies – If We Choose*. Whatever the feasibility, or fantasy, Tom claimed with justification that he was the first war correspondent to push for a Second Front as his initial argument for it appeared in *Picture Post* in August 1941.

Wintringham ended with a chapter entitled 'What Are We Fighting For?' His political prescription combined what he perceived as the strengths of Soviet society with what he saw as a welcome development in Britain: 'Socialism multiplied by democracy'. He hinted at more revolution to come in Britain: 'if the political parties are not ready to express and lead these feelings, we shall have to scrap the present parties and get some new ones'.[36] The next chapter in Tom's extraordinary life was about to begin.

THIRTEEN

Common Wealth

Tom and Kitty married on 25 January 1941 at the Surrey South Eastern Registry Office in Dorking, apparently without telling her parents. Tom's friend since Spain, Kenneth Sinclair Loutit, was the witness. It was four and a half years since they had all met at the Café Rambla in Barcelona and once again they were in the midst of war with bombs falling, troops marching off to the stations and fascists at the gates. The future was uncertain; the present all-important. Tom applied the fatalism of war to love:

'Embarkation Leave'

For each brief embarkation leave
in the changing war that is never over
                        while we have lives,
we have the need to state our need.

We've both known love as a wound's fever;
known, too, the words 'it isn't loaded'
                        that are suicide;
and there's plenty left of childhood's greed;

So this loving's possible, and no other:
bodies' delight in beating death–
                        no fool hope's growth,
none of the waiting, the futile grieving.

We need the sunlight's unhurried loving
that pauses for laughter, or for breath,
                        but takes no oath.
It is impossible? So is our living.[1]

'Now what in hell can we do about this damned world?' demanded Tom. It was 1 June 1941 and the war news was as grim as the year before.

Britain's cities were being blitzed, the navy was losing the battle of the Atlantic, the army was suffering defeat in North Africa and had been evacuated again, this time from Greece and then Crete. People talked of a negotiated peace. A Peace Convention organised by the Communist Party a few months earlier had attracted over two thousand delegates representing, the CPGB claimed, over 1 million voters. 'People are looking for a way out of the present mess' is how Mass Observation summed up the national mood. Despite the prevailing gloom Tom was on good form:

> Action seems a better answer than argument; I have tried both. But no action gets the results desired unless you know what you are doing. I argue that we who live in Britain can end the world's skid towards disaster. I am an optimist who believes that we can understand and act well enough to make the necessary changes.[2]

He was about to found another national grassroots movement, this time a political party called Common Wealth, and he prepared the ground for it in his next book *The Politics of Victory*, published in June 1941, which marked his return to the political arena after five years' soldiering. Tom began by breaking his silence and settling old scores with the Communist Party, but his criticisms were still muted.

Writing more as a quarrelsome friend than an embittered enemy, Tom explained his position in two letters. To his brother John he wrote: 'I am not a member of the Communist Party and violently disagree with them [over their opposition to the war]. But I am still on the "red" or revolutionary side of Socialism and I believe that changes equivalent to at least half a revolution will have to take place.'[3] Therefore, he wrote to Ray Postgate, editor of *Tribune*: 'I do not wish to widen the already serious gap between Communists and other sections of the revolutionary movement. To attack the Communists is to make it less likely that we can develop a united revolutionary movement which will include some or even the majority of them.'[4]

Wintringham was still an unrepentant Marxist and he shared with the Communists a deep suspicion of the British ruling class. In fact, he thought it was quasi-fascist, as he wrote in *The Politics of Victory*:

> The British ruling class armed German Fascism, and continued to support it even when there was a chance 'the gun might go off in the

wrong direction'. They did so in order to use German Fascism as the spearhead of resistance to, and counter-attack against, the working-class and against communism and the Soviet Union.[5]

This was quite a claim, though it was the standard Communist Party line, and Tom repeated it: 'the reactionary section of British finance-capital helps Fascism. . . . Their war against Germany is kept strictly secondary to their opposition to socialism and the working-class revolution.'[6] Wintringham and the Communists believed that what they termed the 'imperial' war Britain was waging was simply a defensive war to protect the empire. India remained unfree while it was expected to fight for Britain's freedom. To them the reason was clear. Tom wrote: 'The British Army, grouped behind its Maginot line of water and its strongholds in the Middle East, is not intended to destroy Hitler but to drive him into an attack on the Soviet Union.'[7]

Tom probably agreed with the Communist Party too that if the Nazis did attack Russia then the British Government would make peace with Germany and let fascism and communism fight it out to the death. But just as *Deadlock War* was published the month of the blitzkreig and therefore proved wrong, so *The Politics of Victory* was published just before Operation Barbarossa, Hitler's invasion of Russia in June 1941, and therefore in this respect instantly out of date. Contrary to Communist expectations Churchill made his famous remark 'if Hitler invaded Hell I would make at least a favourable reference to the Devil in the House of Commons' and forthwith placed Britain's armed forces firmly behind the Soviet Union. The CPGB, driven virtually underground after the suppression of the *Daily Worker*, now offered full-blooded, uncritical support for the war. Tom just had time to add a new preface, conclusion and footnotes to *Politics of Victory* in which he sounded grudging:

I am certain that despite the lead given by Mr Churchill and Mr Roosevelt, powerful forces in Britain and America will work to weaken our actual war effort now that the Germans are doing what the most powerful British financiers intended they should do – go East.[8]

Tom's purpose in *The Politics of Victory* was to outline his case for a united revolutionary movement. His slogan was: 'Turn the imperialist war into an anti-fascist war.' He wanted a popular front of all left-wing parties that would not only fight the enemy but also bring about what he now called 'Victory through Democracy'; a revolution towards socialism, workers' councils, greater discussion of war policy and the freeing of the empire. Only that kind of society, he claimed, would galvanise Britons to defeat the Nazis. It was an argument he had been making ever since he publicised his Four Points at the end of *New Ways of War* and, like George Orwell, he blamed the Communists for failing to seize their revolutionary opportunity in the heady, turbulent atmosphere of 1940. He admitted that Churchill had gone some way to appeal to social democracy by forming a coalition, arming the citizens and pushing to one side the 'most reactionary representatives of finance capital like Chamberlain', and this had temporarily calmed the atmosphere. But now, a year later, he said that Churchill had reverted to his conservative nature and the establishment had regained its confidence. Yet, believed Wintringham, the mood for revolutionary change was still there:

> Anyone who is in contact with the feeling of the army, the factories and the air-raid shelters in 1941 will surely agree with me that there is a volume of discontent and a willingness for action which could be led towards a programme of anti-Fascist war.[9]

Moreover, wrote Wintringham, revolutionary socialists were to be found in the most unlikely quarters. At Malvern in January 1941 a convocation of clergy including the Archbishop of Canterbury, William Temple, had concluded that 'the ultimate ownership of the principal industrial resources of the community in the hands of private owners was a stumbling block to Christianity'. In India, Pandit Nehru, on trial for leading the Quit India movement, declared from the dock: 'Unless the war has a revolutionary aim of ending the present order and substituting something based on freedom and cooperation . . . we must dissociate ourselves from it.' This gave Tom hope and he spotted other groups of dissident socialists looking for a lead:

> The real organs of power and expression of the British people are today the voluntary war organisations; the A.R.P. [Air Raid Precautions] services, the fire-fighters, the Home Guard. In many cases they are practically anarchist. A zone commander (Colonel) in the Home Guard remarks of his battalion commander: 'he's not sufficiently bolshevised yet, he still pays attention to the War Office'. These organisations have few means of even semi-political expression.[10]

Tom was not yet thinking of forming a new political party – that would soon come. For the moment he called for a progressive alliance, a new popular front of disparate and discontented citizens. They would join with Marxists like himself who were dismayed by the Communist Party and Labour voters who felt muzzled by their party's membership of the Coalition Government. Tom wrote dismissively: 'the Labour Party acts as supporter of imperialism and as controller of the working class'.

What should be the attitude of this progressive alliance towards Prime Minister Churchill? He was, wrote Wintringham, an arch imperialist and conservative; but above all he was a patriot. He was still the best bet for eventually winning the war. This was essential, for 'we cannot even speak of socialism if we are robbed of a country in which to practise it',[11] a quote that Tom took from his new Communist hero, Mao Tse-tung. The Chinese example, in which Mao's Communists allied with the Kuomintang under Chiang Kai-shek in order to resist the Japanese, showed, in Tom's words, that 'it is possible to resist a foreign aggressor, and fight alongside a capitalist Government, even though this capitalist Government does its utmost to prevent us gaining our aims'. The aim of Wintringham's new alliance, then, should be to support Churchill in his fight against fascism while campaigning vigorously for its own policies. Moreover, it would also oppose all the bureaucrats and profiteers whose inefficiency impeded the war effort and who had kept Churchill out of power for so long. By these means, he hoped, the opposition of Churchill to the popular front could be neutralised. In the meantime, he continued, 'when it becomes clear to the peoples of Europe that a great body of opinion in Britain is pressing towards an anti-fascist war, the peoples of Europe would begin to stir'.[12] This became Tom Wintringham's political platform for the next four years.

One of the pressure groups for change which Tom identified in *The Politics of Victory* was the 1941 Committee, of which he was a member. In fact, most of the members were journalists or publishers such as Kingsley Martin, editor of the *New Statesman*, Tom Hopkinson, editor of *Picture Post*, David Astor, soon to be editor of the *Observer*, Michael Foot of the *Evening Standard* and the publisher Victor Gollancz. They met under the chairmanship of J.B. Priestley in the London home of Edward Hulton, owner of *Picture Post* and a supporter of Tom since Osterley Park. It was easy to mock this know-all clique of armchair critics. H.G. Wells, a literary giant since Edwardian times, was briefly a member; he characterised the group as 'a well meaning but otherwise meaningless miscellany of people earnestly and obstinately going in every direction under their vehement professions of unity'.[13] Nevertheless, most of the propagation of left-wing views at this time came not from the Labour Party but from people such as these: progressive, some Marxist, professional communicators who saw their role as educating democracy and increasing social understanding. Mass Observation, the Documentary Film Unit, Penguin Books and the Left Book Club, *Picture Post* and the new campaigning *Daily Mirror* all came from this coterie; and standing on its margins was George Orwell himself. It was an alternative establishment. 'We were anti-They, against the privileged classes,' said Allen Lane of Penguin Books. It was an establishment with its own code:

> To read the left-wing propaganda of the late 1930s and war years is to enter a thought world of certainty in which intelligence and justice, however outraged for the time being, are bound to triumph. We might almost be re-living the convictions of the English Puritans in the 1630s. In a diluted fashion, the Marxist vision of the rise of the industrial working class prevailed: and the war seemed to prove that the day of the common man had arrived.[14]

This description fitted Tom exactly and Edward Hulton's sitting room in Mayfair was a more congenial environment than the proletarian base of 16 King Street. Wintringham was now centre stage. Instead of purveying *Daily Worker* agitprop on street corners, he networked with the 1941 Committee collecting informed criticism and passing it on to the Government. In May 1942 it issued a Nine Point Declaration for left-wing candidates prepared to take on the Government at by-elections. Tom was one of its authors and the Declaration advocated all his 'Victory through Democracy' policies. On 25 June the first Independent candidate, Tom Driberg, stood at a by-election at Maldon in Essex with these Nine Declarations as his policy and Wintringham went along to canvass for him. A notorious gossip columnist and homosexual, Driberg was also a sincere socialist and he and Tom became friends. He won a sensational victory, reducing the Tory vote by over 20 per cent.

It was only a short step from advising Independent candidates at by-elections to forming a new political party, but of the 1941 Committee there were few who were professional politicians. In any event, by 1942 many of the Committee were valuable signatories but inactive members, perhaps for the reason that had put off H.G. Wells. Of those who remained Tom was well qualified and impatient to start a new party as encouragement for a popular front grouping. Equally impatient and qualified but with a different agenda was the Liberal MP turned socialist Sir Richard Acland, another member of the Committee. Encouraged by the victory at Maldon, a month later they announced the foundation of Common Wealth. Until the autumn J.B. Priestley was Chairman but he then resigned and Acland became President with Wintringham as Vice-President. From the start it was an unlikely alliance and it never really worked. Reading through the voluminous correspondence between them they emerge more as sparring partners than prophets of the New Order for which Acland was calling.

Richard Acland, like Tom Wintringham, came from a family of Liberal MPs, but there the similarity ended. Acland's background was the landed aristocracy of Devon while Wintringham belonged to the urban middle class of Lincolnshire, with Nonconformist roots not far behind. Above all, while Wintringham had joined the Communist Party, Acland had become a born-again Christian after what he described as a 'physically compelling' conversion in 1940. Marxism and Christianity did not mix, despite enormous efforts to find common ground because, of course, you cannot leave God out of the argument. Related to this was a difference of intellectual approach. Acland was an inspired but intuitive public speaker; Wintringham was rational or 'scientific', as he put it, and deeply suspicious of those who were not. And related to this was a different approach to the discipline required to run a party. Acland, carried away by passionate belief, was both vague and autocratic; Wintringham, after years in the Communist Party, was precise and could be pedantic about the formality of committees. Their language in argument spoke volumes. Acland's invective consisted of: 'By Jove. . . . Look, I'm frightfully sorry. . . . Mark you, it's only a wild guess but . . .' while Wintringham became goadingly pedagogic and practical: 'It would take too much time to list your errors in order of magnitude or deal with all of them. They range from mere slips to general impressions. I deny entirely that . . .'[15] Nor did Tom spare communist rudery, including the phrase 'fascist tendencies'. Finally, even their body language in public debate showed their difference. Acland, tall, lanky and earnest, waved his arms about and shouted exultantly like a revivalist preacher; Wintringham, sometimes aggressive but always considered, stood with military bearing and self-control.

Acland roused suspicion on the left; in fact the Communists compared him to the fascist Oswald Mosley. Both came from country baronetcies, both were powerful orators, and both left their political party in mid-career to convert to socialism. Acland did not discourage this comparison when he wrote a book about his ideals with the title *Unser Kampf* (1940) and gave his movement based on it the militaristic, if not fascist, name Forward March! But there was a world of difference in practice between the national socialism of Mosley and the moral socialism of Acland. H.G. Wells did not trust Acland either. He wrote to Tom:

> I am sorry to see that you and Priestley have pinned yourselves to Acland. He is from the Revolutionary Point of View a thoroughly bad character. His intelligence is very limited and unstable, he is as imitative as a monkey, any claptrap that seems to be popular goes into his bag and any 'religious' cant, and his ambition for leadership is uncontrollable.[16]

Differences arose from the beginning over what to call the new party. Acland suggested to Tom the name REALITY so that members could call themselves 'Realists',[17] which shows just how unrealistic he could be. No wonder Members of Parliament laughed at him even though he held public audiences spellbound. Wintringham suggested to Acland either the People's Common Wealth Movement or the Common Wealth Freedom Movement, because Acland stood for 'collectivism' or common ownership while J.B. Priestley stood for 'vital democracy' or freedom. (Common wealth is derived from the fifteenth-century term 'common weal' or 'good', meaning a body politic founded on law.) It was left to Priestley to adjudicate and he chose the abbreviation Common Wealth. No doubt this pleased Tom because of its resonance with the English revolution and the Commonwealth republic of 1649–60.

Acland and Wintringham agreed more or less on two of the three main principles of Common Wealth. The first was that all major industrial resources and land, in fact all land not required for personal use, should be under 'common ownership'. The second principle was 'vital democracy', meaning that voters should have a far more extensive say in the running of the State by voting for workers' councils at the workplace and for national and regional parliaments; and they should vote under the more democratic system of proportional representation. The two principles were related, for as Priestley said to Tom: 'The compromise of public [i.e. State] control of private enterprise will not work. It is a negative process! You cannot postpone socialism; all the great productive resources must be owned in common.'[18] That meant run by workers' councils, a proposal Tom enthusiastically supported. He made the point that the communist policy of proletarian control was now out of date as industrial workers were no longer a majority. A new class had emerged on which he, Orwell and others pinned their hopes: the salaried managers, senior trade unionists, civil servants and technicians, in short, the white-collared class. He saw them as the new dynamo of democracy. While reading or writing about these aims it is easy to forget just how revolutionary they were. Acland lived up to his principles by giving away all his Devonshire estates to the National Trust, not, he hastened to say, to avoid death duties, but out of the concept of service.

But Acland and Wintringham could not agree over the third principle, 'morality in politics'. In fact their fundamental disagreement undermined the whole concept of Common Wealth. What Acland called for was far more than just higher standards in public life. His vision was of a brotherhood of man, selflessly dedicating itself to the public good. Without this ideal, common ownership and vital democracy would not work. Economic socialism was not enough; it had to be spiritual. He wrote to Tom: 'We have discovered from Keir Hardie the line along which socialism MUST be preached if it is to prevail.' To Acland moral socialism was the defining theme of Common Wealth, what made it different from anything that had gone before. He wrote to Tom again:

> Now this is crucial. It is my view and that of hundreds of others that the key to Common Wealth is that unlike all other political parties we link changes in the structure of society to moral changes in the individual. This IS our strength; this IS the reason for our being; this IS why in the hideous difficulties of wartime we grind and slog at branch work.[19]

Acland was not simply an idealist, for it was he who had persuaded Archbishop Temple at the Malvern Convocation to state that private ownership was a stumbling block to Christianity. He saw Christian votes in common ownership. Essentially, however, he was a deeply committed Christian. 'We assert,' he said, 'that "thou shalt love your neighbour" is not a pious aspiration for an impossible ideal. Common Ownership is *primarily* necessary because without it man cannot live according to his true nature.'[20] This is what Acland preached with messianic zeal – and Wintringham completely rejected it.

Tom could not even bring himself to utter the phrase 'morality in politics'. As an atheist he denied the very existence of either absolute morality or 'Platonic idealism'. He told Acland bluntly: 'there is no "spiritual" side of life outside the material'. What is more, said Tom, it should be no concern of the State to legislate morality over individual life; that was quasi-fascist. What Acland really wanted, he argued provocatively, was a theocracy and not a democracy. Tom loathed the Established Church. He challenged Acland: 'Where in the Gospels did Christ preach common ownership? How can the Church claim over its history to have practised this morality?' The concept Tom accepted was social ethics, meaning the relations between man and society; indeed, he said, 'there has always been a moral aspect to socialist teaching but this means a social good and not an absolute good'.[21] So Tom eschewed morality and used the term 'fellowship' instead, a word that suited his intention of drawing together the groups of the left into a new popular front. Finally, Tom found the emphasis on morality irrelevant because, he said, it had little to do with the working man. 'I find it impossible to advise 60 percent of the population of this country to give up the scramble for profits, because never in their lives do they get the chance of making any profit on anything.' This dismissive argument must have hurt Acland with its implication that he was out of touch.

The argument spat on over the four years of Common Wealth. Some of it was aired, improbably, in the pages of *Town and Country Review* of which Tom was Editor. Because paper was not available for new political magazines, Common Wealth (commonly called CW) bought up a defunct journal and typeset the title ingeniously:

t o W n and
C o u n t r y
review.

Soon the argument took on a seventeenth-century character with Tom and Kitty writing one pamphlet, *Fellowship or Morality?*, and Acland writing another, *It Must Be Christianity*. There was even the equivalent of the Putney Debate, one weekend in June 1944, when the National Committee met to discuss 'Issues which seem to be undecided in Common Wealth at the present time', meaning the 'public morality' deadlock. Perhaps this was the occasion when Tom whiled away a few hours of debate by drawing a diagram that linked all the members of the National Committee to various theoretical standpoints, depending on whether they belonged essentially to the Christianity camp or the 'scientific socialism school'; it looks appropriately tangled. At times the argument became heated. Acland referred to what he called Wintringham's 'ferocity' in debate, but both men were anxious to avoid a public confrontation. Acland wrote again: 'In speech we see the cloud of resentment pass across the face of the other, and we quickly turn aside so as not to tell him the whole of what we mean.'[22] The ill feeling between him and Kitty, who was herself on the National Committee, was less discreetly handled. He wrote to her in exasperation:

You have a more chaotically disorderly brain than anyone I've ever met. Honestly, I just don't know how it is done. You are wholly incapable of holding an organised part in any discussion or argument. You have admitted to me that you find difficulty in expressing your ideas in words and this is indeed so. It produces the most disastrous results.[23]

Kitty retaliated by accusing Acland, in as many words, of sexism. In 1944 she also threatened to present a motion to the National Committee that declared:

C.W. is disintegrating because of attempts to turn it into an autocratic pseudo-religious body with fascist tendencies. To prevent this happening those members of leadership who are responsible for these disruptive tendencies should only make policy suggestions at the National Committee or in writing to sub-committees. They should not attend policy meetings.[24]

She was referring, of course, to Sir Richard Acland, the President of Common Wealth.

In one essential way Acland and Wintringham complemented each other: both appealed to the voters and for different reasons. Acland's revivalist fervour inspired his earnest and idealistic audiences, many of them young white-collar voters who had not voted before and were looking for a way to make the sacrifice of wartime. A typical voter, it was said, was a church-going young teacher living in a salubrious suburb, outside the Labour heartlands. These audiences lined up for Acland's New Order, imagining behind him on the platform great symbolic figures of the present and future: Beveridge, who represented the future welfare state already in the news; international figures such as Nehru and Chiang Kai-shek who stood for the end of empires; Stalin, not only the leader of a country that showed socialism worked but also the general who commanded a heroic people's war; Roosevelt, architect of the New Deal of the mid-1930s who was now showing Churchill the way. 'When we say that we have come to the end of an age and that a new society must emerge from the present world chaos WE MEAN IT!' cried Acland.[25] His audiences identified with a world revolution, a revolution that in Britain, Acland was careful to say, would come in the British way – through the ballot box. The burning sincerity of his sermons fired his audiences; the poster he inspired that consisted simply of the words 'Is it expedient?' crossed out and replaced by 'Is it right?' sent them away converted.

Tom was much lower-key and practical. He was less interested in middle-class political virgins and earnest Christians than in disaffected Labourites and those further to the left; blue-collar workers and Other Ranks in the armed forces. He was after popular front voters more than a New Order and in January 1943, eager as ever to put his ideas into practice, he decided to contest a by-election, the vacant parliamentary seat of Midlothian North in Edinburgh.

His opponent was the Solicitor General for Scotland, Sir David King Murray, and North Midlothian was then a safe Conservative seat. Under the wartime political truce none of the parties in opposition in a constituency put up a candidate so the Tory had the field to himself until Tom made it a contest. His tactics were clear. He denied that Common Wealth was a party, asserting that it was rather a new sort of popular front, a constitutional means whereby voters from others parties could show their opposition to the way the Coalition Government, which was essentially Tory, was running the country and the war. He even claimed that he would not have 'butted in' if Labour had decided to contest the seat. He spoke of an alliance between the working class who had no use for capitalism and the middle class who were now ready for revolutionary changes of society.[26] He made much of a 'People's war such as the Russians are fighting'. He did not speak of 'morality in politics'.

Tom was an impressive candidate. He came endorsed by the intellectual luminaries of the left, H.G. Wells, J.B. Priestley, H.N. Brailsford, Dame Sybil Thorndike, Naomi Mitchison, journalists Vernon Bartlett and Hannen Swaffer. They wrote of his lifelong championing of the people and of his courage. His face on the election poster suggested experience, humanity and determination. He spoke with authority, making much of his war record and his hopes for Scotland in a federal Europe after the war. He referred to the legacy of Gladstone who in the same constituency in 1879 had made seminal speeches calling for an ethical foreign policy; 'Remember the rights of the savage', Gladstone had proclaimed. Wintringham reminded his audiences that he had always spoken against imperial rule. His quiet, undemonstrative manner went down well in this constituency.

The election generated enormous enthusiasm and Tom was helped by the sort of popular front team he could hardly have dreamed of. There were churchmen, civil servants, members of the local Labour and Communist Parties in defiance of their national leadership, even a full colonel, 'a cavalry officer who insisted on canvassing for me on his horse. It was a peculiar form of class alliance.'[27] Tom's sister Jim (now Mrs Elizabeth Neale) welcomed Tom back to the family's liberal roots, as she saw them, by serving as his election agent.

On polling day, 5 February, the voting was evenly balanced. In the end Wintringham lost, just 869 votes short with 48 per cent of the poll. Experts said it was Churchill's last-minute letter of support for King Murray that swung it, plus the fact that most of the voters were over fifty-five, for reasons of the war, and conservative in their loyalties. Several voters wrote to Tom saying he was the best candidate they had ever listened to and Kitty wrote to her mother:

We haven't had so much fun for years! Both of us got flu and ended up ten pounds lighter but we won a moral victory. I've fallen in love with Scotland, both the weather and the people. They have the right angle on life. I get along with them like a house on fire. There's a snap in the air here which is better than eternal damp. I'm going to wangle my way back.[28]

So Tom very nearly won the first by-election victory of Common Wealth. The movement was to win three of the eight by-elections it contested before the general election of 1945, all against a sitting Tory MP. In seven of these, CW, acting as the Labour substitute, gained an increase on the last Labour vote before the war of about 10 per cent. In fact, for a short while in 1943–4 Common Wealth was on a roll, despite disagreements among the leadership. George Orwell, writing for *Partisan Review* in April 1943, went so far as to say:

I think this movement should be watched with attention. It might develop into the new Socialist party we have all been hoping for, or into something very sinister. It needs another revolutionary situation to arise, either through military disaster or at the end of the war.

Orwell shared the left's suspicion of Acland's 'Fuehrer complex' but he had, as always, some shrewd observations to make about the Common Wealth appeal. He approved of what he saw as its propaganda tinged with ethical values, and he noted that it was careful not to use the stock phrases of Marxist ideology such as 'class war' or even 'socialism', thereby reassuring those who wanted fundamental change but were scared off by the hard left. For example, CW called for the confiscation of land but it promised a small amount of compensation; 'in effect the bourgeois is to be given a small life pension instead of a firing squad', Orwell wrote wryly. All in all, he concluded, it did have elements of demagogy and Utopianism but 'it takes a much better account of the balance of forces than any of the older parties of the left have done'. Common Wealth worked for consensus rather than class war. As historian Paul Addison put it: 'Acland was like a violinist playing in a brass band and giving a more sensitive rendering to the wartime theme of "fair shares for all".' Wintringham was down among the brass, playing a ruder instrument but the same tune.

Nevertheless, depression settled slowly over the Wintringham household. At the end of 1942 Kitty had complained to her mother about the strain of war and the uncertain future: 'so many schemes have been put to us which have never come to anything that frankly I don't pay attention any longer; but I expect we'll bounce up'.[29] And so they did with the excitement of the by-election, but a year later Kitty complained again: 'I have been getting progressively more tired and depressed, physically, mentally and emotionally, for the last six months or more. I am thoroughly run down and anaemic.'[30] For the three years of the real war on the home front they had been working flat out; now they experienced the anticlimax of the period when the fear of defeat was past but the hope of victory was premature. It was a long slog with rationing, the blackout and seemingly endless stop–go journeys on public transport. In London, in Paramount Court, they heard the fearsome drone of the V1 bomb and more often they thought they heard it stop, which was worse. In 1944 Janelia Slater stayed with them for a week at their new house, Les Ardennes, Frensham Vale, near Farnham: 'Tom was living in a little house surrounded by fir trees. He had this rather maddening wife Kitty who nagged and badgered. Tom looked pretty worn out by it and a paler version of himself.'[31]

Kitty was very dependent on Tom. The signals had been there in 1937 when she had suffered a breakdown in New York. As with journalism now with politics. An intrepid adventurer in her twenties, she had become a surprisingly insecure woman in her thirties; and Tom appeared to resent it. She wrote him a long and anxious letter:

> We have worked as a team for years believing that this team was the most important thing in our lives, even if one partner had to remain silent and hidden. But now this silent partner is expected to start from scratch and build up a separate reputation, made more difficult because she is a woman, a wife and had done all this teamwork.[32]

Presumably, Tom had told her to make her own way working for Common Wealth, and this brought out her insecurity:

> Tom, is it queer that I should begin to believe that I've lived in a fool's paradise – that I am a pretty useless person in fact – that years of what I thought were revolutionary training are of little importance? Am I to be debarred from work and action because I want to remain the full, active and developing team-mate? I know I am an unreasonable, uncontrolled person in many ways, that is the real problem. But must I fight this out alone with myself, as it were against you instead of with you?

This loss of confidence was indeed part of the problem, for when Kitty felt insecure she became more possessive and tried to tie herself to Tom with strings of words. Her excessive volubility was remarked on by many and, as Acland told her, it limited her effectiveness as a communicator. Moreover, she seemed to resent others encroaching on Tom's affections. While Tom's first wife Elizabeth had been virtually adopted by the Wintringham family and become a close friend of his younger sister Jim, Kitty kept her distance. Some of her jealousy of Tom was not misplaced and she had a point when she referred in her letter to his prejudice against women in politics, 'this "you can't have a woman" business' as she put it. 'Both to me and other women [in Common Wealth] you are saying "accept the handicaps of being a woman and slave for the movement", in a way that men do not have to prove themselves.'

At the same time, April 1944, Tom also received a letter from his loyal friend Christina:

Dear Tom – You kept your promise to let me know of your joys and sorrows, so now I write to tell you that Peter [her husband] is dead. . . . I hope Kitty has taught you the meaning of real love now. It's very, very precious. Yours Christina.[33]

Tom's low spirits are understandable. The longer the war continued, the more likely it seemed that Britain would eventually be on the winning side but without the morale booster of instant socialism; simple patriotism was enough. Radical change had to come, but for the majority of Britons it was sufficient to look forward to a peaceful revolution after the war.

Moreover, Tom's plans to use Common Wealth as an umbrella for a new popular front were falling apart. The CPGB had other ideas. Now that Russia was fighting a people's war the CPGB changed from opposing the war to supporting it without reservation. Harry Pollitt was reinstated as General Secretary, and to him national unity was all that mattered. Genuinely stirred by the suffering and heroism of the Soviet people, he persuaded the Party to offer unconditional support for the Churchill Government. This meant that the Party joined the electoral truce.

Pollitt's rallying call was now 'Everything for the Front'. He went so far as to lecture the miners, of all people, to 'avoid absenteeism or strike stoppages. . . . They are daggers stuck in the back of men of our own class in Europe.'[34] Palme Dutt, as usual, went along with this revisionism and it was certainly popular nationwide for membership of the Party tripled to 60,000. Yet the Party's exaggerated respect for the electoral truce lost it opportunities. Had it opposed the Government at by-elections by combining with Common Wealth or by fielding its own candidates it could have aired popular discontents and put pressure on the Coalition, particularly on Labour ministers.

This, of course, was what Wintringham hoped for, but in vain. It was clear that the CPGB would neither admit to its errors prior to June 1941, when Russia entered the war, nor join a popular front to force through social reform after June 1941. In fact the Communists not only spurned Common Wealth but derided it, calling it 'a new Mosleyite and crypto-fascist party'. Any hopes that Tom may have had of rejoining the Party were now gone.

One of Pollitt's rallies was watched by Sinclair Loutit and afterwards he spoke to Pollitt about Wintringham: '"A good man gone wrong" said Harry Pollitt, "but still a good man". I told Tom this and he said "well that's good to hear and I can say exactly the same for Pollitt".'[35] Some of the affection between the two men, memorably expressed by Pollitt at Tom's first wedding, had survived the past twenty turbulent years. Pollitt was a good man whose dogged devotion to Moscow caused him excruciating contortions; Tom was by no means a good man in some ways yet apart from a few wobbles in the 1930s he kept his revolutionary integrity.

In 1943 Stalin abolished the Comintern. He gave as the reason 'the deep differences in the historical paths of development [towards communism] of various countries', which must have afforded Tom an 'I told you so' moment. Stalin's real reason, however, was to reassure the West that he no longer had ambitions to encourage world revolution. Probably few lamented its passing, except Palme Dutt.

From early on in the life of Common Wealth some of its key members such as Wintringham and the Organising Secretary R.G. Mackay realised that common ownership or moral socialism stood not a chance of success without the support of the working man and that meant without some Labour Party support. In fact, back in September 1942 Wintringham had written in *Left News*:

The Labour Party, the Trade Unions and the Co-operatives represent the worker's movement, which historically has been, and is now, in all countries the basic force for human freedom. . . . We deeply regret its indecision and we count on our allies within the Labour Party who want a more inspiring leadership to support us.

What Common Wealth needed was affiliation with the Labour Party leading to an electoral pact. Otherwise, Tom feared, the left-wing vote in a general election at the end of the war would be split to the advantage of the Tories. Negotiations dragged on for eighteen months with Tom one of the team. He proposed affiliation at the Common Wealth Special Conference in October 1944, proclaiming: 'Labour is not a Socialist Party fighting for international socialism on a real Left Wing programme but C. W. can make it so!' He carried the conference despite only grudging support from Acland. Kitty wrote: 'R.A. damns affiliation with faint praise and mocks it in private. . . . He makes reactionary attacks on socialists and does not know what democracy means.'[36] At heart Acland wanted his New Order without compromise. In November, Tom, Acland and others met a Labour Party delegation to suggest affiliation and an electoral arrangement. This was put in the form of a bid placed unreasonably high, probably at Acland's insistence. CW demanded the sole right to contest forty-three selected Conservative-held seats (i.e. the Labour candidate should stand down) for the price of leaving all other constituencies to Labour. Not surprisingly, the Labour Party rejected this offer and a subsequent one when Wintringham met Herbert Morrison and reduced the demand, in his words, to 'twenty middle-class Tory seats'. That ended negotiations.

In December 1944 Wintringham reported back to CW that the Labour Party Executive had dismissed Common Wealth as 'a party founded by a rich man in order that he should become a political leader, with views based not on Marx but on Marks and Spencer. It was unable to contribute anything to the Labour movement and was only desirous of cheap seats.'[37] This must have stung Tom, whose socialist credentials were completely sincere and hard earned, but he had long suspected the value of his alliance with Acland.

Then R.G. Mackay resigned, rubbing salt in the wound by suggesting in a letter to Tom that he and Acland should resign too and stand as Labour candidates in the forthcoming election: 'Labour is standing near one hundred percent on a socialist ticket. C.W. is out in the cold and confuses the issue! If the mountain won't go to Mahomet, then Mahomet must go to the mountain!'[38] There was no room for a third socialist party between Labour and the Communists; Common Wealth had been elbowed out.

In March 1944, Victor Gollancz asked Tom to write 'a cold, calm, factual and deadly' sequel to *Guilty Men*.[39] The pretext was the publication of a book by the Right Book Club called *The Truth about Munich* which, Gollancz believed, would be used by the Tories in the forthcoming election as a justification for their appeasement of Hitler. Tom relished the task. The result was *Your M.P.* and it became almost as controversial and successful as its predecessor, eventually selling over 200,000 copies. In fact it succeeded in its aim of demolishing the pro-appeasement lobby because it became a best-seller of the 1945 general election. Whereas *Guilty Men* had attacked the twelve most prominent Tory appeasers from Chamberlain down, *Your M.P.* ridiculed the 'average, essential, ordinary Tory MPs', those backbenchers who had supported them and were still in Parliament opposing social reform. Tom gave himself the pseudonym of Tiberius

Gracchus, after the Roman tribune and soldier who had tried to represent the will of the people by redistributing land to the landless and was murdered for his pains. He took on a similar role as people's champion against the landed aristocracy and finance capitalists who had been appeasers; the 'fifth columnists or fellow travellers' of the right.

For once, Tom combined his skill as fiction writer with his experience as an investigative journalist; and he infused the text with genuinely felt mockery. His central character is the fictional Tory MP Maj Robert Patriot who is on a train journey to tell his wife of their son's death of wounds in a prisoner of war camp. In his grief he looks back over his career and concludes that he is guilty of his son's death by supporting appeasement, thereby encouraging Hitler. Tom targets real Tory MPs by sketching in genuine parliamentary moments of the past decade:

The national record, perhaps the world's record, for fatuous placidity must be allowed Sir Thomas Inskip whose figure sways through these years of storm like a barrage balloon in difficulties. He spoke as Minister of Co-ordination of Defence on 31 August 1939, days before war was declared. He said: War today is not only not inevitable, but is unlikely.

Then there was Sir Thomas Moore

who thought well of Hitler: 'peace and justice are the key words of his policy' he said (Sunday Dispatch 22.10.33). The reader must also, clearly, credit him with honesty and sincerity. And with a glowing patriotism. In the Daily Mail of 18.02.34 he praised Mosley's Blackshirts for their 'pride of race, love of country and loyalty'.[40]

The train journey ends with the realisation by Maj Patriot MP that the hagiography of Hitler he has been reading to jog his memory, *Thoughts and Talks*, a Right Book Club reissue of 1938, was written by Sir Arnold Wilson MP. He was the very same man, Patriot realises with horrible empathy, who said when war broke out 'I have got to atone', left Parliament, joined the RAF as a rear gunner and was killed at the time of Dunkirk. Robert Patriot resigns too and tries to work in a factory. 'He never spoke of politics. His politics had killed his son.' It is a shocking last paragraph.

The book has an appendix detailing how 310 Tory MPs voted in eight key debates from upholding Mussolini's invasion of Abyssinia in 1935 to shelving the Beveridge Report in 1943. Today we would call it a consumer's guide but then it was condemned by Conservative MPs. 'The book should be banned,' said Beverley Baxter MP. 'It is muck-spreading, a pack of lies and half truths. And it is published by Gollancz – a Jew.' A wittier criticism came from 'T.C.', short for Tiberius Crackus, who composed a song to the tune of 'A Fine Old English Gentleman':

> I will sing to you a story
> With the blessing of the Lord,
> of a left-wing intellectual
> Whom you may think a fraud.
> He's a self-complacent expert
> At the old axe-grinder's job
> And his writings bear the hallmarks
> Of the intellectual snob. . . .
> . . . Like the left-wing intellectual
> One of the world's worst kind.[41]

Your M.P. had obviously struck home.

The last hurrah for Common Wealth was the general election of July 1945. The Labour Party's policy document, *Let Us Face the Future*, effectively swept the ground from under the feet of CW's twenty-two candidates, unless they were literal believers in moral socialism, because it called for wholesale nationalisation and the adoption of Beveridge's plans for a welfare state. This manifesto caught the public mood and, incidentally, proved wrong Orwell's prediction of two years before. Churchill completely misjudged the public mood in his election broadcast on 4 June when he declared 'from the bottom of my heart' that the introduction of socialism would require some form of Gestapo.

Tom's concern, when he put himself forward as Common Wealth candidate in his home town of Aldershot, was not to split the left-wing vote and hand victory to the Conservatives. He promised Tom Gittins, his Labour opponent, that if he stood down then he, Wintringham, would vote for all Labour measures in the new Parliament; and Parliament, he predicted, would be serving a Labour Government whatever happened in Aldershot. This surely defeated the object for which Wintringham was standing. Remarkably, however, Gittins agreed not to stand although he had announced that 'Common Wealth and the Communist Party are a political crazy gang who have harmed the cause of socialism.'[42] His gesture was a glowing testimonial to Tom's reputation and gave purpose to his campaign as spokesman for socialism.

Wintringham decided to catch the happy mood at war's end with a 'travelling circus of a campaign', as he put it. It showed both his technical innovation and his flair for sloganising. For the first time ever, so the local paper said, loudspeakers were placed on a campaign car while Tom walked behind talking into a microphone. 'He was hailed with delight by young children who followed him from street to street.'[43] His election pamphlet carried the eye-catching headline: 'Is Hitler Hiding In Hampshire?' This capitalised on press speculation that Hitler had escaped from the Berlin bunker; but behind the joke question lay the ugly insinuation, if taken at face value, that Tom's Tory opponent was a neo-Nazi. For while researching *Your M.P.* Tom discovered that Oliver Lyttleton, President of the Board of Trade and Tom's Tory opponent, had been a director of the German metal combine Metalgesellschaft before the war when it had been arming Hitler's forces. He also discovered that the Nazi Foreign Minister Joachim von Ribbentrop, who had been captured by Allied troops, was once Lyttleton's guest in Aldershot! This was a target too obvious to ignore and, after all, Tom was only trading insults since Lyttleton referred to him as 'an ex-gaolbird'.

Kitty added a family note to his election leaflet that may have sounded effusive but was nothing less than the truth:

> There is another side to Tom's character that you should know: the man who loves ideas and clothes them in words which stir our hearts as well as minds. The man who is known among his friends for his kindness, deep understanding and patience, and his ability to make the most unlikely people work together happily and well. All these qualities spring, I believe, from the faith which guides his life, which he sums up as 'I believe in people'.[44]

The election results were announced on 26 July, after the many votes from the armed forces serving abroad had come in, and the final count showed that Labour had won by the surprisingly large margin of 180 seats over the Conservatives. Tom had once again done well, but not well enough. He halved the Conservative vote but still lost by 14,435 votes to 19,456.

Only one Common Wealth candidate won, E. Millington at Chelmsford in Essex, and two Communists, Willie Gallagher and the hero of the East

End direct action over air-raid shelters, Phil Piratin. But both parties polled over 100,000 votes, a rare success for minor parties in a general election. Acland and fifteen other candidates lost their deposits and Kitty did disastrously in Tom's former constituency of Midlothian North. She had been determined to stand, perhaps to show her independence from Tom and despite lukewarm support from her agent. 'There is little enthusiasm to be candid but we will rally round', wrote Anne McGregor. At the count she was shown to have achieved exactly what Tom wanted to avoid. She split the left vote and gave the seat to the Tories: Conservatives 24,834 votes; Labour 23,657; Common Wealth 3,299.

Immediately, Acland and Wintringham decided to close down Common Wealth and recommended that its members join the Labour Party as a left-wing, socialist pressure group. Thus, somewhat ignominiously, ended the life of the only party to oppose the wartime electoral truce (apart from the just-surviving ILP) and one that had preached a revolutionary brand of socialism at that. A few continuing members published a document *Stand Firm* and kept CW going for a few more months. Tom applied to join the Aldershot branch of the Labour Party but said he did not want to stand again as a candidate. His revolutionary options, and energy, were expended.

FOURTEEN

A Prophet without Honour

Tom was waiting for a call that never came. In 1948 he hoped to be sent to Palestine to lead a volunteer force of peace-keepers, a new international brigade. In 1949 he hoped the *Daily Herald* would send him to Peking to report on the new Communist China. Kitty hoped, as did others, that he would become a Labour MP and be appointed a Minister of State in the War Office. And why not? He was still the foremost socialist writer on military matters and an ex-soldier who commanded great respect. His son Oliver, who did his National Service between 1947 and 1949, was often asked, '"Wintringham? – Any relation of Tom Wintringham?" My instructors were regulars who thought Tom a great man, which made me exceedingly proud.' Tom's former membership of the Communist Party was against him, though it is worth noting that John Strachey, who was back in the Labour Party after flirting with the politics of both Oswald Mosley and Harry Pollitt, was made Minister of State for Air in 1950. Tom's frustration was all the greater because his record proved that he made things happen. His was a rare blend of ideas and action; an International Brigade, the Home Guard, the Common Wealth Party, air-raid shelters for the working class, army education, all had existed in Tom's mind before he became one of those who made them real. And now nothing. 'It is intolerable not to be altering history', he wrote in 1948.[1]

Tom and other socialists found Labour's nationalisation programme depressing to behold. His friend Alan Wood wrote in *Tribune* about the 'titled Socialism of today, with the dreams of Keir Hardie translated in terms of stuffy public Boards and Corporations, each presided over by a member of the House of Lords'.[2] What he meant was that the old private industries like coal had not been handed over to the people but were now run by State committees of bureaucrats, ennobled trade unionists and public worthies. In 1948 Tom was asked to become Labour candidate for Brigg, just down the road from Grimsby. He said he would, as it was 'my kind of country . . . agriculture, steel and docks'. He had one condition, however: 'I must put forward a clear socialist policy. We must nationalise steel and land, giving farming first priority.' What he wanted was proper socialism, the common ownership and vital democracy of CW. So Tom moaned to Victor Gollancz about what he saw as the 'dull decay of policies without theory and of Government without colour or warmth'. What depressed him particularly was the Cold War, both the increasing anti-communism in the United States and the 'frozen dogma' of the Kremlin, as he put it. For an optimist such as Tom, who emerged from nearly ten years of anti-fascist war believing that peaceful co-existence and the advance of socialism should be universal goals, the postwar world was a rude shock. 'A lousy mess', he called it.

Tom wrote to Yank Levy admitting that he was feeling 'too fed up with the silly old world to be much use' and Kitty wrote to her old friend the American sculptor Rhys Caparn that she had 'sunk into being a stupid domestic shrew'. Their domestic worry was that for the first time for many years Tom had no job and therefore no income, except for the odd piece of freelance journalism. They had to live off Kitty's capital. Luckily some trust funds in her name became available and Uncle Harry, Henry Wise Miller of the New York stockbroking firm of Miller and Dodge, sent the money over. Between 1945 and 1948 they lived in what O.J. thought of as an 'expensive-looking house', called Pear Trees, at Brick End, Broxted in Essex but late in 1948 they moved up to Scotland, to 19 Laverockbank Road, Edinburgh 5. Tom explained the move to Yank: 'London smells of death and we have a lot of friends up here from the elections.'[3] Was he referring to the clear-up from the war or the decay of his political ambitions? In another letter he said that Edinburgh was 'one of the few lovely cities of Europe of which the beauty has not been destroyed in my lifetime'. Now the Wintringhams lost contact with many of their friends but, in any event, Tom had virtually withdrawn from public life.

On O.J.'s twentieth birthday, in March 1949, his father wrote to him:

Happiness, I feel superstitiously, should never be mentioned in a world such as this that you inherit. Then sometimes it may creep up on you without noticing you are there; and if you politely do not stare at it, may remain about the place. I hope so.[4]

There seem to have been plenty of times when happiness did creep up on Tom unawares, despite his gloom. Photographs show a man looking older than his middle years, his bald head – always eye-catching – sloping up towards the back and longer than before, his features more lined, but often with an engaging smile. He was a scholar, with a dry voice, round spectacles and the manner of a professor, but a sensual man too who indulged his tastes for fine food, sex and driving dangerously. Alan Wood recalled:

> He was a gay companion. I recall driving in his low bodied car [was this his Alvis 22?] with Tom's eye on the needle of the speedometer, flickering over 60, and his noting with cool precision at what speed the back wheels showed a disposition to leave the road. . . . He was a fine poet too, planning the pattern of sounds with the care of a general deploying troops on a battlefield.[5]

O.J. was a schoolboy at Abbotsholme until 1947 and he regarded his father like a favourite uncle:

> I remember Tom came once to take me out for half term in a little sports car designed for racing, with the accelerator as the middle one of the three pedals. He produced an Ordnance Survey map of the Peak district, and we searched it for the steepest roads crowded with contour lines. Then I was allowed to drive. I was probably 13 or 14. Bliss for me and rather brave of him. When dense choking white smoke poured out he only said 'it's a cork clutch, it's meant to do that!'[6]

Another of Tom's treats for O.J. was a trip to a London bookshop. In 1943 Tom bought him two poetry anthologies. 'We agreed,' remembered O.J., 'that we liked *La Marche des Machines* (A.S.J. Tessimond) and that we could, like Rupert Brooke, love "the keen unpassioned beauty of a great machine".'

In 1949, Tom told Yank that O.J. had spent the previous Christmas with him and Kitty in Edinburgh. 'My big lad gave us a lively time and I was able to teach him how to skate a car sideways on a frozen road.' Lesley remembers 'an enormous car, a bright yellow one with a strap holding down the bonnet', and O.J. adds: 'one's view was filled with two vast chrome headlights'. Unlike her brother, Lesley did not get to know her father, 'his choice and making, not mine,' she said, but in adolescence she formed loving and lasting friendships with both Elizabeth and Tom's sister Jim.

Tom's love of machines led Alan Wood to draw an interesting comparison between him and that other motor-bike enthusiast T.E.

Lawrence: 'He had a good deal of T.E. Lawrence in his make-up and presented the same puzzle and paradox, as an intellectual of culture and sensitivity who delighted in all the technicalities of war and slaughter.' Wood made another interesting comparison too, with Frederick Engels: 'neither thought Socialism incompatible with the good things of life, when available. Tom was fastidious, almost fussy, in his tastes in literature, art, food and wine.'[7]

Tom Driberg MP told an anecdote about Wintringham that showed him to have a most attractive quality, the ability to be charming and offensive at the same time:

> He was a friendly, bald, slight man, blinking through his glasses as he held forth, with authority and charm and never boringly. I asked him once why 'spit and polish' Guards regiments were outstanding in battle. His answer was outrageously offensive to all concerned. 'I suppose, broadly speaking', he said in his slow, slightly nasal drawl, 'it's because if you can't get proper officers, gentlemen make the best substitute.'[8]

On 26 January 1947, during a spectacularly cold winter when, according to Tom, the drifts in Lincolnshire were so high that rabbits jumped over the telegraph wires, Benjamin Rhys Wintringham was born. Did Tom and Kitty wait to have a child until they were free from public duties? Once again Tom's account in a letter to friends about Benji's first weeks centres on a car journey. It's a story about freezing fog and driving with the window open to scrape ice off the windscreen and their 'blizzard baby' in his cot on the back seat and the cold he caught. 'Damned awkward if you can't blow your nose', wrote Tom.

He explains in the letter, with increasing excitement, how the Government was mishandling the blizzard crisis by ignoring an 'archangel of a news adventure story' that would have won over public opinion to accept the cuts and restrictions. This is an unexpected example of Tom's revolutionary patriotism and of his ripping yarns approach to English history: it's *Armies of Free Men* all over again. Tom writes that the blizzard should be seen as another blitz, that 'ordinary real people' were fighting it and winning it and deserved 'real democracy and not just the bones of it'. If he had been the Government's spokesman, he said, he would have got a BBC war correspondent out on a collier that was struggling through the iced-up North Sea. He would have told him to give 'the silly names of the little ships like Kipling did on the trawlers mine-sweeping: "Send out Stormcock, Unity, Claribel, Assyrian and Golden Grain."' He would have interviewed a merchant seaman. He would have 'turned out the Elder Brothers of Trinity House – Winston is one and he would have loved it – to welcome the collier captains on Tower Hill, and the Lord Mayor of London to give them all a meal at the Mansion House'. For a moment Tom is no longer an out-of-work journalist on paternal duties but the Minister for National Emergencies harnessing the will of the people for a better Britain; and then it's back to the nappies.

Tom's frustration must have begun soon after the end of the war in the autumn of 1945 when he was banned from visiting the United States. The reason given by the Board of Immigration was his former membership of the CPGB, so it was an augury of the Cold War ahead. Kitty went to the States in January 1946 and fought his case with typical determination. Meanwhile, Tom rallied his influential journalist friends to lobby for him, such as Vernon Bartlett, now an MP, Gerald Barry, editor of the *News Chronicle* and the left-wing American foreign correspondent Herbert Matthews. Tom Driberg wrote a diary piece in *Reynolds News* on 3 February 1946:

Presumably the State Department will reconsider its decision to refuse an entry visa to Tom Wintringham, author of *Your M.P.*, ex C.Per, ex-IBer, ex CWer [*sic*], now member of the Labour Party. The grounds for refusal were political. The State department would have banned Tom Paine and still more Thomas Jefferson had he not been a native of Virginia. Jefferson held that 'a revolution every twenty years or so is very good for a nation' – views far more extreme than Wintringham's. It's amusing to note that just after Pearl Harbour the Governor of California cabled a pressing invitation to Wintringham to set up a Home Guard! Will delegates to the United Nations, meeting in San Francisco, be granted visas?

Kitty wrote to her New York solicitor: 'Damn the man, and God protect one from one's friends!'[9] which seems ungrateful. They succeeded in persuading the Board of Immigration to lift its ban – no mean achievement – only to find it reimposed by the Attorney-General Tom Clark. Kitty claimed it was the most high-profile case for ten to fifteen years and that the last Briton to have been banned for political reasons was John Strachey, who was now a prominent Labour politician. In any event, Tom remained banned and his passport shows he did not leave Britain after he returned from Switzerland in 1938.

Wintringham did have one other connection with the United States at this time. He wrote an article for the *Virginia Quarterly* in 1946 about the new atom bomb and once again his views were prescient. He disagreed with those who thought the devastating weapon would end either war or civilisation or both. Soon, he wrote, more countries than the United States would possess it and fear of retaliation would prevent its use. He did not deploy the term MAD (Mutually Assured Destruction) but that was what he had in mind. Further, said Tom, small wars would still take place when a nuclear bomb was either unavailable or irrelevant; and so it has proved.

Tom loved the radio, partly because its technical possibilities appealed to him, and the BBC records show that he made thirty broadcasts over the last ten years of his life. This was the era when all talk was scripted in advance, including discussions. Photographs show Tom with his friends George Strauss MP and Tom Harrison, the founder of Mass Observation, sitting over piles of paper in front of a large mike. This was *Answering You*, a wartime version of the *Brains Trust* broadcast on the BBC's North American Service. So it was not surprising that the *New Statesman* appointed him its radio critic in 1946 and the next year he accepted the same role in a new and long-running Third Programme series *The Critics*. One of his criticisms was of a Home Service documentary on the battle of Britain by the famous duo Chester Wilmot and Lawrence Gilliam. Wintringham found it lacking in human interest:

> Where were the voices of Sailor Malan and the pilots from our towns and counties? The girls picking apples in Kent? The men ploughing with the bombers and dog fights above them? The firemen in the blazing docks and the sailors on the convoys in the Thames? These were the people who took the Luftwaffe attack. Why weren't sketches of them woven into the programme?[10]

Perhaps he had in mind the poetic film documentary by Humphrey Jennings, *Diary for Timothy*, released the same year. Once again it was the ordinary people and the *Picture Post* approach that appealed to Wintringham. However, being a radio critic was one of Tom's few roles that he found tiresome. O.J. thought that his father's heart was not in it, which was the view, too, of Kingsley Martin, the *New Statesman* editor, who dismissed him after only a few months. 'Dear Tom. This is a horrid letter. You've not written as if you are on top of the subject or enjoyed listening or doing it. I'm sorry about this.'[11]

Tom's mind was as fertile as ever. Over the next two years, with Kitty as his faithful secretary or co-author, he wrote up ingenious ideas that, given the chance, he would be only too ready to implement. For instance, he conceived an International Radio Service, an unofficial people's radio, on which the citizens of the world would air their dissenting views. The programmes would be compiled and recorded by a small independent station such as Radio Luxemburg, with contributors in external studios connected by air lines and their words translated into the main languages of the world; then the sound discs would be freighted out by air. As a matter of fact a few years later BBC External Services did set up a department that compiled tapes, in English, and air freighted them around the Commonwealth. Then Tom wrote a paper on extracting engine oil from peat. More controversial was another of his letters, printed by *The Times*, in which he suggested that parts of the British Empire should be sold to the United States under a lease-back arrangement in order to pay off the war loan. O.J. remembers listening to a radio programme with Tom called *Are You Open to New Ideas?* Tom said afterwards: 'How easy it is to put an innovator down!'

One practical idea stands out from the others as considerably more than a brainwave cooked up by an inventor sitting at home with a typewriter. This was Wintringham's plan to send a peace-keeping force to Palestine in 1948. Once again, for the last time, he combined his political beliefs with his war experience; and he used both his journalism and networking to put pressure on the Government.

British soldiers in Palestine were being kidnapped, murdered and caught in cross-fire between Zionists and Arab Nationalists battling for a homeland. Under a League of Nations mandate dating back to 1919 Britain was trying to keep the peace between the two, but the Holocaust had finally made this impossible. Zionists were determined to make a state in their land of the Old Testament and thousands of survivors from Europe were packing refugee ships to join them. Their arrival was fiercely resisted by Arabs in Palestine who feared they would be swamped or squeezed out from their land which they had occupied for centuries. What could Britain do? One notorious incident dramatised its predicament. In July 1947, 4,500 Holocaust survivors from Germany and Poland on board the ship *Exodus* arrived in Haifa but the British Foreign Secretary, Ernie Bevin, ordered them to turn round and go back to Europe. They refused, so British soldiers used rifle butts, hosepipes and tear gas against survivors of the death camps. Members of UNSCOP (United Nations Special Committee On Palestine) watched the incident, pale with shock, and reported back: 'It is the best possible evidence we have of allowing Jews into Palestine.'[12]

In November 1947 the United Nations General Assembly voted to partition Palestine and to allow a small Jewish state, as yet unnamed; a free port for Jewish immigrants, Haifa, would open on 1 February 1948 and Jerusalem would remain under UN control. Partition would take place not later than 1 August. The neighbouring Arab states all rejected partition and the delay in implementation was the recipe for six months of escalating terrorism and violence. The British Army was stuck in the middle; all the troops wanted to do was to return home and both British Government and people sympathised with them. Churchill called it 'a squalid war'. The United States asked for a ceasefire but the Jewish Provisional Council rejected one. The UN had no peace-keeping force. Without help and without hope, Britain threw in the towel and ordered the phasing out of British troops, initially without a final timetable but then by 14 May 1948. A bloodbath was expected to follow.

Wintringham was probably unaware that his *New Ways of War* was being used as a handbook by Jewish fighters. One member of the Irgun said recently: 'Wintringham taught me all I knew.'[13] He was aware that a peace-keeping force was urgently needed as, of course, were many others. They knew that for political and legal reasons a peace-keeping force would not come through the Security Council of the new UN, at least in time, although Article 43 of the Charter did allow for one. One proposal from Canada was for a force similar to the French Foreign Legion. The Jewish Agency, the organisation through which Jews in Palestine were formally in contact with Jews outside, called for an international militia. Tom had another plan.

'For over a year', Wintringham wrote in January 1947, 'I have been trying to make friends in the Labour Party realise the need for a small international standing army, a World Guard, but they refuse to think about military things.'[14] Now he circulated a detailed paper calling for an international brigade of volunteers that would come from countries outside the Middle East and would work under a nominal country for legal reasons. He suggested Sweden, France and Czechoslovakia as possibilities. The key here was 'volunteers' because, Wintringham argued, this status would get round all kinds of diplomatic and legal difficulties. Britain should supply the arms, simply by leaving them behind when it left Palestine, the United States should provide the cash and the Soviet Union should provide other resources in kind. Tom said that he knew from experience that such a force would rapidly become effective. It would cost about $20 million and 'finish the job this year. Official blessing would come from the World Guard being at the disposal of UNSCOP'.

Over fifty years later and with the Palestinian issue as intractable as ever, Tom's whole plan must appear laughable; but he did not have the benefit of hindsight. What he did have was a belief in what he called 'the deep and widespread longing for peace in the world'. Just as a desire to stop fascism had led volunteers to risk their lives in Spain, so now a longing for peace would draw volunteers to Palestine. It was a question of 'morale', Tom said. Moreover, if his World Guard succeeded, then morale would be all the greater and the Guard could turn to other wars over sovereignty, such as that being waged in Kashmir. Eventually it could become a standing army seconded to the UN.

Desperate situations bring forth desperate solutions and what else was on offer? Tom's plan was publicised by the American League for a Free Palestine, run by Rhys Caparn's husband Johannes Steel, and sent to influential Zionists by Professor L.B. Namier. Incidentally, Tom was asked by the Jewish Legion to advise and support a Hebrew State in the whole of Palestine. He declined, saying that the ultimate solution should be a Palestine with equal rights for Jews and Arabs, and he drew a comparison with the Walloons and Flemings in Belgium.[15] On 16 February 1948, Tom outlined his proposal in a letter to *The Times*. Correspondence between the paper and Tom suggests that *The Times* wanted to print his letter as a pretext to write a leader and provoke some kind of response. This happened. *The Times* leader called for 'an international force to discharge the duty of maintaining order in Palestine until a succession state or states can emerge. The British are going and some authority must step in to take their place'. The next day the paper carried a response in the form of a letter signed by MPs from all parties led by Richard Crossman (Labour), Robert Boothby (Conservative) and Tom's old friend since school days Wilfred Roberts (Liberal). They took up Tom's call for an international force from what they designated the 'lesser powers using the vast stores of arms and equipment to be left by the British'; they did not put forward his all-important call for a volunteer brigade.

Then there was silence. The Wintringham file closes except for a further letter from Tom to Wilfred Roberts and a note to Tom from Lt Col P.R. Butler: 'God forbid that what the International Brigade inflicted upon Christian Spain should be repeated in the Holy Land!' With public reaction of this kind, what hope was there?

On 14 May the last British soldier left Palestine (apart from a small garrison at Haifa) and Prime Minister Ben Gurion inaugurated the new State of Israel. It was immediately recognised by the United States. By this time it controlled about 20 per cent of mandated Palestine but 1,200 Jews had already been killed in battle. Now the fighting intensified, as predicted, until in the spring of 1949 armistices were signed between Israel and its Arab neighbours. By Independence Day on 15 May 1949 Israel governed more territory than it had been granted under the UN's partition plan nineteen months before. Jerusalem remained divided.

As if in retreat from the world Tom turned to fiction. He was in the middle of what Kitty later described as 'three years of heart-rending work, of trying to become the pure creative writer at 49 – three started novels and a world history'.[16] One of these unfinished novels, *More Fun, More People Killed*, set in London in 1940, was, as Tom put it to Victor Gollancz, 'more melodramatic and more obscene than I expected'. More erotic would have been a better description, but obscene enough to shock the comrades of King Street and the priggish Richard Acland. Not surprisingly, Tom had quite a flair for mildly pornographic romantic fiction, sufficient these days to make a lot of money:

'Eddie's not coming back here, not till midnight,' she said. His fingers were on the bath-towel wrap, between her shoulders and her breasts. She did not resist or move backward when he pulled the wrap gently open. But in the same reasonable voice she said 'a bargain, darlin' – three kisses and then be good – till we've eaten'.

He kissed her lips; her mouth answered his, but her body kept a little away from his. He put his hand behind her back to pull her towards him, but as she came to him she touched his lips with her tongue, then twitched her head back. She kissed him fiercely and briefly, pressing all her tiptoe strength against him, then broke away. 'Count's two,' she whispered, and raised her hands to his face, checking him.

'Not my mouth again,' she said, very quietly and pulled his face down towards her left breast. He went down on one knee, putting his lips to the soft curve just above her navel, and then she waited a moment before she evaded him again. Then she was out of his grasp and past him towards the door. 'You move when you feel able to!' she flung back at him, with a chuckle.[17]

Tom's ambitious literary project was a 300,000 word book on 'the tendencies, ideas, efforts and material achievements leading towards the unity of the human race'. He called it a 'One World History' and it was the result, he told his brother John, of four years reading history and philosophy. Tom only completed 25,000 words about which, he said, Gollancz was 'severely non-committal', but it is of importance because of what he wrote in the introduction; his vision statement we might call it today:

Many of us believe good the growth of science, understanding of the universe, mastery of the natural world. There are even still a number of us who believe in human progress. I hold it strongly and I believe in people. I can see no earthly reason, and can believe in no heavenly one, why human beings should not again make progress towards living 'more abundantly' on every level that life can reach.[18]

Tom was a secular humanist who believed that science, not religion, explained how the world worked and that mankind was capable of progress. The practical philosophy guiding progress, of course, was socialism, and the all-important question that he intended 'One World History' to answer he framed like this: 'Can Marxism become scientific socialism? Can it be so changed and developed that it embodies the "something to believe in" for which so much of the world is longing? Can it combine the beliefs in science and in human brotherhood?' Optimist that he was, presumably Tom thought the answer was yes: an affirmation that the history of the next fifty years would show, sadly, to be built on sand.

He came nearest to providing his answers in his final essay, 'Communist Dilemmas'. Kitty said he completed it 'that last afternoon of his life'. It was published posthumously as 'Tom Wintringham's Last Testament' in three *Picture Post* articles between 3 and 25 March 1950: 'Revolt against Moscow', 'Victims of a Frozen Theory' and 'The Kremlin is Divided Too'. He never intended it as a last testament, of course, but it serves the purpose well. It shows how a progressive and non-doctrinaire Marxist reviews the ideology that has dominated his life, written when the supremacy of the Soviet Union in the communist world was being challenged for the first time, but the truth about Stalin's dictatorship was still concealed.

In 1945 Wintringham said that the world had not outgrown Marxism but that Marxism had ceased to grow. The Russian Revolution had shown the way and Marxism had come nearer than any other ideology to filling man's need to believe in brotherhood and science, but then in the 1930s it had got stuck; the believers had become 'victims of a frozen theory'. In 1949 he renewed his own faith because of the Chinese and Yugoslav communist revolutions, but these convinced him further that classical Marxism, the Marxism of the *Communist Manifesto* of 1848, needed radical updating.

Orthodox Marxists, said Wintringham, were like Victorian theologians still dogmatically applying Old Testament teaching when it was long out of date. In particular, the founding text of the *Communist Manifesto* was now redundant when it proclaimed that 'Society is more and more splitting into two hostile camps, into two great classes directly facing each other, bourgeoisie and proletariat. The proletariat alone is the really revolutionary class.' Further, Orthodox Marxists were wrong to hold to the corollary of this; that a crisis in capitalism would lead to a war between bourgeoisie and proletariat out of which the proletariat, led by the Communist Party, would emerge victorious. This, wrote Tom, was out of date, too. He had believed it until the mid-1930s. He had been a revolutionary as opposed to a reformist but then the Orthodox Marxists, including his former comrades in King Street, had failed to grasp three realities that had not only made the dogma redundant, but had led to a world war.

The first reality was that the industrial proletariat was no longer the majority class. By maintaining their insistence that the proletariat was the only revolutionary mass that mattered, the Kremlin had set 'class against class' and so allowed fascism into power. Later in the 1930s the Kremlin had cynically manipulated the Popular Front between progressive classes, treating it, in Tom's words, as 'a manoeuvre not a reality', with the result that the Kremlin had undermined the all-important communist fight against fascism. Secondly, Orthodox Marxists had failed to face up to the unwelcome reality that during these years the proletariat appeared to prefer being downtrodden by capitalism to revolting against it, as the minuscule membership of the CPGB at the height of the Depression had shown.

Hence exploitation leading to revolution was a Marxist myth as much as the myth of the proletariat.

The third reality was the advent of fascism, an ideology that Marx could not have foreseen but that Marxists eighty years later ought to have anticipated. The fascist combination of nationalism, a supposed modernity and a corrupted form of socialism had exerted a strong appeal. Faced by the collapse of capitalism many workers had either accepted fascism or been coerced into it, at the expense of communism.

These were powerful criticisms and surely no less than the truth. How might Pollitt or Palme Dutt have responded? Not that Wintringham was disillusioned, for he saw the Chinese and Yugoslav revolutions as a way ahead. Both were based on an alliance of classes; both rejected the proletarian fallacy and both were succeeding because they had put fighting fascism as the first priority. Tom liked the Chinese, he told O.J., because they were a practical people without 'the sad Slav introspection. A people who have never worshipped god will take Communism differently from our Messianic Russian pals.' As for the Yugoslavs, he was heartened by Tito's belief in 'the multiformity of revolutions and the construction of socialism'.[19] Tom believed, he said, in what Gerrard Winstanley the Leveller had advised three hundred years ago: 'What other lands do, England is not to take pattern of.'[20] Tito had followed this principle by rejecting the Russian road to communism and setting out on his own.

What then should be the English way to Marxism in 1949? Tom said that he believed socialism was as necessary as ever and that a socialist state was 'possible'. It was possible not because of poverty or material frustrations for in his view they seemed to lead to 'sterile struggle based on the proletarian fallacy' (a dig at the CPGB), but because of war. Almost everybody longed for peace and socialism was the way of providing it. Here, Tom said, generations of Orthodox Marxists had omitted to consider a crucial clause of the *Communist Manifesto*:

The history of all hitherto existing society is the history of class struggle, of oppressor and oppressed . . . ending in either a revolutionary reconstitution of society or *in the common ruin of the contending classes.*[21]

The international class struggle, wrote Tom during the Cold War, was about to pitch America, which he considered capitalist and quasi-fascist, against proletarian Russia and if this did lead to war then the 'common ruin of the contending classes' would be the outcome for everybody – a third, nuclear, world war. Socialism was an ideology of peace, concluded Wintringham, because it was based on the classless society. A revitalised Marxism should bring this about by a peaceful striving for class alliances rather than pitching in again to foment a terminal class struggle.

Wintringham was not to know that the Chinese revolution would lead to millions of deaths and widespread destruction, despite its socialist achievements, but he had less excuse for misreading postwar Russia. In 'Revolt against Moscow' and 'The Kremlin is Divided Too' his defence of Stalin was absurd. He saw a great divide in the Kremlin between the majority, the Orthodox Marxists or 'theologians' who were determined to advance their fossilised theories, and the minority, the administrators and industrialists who were moving with the times. The majority were Greater Russians who, with the Red Army, were preparing for another stage in the proletarian revolution: a war on the capitalist West. The minority, mostly non-Russian, were the advocates of peaceful co-existence. Stalin was their champion.

> Stalin called the 1939–1945 war a 'just war of liberation' from the beginning implying that the allies had right on their side and the C.P.G.B. and Comintern was wrong. Now the pundits of the dead International were proclaiming that capitalism produced war and therefore capitalists everywhere had to be fought as such, and to be fought soon. The minority led by Stalin were emphasising the possibility of, and need for, a long period of peaceful co-existence with America and the West.[22]

Not content with this distortion of history, Wintringham went on to remind *Picture Post* readers that Stalin was a Georgian who was defending the rights of national minorities against the centralisation of Moscow. His failure, Wintringham admitted, was that because 'he was weak on culture' he had not prevented attacks on intellectuals in the name of proletarianism by the Party dogmatists. He meant the purges, in so far as he knew about them.

All this, of course, was rubbish. Stalin did not defend national minorities: he took away their autonomous status, destroyed their leadership, transported whole peoples like the Crimean Tartars to the east. He did not defend the intellectuals: he accused them of treason, threw them into prison, encouraged their slaughter both before and after the war. He was not leading a minority dedicated to peaceful co-existence; he was the absolute dictator who planned Russia's Cold War. He acted in the tradition of greater

Russia, cutting it off with an iron curtain (Churchill's description) from the West and extending its borders by force to establish socialism in one zone as opposed to in one country. Wintringham had always defended Stalin but this final whitewash was embarrassing. He was not alone, of course. As ever, George Orwell was acute in identifying the continuing widespread allegiance to Stalinism on the British left, despite all the evidence to the contrary. He wrote in 1948 when revising his first draft of *1984*:

> Nearly the whole of the English Left has been driven to accept the Russian regime as Socialist, while silently recognising that its spirit and practice are quite alien to what is meant by Socialism in this country. There is a schizophrenic manner of thinking in which words like 'democracy' can bear two irreconcilable meanings and such things as concentration camps and deportations can be right and wrong simultaneously.[23]

This schizophrenia became the double-think of *1984* and Wintringham's use of the dialectic was not very different. His defence of Stalin was at least consistent compared to the Labour politician who was pro-Stalin in 1938, anti-Stalin in 1940, lyrically pro-Stalin in 1944 and violently anti-Stalin in 1948. But how to explain Tom's myopia? He was certainly a better theorist than he was a politician and, too, he just could not shake off the father figure who had commanded his allegiance all those years; a good thing he died before Khrushchev's exposure of Stalin in 1956.

What political path might Wintringham have taken had he lived? In the late 1950s I see him as a founder member of the Campaign for Nuclear Disarmament, by far the largest postwar public mobilisation by the left. In the late 1960s I see him writing for *Marxism Today*, an optimistic supporter of Eurocommunism, the Prague Spring and the Italian way. He would clearly have been an enthusiastic supporter of guerrilla armies fighting wars of national liberation from colonial rule. Israeli and Indonesian guerrillas used Tom's *New Ways of War* in the late 1940s. Is it fanciful to see the next generation in Latin America and South East Asia studying dog-eared copies of Tom's manual or Yank Levy's *Guerrilla Warfare*, which Tom wrote? It is a legacy he would have been proud of.

In August 1949 the Wintringhams were on holiday at Searby Manor in North Lincolnshire. Tom was there with Kitty and Ben; O.J. had come too and Lesley was expected; Tom's sister Meg (still a Communist) had brought her three children. It was the first time Kitty had joined the family party and the atmosphere, remembered O.J., was tense. Kitty said she felt uncomfortable and Jim was anxious because Kitty was not fitting in.

On Tuesday 16 August Tom volunteered to help with the harvest at Owmby Farm and the foreman, concerned that as a townsman Tom would not be strong enough to fork sheaves from the trailer up onto the corn stack, put him on the stack arranging the sheaves. Tom had admitted to O.J. that he was very unfit and Lesley remembers him in his last years as rather pale and pudgy. Tom stood on the stack and saw his sister Jim drive past. He said, 'There goes my sister to the W.I. [Women's Institute]'. Those were his last words because he slowly sank to his knees, and died. It was a peaceful death for a very English revolutionary.

The post-mortem showed that Tom died of a ruptured aneurism of the right coronary artery. His public, completely unexpected death, for he was only fifty-one, obviously came as a great shock. The atmosphere cannot have been helped by Kitty's insistence that the wider Wintringham family should not attend the funeral, although Tom had died during a family gathering. Jim agreed. O.J. wrote to Elizabeth, who replied: 'Thank you for telling me but, you know, I lost him long ago.' The unhappy atmosphere was lifted a little by the poet John Betjeman, a former lover of Meg's, who took some of the family off to Cleethorpes for the afternoon.

The funeral took place at Leeds crematorium three days later. Only Kitty, O.J. and John (Tom's brother) attended, while little Ben waited in the car outside. There was no priest, no ceremony, no speeches; nothing distinctive to mark the end of such a remarkable life, except that Kitty gave the communist clenched fist salute. She and Ben alone went up Arthur's Seat in Edinburgh to scatter the ashes. Afterwards she wrote to Rhys Caparn, the sculptor and now Ben's 'anti-godmother':

> The time I thought of you most vividly was when they finally allowed me to go back and see him after the post mortem. I went to see his hands, hands don't die. And then it was the face that was so wonderful – not my private Tom, but all the fine strength of him – the man who could and did – and so many believed would do so again and he was about ready to – could lead and inspire men. And then I wanted you so, to sculpt that, the fine strong bones.[24]

Kitty could not settle to anything after Tom's death. In the 1950s she took Ben to the United States and lived with her mother in Hawaii, but this did not work. For one thing her politics were too left-wing for McCarthyite America; ironic considering she had been refused membership of the American Communist Party. She and Ben returned to England and in 1966, as soon as he was off her hands, she killed herself. She wrote in her suicide note to O.J. that life without his father was not worth living.

Elizabeth eventually married again; to her cousin, the Shakespearian critic John Dover Wilson. For fear of social embarrassment she dropped her old Communist friends like the Page Arnots and burned Tom's press cuttings.

Tom's funeral obsequies had been as sparse as his death had been sudden, and now the end of this man who had been a household name just a few years before, and a conspicuous figure in some of the dramatic events of the first half of the century, was hardly noticed. Tom's death was announced on the BBC but the only obituary of note in a national newspaper was in *The Times*. The *Daily Worker* ignored his passing. The Party had regarded him as a non-person for a decade but nevertheless the editorial office must surely have felt just a tremor of guilt; he had founded the paper and been a salaried Communist editor for many years. Alan Wood complained in *Tribune*:

I will never understand the news values of Fleet Street, the blank ignorance of newpaper editors on what sort of things the public are interested in. Here was a man who, during the war, was known to millions through the *Picture Post* and *Daily Mirror* and Penguin Books; as the prophet of the Home Guard his was an essential part in our finest hour. Could not one newspaper editor at least see an interest in the leader of that select band of Englishmen who had the honour of actively fighting for Spanish democracy? That is something for which he will always be remembered.[25]

Alan Wood's obituary of Tom compensated for the silence or ignorance of others. (The *New Statesman* carried a Diary item but said Wintringham had been a famous novelist in the 1930s!) Wood made the essential point. Tom was convinced that few things in life could be achieved unless you were prepared to fight for them. Unlike those who advocated Utopian policies in the *New Statesman* or *Tribune* but then did nothing, Tom realised that socialism would not just happen. His activism changed from strike and mutiny in the 1920s to the Popular Front in the 1930s, to the Home Guard and Common Wealth in the 1940s. In each decade Tom was in the vanguard of the movement towards revolutionary socialism.

'Wintringham', Wood went on, 'believed passionately in two things, Socialism and Freedom; and he would sacrifice neither.' He quoted from Tom's *Armies of Free Men*: 'Freedom is a force . . . that is the essential thing that is England: that throughout centuries a people has made of its freedom not weakness but a strength.' Wintringham's freedom, however, needs qualification rather than a sentimental acceptance at face value. Here was a man, after all, who followed the democratic centralism of the Communist Party during its hardest period and supported discipline, even execution, for deviants from the Party line in Spain. The point is that while his fellow revolutionary George Orwell believed passionately in the freedom of the individual, Tom Wintringham believed in the freedom of a class: the working class or, as Orwell put it, 'the ineradicable decency of the working man'. Tom believed in freedom *from* more than freedom *for*: from oppression, from poverty, from ignorance. That was the Marxist way to progress.

> Can you not feel it? The long tide stirring,
> The people passing, pausing, returning,
> Swaying and surging in the cold wet streets?
> And the fear in the faces of the fat? And the burning
> Hope in the eyes where, terrible in hopelessness,
> Lonely and cold a ghost of hunger sat?
>   Men will remember!

So wrote Tom in his poem 'Revolution' of 1925. I see Wintringham in a long line of English revolutionaries. Like John Lilburne he went to prison for his beliefs; like Oliver Cromwell's English captains he came from Lincolnshire stock and tried to bring about an English revolution; and like George Byron he was a poet who fought for a lost cause in a foreign country.

Wintringham was the last *English* revolutionary. He drew very consciously on the 1,000-year history of the English nation with its distinct radical tradition that he saw rightly as still alive. The Popular Front gave him the opportunity to appeal to a specifically English heritage and this he did with his essay 'Who is for Liberty?'. The war cast him first in the role of revolutionary patriot, as inspirer of another army of free men; and then as a new kind of revolutionary socialist, as the co-founder of Common Wealth. Tom believed, as the Leveller Gerrard Winstanley wrote 300 years before, 'What other lands do, England is not to take pattern of'.

After the war the subservience of the CPGB to Moscow continued. Stalin reconstituted the Comintern in the form of the Cominform and continued to give orders through it. In 1948, for example, he gave the order to denounce Tito and British Communists obeyed at once; so much for the 'multiformity of revolutions' that Wintringham believed in. Tom, meanwhile, was at least attempting to adapt Marxism to the changing conditions of the postwar world. He regarded the major reforms of the Labour Government after the war, instituted by the leading socialist politicians of his generation such as Ernie Bevin and Stafford Cripps, as falling far short of a socialist revolution.

Then, only seven years after Tom's death, the revolutionary aspirations of his generation finally went up in smoke. Stalin died in 1953 and in 1956 Krushchev's revelations about Stalin's Great Terror to the Twentieth Congress ended a world communist movement. As historian Eric Hobsbawm, at that time a member of the CPGB, wrote:

> The ten days of the October Revolution and the ten days of the Twentieth Congress of the Communist Party of the Soviet Union divided the revolutionary movement irrevocably into a 'before' and 'after'. To put it in its simplest terms, the October Revolution created a world communist movement, the Twentieth Congress destroyed it.[26]

The same year Russia invaded Hungary and seven thousand members of the CPGB handed in their cards, one-quarter of the membership. The old order had ended.

Whether Tom Wintringham is the last English revolutionary or 'a unique English revolutionary', as the *Dictionary of National Biography* now describes him, I hope I have elevated him from a footnote to the main text of British history of the first half of the twentieth century. He was a figure of national importance, albeit a figure in the second rank. History has not given him his due. He has no monument. But he does have his poem 'Monument', arguably his best, which he wrote in Spain in August 1937. It begins and ends thus:

> When from the deep sky
> And digging in the harsh earth,
> When by words hard as bullets,
> Thoughts simple as death,

You have won victory,
People of Spain,
You will remember the free men who fought beside you,
    enduring and dying with you, the strangers
Whose breath was your breath. . . .

Bring together under the deep sky
Metal and earth:
Metal from which you made bullets
And weapons against death,
And earth in which, for victory,
Across all Spain,
Your blood and ours was mingled, Huesca to Malaga:
    earth to which your sons and strangers
Gave up the same breath. . . .

Take then these metals, under the deep sky
Melt them together; take these pieces of earth
And mix them; add your bullets
And memories of death:
You have won victory,
People of Spain,
And the tower into which your earth is built, and
Your blood and ours, shall state Spain's
Unity, happiness and strength; it shall face the breath
Of the east, of the dawn, of the future, when there will be
    no more strangers. . . .[27]

A motor-racing track is being built near the River Jarama with a museum next to it. A monument to the British Battalion should be erected on the battlefield too, a monument to the ideals of a generation. Tom's poem should be engraved on it.

Appendix
Books by Tom Wintringham

The Coming World War, Wishart, 1935; revised edn, Lawrence & Wishart, 1936.

Mutiny – a Survey of Mutinies from Spartacus to Invergordon, Stanley Nott Books, 1936.

English Captain, Faber & Faber, 1939; Penguin, 1941.

Deadlock War, Faber & Faber, 1940.

Armies of Free Men, Routledge, 1940.

New Ways of War, Penguin, 1940.

Freedom is Our Weapon – A Policy of Army Reform, Kegan Paul, 1941.

The Politics of Victory, Routledge, 1941.

People's War, Penguin, 1942.

Weapons and Tactics, Faber & Faber, 1943; reprinted, Penguin, 1973.

Your M.P. ('Gracchus'), Gollancz, 1944.

Blitzkreig by F.O. Miksche, Faber & Faber, 1941; translated from German and with an introduction by Tom Wintringham.

Guerrilla Warfare by Yank Levy, Penguin, 1941; ghosted and with an introduction by Tom Wintringham.

Notes

Chapter One

1. John Lepper, 'Battle of Jarama', *Penguin Book of Spanish Civil War Verse*, Penguin, 1980, p. 133.
2. Tom Wintringham, *English Captain*, Faber & Faber, 1939, p. 204.
3. 'Tom. A Brief Memoir' by Hugh Williamson. THW archive; Small Black Suitcase File 22. LHCMA.
4. 'T.H. Wintringham; a short autobiography', 1937. THW archive; Small Black Suitcase File 26. LHCMA.
5. Martin Lancaster, 'Thomas Henry Wintringham; his politics and life'. Unpublished thesis, Grimsby College, 1997.
6. 'T.H. Wintringham; a short autobiography'.
7. Kenneth Sinclair Loutit in a letter to David Fernbach, 1978.
8. 'Tom Wintringham; outline biography', 1936. RGASPA Moscow. 545/6/216.
9. 'T.H. Wintringham; a short autobiography'.
10. 'The death of Leveller William Thompson' in *Mutiny* by Tom Wintringham, Stanley Nott, 1936, p. 61.
11. Review of Tom Wintringham, *Armies of Free Men* (Routledge, 1940) by George Orwell. Published in the *New Statesman*, vol. 20, p. 632 and quoted by Shaun Spiers in 'Tom Wintringham and the Socialist Way of War', unpublished MS, 1980.
12. 'White Paper', unpublished short story by Tom Wintringham. THW archive; Larger Black Suitcase File 36. LHCMA.
13. Kevin Morgan, *Harry Pollitt*, Manchester University Press, 1993, p. 2.
14. Harry Pollitt, *Serving My Time*, Lawrence & Wishart, 1940, p. 9.
15. Quoted by Steve Benson in *I Will Plant Me a Tree. The History of Gresham's School*, p. 202.
16. *The Gresham* (1915) in school library.
17. Tom Wintringham, *How to Reform the Army FACT* booklet, April 1939.
18. THW archive. THW 2; File 37. LHCMA.
19. *Ibid.*
20. Letter from Wilfred Roberts to David Fernbach, 1977.
21. THW archive. THW2; File 28, LHCMA.
22. *War in the Air*, vol. 4 by H.A. Jones. Imperial War Museum, 1934.
23. *Official History of the War: Military Operations, France & Belgium 1917*. Imperial War Museum.
24. 'Dawn Near Vinny: April/May 1917', THW archive. THW2; File 28. LHCMA.

25. THW's pocket book owned by O.J. Wintringham.
26. *Ibid.*
27. THW archive. THW 2; File 37. LHCMA.
28. *Ibid.*
29. *Ibid.*
30. *Mutiny* by THW, Stanley Nott, 1936, p. 10.
31. *Mutiny* by THW. *Left Review*, 1935.
32. Pollitt, *Serving My Time*, p. 65f.
33. THW archive. Larger Black Suitcase; File 22. LHCMA 34.
34. *Ibid.*
35. THW archive. THW 2; File 37. LHCMA.
36. 'T.H. Wintringham; a short autobiography'.

Chapter Two

1. THW archive. THW 2; File 28. LHCMA.
2. Letter from Andrew Rothstein to David Fernbach, 1977.
3. 'T.H. Wintringham; a short autobiography'. THW archive. Small Black Suitcase; File 26. LHCMA.
4. G.D.H. Cole and Raymond Postgate, *The Common People 1746–1946*, Methuen, 1946, p. 423.
5. Harry Pollitt, *Serving My Time*, Lawrence & Wishart, 1940, p. 71.
6. *The New Oxford*, November 1920. Bodleian Library.
7. 'T.H. Wintringham; a short autobiography'. LHCMA.
8. Dr Kenneth Sinclair Loutit, letter to David Fernbach, 1978.
9. THW archive. THW 2; File 37. LHCMA.
10. Letter from Andrew Rothstein to David Fernbach.
11. Quoted in John Callaghan, *Rajani Palme Dutt: A Study in British Stalinism*, Lawrence & Wishart, 1993, p. 24.
12. Quoted in Henry Pelling, *The British Communist Party*, A. & C. Black, 1975, p. 9.
13. *Ibid.*, p. 10.
14. A.J.P. Taylor, *English History 1914–1945*, Penguin, 1975, p. 193.
15. Wintringham's Russian Diary. THW archive. Larger Black Suitcase; File 36. LHCMA.
16. *Ibid.*
17. Tom Wintringham, 'Artists in Uniform', *Left Review*, February 1935.
18. Wintringham's Russian Diary.
19. THW archive. THW 2; File 28. LHCMA.
20. THW archive. Larger Black Suitcase; File 36. LHCMA.
21. *Evening Post*, 30 September 1950. Quoted in Callaghan, *Rajani Palme Dutt*, p. 12.
22. Quoted in Francis Beckett, *The Enemy Within*, Merlin Press, 1995, p. 30.
23. This and preceding quotations from Callaghan, *Rajani Palme Dutt*, pp. 37–9.
24. *Free Oxford*, 10 December 1921. Bodleian Library.

25. Letters between Salme Murrik and Palme Dutt in Palme Dutt File, Working Class Movement Library (WCML), Salford.

Chapter Three

1. THW archive. THW 2; File 37. LHCMA.
2. Palme Dutt Papers in Working Class Movement Library (WCML), Salford.
3. Quoted in Henry Pelling, *The British Communist Party*, A. & C. Black, 1975, p. xi.
4. THW archive, 1925. Larger Black Suitcase; File 21. LHCMA.
5. Report on Organisation, 7 October 1922. Quoted in John Callaghan, *Rajani Palme Dutt: A Study in Stalinism*, Lawrence & Wishart, 1993, p. 49.
6. *Workers' Weekly*, 16 June 1923.
7. THW archive. THW 2; File 37. LHCMA.
8. *Ibid.*
9. *Ibid.*
10. Palme Dutt Papers, WCML.
11. *Ibid.*
12. *Ibid.*
13. THW archive. THW 2; File 37.
14. *Ibid.*
15. *Ibid.*
16. Palme Dutt Papers, WCML.
17. *Ibid.*
18. *Ibid.*
19. THW archive. Larger Black Suitcase; File 21. LHCMA.
20. Harold Nicolson, *King George V*, quoted in James Klugmann, *History of C.P.G.B., Vol. 1 1919–1924*, Lawrence & Wishart, 1969, p. 249.
21. Ramsay MacDonald, Preface to 1924 reprint of *Socialism: Critical and Constructive*, quoted in Klugmann, *History of C.P.G.B., Vol. 1*, p. 266.
22. J.H. Thomas, 'My Story', quoted in Klugmann, *History of C.P.G.B., Vol. 1*, p. 249.
23. Palme Dutt Papers, WCML.
24. *Ibid.*
25. Appendix 6 in Klugmann, *History of C.P.G.B., Vol. 1*, p. 366.
26. Report of 24th Annual Conference of the British Labour Party, pp. 123–31; quoted in *ibid.*, p. 318.
27. Quoted by David Fernbach in 'Tom Wintringham and the People's Army', unpublished MS.

Chapter Four

1. *Sunday Worker*, 18 October 1925.
2. THW archive. THW 2; File 37. LHCMA.
3. Graham Pollard Papers, Special Collections, Bodleian Library, Oxford.
4. *Workers' Weekly*, 20 November 1925.

5. J.C. Davidson, Parliamentary Secretary to the Admiralty. Quoted in Margaret Morris, *The General Strike*, Pelican, 1976, p. 162.
6. *Workers' Weekly*, 13 November 1925.
7. *Ibid.*
8. *Workers' Weekly*, 20 November 1925.
9. *Workers' Weekly*, 4 December 1925.
10. *Ibid.*
11. THW archive. Tom's prison letters are not yet filed. LHCMA.
12. 'Jim', unfinished novel by Tom Wintringham. THW archive. Larger Black Suitcase; File 36. LHCMA.
13. *Left Review* (1st edn), vol. 1, no. 1, October 1934.
14. THW prison letters. THW archive. LHCMA.
15. *Ibid.*
16. *Ibid.*
17. Palme Dutt Papers in British Library (BL) CUP 1262. K4 MS 1922–27.
18. Quoted in Morris, *The General Strike*, p. 176.
19. Palme Dutt Papers in BL.
20. Graham Pollard Papers, Special Collections, Bodleian Library, Oxford.
21. *New York World*; quoted in Julian Symons, *The General Strike*, Cresset Press, 1957, p. 193.
22. Russian Centre for the Preservation and Study of Contemporary Historical Documents (RGASPI), Moscow 495/100/333.
23. Quoted in James Klugmann, *History of C.P.G.B.*, *Vol. 2 The General Strike*, Lawrence & Wishart, 1980, p. 124.
24. *Ibid.*, p 143.
25. RGASPI Moscow, 495/100/299.
26. Bob Edwards (later Labour MP then ILP and Merseyside Council of Action); quoted in Morris, *The General Strike*, p. 92.
27. Klugmann, *History of C.P.G.B.*, *Vol. 2*, p. 169.
28. *Ibid.*, p. 185.
29. *Workers' Weekly*, 6 June 1926.
30. National Museum of Labour History (NMLH), Manchester. Report of ECCI Presidium on microfilm. Reel 26.
31. Quoted in Symons, *The General Strike*, p. 134.

Chapter Five

1. 'Before Prison', 1932. THW archive. Larger Black Suitcase; File 21. LHCMA.
2. 'Notes for J.S.' (Johannes Steel). This is a twelve-page autobiographical synopsis written by THW in 1941. THW archive. LHCMA.
3. Elizabeth Arkwright, 1928. THW archive. Larger Black Suitcase. File 21. LHCMA.
4. Quoted in Andrew Thorpe, *The British Communist Party and Moscow 1920–1943*, Manchester University Press, 2000, p. 122.

5. London and District Committee of CPGB, February 1930. Papers in Graham Pollard Collection, Special Collections, Bodleian Library, Oxford.

6. Quoted in Noreen Branson, *History of the Communist Party of Great Britain 1927–1941*, Lawrence and Wishart, 1978, p. 49.

7. THW file in RGASPI, Moscow.

8. Quoted in Henry Pelling, *The British Communist Party*, A. & C. Black, 1975, p. 56.

9. T.H. Wintringham, *Facing Both Ways; The I.L.P. and the Workers' Struggle*, CPGB/Dorritt Press, 1932.

10. T.H. Wintringham, *War! – And the Way to Fight Against It*, CPGB/The Peoples' Press, 1932.

11. Quoted in Frances Beckett, *The Enemy Within*, Merlin Press, p. 45.

12. Palme Dutt Papers, WCML, University of Salford.

13. Autobiographical note in THW archive. Smaller Black Suitcase; File 26. LHCMA.

14. *Ibid*. See also article in *Daily Worker*, 7 January 1930.

15. 'British Freedom'; article by THW in *Labour Monthly*, February 1932.

16. *Ibid*.

17. The High Cross Folder in THW archive. Smaller Black Suitcase; File 21. LHCMA.

18. Elizabeth Wintringham, 'The Game'; THW archive. Larger Black Suitcase; File 21. LHCMA.

19. *Ibid*.

20. Palme Dutt Papers in WCML, University of Salford.

21. THW archive. Larger Black Suitcase; File 36. LHCMA.

22. Lesley Wintringham to the author.

Chapter Six

1. Tom Wintringham, *The Coming World War*, Wishart Books, 1935, p. 12.

2. Letter from THW archive quoted by David Fernbach in unpublished MS, 'Tom Wintringham and the People's Army'.

3. Tom Wintringham, *War! – and the Way to Fight Against It*, CPGB/The People's Press, 1932.

4. Tom Wintringham, *The Politics of Victory*, Routledge, 1941, pp. 109–10.

5. *The Coming World War*, p. 221.

6. Tom Wintringham, *Mutiny*, Stanley Nott, 1936, pp. 38–9.

7. *The Coming World War*, p. 152.

8. *Ibid*., p. 142.

9. *Ibid*., pp. 20–1.

10. Tom Wintringham, *Mutiny*, pp. 348–9.

11. Tom Wintringham, 'Modern Weapons and Revolution', *Labour Monthly*, January 1932.

12. Tom Wintringham, 'Modern Weapons and Warfare', *Labour Monthly*, August 1932.

13. Tom Wintringham, 'War is also an Art', *Left Review*, February 1936.

14. See 'The Military Principles of Mao Tse-tung' in Stuart R. Schram (ed.), *The Political Thought of Mao Tse-tung*, Penguin, 1969.

15. Tom Wintringham, 'The Road to Caporetto', *Left Review*, November 1935.

16. Public Record Office FO 371/16336.

17. *Ibid.*
18. THW archive. Larger Black Suitcase; File 21. LHCMA.
19. THW archive. Small Black Suitcase; File 21. LHCMA.
20. *Left Review*, October 1934, p. 38.
21. Palme Dutt Papers, WCML, University of Salford.
22. THW archive. Small Black Suitcase; File 15. LHCMA.
23. Quoted in Julian Symons, *The Thirties – A Dream Revolved*, Faber Paperbacks, 1975, p. 74.
24. C. Day Lewis, 'The Road These Times Must Take', *Left Review, November 1934*; also Symons, *The Thirties*, p. 74.
25. THW archive. Spanish Civil War (SCW) File 4. LHCMA.

Chapter Seven

1. Tom Wintringham, *English Captain*, Faber & Faber, 1939, pp. 164–5.
2. Quoted in R. Dan Richardson, *Comintern Army: The International Brigades and the Spanish Civil War*, University of Kentucky Press, 1982, p. 4.
3. THW archive. Spanish Civil War (SCW) File 7. Short story for Leslie Reade. LHCMA.
4. George Orwell, *Homage to Catalonia*, Penguin, 1962, p. 8.
5. Quoted in Richardson, *Comintern Army*, p. 11.
6. *Ibid.*, p. 9.
7. *Ibid.*, p. 14.
8. Jason Gurney, *Crusade in Spain*, Faber & Faber, 1974, p. 73.
9. THW archive. SCW, File 4. LHCMA.
10. *Ibid.*, SCW, File 11.
11. Hugh Thomas, *The Spanish Civil War*, Pelican, 1965, p. 379, note.
12. *English Captain*, pp. 26–7.
13. THW archive. SCW, File 11. LHCMA.
14. Quoted by David Fernbach in unpublished MS, 'Tom Wintringham and the People's Army'.
15. Letter, Dr K. Sinclair Loutit to David Fernbach, 1978.
16. *English Captain*, p. 40.
17. Letter, THW to Harry Pollitt. SCW Box C, File 5. Marx Memorial Library (M.M. Lib).
18. *English Captain*, p. 34.
19. Quoted in Tom Buchanan, *Britain and the Spanish Civil War*, Cambridge University Press, 1997, p. 121.
20. THW private archive.
21. Letter, THW to Harry Pollitt. SCW Box C, File 5. M.M. Lib.
22. Wintringham File 545/3/456. Russian Centre for Preservation and Study of Contemporary Documents (RGASPI).
23. THW archive. SCW, File 7. LHCMA.
24. Dr K. Sinclair Loutit, letter to David Fernbach, 1978.
25. Box C, File 7. M.M. Lib.

26. *Old Colony Memorial* newspaper, Massachusetts. 25 August 1937.
27. Dr Sinclair Loutit, letter to David Fernbach, 1978.
28. THW archive. SCW File. LHCMA.
29. THW archive, File 4.
30. Kitty Bowler, 'Just Try To Get In', THW Archive 1, File 3. LHCMA.
31. *Spanish Civil War Verse*, ed. Valentine Cunningham, Penguin, 1980, p. 149.
32. Box C, File 7. M.M. Lib.
33. Dr Sinclair Loutit, letter to David Fernbach.
34. THW. Private archive.
35. William Rust, *Britons in Spain*, Lawrence & Wishart, 1939, p. 4.
36. *English Captain*, p. 54.
37. THW. SCW archive. File 11. LHCMA.
38. *Ibid.*
39. *Ibid.*
40. John Cornford, 'Full Moon at Tierz' (1936) in Cunningham (ed.), *Spanish Civil War Verse*, p. 130.
41. Private correspondence.
42. THW archive. SCW File 7. LHCMA.
43. Gurney, *Crusade in Spain*, p. 59.
44. *Ibid.*, p. 63.
45. Quoted in Buchanan, *Britain and the Spanish Civil War*, p. 128.
46. *Voices from the Spanish Civil War: Personal Recollections of Scottish Volunteers in Republican Spain*, ed. Ian MacDougall, Polygon, Edinburgh, 1986.
47. THW archive. SCW File 4. LHCMA.
48. Letter, THW to Victor Gollancz, 10 August 1941. THW archive 1; File 34. LHCMA.
49. THW archive. SCW File 11. LHCMA.
50. *Ibid.*
51. *Ibid.*
52. SCW Box C, File 9/9. M.M. Lib.
53. *Ibid.*
54. *Ibid.*
55. SCW Box C, File 10. M.M. Lib.
56. THW archive. SCW File 11. LHCMA.
57. *The Spanish Civil War Collection*, Imperial War Museum Sound Archives, 803/4.
58. SCW Box C, File 10. M.M. Lib.

Chapter Eight

1. THW archive. SCW File 10. LHCMA.
2. George Leeson; Imperial War Museum Sound Archives 803/4.
3. Jason Gurney, *Crusade in Spain*, Readers Union Book Clubs, 1974, p. 112.
4. Tom Wintringham, *English Captain*, Faber & Faber, 1939, p. 164.
5. *Crusade in Spain*, p. 106.

6. *Ibid.*, p. 107.

7. *English Captain*, p. 258.

8. *Ibid.*, pp. 106–7.

9. *Crusade in Spain*, p. 117.

10. *Ibid.*, p. 184.

11. *English Captain*, p. 184.

12. *Crusade in Spain*, p. 114.

13. *English Captain*, p. 214.

14. Tom Wintringham, *New Ways of War*, Penguin, 1940, p. 124.

15. *Crusade in Spain*, p. 121.

16. Fred Copeman, Imperial War Museum Sound Archives, 794/13, reel 2.

17. SCW Box C, 10/9. M.M. Lib.

18. *English Captain*, p. 238.

19. *Crusade in Spain*, p. 127.

20. Quoted in Bill Alexander, *British Volunteers for Spain*, Lawrence & Wishart, 1982, pp. 106–7.

21. Review by Guy Chapman in Tom Wintringham, *How to Reform the Army*, FACT, No. 25, April 1939.

Chapter Nine

1. Fred Copeman; Imperial War Museum Sound Archives, Tape 2 794/13.

2. THW file 546/6/216. RGASPI Moscow.

3. Patricia Edney (née Darton), Imperial War Museum Sound Archives, Tape 4 8398/13. All other quotations from Patricia Edney are from the same source.

4. Account of Kitty Bowler. Item 83. THW file 546/6/216. RGASPI Moscow.

5. THW archive. SCW File 10. LHCMA.

6. THW's correspondence with Victor Gollancz of 10 and 11 August 1941. THW archive 1; File 34. LHCMA.

7. THW archive. SCW File 11. LHCMA.

8. Unpublished poem by THW in his archive. Small Black Suitcase; File 26. LHCMA.

9. Letter 88; 7/6/37. THW file 545/6/216. RGASPI Moscow.

10. THW to Charlotte Bowler, 25 June 1937. THW archive. Small Black Suitcase; File 26. LHCMA.

11. George Orwell, *Homage to Catalonia*, Harcourt Brace, New York, 1952, p. 180.

12. *Our Fight*, no. 45, 16 May 1937.

13. THW. SCW File 11. LHCMA.

14. *Ibid.*

15. THW. SCW File 18. LHCMA.

16. Tom Wintringham, *English Captain*, Faber & Faber, 1939, p. 277.

17. *Ibid.*

18. *Ibid.*, p. 306.

19. Ephraim Lessor, Imperial War Museum Sound Archives. 9408. Recording 1986.

20. THW. SCW File 7. LHCMA.

21. *Ibid.*, File 18.

22. *Ibid.*, File 11.

23. *Ibid.*, File 19.

24. *Ibid.*, File 18.

25. *Ibid.*, File 11.

26. THW, 'Hospital in August' (second verse), unpublished poem. THW archive. Larger Black Suitcase; File 21. LHCMA.

27. THW; SCW File 11. LHCMA.

28. *Ibid.*, File 18.

29. *Ibid.*, File 11.

30. From THW's unpublished poem, 'Hospital in August'.

31. Gustav Regler, *The Owl of Minerva*, Rupert Hart Davis, 1959, p. 261.

32. 'Notes to Johannes Steel', 22 May 1941. THW archive. LHCMA.

Chapter Ten

1. THW; SCW File 10. LHCMA.

2. THW. Larger Black Suitcase; File 36. LHCMA.

3. Geoffrey Trease, *Red Comet*, Lawrence & Wishart, 1937, pp. 36–8.

4. CPGB Reel 7 microfilm; Appeals Comm. of 9/19/38. National Archive of Labour History (NMLH).

5. Quoted by THW in letter to Kitty Bowler. SCW File 11. LHCMA.

6. NMLH, CPGB Reel 7.

7. J.R. Campbell, 'A Statement on the Purges', Politburo 5/3/38, Reel 5 CPGB in NMLH.

8. Private correspondence between Rose Cohen and her sister Nellie Rathbone, shown to the author by Nellie's daughter, Joyce Rathbone.

9. William Campbell, *Villie the Clown*, Faber & Faber, 1981, p. 144; and in conversation with the author.

10. THW archive. Small Black Suitcase; File 26. LHCMA.

11. THW archive. SCW File 16. LHCMA.

12. THW review of *Puritanism and Liberty*, ed. A.S.P. Woodhouse, 1938. LHCMA.

13. THW archive. Larger Black Suitcase; File 36. LHCMA.

14. Quoted in Noreen Branson, *History of Communist Party of Great Britain*, Lawrence & Wishart, 1985, pp. 265–6.

15. Quoted in Kevin Morgan, *Harry Pollitt*, Manchester University Press, 1993, p. 108.

16. All quotations from C.C. meeting in Andrew Thorpe, *The British Communist Party and Moscow 1920–1943*, Manchester University Press, 2000, pp. 259–60.

17. Tom Wintringham, *The Politics of Victory*, Routledge & Sons, 1941, pp. xvii and xix.

Chapter Eleven

1. Tom Wintringham, *New Ways of War*, Penguin Special edn, 1940, p. 127.
2. George Orwell, letter to *Partisan Review*, 3 January 1941. *The Collected Essays and Letters of George Orwell, Vol. 2 1940–1943*, eds Sonia Orwell and Ian Angus, Penguin, 1970, p. 71.
3. *Tribune*, 20 December 1940.
4. Paul Addison, *The Road to 1945*, Quartet Books, 1977, p. 104.
5. Quoted in Basil Liddell Hart, *Memoirs, Vol. 2*, p. 271.
6. Tom Wintringham, *How to Reform the Army*, FACT, No. 25, April 1939, p. 75.
7. *Ibid.*, p. 74.
8. *Ibid.*, pp. 33 and 44.
9. *Ibid.*, pp. 5 and 35.
10. THW to B. Liddell Hart, 19 December 1938. LHLetters 1/758. LHCMA.
11. *How to Reform the Army*, p. 47.
12. Tom Wintringham, *Deadlock War*, Faber & Faber, 1940, p. 187.
13. Interview with the author, January 2003.
14. Quoted in Addison, *The Road to 1945*, p. 72.
15. *Ibid.*, p. 107.
16. Quotations from Orwell's diary entries here and subsequently from his *Collected Essays and Letters . . . 1940–1943*, pp. 398–419.
17. *The English Revolution*. Part Three of George Orwell, *The Lion and the Unicorn*, pp. 112–18.
18. THW archive 1; File 21. LHCMA.
19. *Ibid.*
20. *New Ways of War*, pp. 122–3.
21. THW archive 1; File 7. LHCMA.
22. *Partisan Review*, 17 August 1941; *Collected Essays and Letters of George Orwell*, p. 180.
23. J. Walker Papers in Liddle Collection, Leeds University. YA 7517/5 and YA 7517/7.
24. Alexander Maxwell; quoted in F.H. Hindsley and C.A.G. Simkins, *British Intelligence in World War Two*, HMSO, 1990, p. 57.
25. Charles Graves, *The Home Guard of Britain*, Hutchinson & Co., 1943, p. 79.
26. Sir Edward Grigg; quoted in S.P. MacKenzie, *The Home Guard*, Oxford University Press, 1995, pp. 74–8.
27. Hugh Slater, *Home Guard for Victory*, Victory Books, Victor Gollancz, 1941.
28. THW archive. 'Notes for J.S. on Tom Wintringham', p. 6. LHCMA.
29. Clement Attlee; quoted in Addison, *The Road to 1945*, pp. 121–2.

Chapter Twelve

1. Janelia Parlade, letter to David Fernbach, 26 November 1978.
2. Noel Thompson in the *Sphere* magazine, 10 August 1940.

3. Tom Hopkinson, *Of This Our Time*, Hutchinson, 1982, pp. 177–8.

4. Letter, THW to brother John; THW archive. Large Black Suitcase; File 32. LHCMA.

5. Edmund Ironside, Commander-in-Chief Home Forces; quoted in S.P. Mackenzie, *The Home Guard*, Oxford University Press, 1995, p. 56.

6. George Orwell, *Collected Essays and Letters 1940–43*, Penguin, 1970. Wartime Diary, 23 August, p. 417.

7. Quoted in THW, 'Notes for J.S.', LHCMA.

8. Noel Thompson in the *Sphere*.

9. Yank Levy, *Guerrilla Warfare*, Penguin, 1941, p. 11.

10. THW, 'The Question of Street Fighting', *Picture Post*, 24 January 1942.

11. THW archive 1; File 7. LHCMA.

12. THW, 'Notes for J.S.', LHCMA.

13. Hopkinson, *Of This Our Time*, p. 179.

14. MacKenzie, *Home Guard*, p. 98.

15. PRO W/O 165/92; Inspectorate Meetings of LDV.

16. PRO WO 199/3237 No. 352.

17. PRO WO 199/3237 No. 400.

18. Letter to George Strauss. THW archive 1; File 34. L-H Lib.

19. PRO T 162/864/E41628/I.

20. Tom Wintringham, *People's War*, Penguin Special edn, 1942, p. 39.

21. THW archive 1; File 34. LHCMA.

22. THW archive 2; File 6. LHCMA.

23. Original in THW archive 2; File 5. LHCMA.

24. Complete account in Large Black Suitcase File 32. LHCMA.

25. Complete account in Large Black Suitcase File 28. LHCMA.

26. Quoted in Peter Clarke, *The Cripps Version; The Life of Sir Stafford Cripps*, Allen Lane, 2002.

27. Account in Hanban Patel, *Cripps Mission – The Whole Truth*, Indus Publishing Co., New Delhi, 1990, p. 64.

28. All sources in THW archive. Large Black Suitcase File 28. LHCMA.

29. *Ibid.*

30. Trevor Royle, *Orde Wingate: Irregular Soldier*, Weidenfeld & Nicolson, 1995, p. 238.

31. Tom Wintringham, *Freedom Is Our Weapon*, Kegan Paul, 1941, pp. 62–3.

32. Liddell Hart/Wintringham correspondence in Liddell Hart File 1/758. LHCMA.

33. Tom Wintringham in *People's War*, p. 26.

34. *Ibid.*, p. 47.

35. *Ibid.*, p. 61.

36. *Ibid.*, p. 96.

Chapter Thirteen

1. *Penguin New Writing*, ed. John Lehmann, 1946, p. 82.

2. T.H. Wintringham, *The Politics of Victory*, George Routledge & Sons, 1941, p. viii.

3. THW archive 1; File 34.LHCMA.

4. THW archive 1; File 26. LHCMA.

5. *The Politics of Victory*, p. 12.

6. *Ibid.*, p. 41.

7. *Ibid.*, p. 43.

8. *Ibid.*, p. 116 fn.

9. *Ibid.*, p. 53.

10. 'Notes on British Politics', THW archive 2; File 5. LHCMA.

11. *The Politics of Victory*, p. 117.

12. *Ibid.*, p. 122.

13. H.G. Wells; quoted in Paul Addison, *The Road to 1945*, Quartet Books, 1977, p. 189.

14. *Ibid.*, p. 154.

15. These and the following quotations are taken from a file labelled 'Morality' by Kitty Wintringham now in the possession of her son, Ben.

16. THW archive 1; File 30. LHCMA.

17. Letter from Sir R. Acland to THW. THW archive 2; File 6. LHCMA.

18. *Ibid.* File 17.

19. Kitty Wintringham's 'Morality' file.

20. R. Acland, *It Must Be Christianity*. CW pamphlet, 'Morality' file.

21. *Ibid.* Letter THW to R. Acland.

22. THW archive 2; File 17. LHCMA.

23. THW archive 1; File 30. LHCMA.

24. 'Morality' file.

25. Quoted in Angus Calder, *The People's War*, Literary Guild, 1969, p. 548.

26. THW, 'Why I Fight Scots By-Election', *Forward* (Glasgow Press), 2 January 1943.

27. 'By-Elections and National Unity', *Left News*, March 1943.

28. THW archive 2; File 6. LHCMA.

29. *Ibid.*

30. THW archive. Larger Black Suitcase File 37. LHCMA.

31. Janelia Slater, letter to David Fernbach, 1978.

32. THW archive. Small Black Suitcase File 26. LHCMA.

33. THW archive. Larger Black Suitcase File 37. LHCMA.

34. Quoted in Kevin Morgan, *Harry Pollitt*, Manchester University Press, 1993, p. 130.

35. Dr K. Sinclair Loutit, letter to David Fernbach.

36. This and the previous quotation are from THW archive. Archive 2; File 17. LHCMA.

37. Report by Negotiating Committee, *ibid.*

38. THW archive 1; File 30. LHCMA.

39. THW archive 1; File 2. LHCMA.

40. Gracchus, *Your M.P.*, Victor Gollancz, 1944, two quotations pp. 39 and 48.

41. THW archive 1; File 2. LHCMA.

42. Aldershot election: THW archive 1; File 24. LHCMA.

43. *Aldershot News*, 6 July 1945.

44. THW archive 1; File 24. LHCMA.

Chapter Fourteen

1. Letter to Prof. L.B. Namier. THW archive 1; File 1. LHCMA.

2. *Tribune*, 'End Piece', 26 August 1949.

3. Letter to Yank Levy, 21 January 1949. THW archive 2; File 24. LHCMA.

4. Letter to O.J., March 1949; THW archive 2; File 24. LHCMA.

5. Cf. *Tribune*, 26 August 1949.

6. Oliver Wintringham, 'Tom Wintringham: a memoir of my father', October 1995. THW archive. LHCMA.

7. Cf. *Tribune*, 26 August 1949.

8. *Reynolds News*, 21 August 1949.

9. THW archive 1; File 13. LHCMA.

10. THW as radio critic. THW archive 1; File 11. LHCMA.

11. *Ibid.*

12. Quoted in Martin Gilbert, *Israel: A history*, Black Swan Publications, 1998, p. 146.

13. Conversation with author.

14. Letter to Prof. L.B. Namier. THW archive 1; File 1. LHCMA.

15. *Ibid.*

16. Letter to Rhys Caparn, 10 September 1949. THW archive 1; File 24. LHCMA.

17. THW archive 2; File 36. LHCMA.

18. THW archive 1; File 35. LHCMA.

19. 'Communist Dilemmas', THW archive 2; File 24. LHCMA.

20. 'Victims of a Frozen Theory', *Picture Post*, 18 March 1950.

21. Notes on 'Socialist Myths'. THW archive 2; File 24. LHCMA.

22. 'Revolt Against Moscow', *Picture Post*, 11 March 1950.

23. G. Orwell; quoted in Thomas Pynchon, 'The Road to 1984', *Guardian Review*, 3 May 2003.

24. Kitty Bowler, letter to Rhys Caparn, 10 September 1949. THW archive. Larger Black Suitcase; File 34. LHCMA.

25. Obituary in *Tribune*, 25 August 1949 and in THW archive. Small Black Suitcase; File 24. LHCMA.

26. Eric Hobsbawm; *Interesting Times: A Twentieth Century Life*, Allen Lane Books, 2002, p. 201.

27. *The Penguin Book of Spanish War Verse*, ed. Valentine Cunningham, Penguin, 1980, pp. 305–7.

Index

Sub-entries are ordered chronologically.

PRAISE FOR
A QUICK TING ON...

'Groundbreaking,' *The Guardian*

'Amazing,' *The Metro*

'Timely and needed,' BBC Radio 5

'Spearheaded by the hugely impressive Magdalene Abraha,
the heartening launch of a phenomenal new series,'
Mellville House

'There is nothing like this,' *The Bookseller*

'What better way to begin Black History Month than with the
announcement of a book series celebrating Black British life?'
Bustle Magazine

'Magdalene Abraha will launch her long-awaited book series,
A Quick Ting On... it's brilliant,' *Elle*

'Exciting,' *Refinery29*

'The first ever non-fiction book of its kind', *The Voice*

'*A Quick Ting On...* is set to be behind some of the most
exciting books.' *Stylist* Magazine

'A game changer,' BBC World Service

'Bringing Black Britishness to the fore,' *The Blacklist*

'How much do you know about plantains? Or Black British
Businesses? Or Afrobeats? If your answer is not enough, that
could soon be rectified,' *Evening Standard*

A QUICK TING ON...
...ABOUT THE SERIES

A Quick Ting On is an idea rooted in archiving all things Black British culture. It is a book series dedicated to Black Britishness and all the ways this identity expands and grows. Each book in the series focuses on a singular topic that is of cultural importance to Black Britishness (and beyond), giving it the sole focus it deserves. The series was inspired by everyday conversations had with Black British folk far and wide, whether that be in WhatsApp group chats, in person, on social media, at parties, barbecues and so on.

    A Quick Ting On is about providing an arena for Black people to archive things that they deem important to them and in turn allowing these explorations to exist long after we are here.

A bundle of joy, learning, nostalgia and home.

Magdalene Abraha FRSA (Mags)
xx

JACARANDA

This edition first published in Great Britain 2024
Jacaranda Books Art Music Ltd
27 Old Gloucester Street,
London WC1N 3AX
www.jacarandabooksartmusic.co.uk

A CIP catalogue record for this book is available from the British
Library

ISBN: 9781913090524
eISBN: 9781913090555

Cover Illustration: Camilla Ru
Cover Design: Baker, bplanb.co.uk
Typeset by: Kamillah Brandes

A QUICK TING ON...

GRIME

FRANKLYN
ADDO

AQ
TO

TABLE OF CONTENTS

PREFACE

Throughout the process of writing this book, the landscape of UK music has continued to evolve as rapidly as the tempo of Grime. The saturation of the streaming era means that the slew of new releases can sometimes even be challenging to keep up with. Though it's no longer the most popular genre of today, many new events have continued to highlight Grime's impact and stunning success since its grassroots origins. Grime got its first Grammy in February 2024; Flowdan and Skrillex's song 'Rumble' won the award for Best Dance/Electronic Recording. Grime's spirit remains discernible today, whether in young MCs' instrumental selection, or in the DIY approach of independent new-gen artists. The genre grew from the ground up in hostile conditions, and has ended up proving instructive. It demonstrated the success that can be achieved on artists' own terms, with gruelling graft, without any external investment. Today, the careers of veteran Grime artists like Skepta and Kano are still fruitful, with forays into fields like fashion and TV.

Such success may seem unlikely given Grime's humble and obscure origins, which are narrated in this book. But commercial performance and mainstream validation are not true barometers of success. Grime's cultural impact is indelible. The genre both reflects and has garnered a committed community.

Before producing such significant profits or attracting widespread accolades, Grime has long been dear to people like me, those of us really from the ends, who can relate to its gritty sound and unflinching attitudes. We intimately understand its culturally specific references. We were fashioned of Grime, in that our tastes were informed by its aesthetic from early on. Grime represented our lives, our social circumstances, our lingo, our style. Grime was our very own proudly homegrown sound, which blossomed into a vibrant scene.

Since Grime was so momentous and foundational, it's only right that it would feature in a book series archiving Black British culture. I was honoured to have been trusted by my peoples Mags, who I went to college with, to write this contribution. I felt equipped for the undertaking because of my lived experience of Grime, my own participation in music, and academic background in Sociology and Cultural Studies. All these factors informed my perspective and approach.

I was born in '93; I was just entering double digits in age by the time Grime had germinated and was settling into its golden era. Although I was still in secondary school and not quite 'outside' when Grime blew up, I lived and loved it all the same. For those who may be unaware of Grime, this book endeavours to communicate the genre's essence, although I fear that mere description ultimately won't suffice. Grime was an experience. You kinda had to be there, still. I do my best nevertheless to distil Grime into some of its core elements and present them in this book. For those of us lucky enough to have grown with Grime, this is a memoir of all its glory. I trust this book will bring to mind fond memories of the golden age of a generational genre.

A Quick Ting On: Grime explores how the genre first came to be, in the transitory period between the late '90s and early

2000s. It emerged in unique circumstances at the turn of the millennium, but Grime is timeless. This book examines the sociopolitical landscape that the genre was incubated in, as well as the musical context that it evolved from. One chapter examines underground sounds like UK Garage and Jungle, which mutated into Grime. Another traces the transition from the analogue age and from platforms like pirate radio into the digital era. The ubiquity of the internet, which may be unremarkable for younger readers, is a far cry from the time when Grime was first born. This book describes how the advent of new digital technologies democratised access to creativity and were critical for Grime's aesthetic and ascent.

Culture chronicles the times. If one listens to Grime lyrics intently, incisive social commentary can be heard in abundance. Although Grime is distinctly, patriotically British, this book acknowledges the context of migration and the African and Caribbean influences which Grime could not exist without. Themes of race and class are necessarily engaged with throughout. Grime is a product of multiculturalism, spearheaded by young Britons from working-class backgrounds. The innovative youngsters behind Grime did not have ready access to the formal entertainment industry. Nevertheless, they resolved to express their truths and share their art with the world. They went on to produce records which are now certified classics.

One of the things that most excites me about this book is its spotlighting of some of the greatest Grime records, from seminal instrumentals, to famous dubs. I encourage readers to get lost in the playlist the prose produces, compiled of all the songs mentioned across the chapters.

Many of us will now forever cherish many of the gems which make up the Grime catalogue. Although Grime is now taken for granted and widely celebrated, it's important to remember that this was a genre that was first rejected by the mainstream. From its inception, Grime was misunderstood, much like the group of people who produced it. In any case, the genre was unstoppable. Grime is a formidable force, whose impact has inspiringly been intergenerational, and extended beyond sound.

I enjoyed writing, for instance, about the style of Grime. Grime's style still informs fashion today, not just in the UK but globally, both on an individual level and in terms of influencing the industry. The aesthetic and attire of Grime are articulated and appreciated within this book. This book also celebrates the enterpreprenurialism of Grime's pioneers, who established a commercial infrastructure to attract attention and investment to a budding scene. Today, British rap music is proving profitable for participants. Grime ascended from grassroots obscurity to become a national treasure, helping to kick down doors and shatter glass ceilings for subsequent subcultures.

This book doesn't claim to be a complete history of Grime. It's c. 50,000 words written from the inevitably subjective perspective of a fan. It's not exhaustive or encyclopaedic, it probably only scratches the surface of such a rich scene. I couldn't possibly have featured every Grime artist or release there's ever been. So if I missed out your favourite MC or record, you're gonna have to allow me. This book is but a contribution to a small but growing canon of literature that commemorates Grime, chiming in alongside the works of Jeffery Boakye, Dan Hancox and Aniefiok Ekpoudom, whose in-depth history of rap is immersive and intimate.

AQTO: Grime is a documentation of what Grime meant on an individual level, a homage to a culture whose impact is enduring. This book is a celebration of the community that Grime came from. It honours the foundational acts and actors of the Grime scene. I hope that those who feature within it are proud to be immortalised in literature. The hope is that this book contributes to the preservation of Grime's history. Our work deserves proper archiving instead of remaining as disparate fragments dispersed across dusty corners of the internet. But this is more than just a work of mere nostalgia.

Grime is not dead; it lives on in the DNA of British music. And Grime is much more than just a music genre. It was a moment, and remains a movement. Grime provided a blueprint for subsequent subcultures to follow. Grime is an essence, an identity. It may sound grandiose, but some of us wouldn't be who or where we are today without Grime's influence. It contributed to our self-esteem at a critical time of coming of age, enabling us to assert our existence and articulate our experiences. Grime compelled some of us to venture along our own creative pathways. When I started making my own music, the first genre I ever experimented with was Grime. Similar to how I learned basic HTML coding and graphic design to customise my Piczo profile, I started producing instrumentals for fun. I emulated my favourite MCs like Kano as I learned to use lyricism to express my own thoughts and feelings.

MY PERSONAL RELATIONSHIP WITH GRIME

NEEDLE DROP: N.A.S.T.Y. CREW, 'TAKE YOU OUT'

Three things that have always been important to me: words, music, and community. Words came first. English was my favourite subject in primary school. I found peace in the stillness that reading requires, and appreciated the art of communicating through language. Music came second, although it was still the writing that drew me in first and foremost.

As much as many are moved by its explosive sound, Grime is a genre which equally embraces lyricism. This is perfect for someone like me, whose brain foregrounds words. I keep a lyrical reference on deck. I really do reflect on artists' words, and retain those which resonate with me. When I interact with others, I amuse myself with my own ability to have whole conversations using just song lyrics.

Anyone who knows me well will know. I've often said only half-jokingly that I might prefer headphones over humans. More time, I'm definitely doubling back home to grab my headphones if I happened to forget them as I left out. I'd probably pick being late wherever over the prospect of going without music for the day.

With age, I've come to appreciate a real range of genres.

I recall first being exposed to Soul songs from groups like En Vogue, or Soul II Soul, whose Britishness surprised me given the scale of their success. I engaged even more with American Rap. I was impressed by Ludacris' flows, and moved by Tupac's conviction. I vibed with Ja Rule's fusion of Hip Hop and R&B, and was amused by Eminem's hyperbolic performances. I started buying copies of albums from the barbershop across the road from my house. Colin, the bossman who owned it, was a bonafide hustler. He diversified his services from offering haircuts and grooming products to selling bootleg CDs and facilitating international money transfers.

The first genre I really became obsessive about was Grime. Perhaps this was a rite of passage, growing up as a young Black boy on an East London council estate. It was around 2004. Dial up internet had just phased out. We were broadband babies; our horizons had been broadened by the internet's boundless possibilities. Outside of first hearing Dizzee Rascal's debut album on CD in 2003, it's hard to pinpoint the exact moment I became aware of Grime. It was just a fact of life. At some stage, it would become basically omnipresent around my peers and I. We found ourselves almost inevitably immersed in it.

Another passion of mine, and pillar of this book, is community. Community has been crucial for Grime. Some artists like Wiley are self-sufficient and can manage their own musical process from production through to release. But Grime has always been a collaborative effort, thriving precisely because of this collective approach. Grime exemplifies the old adage of there being strength in numbers. Grime crews cliqued up, pooling their talents, resources and networks to extend their reach and magnify their impact. Producers, DJs and MCs were all crucial collaborators in the process of making and breaking new riddims, as were promoters, who provided lively spaces for the scene to congregate in.

Indeed, Grime is also consumed largely in community. Raves and clashes channel Grime's eruptive energy. In school playgrounds or on commutes, young people grouped together around Grime music. My bredrins and I excitedly shared early instrumentals and freestyles between our devices. It was Nokias and Sony Ericsons. It was via infrared before bluetooth became popular. We swapped songs in manic group chats on MSN messenger, as well as funny videos, and excerpts of *Keisha Da Sket* (a series of sultry stories which went viral before the term existed). These early experiences of sharing digital content is how instrumentals like Rhythm and Gash by Rebound X have become permanent fixtures in the museum of my memory. We insatiably consumed Grime wherever and whenever we could, whether through downloading dubs onto our PCs, or watching Channel U on Sky TV for hours on end.

Grime soundtracked our youth. MCs became community celebrities, OG influencers long before the Instagram era. A distinguishable culture grew around Grime, which informed how we spoke, dressed and carried ourselves. We connected with Grime aesthetically and attitudinally. Up until today, you're still liable to see me cutting through in a Nike trackie and Black TNs, probably my favourite creps of all time, next to White Air Force 1s. I couldn't tell you when I last wore a hard sole shoe, and I could count on one hand the occasions I've put on a collared shirt. My commitment to comfort and to remaining as authentic as possible in any space I might find myself in was encouraged early on by Grime. COVID is only the most recent reason I roll around masked up. Long before the 2020 pandemic, my head stayed in a hood, just how Grime and the ends had taught me. Anonymity is the preference. The idea is to be inconspicuous, although recently, I'm reluctantly starting to concede that the effect is probably the opposite.

Beyond aesthetic appreciation, I connected with Grime even more deeply when I understood how the music intimately reflected our social circumstances. MCs compellingly described both the mundane aspects of the ends, as well as the more sensational, and sometimes, sinister. Grime often emits a wholesome, youthful energy, with its singalong sensibilities and regular references to video games, for example. At the same time, it can be saturated with depictions of robberies, drug-dealing, and violence, all unfortunate realities which have disproportionately affected relatively impoverished areas like my own, Hackney, or Tower Hamlets, where Grime was born.

I can see how Grime could sound grating and gruesome to the unfamiliar ear. Devoid of context, some songs might alarm some listeners. Apart from being harmonically harsh, Grime is unconcerned with euphemism or etiquette as it openly grapples with the taboo. If Grime's content is unsettling, however, this is but a reflection of the society that it is birthed in. While there may be important internal conversations to be had about artists' responsibility to make thoughtful, progressive work, it's reductive and all but racist to claim that genres like Rap and Grime only glorify violence. Far from being exclusive to our genres, geographies or demographics, violence, drugs and sex have long been themes and features of society and popular entertainment.

There are many examples of substance and sophistication in Grime which are overlooked to focus on its more graphic moments. I recall, for example, having Kano's 'Over and Over' on repeat for quite some time from Winter 2007. The track deserves its title. Instead of thoughtlessly glamorising the streets, Kano on 'Over and Over' presents *knowledge and facts for the youths*', as ever. At a laid back rap tempo of 99 bpm, 'Over and Over' isn't strictly Grime, but the *London Town* album whose tracklist it features on is by all means a product of the scene. Kano sounds listless and disaffected on the tune. His lethargic energy proved relatable. The track embodies a sense of monotony as Kano describes feeling trapped within an empty routine he seems to want to transcend. Kano sounds pensive and philosophical; 'Over and Over' is like a confessional. Kano's references to being sent home from school and feeling conflicted about religion resonated with me as a Year 10 student who was raised in the church. His name dropping of Air Max trainers embolden me to bop in mine with extra conviction. The vivid details about the ambience of sirens and lines about petty crime, police and prisons reflected what I was seeing around me in Hackney as we settled into adolescence. Although the song is not coy in its mentioning of guns, drugs, and doing the dirty doggystyle, 'Over and Over' is a stunning example of Grime's capacity for reflectiveness and insight.

It's also an outstanding example of Grime's sonic range. The production on 'Over and Over' is sombre and stripped back, which confounds Grime's characteristic clamorous style. 'Over and Over' sounds cinematic and is arranged dynamically. One section has calming keys subtly adlibbing in the background. A rich string section is introduced in the second half of the song. There is a dramatic pause of silence at 3 minutes and 22 seconds lasting for two seconds. It's almost like an abrupt, false ending. There are also smooth additional vocals sung by both a male and a female, layered over Kano's solemn raps. The track sounds serene, although it describes some extent of chaos. Almost two decades on and I still have 'Over and Over' in heavy rotation. It's a personal favourite across all genres, and one of the songs I might listen to if I'm contemplating life, yearning for change or growth.

At various moments throughout this book, especially in the final chapter which envisions the future of Black British music, I examine the heightened scrutiny that Grime and its associated genres have been subjected to. I have personal experience of the lack of nuance with which Black art is received. I was 16 when a national tabloid described me as a 'gangster rapper'. Today, I might just embrace such a label, understanding how stereotypes can be satirised and subverted. At the time, I was mainly unimpressed by the misrepresentation of my music. I started reflecting on the potential repercussions of uncritically brandishing all types of art with the same brush. My musical style then was derived from Grime, while my lyrics were influenced by faith and conscious rap. The headlines were almost laughably inaccurate. The racist and classist discourse they generated highlighted to me how Black art forms are dismissed as vulgar and valueless. I learned from experience that Black artists are liable to be ridiculed or vilified for making decisions that don't align with the mainstream.

Today, music is a core component of my work with young people, as well as visual forms of media, and of course, literature. I use all kinds of creativity in spaces like schools and prisons, to engage young people in discussions about their own lives and their society. For me, words, sound and visual art are cathartic and therapeutic, as is the creative process. I know from experience how deeply art can both affect people and reflect their realities. I also advocate against censorship, instead curating safe spaces for young people to write and immerse themselves in creative practice. This work seems all the more important in such a regressive social context, with less and less physical space for communities to come together, and creative courses being scrapped at universities. I've written elsewhere about my work defending against the misuse of rap lyrics in criminal court cases.

It was Grime that first gave me my perspective and set me upon my present pathway. Of course, I could never have known it at the time. Although the young people I work with today are generally only vaguely aware of the millennial genre, its resourceful, rebellious spirit surely lives on. Grime's foundational contribution is certainly cemented. Important lessons can still be derived from its content, and its legacy has lent to genres which have followed. The music I make now is far from Grime, but my wordier style of rap is definitely informed by it, as is my commitment to candour in my content and to community. For me, it's always been about much more than just music or entertainment. Grime spoke to my conscience, and ignited my own creativity.

Personally, I'll forever appreciate Grime for awakening my artistic ambitions, and priming some of my political persuasions before I could more consciously contemplate them. Grime gave me a sense of comfort and camaraderie. Through Grime, I started to understand that the circumstances I was living within and witnessing around me were not necessarily unique. Many of our experiences as young, working class Londoners from diverse ethnic backgrounds were shared. I felt like Grime artists and fellow fans led parallel lives to me, even if I'd never met or spoken with them individually. Grime provided a platform for expression and a channel of communication for a demographic otherwise unheard and unrepresented. It told me early on that my voice mattered, that what I may have to say deserves to be heeded, that exactly how I might be inclined to communicate something may be exactly the way that someone somewhere needs to receive it. Long live Grime, then, in spirit and within the hearts of people like myself if not within the fickle, money-hungry music industry.

277 TO LEAMOUTH

NEEDLE DROP: DIZZEE RASCAL, 'CUT 'EM OFF'

———————————

'*My name is Raskit, listen to my flow,*' declares Grime pioneer Dizzee Rascal on his song 'Cut 'Em Off'. His voice has not yet shed altogether the higher frequencies of adolescence. 'Cut 'Em Off' is track 7 on his debut album, *Boy In Da Corner*. Released in July 2003 by XL recordings, the 15 track album would be a commercial success and garner critical acclaim. Almost entirely produced by Dizzee, *Boy In Da Corner* stands as a seminal moment in both Dizzee's career and the evolution of Grime music as a whole. More than two decades since its release, the record is hailed as a bona fide classic in the rich archive of British music. Its influence and impact is so pervasive, that Dizzee Rascal has occasionally voiced frustration with the nation's fixation on his historical work.

It is rare for a body of work to be so enduringly celebrated by audiences that it merits a live performance of every track, decades after its release. Yet the excellence and success of *Boy In Da Corner* is such that Dizzee Rascal has been able to perform the record in full not only in London at the Copper Box Arena, but also in New York, a city where British music traditionally garners less attention.

It remains remarkable that Dizzee Rascal was just about

17 years old when he produced and recorded the bulk of the songs that would constitute the album. Although his tender age is apparent upon listening, the breakthrough MC delivers his lyrics with a reflective passion beyond his years. The album would come to be widely analysed as an incisive and vital piece of social commentary, a raw reflection of the challenges of inner-city life.

I was just about to enter secondary school when I received the *Boy In Da Corner* CD as a gift from my older sister, Cella. Cella loved music; she sang in her school's choir and avidly listened to everything from Gospel and old school Soul to R&B and Rap. Albums like Beverley Knight's *Who I Am* and Nas' *God's Son* are examples of the staples that could be heard blaring through our house at any given time. Also on Cella's palate were the rapidly mutating sounds of the UK underground, freshly ripped from pirate radio sets and recorded onto tapes and minidiscs. A 7-year age gap meant that I was too young to accompany her to the raves where UK Garage reigned. Instead, I lived vicariously through my big sister, inheriting and fusing some of her music tastes with my own. With its spacey synthesis and pulsing bass, UK Garage classics like Sia's *Little Man* would become some of my forever faves. The arrival of Grime as a genre, however, would prove transformative for my generation.

'*I socialise in Hackney and Bow,*' Dizzee continues to rap on 'Cut 'Em Off'; his voice unsettlingly shrill, his delivery animated and authoritative. Much of the rich history of Grime music is rooted in the post-industrial valleys of East London. While the widespread recognition the genre would eventually achieve owes to contributions from across the capital and wider country, it is the inner-city enclaves like Bow and Stratford in boroughs like Newham in Tower Hamlets that are especially central to Grime's story.

The Hackney secondary school I attended in the early 2000s neighboured the housing estates that Grime figureheads like Dizzee Rascal and Wiley traversed. Growing up, I was blissfully ignorant of my local area's notorious reputation as a deprived hot-spot for crime. Before my beloved borough became the coveted zone-2 location it is romanticised as today, it was considered by many as an area to be avoided. For me, though, Hackney was always just home—and ain't no place like Home Sweet Home.

Long before the area would become infamous, and nightclubs like Palace Pavilion emerged along what became known as the 'murder mile', neighbourhoods like Clapton and Mare Street were once the favoured residences of monied elites and the political class. They settled in grand dwellings. Sutton House on Homerton High Street stands as the oldest surviving example. Built in 1535 by a colleague of Edward VIII, the impressive manor house once hosted diplomats before becoming home to a succession of merchants and church clergy.

Today, Sutton House is a Grade II listed building owned by the National Trust. While concrete is all I have known, the building's brickwork at the time of its construction would have been an extraordinary display of wealth and status compared with the feebler wattle and daub homes which were common. Despite being built of similarly sturdy materials, and situated just a short walk from each other, the scale and grandeur of the private, 3-storey Sutton House is incomparable to the humble public housing estate I was raised on.

Hackney continued to become more populous over time, with areas like Kingsland and Dalston Lane being among the first to develop. The region grew into a bustling hub of manufacturing and commerce with the industrialisation of the 19th century. In 1872, train stations were built by Great Eastern

Railway in locations like Stoke Newington, Cambridge Heath and London Fields, where Hackney's leather and shoe factories flourished. The furniture district, meanwhile, was based nearby in South Shoreditch. Economic migrants flocked seeking financial opportunity, diversifying the demography of the East End. Abundance and deprivation would, for a time, live side-by-side, per the inevitably unequal and unsustainable advancement of capitalism.

By the arrival of the 20th century, East London was more definitively working-class. London's overall population had surged at an unprecedented rate, leaving the city's infrastructure unprepared for such rapid growth. The housing situation became desperate; destitute individuals and families seeking affordable accommodation found themselves living in impoverished pockets of town, so-called slums, where disease was rampant, and both infant mortality and crime rates were high.

Similar circumstances befell increasingly urban areas across the country. Profiteering landlords left properties in states of dangerous disrepair. Some slums were makeshift shanty towns, whose shaky buildings had no drainage systems and were liable to fatally collapse. Others featured unsanitary tenements crammed with as many people as physically possible.

By the end of the Victorian era, the landscape and character of the East End of London had transformed. The earliest settlers in rural Hackney were attracted to the fresh air and spring waters of the marshland. The fresh air and spring water of old gave way to a distinct 20th century griminess as clouds of industrial pollution enshrouded the capital. The changing times are as ever archived in cultural artefacts like literature. Dickensian portrayals of slum squalor illustrate the abject poverty and crime that plagued areas like Bethnal Green, contrasting the images of monarchic opulence commonly associated with England. The stunning, spacious homes that surround Victoria Park today are a far cry from the grim realities of the workhouses that once operated nearby, where labourers were paid poverty wages to perform gruelling tasks.

Today, Hackney is well-known for its ethnic diversity, with records of Black residents dating back to 1630. It was key 20th century events, however, like World War II and the 1948 arrival of the HMS Windrush at Tilbury docks which significantly accelerated the transformation of the UK's cities into the cosmopolitan melting pots they are today. After the war, former constituents of the British Empire were invited to England to help rebuild the country and address labour short-ages in the NHS and public transportation. Migrants arriving in Britain from the Caribbean throughout the '70s and '80s found employment at companies like Tate & Lyle which oper-ated by East London's docklands, or Ford, whose cars were produced at a factory in Dagenham.

By the time I was born in the early '90s, Hackney had already become home to substantial communities from the Black diaspora so much so that I never truly felt like an ethnic minority during my childhood. It wasn't until ventured further out into the world that I realised how culturally specific my upbringing had been. I recall regularly being dragged along for example to Dalston Market with my mother to buy West African food produce. These Saturday morning pilgrimages were often met by my reluctance then, however wiser and older, I no longer take for granted the luxury of plantain being available for purchase nearby. Ridley Road memories are embedded within my brain's grey matter—the bellowing voices of sellers trying to attract custom; the hustle and bustle of the crowds meandering from stall to stall. My recollections are vivid and embodied—the pungent smell of meat and fish at the butchers; the vibrant reds and yellows of bell peppers and scotch bonnets.

While the ornate, semi-detached Victorian townhouses of the De Beauvoir area near Dalston starkly contrast the modest simplicity of the council flats where many of my peers and I were raised, as a child I was largely unaware of my working-class status. This blissful ignorance of race and class was both a product privilege and the enchantment of youth. Young people often have little to compare their experiences to; one may not challenge their circumstances if they've known and can envision no alternative. Yet, the boundless imagination of youth remains untethered. Unburdened by the cautious pragmatism required by adulthood, young people are freer to dream and explore fearlessly. This visceral, youthful energy not only helped give birth to Grime but also made the genre unforgettable for those of us who had the privilege of growing up alongside it.

Songs from albums like *Boy In Da Corner* profoundly shaped my musical sensibilities. I played the album repeatedly on my Sony Walkman, which would whir and stutter mechanically, as if it was working hard to deliver sound. Admittedly, the explicit content of Dizzee's now seminal album may not have been age-appropriate for my consumption at barely 11 years old. The naivety of youth meant that any profanity in the music was as lost on me as were its poignant and at times political themes. It was not until later years that I would grow to appreciate Dizzee's insightful musings. From tackling issues of heavy-handed policing and the use of violence right through to illustrating societal inequalities—Raskit's songs broached it all.

Even as a youngster, I recognised my copy of *Boy In Da Corner* as one of the most meaningful presents I'd ever received, and cherished it as such. It felt important to have a physical product that prominently featured someone like me—not just a young Black man, but one with whom I seemed to share cultural and contextual affinity. The album's artwork, designed by Ben Drury and photographed on film by Dean Chalkley, features a grayscale image of a young Dizzee Rascal sitting in the bottom right of the composition. Digital photography had not yet proliferated by this time. The monochrome portraiture contrasts with the cover's luminous yellow background which demands attention and gives a sense of danger and urgency. In the photo, Dizzee is dressed in a loose-fitted Nike tracksuit with Air Max BW trainers, sporting a stern screw-face, all of which were staples in my own teenage wardrobe.

The sharp geometric lines and bold, angular typeface on the album's front cover align with the brutalist style of architecture common in social housing estates of the era. The inharmonious sound of Dizzee's songs and his tongue-in-cheek, provocative lyrics were influenced by the aesthetic and social context of his urban environment. A single listen to the classic album makes it clear how Dizzee's artistry was inspired by his surroundings. Like Tinchy Stryder, the frontman of prominent Grime crew Ruff Sqwad, Dizzee Rascal also grew up on a Tower Hamlets estate called the Crossways. Erected in the '70s, the Crossways estate was locally nicknamed 'the pride of Bow', or 'the 3 flats' because the development is formed mainly of 3 tower blocks. Each looms 25 storeys high. Consisting mostly of 3 bedroom, family-sized units, the estate provides a total of 298 homes. Such was the dense populousness of a rapidly evolving London.

Hearing Dizzee Rascal mention specific East London areas in his tracks might not resonate with someone unfamiliar with the local area. But, for those of us familiar with bus routes like the D6 and the 277, which run from Hackney locations like Mare Street and Dalston Junction through Mile

End and Canary Wharf, to the Isle of Dogs—these references meant everything. For those of us also inclined to 'buss low batties', a term used to describe the fashion of wearing trousers *'ridiculously low'* as Dizzee narrates in 'Cut 'Em Off', it was particularly special to hear our culture, fashion, and lifestyle so accurately depicted in music.

Grime provided an indisputable and presiding soundscape for my demographic. We'd all been bedazzled by the global appeal of American celebrities like 50 Cent, whose 2003 smash hit 'In da Club' entered the running as one of the top 3 most popular birthday songs of all time (alongside the traditional 'Happy Birthday' song and Stevie Wonder's more soulful rendition). 50 Cent's allure was irresistible; his rags to riches tale and branding as an invincible gangster as depicted in the *Get Rich or Die Tryin'* blockbuster captured imaginations far and wide. Although the significance and influence of such US rappers were clear, the personal connection we could forge with them was always limited. They spoke ultimately to a different context not directly translatable to ours. They were of a different geography and generation; they talked and dressed differently; the Hollywood scale of their success seemed out of reach to those of us across the pond.

Before rappers like 50 Cent became international icons, many of us had sung along at family gatherings and in our primary school playgrounds to UK Classics from 'Wannabe' by The Spice Girls, 'Flowers' by Sweet Female Attitude and '21 seconds' by So Solid Crew. The impact of these homegrown hits was intergenerational; they transcended demographics to leave an unerasable mark on the landscape of British music. The pop appeal and summery romanticism of songs like 'Wannabe' and 'Flowers' did not resonate with the long, wet winters ahead, however, nor the volatility of the years we were entering.

So Solid Crew's grittier aesthetic and content connected more, as they reflected the experience of navigating society as young, Black, working-class Londoners. We recognised ourselves in them; they looked like us, moved like us, sounded like us. They described circumstances we could relate to, using language we intimately understood. Even So Solid Crew's music was not completely without its Americanisms, though, and their aspirational bars about 'ice', 'dough' and whipping Audi TTs felt out of reach to so many of us still living in deprivation.

Against the backdrop of the Conservative government's 18-year reign, before Labour leader Tony Blair would enter Downing Street, the full, unabashed representation of our experiences in the UK had not yet fully emerged on the public stage. The Grime generation changed this. Compared to their predecessors, they were even more decidedly anti-establishment, eschewing convention to unapologetically express their unique perspectives. Certified Grime anthems like Lethal B's 'Pow!' for instance expose an intensifying angst among the inner-city's youth. Grime grew raw and unrefined from the concrete. Its early artists chose absolute authenticity over commercial aspiration. The cockney diction of an MC like Bruza, for instance, is unmistakably British.

With their use of familiar colloquialisms, and regular references to familiar fashion accessories like New Era caps and Nike trainers, Grime MCs reflected our culture and described our social experiences. They emerged as the unapologetic spokespersons of our community and heroes of a generation. Grime confounded the existing order of the music industry, embracing abstraction, with its manic drum patterns, growling basslines and warping pads. Its urgent, racing tempo better reflected the frenzied pace of the capital compared with the leisureliness of the Garage era before it.

The restlessness that Grime channelled mirrored the restlessness within me as a teenager, growing up as part of an antisocial generation at the turn of the millennium. This was a period marked by exponential social and technological evolution. Grime was the explosive musical score for our layered experiences whilst coming of age in the endz amid societal uncertainty.

To get to school when I was in Years 7 and 8, I'd bop to the bus stop opposite Hackney Town Hall to board the 277 which terminated at Leamouth. Although we were sweet at heart, my friends and I were at times irreverent and inconsiderate, sometimes disturbing the peace by blasting music from the back of the bus. Our early morning energy undoubtedly irritated some of the corporate commuters we shared public transport with, fueled surely by the copious amounts of glucose in our diets. Some of us stopped by Greggs in the mornings for Tottenham Cakes or Yum Yums. Others bought the signature glazed donut from the much-loved but now defunct East London bakery chain, Percy Ingle, or cookies from the Tescos on Morning Lane or on Well Street. Alternatively, you could grab sugary sweets from the playground tuck shop, or wait until lunchtime to claim a free school meal, if eligible. It was always a delight to be told by a dinner lady that your favourite cake and custard was on the day's menu for pudding. Despite Jamie Oliver's campaigns to make school dinners healthier, nothing could deter us from indulging in baked treats for breakfast, scoffing penny sweets, sherbets, and Freddos from the local corner shop, and washing it all down with a sweet can of KA before our first lesson even began.

Journeys home from school were even more eventful, and rarely direct. Rather than heading straight to our houses, we'd often loiter around the neighbourhood in our friendship groups. With leftover lunch money, or cash earned from playground scrambles or the early entrepreneurial venture of reselling confectionery to fellow students from multipacks at inflated prices, we'd indulge in chicken wings and chips from local favourites like Dixy's or Sam's Chicken. £2 could get you a whole feast. If you were a regular customer, or polite and personable when ordering, bossman might nice you with an extra piece of chicken free of charge. We'd smother our greasy meals in ketchup, mayonnaise and burger sauce, intermittently taking big swigs from cans of Mirinda.

With few options for indoor spaces to congregate, some of us visited local libraries, accessing the internet to play computer games or watch music videos on YouTube. Others would pass by other schools like Hackney Free or Our Lady's to visit friends or fraternise with girls. Some schools started stationing teachers around their buildings at hometime to discourage students from lingering. But even this adult vigilance could not safeguard us from the realities of our neighbourhoods outside of school.

The innocence of early pubescence would at some point diminish. The shops we once frequented now only allowed two young people in at any one time for fear of theft. Issues like phone robberies became more rife and the general threat of violence from our peers increased; Grime reflected on the realities of life in such shifting social conditions.

'You never got jacked just because your phone's crap,' Vortex spits on 'On the Block', a classic Grime dub featuring a packed line up of MCs.

'Sometimes I jack bres but I hate it when it's just keys and a bus pass,' raps a young Ice Kid in a famous 2007 freestyle on BBC Radio alongside Chipmunk.

Grime lyrics trace the transition from the blissful innocence of childhood into the turbulence of inner-city adolescence and young adulthood.

As Grime became the defining sound of our generation, we connected deeply with the genre and its creators. Grime itself was a conduit for relationships, with kinship formed over shared appreciation for the music or jovial divisions created along lines of allegiance towards different Grime artists or crews. Instead of paying attention in Geography, I had long Grime debates with my classmate Muyiwa. I thought Wretch 32 was the best in The Movement; Muyiwa was a massive Scorcher fan. Our spirited discussions certainly frustrated our teacher, Mr. Crotty, but Grime was far more captivating to us than sedimentary rocks. The 277 bus was also my commute for my Year 10 work experience in Canary Wharf. I'd absorb the wisdom of Wretch 32's *Learn From My Mixtape* on the upper deck, finding more inspiration in his insightful lyrics than in a conventional 9-5 job. On eventually getting home from school, my peers and I would rush to download new Grime songs on Limewire. This legendary software allowed us to freely access and store all kinds of media on our devices. We'd excitedly share Grime mp3s with each other on MSN messenger, or fiddle with HTML and CSS codes to embed them on our MySpace profiles. We'd spend evenings watching the latest videos on YouTube channels like SBTV, or on Channel U. Established in 2003, and viewable through Sky digital, Channel U pivotally provided a window into the Grime scene. For the first time, it afforded British urban acts the opportunity to have their music videos broadcast on TV.

Radio was by this point outgoing, but not completely history. Many of us stayed awake each week into the early hours of Tuesday morning as we locked in to DJ Logan Sama's Monday night Grime show on Kiss FM, where our favourite MCs passed through to spray new bars live or debut new tracks. It didn't matter if we were tired at school the next day. Keeping up with the latest in the Grime scene was the priority. Sleep meanwhile could be caught up on at any time—during lessons if necessary.

The influence of Grime became simply inescapable. Its slang at once mirrored and shaped the way we spoke. We used terms like 'nang' to describe things we thought were cool, 'peng' to refer to someone being attractive, and 'par' to describe an interaction or situation in which we felt slighted. When it was Own Clothes day at school, we dressed according to trends popularised by Grime. We wore tracksuits and colour coordinated outfits. We completed our ensembles with accessories like baseball caps and headbands, as seen on our favourite artists.. Many of us, inspired by Grime MCs, adopted tag names, using these instead of our given names.

We assembled local crews. Some of us were inspired to try writing our own lyrics. My bredrin Richard for example wrote a 16 that always got us gassed:

'...Heads, shoulders, knees and toes, knees and toes
It's Panik, that top boy from N1 that everybody knows.'

Grime often appropriated melodies from well-known songs or nursery rhymes, which contributed to its singalong, participatory appeal. Of course, not all of us would try to MC. Some of us became budding producers instead. We emulated our idols by getting our hands on cracked versions of production softwares like Reason or Fruity Loops. We spent countless hours with our eyes glued to our computer screens as we eagerly experimented with sound. FL Studio's user-friendly interface for instance made music production feel more like an engaging game than a strenuous technical endeavour. There is such satisfaction to be found in the process of translating an idea from one's mind into tangible creative output that can be enjoyed by others. Like the pioneers of the Grime era, we focused on creating beats, often overlooking technical processes like mixing or mastering. We rolled around listening to our own creations, feeling inspired by and proud of our own abilities.

Whether or not one was moved to more actively participate in Grime culture by crafting their own lyrics or producing beats,, the genre's cultural impact of the genre was felt far and wide. At various points, the future of Grime seemed uncertain amid attempts to censor its alleged glorification of violence and sanitise its consumption. Nevertheless, Grime's unrefined, confrontational, essence persisted, leaving an undeniable mark on British culture.

3

I DON'T CARE ABOUT GARAGE

NEEDLE DROP: AMIRA, 'MY DESIRE (DREEM TEAM REMIX)'

In December 2000, So Solid Crew joined the esteemed list of performers on *Top of the Pops*. The UK Garage group delivered an electrifying performance of their hit single 'Oh No (Sentimental Things)'. Quintessentially British, and a key arbiter of the mainstream, *Top of the Pops* was a popular music show on the BBC, broadcast between 1964 and 2006. At its peak, the TV programme garnered a viewership of 19 million people. Featuring performances based on UK chart music, the show hosted the hottest international music acts, showcasing their biggest songs. So Solid Crew's smash hit '21 seconds' earned them a second invitation to *Top of the Pops* in 2001. In contrast to pop acts like Ronan Keating and Wheatus who also appeared on the programme around this time, the South London posse seem unlikely candidates for such primetime placement.

By the time So Solid Crew rose to prominence, UK Garage had already started to generate significant buzz. Just before the turn of the millennium, acts like DJ Luck & MC Neat had introduced mainstream audiences to the genre with their Top 10 single, 'A Little Bit of Luck'. Oxide and Neutrino also enjoyed success with 'Bound 4 Da Reload' in 2000. The Caribbean diction audible on both of these songs highlight the influence of the Black diaspora on British culture, a testament to rich histories of migration in the UK. 'Bound 4 Da Reload' was particularly pivotal, reaching the top of the Official UK Singles Chart. It drew from a range of influences, notably sampling the theme music from the BBC's medical drama series *Casualty*. Aside from pointing to a cultural cross-pollination that would increasingly be seen in British art as a consequence of multiculturalism, 'Bound 4 Da Reload' marks a decisive moment in the evolution of the UK Garage sound into a more muted, experimental style.

Traditionally, Garage had been brighter in sound and sentiment. UK Garage, a cousin to the US genre of the same name, emerged from subcultures like Chicago House music and featured straight 4x4 drum patterns instead of the complex breakbeats which came to typify British output. With limited access to instrumentalists and vocalists, UK Garage productions primarily relied on samples, especially those of American singers. The smooth vocals and funky basslines of early Garage tunes were wholesome, as was the so-called Sunday Scene where such sounds started to thrive.

Apart from the Elephant and Castle based club Ministry of Sound, whose Saturday events were a staple of London's nightlife, there were few alternative venues in the early '90s for experiencing music beyond the chart-toppers. To fill this gap, passionate promoters began organising their own smaller parties. These independently organised events typically took place on Sundays, in daytime hours, in peripheral venues like small, South-East London pubs. This so-called Sunday scene quickly became a key site of underground culture as the growing range of DJs and performers platformed attracted larger, ever more diverse audiences.

Located more centrally, in Leicester square, The Gass Club launched an event that championed underground Garage music emerging throughout the city. These events served as incubators for musical experimentation and evolution. DJs kept the crowds energised, playing records at faster speeds or altering pitches in unexpected mixes to create a dynamic atmosphere. The club began to attract a diverse array of attendees, from ordinary revellers and music lovers with day jobs to celebrity patrons, including musicians and footballers. Even when the gangsters of the illegal economy began frequenting these events, spending their dubiously earned cash, the convergence of crowds remained convivial. People from various walks of life coexisted harmoniously, united by their shared love of music.

Where DJs had previously been more like song selectors, playing records relatively uninterrupted, they began to increasingly manipulate and mix tracks together at these new UK Garage events. The clean, polished sound first inherited from the US soon evolved as DJs continued to innovate and producers switched up the style further. There was a departure from predictable loops and traditional song structures towards glitchier, more fragmented drum patterns, and abstract melodies. The extensive, interconnected genealogy of this increasingly experimental music implicated styles ranging from Disco, Dance, and House to Jungle and Drum and Bass. Mid-'90s releases like Todd Edwards's 'Steal Your Heart' gave way to bouncier, bassier numbers like the Artful Dodger's 1997 dub edit of Tina Moore's 'Never Gonna Let You Go'. Chart success became more common as Garage definitively crossed over into pop territory.

Foundational MCs like Creed began being platformed alongside DJs, introducing a new dynamism to events by acting as their hosts, captivatingly rhyming along to DJs' selections. Born Christopher Reed, MC Creed is a UK Garage veteran who was among the early pioneers credited with propelling the genre into the mainstream. His stuttering vocals and animated sound effects would become iconic across generations. Regularly appearing at The Gass Club early in his career, Creed along with other acts like DJ EZ and MC Kie attracted large crowds to comparable nights at club venues like Colosseum, Liberty and the ECI which refreshed London's nightlife landscape. UK Garage culture continued to spread; the genre soon reached cities like Birmingham, Sheffield and Leeds, before being exported to holiday destinations like Ayia Napa where it soundtracked the hedonistic indulgence of party pilgrims. The rest, as they say, is history.

Opportunities opened up for budding DJs and producers, while more MCs began pioneering fresh styles. Between the late '90s and early 2000s, crews like Heartless and Pay As U Go started to generate serious buzz. Events such as Garage Nation, Exposure, and Sun City routinely sold out within minutes of ticket releases. UK Garage also began getting airplay on radio stations like Kiss 100 in the years leading up to the new millennium. In 2000, British DJ and production trio the Dreem Teem joined BBC Radio 1, representing UK Garage. Soon after, the mainstream machine began churning out Garage hits at an unprecedented rate, with major labels both domestically and in the US, commissioning UK producers to remix songs.

Amid the shiny commercialism of the increasingly mainstream UK Garage scene, a rawer undercurrent in electronic music emerged, characterised by a generally more abrasive and boldly

British sound. Described as 'deliciously dark' in a YouTube comment, Groove Chronicles's skippy 'Millennium Funk', released in 2000, exemplifies this trend and sound. During this period, producers like Wookie pivoted from producing Hip Hop and R&B for British acts like Soul II Soul and Lamar to creating racier, more bottom-heavy music which married Drum n' Bass with Garage elements. Played in sets alongside records like Monsta Boy's 'Sorry (I Didn't Know)', Wookie's 'Back up to Me' and 'Battle' are two classic examples of his melodic and rhythmic experimentations in the 125-130bpm range. Such songs reflect the tugging of UK Garage towards a gloomier aesthetic, in parallel with worsening social conditions. Song structures became less conventional as producers premised their songs with intricate, extended drum intros before climactic drops.

The evolution continued. MCing became more central to the scene; mic men like Asher D and Romeo from So Solid Crew took the baton from foundational forerunners like MC Creed and Viper. The realities reflected in the music produced by the newer generation was different to the happy-go-lucky, romanticised content that had saturated Garage up until then. On tracks like 'Envy', also known as 'They Don't Know' per the title of their debut album, So Solid Crew observe how some ravers seemed to prefer to watch face, *'stand and screw,'* mean-mugging each other rather than enjoying themselves to the music. Ms. Dynamite's mesmerising melodies on the song's intro strikingly contrast the prospect of physical violence raised in her lyrics.

The established institutions of UK Garage opposed this new musical moodiness and desperately resisted the looming cultural shift. Those of the old guard felt that musings about street life, regardless of their relevance to lived realities, were misplaced in music. The fact that the entertainment industry did not at first accept this darker, more pensive music makes So Solid's success all the more impressive. While Wookie's records like 'Battle' retained a warmth and maturity with their emphasis on melody and uplifting lyrics, they were more muted and experimental in production compared to earlier UK Garage tunes. So Solid Crew, meanwhile, were a dense mob of youngsters, rapping about being tougher than lead and telling their testers to kiss their asses on primetime TV. In their second *Top of the Pops* appearance in 2001, the group performed their hit single '21 seconds', brazenly rapping lyrics about avoiding feds, smoking trees and worshipping the devil live on BBC1.

So Solid Crew began facing criticism and protests similar to those experienced by Oxide and Neutrino. Their chart-topping hit 'Bound 4 Da Reload' was initially banned from many mainstream radio stations for allegedly glorifying violence. It was not until pirate support eventually snowballed into a play on Kiss that the track took off more widely. Aside from the very name of the song being misinterpreted as referring to ammunition, its inclusion of gunshot sound effects and a skit which refers to a shooting also contributed to its hostile reception. The skit samples dialogue from British director Guy Ritchie's 1998 film *Lock, Stock and Two Smoking Barrels*; the voices belong to actors Tony McMahon and Frank Harper. This highlights a double standard where the vivid portrayals of gangsterism in Ritchie's film were celebrated, whereas Oxide & Neutrino's track was treated as ominous and subjected to censorship. While Ritchie's films are embraced as British, the multicultural influences audible on 'Bound 4 Da Reload' were met with discomfort among traditional audiences. The song pointed to something of a cultural revolution taking place on the youthful streets of London, where Caribbean and West African diction and forms of expression were increasingly integrated into everyday language. This hybridised style of communication felt foreign, impenetrable and 'improper' to the mainstream, as did the sportier attire worn by the young people involved in the underground UK music scene. The sleek, tidy clothing once common within UK Garage night-life was gradually replaced by sportier, more casual styles of dressing, which were unwelcome in the West End clubs where the genre had reigned strong prior.

A series of unfortunate events exacerbated the negative reception of the evolving UK Garage scene, and was used as a justification for heavy policing. In May 2001, Neutrino sustained a gunshot wound to his calf outside the Velvet Room nightclub in Soho during an attempted mugging. Six months later, a double shooting occurred at MC Romeo's birthday party, leading to the cancellation of So Solid Crew's entire British tour amid safety concerns, despite the group's noninvolvement in the incident. The following year, 19 year old So Solid Crew member Ashley Walters would be arrested for firearm possession. Although these moments of violence were not negligible, they were, in the grand scheme, exceptions rather than the norm. Just as football events aren't alto-gether cancelled because of a few eruptions of hooliganism, these relatively anomalous incidents that transpired at some UK Garage nights should not have been allowed to tarnish the standing of the genre as a whole.

Much to the detriment of Oxide and Neutrino, and the ultimate destruction of So Solid Crew, venue owners and club night promoters joined radio stations in prohibiting this newer, edgier music from being played at events, in efforts to repel the more boisterous, inner-city demographic they believed it would invite. Police began refusing licences to events at which they or comparable acts were scheduled to appear. This marginalisation endured for years, frustrating the ambitions of many aspiring artists influenced by the more experimental electronic music sweeping the city.

The cultural shifts as described above contributed to the rejection of Grime from the established spaces of UK Garage. Concerns that the existing musical order might be overshadowed by the new sounds of Grime also fueled this rejection, It became clear that the newly developing music of the underground was not going to be welcomed by the presiding powers. The young artists and the rapidly growing fan base were disregarded as too uncouth and boisterous.

So the disregard became mutual. Although UK Garage was the preeminent sound at the time, it was by no means the single or even the main influence for this new generation of artists. Histories of migration meant that artists were raised in their households on genres like Reggae and Dub, which all bled into UK Garage. Jungle tunes like UK Apache and Shy FX's 'Original Nuttah' illustrate the art of MCing and have informed the uncontainable energy of Grime. Veteran MCs including Wiley and D Double E have long cited Jungle as being more formative to their artistry and careers than Garage. The skippiness of Wiley's formative 'Eskimo' instrumental for example is distinct from the traditional glide of UK Garage; its thudding bass owes more to histories of sound system culture. Instrumentals like 'Pulse X' released by West London Crew Musical Mob were also early indicators of how skeletal and brutalist British music would soon become, compared with the glide and harmoniousness of UK Garage. Despite its simplicity, 'Pulse X' was revolutionary—a minimalistic, 16-bar loop consisting of swinging drums, a powerful bassline, and a brief vocal tag that marked it as a Musical Mob release.

'I don't care about Garage', Wiley famously spat on 'Wot Do U Call It', his first official studio single from his debut album in 2004. He'd previously been part of the UK Garage Crew Pay As U Go, but now fronted his own, which he called Roll Deep in reference to its large membership. Renowned today for selflessly platforming new talent, Wiley recruited a mammoth roster of producers and MCs to his team. Per the competitive spirit inherent within Grime, Wiley wanted Roll Deep to become the preeminent Grime crew, selling the most dubplates and securing the most bookings for raves.

On 'Wot Do U Call It', Wiley describes his determination to create his own musical style and infrastructure outside of an exclusionary entertainment industry. He felt he didn't really belong within the UK Garage scene, believing his versatile output could not be confined to the more generic releases of the time. He continued to experiment musically, independently producing, recording, and releasing his own records on the underground circuit. He acted according to his own creative impulses instead of conforming to the commercial demands of the established industry. Wiley's boundless creativity and relentless, DIY work ethic inspired a generation of artists to pursue similarly enterprising paths.

'Wot Do U Call It' traces the splintering of UK Garage into its less definable offshoots. During this period, the production of underground electronic music ventured further into unconventional territory , with erratically placed snares and percussive elements driving unlikely melodies. Early on, no agreement could be reached on a name to collectively describe what would be called Grime. The sounds were still too emergent and disparate. 'Sub-low', some commentators would suggest, due to the rumbling, bass-heavy character of so many of the tunes. Others would adopt '2-step' as an umbrella title, as rhythms often deviated from the traditional four-to-the-floor pattern of earlier Garage. Some would lazily group these new sounds together as 'Urban', in lazy reference to the concrete, inner-city environment they emerged from.

Wiley personally dubbed his style Eski-beat, or the Eskimo sound and referred to himself as the Eski-boy. Song titles like 'Ice Rink', 'Igloo', and 'Treddin' on Thin Ice' reflect his use of glacial metaphors to describe a certain coldness in his music compared to the soulful, melodic warmth of UK Garage. The muddy lower frequencies and icy synths that characterised this new sound seemed somehow apt for London's dreary climate. It better reflected social realities like widening inequality and high rates of unemployment, addiction and teenage preg-nancy, as well the mood of young artists like Wiley navigating these challenges alongside personal and familial issues.

As personal computers became more affordable and production software more accessible—even through illicit means—young people increasingly experimented with music for leisure. This helped democratise access to creativity. Inspiration spread,and the sonic landscape continued to shift. Producers like DJ Target from Roll Deep and Prince Rapid of Ruff Sqwad were prolific; their creations would help shape a new sound and be remembered as classics.

The music got faster and the vocalists' delivery more intense. Typically in the ballpark of 140 beats per minute, Grime is rapid and urgent, guided by syncopated drums and disjointed breakbeats of all configurations. The name Grime is said to have come about from a journalist's description of the grunginess characterising London's new sound. Indeed, much of the early Grime output was created on entry level equipment in informal spaces, such as youth clubs, bedrooms and classrooms, rather than professional music studios. The first Grime tunes were bounced to audio and released without even being mixed down, lending the genre a distinct grit and edge. The crackles and pops of peaking audio underscore how Grime pushed the boundaries of creativity, daring to explore the extremities of sonic possibility. Grime's sound is defined by thick, booming bass lines and midrange frequencies filled with warping pads and synthesised leads. These abstract, alien sounds and digitally simulated instruments contrasted the more conventional musicality and joyous gloss of UK Garage, marking Grime as a bold and innovative departure from its musical predecessor.

If the mainstream gatekeepers had been shocked by So Solid Crew, they were to be flabbergasted by the new generation of Grime MCs, who were more decidedly anti-social and angsty. Unlike So Solid's tracks which featured shimmery, memorable choruses, often sung by crew member Lisa Maffia, the newer Grime songs neglected such elements. Maffia's hook on 'Oh No' for instance reflects on *the sentimental things in life* with a cheerful melody that almost makes it feel like a South London interpretation of Annie's 'It's the Hard Knock Life'.

While So Solid's rudeboy energy may have been perceived as risque by an uptight, mainstream audience, 'Oh No' is actually just a party tune, one which, true to UK Garage tradition bigs up the ladies, invites listeners to *feel the vibes* and demands respect for the MCs' lyrical prowess. Though out of the ordinary for the show's usual viewership, So Solid's *Top of the Pops* performance of 'Oh No' was theatrical, complete with choreographed movements and coordinated clothing.

Frontman MegaMan wore a white, tailored suit while MC Romeo's less formal trousers and sweater were still neatly assembled, accessorised with a chain and multiple rings, presenting him as a bonafide star. So Solid's polished aesthetic contrasted greatly with the facial coverings and low batties rocked by the generation of Grime. For all the controversy they generated, So Solid Crew's hit singles contained mild content compared to the graphic vignettes of violence and drug dealing that would become abundant in Grime lyrics.

Early UK Garage music was easy listening. Even when the sound became more experimental, later examples from the Garage catalogue were still in some ways palatable to mainstream audiences, whether through their refined production, jovial themes, or shiny choruses. Grime was in many ways the polar opposite. The culture of clashing integral to Grime, for example, was too explosive for the serenity of the Garage scene. Intergenerationally imported to the UK from Jamaican Dancehall culture, a soundclash involves two opposing sound systems or MCs engaging in a head-to-head exchange of riddims or bars to elicit the most energetic reaction from the audience. Clashes are energetic and unpredictable; no holds are barred as MCs unleash witty insults and ego-bruising slurs against their opponents. Just as the word 'reload' in the title of Oxide & Neutrino's millenial banger was assumed to refer to firearms rather than DJ culture, the diasporic culture of clashing has been misunderstood as disorderly and violent, rather than vibrant performance.

The cultural dissonance grew more pronounced; and Garage's relevance for later-born millennials began to wane. Just as those from UK Garage thought of the new scene as crude and vulgar, the Grime generation felt disconnected from the opulent nightlife of champagne popping and sporting high fashion brands in West End Clubs. This new generation were not jet setting to Cyprus and Napa for escapist party holidays. Deciding they did not need the frills of UK Garage, they set out to carve their own niche on home soil. They would build a scene from scratch—needing only mixing decks and a microphone.

And so Grime music became a genuine sensation of its own. Not yet able to achieve mainstream airplay, Grime relied on pirate radio to transcend the local communities it was created within. Like Garage prior, its reach would grow, extending far and wide across the city and country to captivate the minds of the next generation of DJs, producers, artists, and entrepreneurs. Except, Grime's impact would be even more enduring. The aspiring MCs who surfaced in large numbers obsessively scribbled and practised their bars in preparation for the ultimate mainstage, the live pirate airwaves. Pirate radio sets were like lyrical dojos, where MCs would train to become microphone jedis. Promoters and stations arranged and marketed clashes like WWE events. At such sets and at live shows, MCs eagerly awaited their turn to deliver verses back-to-back alongside their peers, scrambling to grab the mic in hopes of getting a reload. Their imaginations ignited, thousands of teenagers in London would grow with Grime music and the art of MCing omnipresent around them.

Of course when speaking about Grime, the legacy and importance of UK Garage cannot be forgotten about. As its direct precursor, Garage definitely helped shape the new sound of Britain. When in 2007 a young North London MC Chipmunk released his hotly anticipated Grimey mixtape *League of My Own*, its tracklist featured a record called 'Fire Alie'. 'Fire Alie' is a jumpy, succinct freestyle, sentimentally akin to the dubs of old. On the tune, Chipmunk exhibits his lyrical prowess with the braggadocio that is formative to the Grime genre. Fresh out of secondary school at 16 just years of age, Chipmunk's raw talent was beyond his years, reminiscent of the prodigiousness of Dizzee Rascal who had helped usher in the transition from the Garage to the Grime era a generation before.

'Fire Alie's instrumental is one of the seven versions of the

Cleptomaniacs's 'All I Do' single, released by an independent electronic music label Defected Records in the year 2000. The song has its origins in Soul singer Tammi Terelle's recording of the same title four decades prior, which would in the future become a classic due to Stevie Wonder's 1980 iteration. The Cleptomaniacs's numerous reworks of 'All I Do' included club mixes, a 'ghost' mix, a radio edit, and the Bump n Flex Dance Floor Dub version, over which Chipmunk memorably performed. The record's skippy drums are littered with scattered, rhythmic hi-hats. The squelching bass dictates movement, while the chopped, melodic vocal samples on the track adds a brightness. In spitting over this instrumental, Chipmunk paid homage to his musical predecessors and continued in the tradition which saw performers increasingly foregrounded compared to DJs or unvocalled instrumentals. 'Fire Alie' is an example of the constant evolution of Black music, telling a story of rich musical lineage even across seas. It situates Grime within a particular historical and cultural context and highlights a unique temporal juncture, exemplifying how UK Garage is integral to Grime's story.

So Solid Crew's '21 seconds' is a precious artefact in British music history. It can be filed next to releases like Sweet Female Attitude's 'Flowers' or Daniel Bedingfield's 'Gotta Get Thru This' as a classic Garage tune sung in spaces from nightclubs to school playgrounds. Yet while I certainly enjoyed such songs while growing up, and still appreciate many of the genre's contributions today, I couldn't by the time I'd reached adolescence claim with any honesty to particularly 'care' about UK Garage as a whole. I found myself more drawn to American rap as it grappled with street realities of poverty and violence that I observed around me, albeit in a different geographical context. Yet, no music connected with my peers and I more-than Grime.

4

DAVID CAMERON IS A DONUT

NEEDLE DROP: BASHY FT. BRUZA, 'FUCK THE GOVERNMENT'

Mischievous impulses and a degree of defiance are normal parts of coming of age. Yet, every generation resists this truth, often insisting that their successors are more unruly than they ever were. I mean, on reflection, I can concede that letting off stink bombs on buses or pressing the emergency exit button to get off between stops was far from exemplary behaviour. Today, I might even be pissed off if I were to encounter a group of kids engaging in the same antics during my morning commute. Yet, the misadventures of my teenage years stemmed from boredom and a lack of maturity not malignancy. Rooted mainly in misdirected youthful energy and underdeveloped consequential thinking, our mild misbehaviour hardly signalled the end of the world or breakdown of society.

The all black sportswear that my peers and I often wore, almost as a uniform, probably contributed to us being seen as more threatening than we actually were. The British media and political landscape around this time inflamed a panic about 'feral' working-class youth who wore hooded garments, caused chaos, and were predisposed to criminality and violence.

News articles often exaggerated incidents and overstated their frequency, using loaded terms like 'thugs' to promote a sense of fright among the public. Politicians raved about 'law and order'. In 2005, the UK's fifth largest shopping centre Bluewater banned hoodies and baseball caps from being worn on its premises as part of a clampdown on antisocial behaviour. Such policy was characteristic of this age and the state's attempt to encroach on public space and private life.

TV programmes like *Little Britain* and *The Jeremy Kyle Show* fed the public imagination with caricatures of working-class people as barely literate, dim-witted drunkards, vehemently opposed to employment. Such media portrayals were one-dimensional and offensive, reminiscent of the voyeurism of the 19th century when citizens took touristic excursions into London's slums for amusement. This tradition of mockery continued as the underprivileged populations of the inner-city were depicted as vulgar, sofa-bound benefit scroungers. These portrayals were more than just harmless satire; they shaped society's perception and treatment of the working class. Sociologist Imogen Taylor's book *Revolting Subjects* powerfully explores how poorer people are treated as objects of disgust. Tragically, they are viewed as insufferable liabilities, treated with contempt and suspicion.

While our communities were far from the one-dimensional hell-holes they were painted as by the British media, there was undeniably a period during my school years when the risk of being robbed felt very real. Vigilance became necessary as encountering a group of young people ready to rummage through your belongings and steal items of value was likely.

To avoid such incidents, some of us sometimes took convoluted routes home from school, being careful not to cut through the wrong estate, end up on the wrong road, or board the wrong bus. We learned to walk with purpose and keep to ourselves. If you got caught slipping, you could lose your possessions, from the cash you carried to the new phone your mother had worked hard to buy. Rumours would even circulate of people being robbed of their footwear.

There was a phase of 'happy slapping', a troubling trend of attacking unsuspecting passers-by. These sudden assaults were captured on video and shared online. Enabled by mobile video recording technology, this distinctly modern craze swept through school playgrounds and public spaces like bus stops and train stations, proving more worrisome than our earlier, more juvenile forms of rebellion. *The Guardian* reported that the British Transport Police had investigated 200 such incidents in the sixth months leading up to April 2005.

Most happy slap incidents were, however, trivial and the fad was ultimately short lived. In the grand scheme, the incidents were rare compared to the vast majority of people who travelled on public transport without encountering any issues. It wasn't until later years that I would become conscious of the more serious, weapon-enabled violence that seemed to proliferate in the inner-city, disproportionately affecting people from deprived socioeconomic and diverse ethnic backgrounds, and of depressingly decreasing ages.

What could cause such social angst? The lasting legacy of the Conservative administration of Margaret Thatcher, who in 1987 famously asserted that 'there is no such thing' as society, offers some insights. During the 1980's Britain's coal, steel and railway industries were decimated due to the deindustrialization and privatisation processes spearheaded by Thatcher. This led to a sharp rise in unemployment which in turn contributed to increases in social ills such as property crime. Believing that British citizens were overly dependent on a 'nanny' welfare state, Thatcher's government implemented a relentless regime of restructure.

As a result, access to social security was tightened and state expenditure per capita was reduced. The significant cuts to public services stoked substantial increases in health and socioeconomic inequalities. By the time Labour took power in 1997, the income disparity had widened significantly; the top tenth of British earners made 10 times as much income after tax than the bottom tenth, doubling the gap that existed when Thatcher first became Prime Minister. Child poverty more than doubled, while taxation was reduced by more than half.

The secondary I attended was among many state schools in Hackney and across the capital with a high proportion of students receiving free school meals. Many of these students came from households earning well below the national median income. Almost half of London's social housing was concentrated in East London local authorities, as well as in boroughs like Haringey in the North, and Lambeth and Lewisham in the south. Estates like the Crossways had long been left in states of disrepair despite promises of regeneration. In the mid 1990's, the UK was still contending with the woes of post-industrial decline and labour market turmoil, leading to a higher number of children growing up in unemployed households in Britain than anywhere else on the continent. Given this context, it's not difficult to see how some young people living in an environment of scarcity might resort to snatching a phone for a quick buck. Illicit activity booms where legitimate opportunity lacks.

Led by Tony Blair, the more centrist, 'New' Labour government of my youth was problematic in its own ways. Blair served as the nation's Prime Minister for 10 years up until 2007, adopting conventionally conservative approaches to some areas of social policy. The 2005 Respect agenda saw a cross-governmental task force constituted to strategise about ensuring that law and order was enforced more effectively in spaces from classrooms to street corners. The aim was to crack down on behaviours like vandalism and the public consumption of alcohol in the evenings and on weekends.

In his final year of office, Tony Blair delivered a speech in Cardiff commemorating the late James Calaghan, former Labour leader and Prime Minister of the UK from 1976-1979. Blair's speech highlighted Callaghan's patriotism and his firm rejection of what he believed to be excessive liberalism. He feared that relaxed attitudes could lead to absurd outcomes like Britain legalising cannabis. Blair praised his predecessor's tough stance on law and order and his promotion of values like self-discipline and respect for authority. In his address, Blair presented a picture of contemporary social decline but also boasted of a business and culture renaissance and the regeneration of public services brought about by Labour's investments. He contrasted these laudable developments with the rampant hooliganism, classless bingeing and mindless violence of a lawless minority. On one hand, Blair seemed to accept that issues like street loitering, fly-tipping, and graffiti were not major in the grand scheme. On the other, he dramatically suggested that such low-level misdemeanours threatened to destroy civil society.

Tensions of social class and culture are ever-present in Blair's rhetoric; throughout his address, he fosters a sure sense of 'us' and 'them'. The then Prime Minister demarcates an irreconcilable split between a decent, law-abiding majority and those with antisocial and criminal impulses, stemming from their dysfunctional upbringing. His solution targeted this latter group with measures such as intensive policing and the creation of structured frameworks of discipline combining 'pressure and support' for problem families to improve in order to continue receiving financial aid from the state. In addition to night-time curfews, culprits of what was deemed to be unacceptable behaviour might expect to receive fixed monetary fines, unpaid community service or parenting orders. Another proposed policy would empower local authorities to evict troublesome tenants who committed antisocial behaviour twice within a three year period from their homes . Such levers would join existing policies like Anti-Social Behaviour Orders, also known as ASBOs, which were already being routinely issued to those deemed to be disruptive members of society , even if only with very limited effect.

The rise of this kind of surveillance and control would become an unfortunate feature in the story of Grime. Early pioneer DJ Slimzee famously received an ASBO banning him from entering any building more than four storeys high in the London Borough of Tower Hamlets without permission. The resourcefulness of Grime was demonised. The young people who entered disused buildings and found ways to access roofs across the city to configure pirate radio broadcasts were considered nuisances, even criminals, instead of the innovators that they were.

Blair's initial allusions to race in his speech, conjured by his mentioning of Labour's anti-discrimination laws of the '60s and '70s and concealed in the language of 'tolerance', were eventually made explicit as he broached the topic of youth violence in London.

'The Black community need to be mobilised in denunciation of... gang culture', Blair said.

'We won't stop this by pretending it isn't young Black kids doing it.'

Although neither poor, Black, nor young people have ever

held a monopoly on crime or violence, it was these marginalised demographics who Blair chose to target both in his speech and policy efforts. As explored in the seminal work *Policing the Crisis* by the late cultural theorist Stuart Hall, discourse around law and order is deliberately manipulated as a political tool. Narratives about criminal offences are routinely racialised, with Black youth being disproportionately vilified in the process. Stuart Hall explained how the visceral, knee-jerk reactions of politicians, the media, and, in turn, public citizens to criminal acts like 'mugging' were 'at odds with the scale of the threat.' Blair likewise conceded in his speech that an irrational fear of crime had seemed to grip society in a way that did not correlate with the number or seriousness of offences being committed.

Social anxieties around migration, economic crisis, and a shifting cultural landscape all converged, to create an environment of uncertainty, fear and frustration. Racialised and working-class young people with an incidental preference for sporty attire became the scapegoats. The rich ethnic diversity of places like Hackney contributed to such areas being considered dangerous and undesirable. A support base developed for more authoritarian measures to be directed against these 'difficult' neighbourhoods, such as more police and community support officers being deployed there.

Considering their political leanings, it was perhaps surprising that Conservative party leader David Cameron had articulated a marginally more compassionate perspective about the apparent problem of antisocial behaviour than Blair's punitive posturing. In 2006, Cameron delivered a speech invoking the image of a hoodie explaining it was a 'vivid symbol' of what had 'gone wrong with young people in Britain.' Despite extending an extent of empathy towards disadvantaged young people, the Tory leader still pathologized working-class individuals and their communities. He described them as 'out of control' and blamed them for turning town centres into 'war zones' asserting they created a 'sense of menace in the air.' Cameron ultimately framed wider social issues like mental health and addiction as exclusively the problems of the poor. His analysis and understanding of the social fabric of the poor Black communities were reductive and lacked depth. He denounced crime, drugs and underage sex, as wrong, albeit with one caveat.

'Simply blaming the kids who get involved in it doesn't really get us much further,' he added. 'It is what the culture around them encourages.'

What exactly is this culture that David Cameron placed blame on? From the underrepresented perspective of the fringes, Grime intimately and unflinchingly chronicled these social changes and challenges that we were experiencing. Grime music offered unsightly reflection of the society it had been incubated in which directly contrasted the nation's pristine self-image. It's no wonder, then, that the genre and culture were not warmly accepted by the established order.

When Lethal Bizzle's 'Pow!' was released in 2004, for example, it was met with extreme censorship. It was barred from national radio play as well as music venues throughout the capital. The reason? The song was said to incite violence. 'Pow!' is exactly the kind of music Cameron took issue with. The insuppressible reaction that 'Pow!' provokes may have led to one too many a scuffle across London's dancefloors. It remains silly to blame disparate incidents of violence on one song, or to imagine that banning it would prevent further violence across British society. This was the same scapegoating that had affected UK Garage a few years earlier.

In 1998, amid a heavily racialised moral panic about 'Yardie' gangs, the Metropolitan Police Unit established Operation Tridentto address what they termed as black-on-black gun crime, later expanding its focus to tackle broader gang-related issues. The formation of Operation Trident emerged pretty much concurrently with the rise of Grime and UK rap. Lethal Bizzle's 'Pow!' is a Grime classic that quickly cemented itself as an igniter of the dancefloor. The song, however, was entangled in controversy far too extreme considering that it was, after all, just one song from an ever expanding catalogue of similarly abrasive music. What's more is that these songs were being created by aspirational, entre-preneurial young people, who were directing their energies towards becoming successful artists rather than the shooters hyperbolically depicted in their lyrics.

The gatekeepers of the UK's established music industry were never going to have taken warmly to MCs name-dropping a full arsenal of weapons from nunchucks and belt buckles to Desert Eagles and AKs, all delivered in thick Jamaican accents. They were to be even more mortified by 'Pow!'s extended version, which features an infamous verse from an MC called Hotshot. The verse ends with Hotshot listing what sounds like every variation of firearm to exist, separating each item with the instruction to shoot. While this final verse invariably ignites crowds, any rendition of 'Forward Riddim' is guaranteed to incite incredible scenes of skanking and moshpitting. Hence, 'Pow!' stands as perhaps the quintessential example from the genre's catalogue, lending credence to comparisons that several commentators have made between Grime and Punk—both visceral cultures that proudly defy expectation.

'Pow!' undoubtedly emerged from feelings of frustration.

'It almost felt like we was kind of being alienated,' Lethal B told British *GQ* in a 2016.

'My reaction to that was, "well fuck that, I'm gonna start my own label and I'm gonna make music I wanna make and I'm just gonna find as much ways as possible to promote the music."'

Lethal B's group More Fire Crew had enjoyed previous success with their song 'Oi!', which peaked at number 8 in the Official Singles Charts and remained in the top 100 for 8 weeks. Just as So Solid Crew's hits had propelled them to the Top of the Pops stage, 'Oi!' enabled More Fire Crew in 2002 to follow suit. By the time 'Pow!' arrived just two years later, however, the doors of the mainstream were firmly closed to such Black British music. The spectacle had gone too far, the sense of danger now felt far too real. The music could no longer be treated as entertainment like it once was.

Even if the disconcerting discordance of 'Pow!' was reflective of the darker direction that Black British underground music had been pulled in, and it highlighted a heightening frustration and deepening cultural divide in Britain, Lethal B and the More Fire Crew had not necessarily set out to make such a riotous anthem. 'Pow!' was put together very quickly and as on-the-fly as its similarly onomatopoeic predecessor.

Shut out of the mainstream industry he'd once had a taste of, Lethal B would act as his own A&R. He'd first heard 'Pow!'s manic instrumental played by a DJ, and made arrangements with its producer Dexplicit to use it for a dub. He swiftly assembled an all-star line up to feature on the song that would become 'Pow!' The rotation of MCs that follow after Lethal's volcanic intro each deliver an engaging 8 bars of their own. An ardent overseer; Lethal directed each of them to spray their biggest bar, i.e., the lyrics for which they were best known.

He was sure that this would make their dub as big as possible, earning them the most hype reactions from audiences.

Sure, some of 'Pow!'s content does sound brutal.

'I'llll crack your skull,' Napper all but screams when it's his turn to drop a verse.

The specificity of his threat plus the conviction in his voice make him sound very believable. But the violent references in this exaggerated performance are generally arbitrary. According to the 2005 Pow Pow documentary released on DVD by early Grime platform, Nu Era, Lethal had in fact asked one of the artists, Fumin, to recite his particular verse precisely because it was so different from the violent fantasy so common in rap.

'You're barking up the wrong tree,' Fumin screeches, appearing second on the track after Lethal.

Next up is the dynamic, veteran MC, D Double E, whose verse comes complete with his trademark sound effects. Even back then, Double sounds conscious of his iconic status. He is unimpressed by the long-winded efforts of other MCs: *'It's me the kids are mad ooon, while your lyrics dem ah just drag ooon',* he teases, dramatically extending his words, full as ever of presence and character.

The underground hype generated by the track, with its all-star roster culminated in a single deal with Relentless Records. Although the boutique label was just 5 years old at the time, it had a proven track record of success with acts like So Solid Crew and had delivered Garage hits from Artful Dodger's 'Re-Rewind' featuring Craig David to B15's 'Girls Like Us'. This signing was only incidental, however, to 'Pow!'s ascent. More Fire Crew had already leveraged their own personal resources and networks to prepare and promote the track. Lethal Bizzle invested personal funds into a music video which was put into heavy rotation on Channel U in

2004, a popular new TV Channel that was launched in 2003 by Darren Platt. As pirate radio expanded the sonic reach of Grime music, Channel U did the same for the visual dimension of the genre. Instantly, the channel became a window into the scene, reflecting and shaping the aesthetic of Grime culture. An updated version of 'Pow!'s initial independent video was released by Relentless in December of 2004, achieving playlisting on the aspirational MTV Base.

Also released on 12 inch vinyl, the official CD version of 'Pow!' which landed in December 2004 contained both videos. The illustration printed on the CD had a comic book, youthful quality. The song's title is written in all caps in playful typography atop a cartoonist's depiction of a smash impact illustration. But even this neatly packaged re-release of 'Pow!' delivered with label backing would be collectively shunned by mainstream radio outlets and venues, which prohibited its play or performance. Police mechanisms like Form 696 were more frequently used to deny licences to events where Grime records like 'Pow!' might play. Venues posted signs warning DJs that this kind of music was unwelcome. Oral accounts of Lethal B's 'Pow!' suggest that certain venues went as far as banning the instrumental version of 'Forward Riddim' from being played.

Such censorship, however, often only serves to make its objects more intriguing and widely sought-after. Indeed, 'Pow!'s notoriety only adds to its legend. The clampdown on the record was as disproportionate as it was ineffective, both in terms of its commercial performance and enduring impact. 'Pow!' sold well in spite of being black-balled, ending up falling just one position short of becoming a UK Top 10. This was a remarkable feat given its release in Christmas week against competition by established pop acts like Ronan Keating and Morrissey. 'Pow!' was an unexpected contender in the Charts alongside the monumental albeit problematic Band Aid single, 'Do They Know It's Christmas'. Yet, its raw and explosive energy, enabled the record to resonate with a whole generation of disenfranchised young people. Brimming with familiar youthful rebellion, the song facilitates catharsis and captures a sentiment of disgruntlement and discontent shared across a section of young people living in an ever more alienating social landscape. Somehow simultaneously confrontational and euphoric, 'Pow!' marks a clear cultural turning point.

In perhaps an unlikely turn of events, Grime MC Lethal Bizzle and Prime Minister David Cameron would go back and forth in newspapers, debating the issue of crime. Each penned articles stating their position. 'David Cameron is a donut', Lethal B's June 2006 opinion piece in *The Guardian* was headlined. 'You're talking rubbish, Lethal Bizzle...' Cameron responded a few days later in a *Daily Mail* column. Embarrassingly, Cameron's article quotes lines from More Fire Crew member Neeko's verse on 'Pow!', misattributing them to Lethal Bizzle. Perhaps in an attempt to to redeem himself, Cameron in his hug-a-hoodie speech a month later, acknowledged the differential experiences of those living in housing estates, who often lacked access to the city's entertainment and leisure amenities and had sometimes survived abuse and neglect.

The 'renaissance' touted by Tony Blair in 2007 was a romanticised cover up of a divided reality. It was more accurately a time of harrowing social histories and experiences that songs like 'Pow!' emerged from. Blair listed what he considered to be Labour's successes such as a revitalised labour market, but the economic progress and the thriving cultural institutions he celebrated did not equally benefit all British citizens. Instead, opportunity and access were unevenly distributed along lines of class and race. Despite having spoken of the importance of amplifying young peoples' perspectives and offering them meaningful, constructive activities, the Tory party under Cameron's leadership would in fact close hundreds of youth centres after assuming power from Labour.

While political leaders courted votes with their promises, the youth of Grime remained largely overlooked. 'Pow!' represented, then, another kind of renaissance unfolding on London's streets, away from Blair's cultural institutions of the mainstream, which were as disconnected from the working-class youth as they were inaccessible. Both the song and the Grime movement were examples of true DIY endeavours of youth before any kind of label investment or mainstream interest.

Dexplicit, the producer of 'Pow!' recalls a time when he struggled with mixing the audio of songs. He'd had no formal training and at that time less conversant with more advanced audio processing tools like EQ and compression. Grime music attracted an onslaught of staunch criticism for its content. Was it not preferable, though, for young people were engaging in creativity, camping in makeshift studios and learning skills like audio engineering rather than actually engaging in some of the more destructive realities that some of their music described?

5

THE TECHNOLOGY
OF GRIME

NEEDLE DROP: PRINCE RAPID/RUFF
SQWAD, 'PIED PIPER'

In addition to reshaping our connections with the world, each other and even to ourselves, technology also mediates power. Technology empowers individuals to speak out against injustice and challenge traditional hierarchies. Just as culture serves as an arena for social tensions and creativity to be expressed, like music providing a voice for underrepresented groups, technology similarly facilitates resistance.

Excluded from full participation in the capital's opportunities and amenities, the resourceful youngsters of the Grime generation turned to technology. Whole-heartedly committing themselves to what initially may have been creative pastimes, they developed invaluable technical skills .

Those who set up the early pirate radio shows and stations of the early Grime scene, for example, are owed credit as self-taught communications and audio engineers. Many were influenced by the rich heritage of Jamaican soundsystem culture and had inherited the context of unlicensed broadcasting traceable in Britain. They would audaciously scale buildings with their wire strippers and soldering irons, learning on-the-fly to construct the broadcasting systems which proved vital for the spread of Grime. Faced with rising unemployment, many young men dedicated themselves to radio as a medium and Grime as a lifestyle. Taking legal and financial risks to run their own radio shows and stations, their activities required bravery, technical know-how and business acumen.

Pirate radio was distinctly an analogue affair, far removed from the more immediate and incessant nature of today's hyper-digital age. Several hardware materials are needed to start broadcasting, including a transmitter, an antenna, and lengths of wire. Stronger power sources allow for audio signals to be transmitted over greater distances, but the general rule of one watt equating to one square mile of coverage fails to account for the environmental factors which might also affect affairs. AM radio signals transmit more effectively at night, free from interference from sun rays, which aligned perfectly with the covert activities of the Grime pirates and contributed to the genre's nocturnality. The presence of nearby competing trans-missions, further complicated matters, impeding clear signals and limiting broadcasting range. The technology facilitated the hijacking of existing broadcasts and the hostile taking over of occupied frequencies, which fittingly served the disruptive energy of Grime.

Antenna placement was another critical variable; the higher one could be erected, the better. Venturing as far as possible away from the congested frequencies on the ground, the budding broadcasters of the burgeoning Grime scene scaled the heights of the city, scouring for optimal vantage points to make strongholds for their radio endeavours. They besieged London's rooftops to mount their equipment, precariously hanging antennas out of tower block windows to achieve transmission.

Microwave technology soon allowed for antennas and transmitters to be placed remotely from each other. It became harder, therefore, to pinpoint the exact location that broadcasting signals were originating from, helping the pirates to evade the intensifying enforcement activities of the Department and Trade Industry. Even if the individual components that comprised broadcasting rigs were seized by the authorities, replacements could be swiftly configured so shows could resume with minimal disruption.

Younger Grime fans might not remember having to carefully sift through radio frequencies to find their favourite pirate stations, or haphazardly balancing aerials against other household objects to stabilise signal. By the time I was coming of age, such technology was becoming obsolete, overtaken by the reign of the internet and increasing ubiquity of advanced mobile phones.

The first mobile phone I owned was the Nokia 3410, a curved, compact device released in 2002 equipped with basic calling, text messaging and contact storage features. Far more novel to me than these elementary functions, though, was the fun fact that the phone's customisable outer casing allowed owners to express their individual style with different colours or patterns. It was also more exciting that the 3410 came preloaded with *Snake*, an ingeniously simple game that signalled a new era of digital entertainment and foreshadowed later Nokia products like the N-Gage phone and gaming system. The aim of the game is straightforward: the player is to 'feed' the snake as much as possible i.e., to guide it accurately towards pixelated dots which pop up in variable positions on-screen. As the snake is fed more and more, its length increases along with the player's score, making it harder to control over time. The challenge is to avoid causing the gradually elongating snake to collide with itself, which results in the game ending.

Despite its simplicity, *Snake* could be wildly addicting. Like many young people I found myself spending countless hours engrossed in the game, obsessively thumbing the directional buttons on my phone in hopes of outdoing my highest score. We'd officially entered an era wherein the function of phones was no longer restricted to communication. The mobile phone became an indispensable hub for personal entertainment.

In secondary school, my friends and I would compose our own custom ringtones to use instead of the selection or default monophonic melodies standard of Nokia phones at the time. Some searched the internet for instructions to recreate popular songs like Nelly's 'Dilemma', ft. Kelly Rowland, or Jay Z's 'Big Pimpin'', ft. UGK. This time marked the relatively new, democratic nature of the online world,where information and media could be easily shared with just a few clicks.

By the time I upgraded my phone to the Sony Ericsson W810i around 2006, technology had advanced significantly and the internet had become even more enormous and ubiquitous. Interestingly, it was music that was my new device's unique selling point. As CDs began to fade into obscurity, the W810i represented a modern iteration of Sony's earlier Walkman stereos. Perfect for my introverted disposition, the W810i even enabled users to deactivate its communication functions, transforming it into a dedicated music player.

The LCD colour screen of my new phone measured 176 by 220 pixels, rendering the tiny, monochrome display of my old Nokia archaic. Not only was the 20MB memory integrated within the Sony Ericsson more than 100x the capacity of my old 3410, it also supported the insertion of external memory cards up to 4GB so that users could store about six albums worth of songs. Apart from being able to play .mp3, .wav and even .MIDI files, the W810i boasted a 2 megapixel camera, equipped with autofocus and flash, so the phone could capture images and videos of unprecedented quality.

The introduction of infrared and later bluetooth connectivity, which eventually became standard on devices of the era made it easier for music to be transferred peer-to-peer. My friends and I eagerly sent each other Grime riddims as we travelled or hung out together. Just as the distribution and consumption of music was revolutionised through developing technologies and the vast expansion of the internet, so too was the process of creating music for those of the Grime generation.

Before studio simulators and digital sound synthesis proliferated, professional music equipment was more prohibitively priced and not widely available. Quality audio capture relied on expensive, sometimes hefty hardware, which wrote recordings onto reels of tape or cassettes. Some of the earliest devices made available to retail customers by leading audio brands like Tascam provided merely 4 channels of sound recording. While this may have sufficed for Grime's earlier, more minimal compositions, some of the genre's output would be programmed more intricately and incorporate numerous disparate elements. Later hardware recorders offering up to 8 and 16 tracks of audio would cost significantly more to purchase.

Music production, before the online age, was usually undertaken using physical workstations as sold by companies like Moog and Korg. The funky sounds of the Minimoog, for instance, informed the Jazz and Disco of the 1970s, whereas the futuristic Korg Triton can be heard in some of the first songs that signalled the arrival of Grime. Pushing existing keyboard technology to new and improved heights, the Korg Triton boasted enhanced sampling and digital sequencing abilities, in addition to an impressive array of stock sounds within its expandable storage. Although presets such as the Triton's distinctive Gliding Squares bass are recognisable in formative Grime instrumentals, the synth also allowed users to extensively customise and modulate their own unique sounds.

While companies like Korg, Moog and Tascam innovated in the realm of hardware, others focussed on developing the digital applications that would go on to transform the music industry. Steinberg's 1996 Cubase was an early example of Virtual Studio Technology (VST), offering an extraordinary 32 tracks of audio, seamlessly integrating a range of effects and processing tools.

This groundbreaking software enabled users to stack multiple layers of sound, adjust volumes precisely and 'pan' elements left or right to achieve rich, expansive stereo images. With VST Plugins integrable within digital audio workstations (DAWs), creators were no longer reliant on pricey, space-consuming physical instruments for music production. Instead, they could easily experiment with the growing range of sounds, unlocking new creative possibilities.

As well as transforming the creative process, these technological advancements also expanded musical possibilities, popularising altogether unprecedented sounds and styles. Propellerhead's 1994 ReCycle brought time-stretching, which allowed users to manipulate the speed and length of audio files without affecting their pitch. This opened up a host of previously unexplored sonic avenues, fostering further evolution within electronic genres like UK Garage which relied heavily on sampling. Another notable Propellerhead application, ReBirth, launched in 1996, played a key role in making the iconic Roland 808 bass a staple across contemporary music.

When the company's flagship product Reason arrived in 2001, the sound suite attracted criticism from some commentators for its lack of audio recording capabilities. That Reason enabled individuals to create music entirely within a computer, without the need for any external sources of sound, perfectly reflected the essence of this new, digital era.

Reason was designed to emulate the aesthetic of old analogue audio equipment. Pressing the 'tab' button on one's QWERTY keyboard revealed the rear panels of any digital instruments loaded, allowing users to rig them as necessary using virtual wires. Apart from stock patches like resonant horns and grand pianos which could be played in virtual instruments like Reason's NN-XT sampler, the application also enabled more granular digital synthesis, allowing users to manipulate oscillators and modify raw sound signals. Synthesisers blend instructions from multiple oscillators regarding waveform shape, frequency, and amplitude to create layered sonic output. By stacking, tuning, and filtering two or three oscillators slightly differently, users could create cohesive, unique sounds. Waveform shape plays a crucial role in determining sound texture. Sine waves, pure in tone and devoid of distortion, serve as the fundamental building blocks of audio, producing smooth and clear sounds. While ideal for subtle sub-basses, sine waves may appear too pristine for grittier tastes and productions with a darker edge. On the other hand, square and triangle waveforms generate noisier, buzzier tones characterized by odd harmonics and partial tones, often used for grating leads, dusty brasses, and powerful kick drums typical in Grime music. Sawtooth waves, with their jagged shape and harsh sonic quality, intensify this effect, offering saturated sound with a fuller range of frequencies and harmonics.

Digital synthesisers provide users with flexibility to adjust sounds according to their preferences. Parameters like 'attack' affect how quickly a sound reaches maximum volume, while 'sustain' and 'release' values determine the duration sounds last when notes are played. Such technology proved transformative for Grime's pioneers, who invested countless hours experimenting with these processes. The primary instrument for these new-age musicians would be their computers; they'd strum digital guitars using their PC's mouse as a pick. MIDI technology, which became central to digital music production, kept CPU usage light compared to the computing power and storage traditionally required for processing large audio files.

Some of the earliest Grime music was produced on 'cracked' copies of such software as described above, downloaded illegally via peer-to-peer sharing platforms like Limewire. Beyond the technical nuances of digital sound synthesis, one of the most important technological advancements in the story of Grime is the explosion of the Internet. The Internet connected communities across the world, promoting the free dissemination of information, ideas and resources. Pirated programs were installed (often along with all kinds of malware) on parents' PCs or on laptops originally purchased for educational purposes. Many panicked hours were spent trying to purge systems and prevent the frustrating popups caused by dubious downloads.

Pirating extended beyond radio. Pirated software applications regularly came compressed within .zip files. Installers came bundled together with serial generators and step-by-step instructions to successfully activate the shadily acquired applications. Often, the hackers responsible for compromising programs and sharing them with the world would proudly take credit, leaving their monikers in the .txt. files. Piracy became another heated frontier of philosophical debate about the unequal distribution of resources and the democratisation of knowledge. Much like the pioneers of the scene who mastered transmitters and constructed broadcasting rigs, generations of young people would be led by their passion for music to develop fairly advanced technical skills like the ability to tamper with digital applications' core files. Sometimes, one would need to change file extensions to trick computer systems into believing that valid licences were held for softwares. Other tactics involved disconnecting computers from the Internet before installation to thwart communication between software and company servers during authentication processes. The illicit ingeniousness of the digital generation meant that the youth of Grime had at their fingertips an ever-growing array of tools they could use in their creative pursuits.

It was an unlikely application called Fruity Loops, however, released in 1998, which would become the holy grail of music production in Grime. Fruity Loops would become wildly popular. The program's inviting, user-friendly interface distinguished it from other music production packages like Reason which mimicked professional analogue equipment. Fruity Loops simplified its step-sequencer and piano roll, making them more accessible to newcomers. This allowed users to swiftly dive into rhythmic and melodic experimentation without grappling with complex audio chain configurations.

In some ways, with its entry-level positioning and prioritising of .MIDI over audio processing, Fruity Loops could perhaps have been considered the polar opposite of Avid Technology's Pro-Tools, which since its 1989 release has become the music industry standard for recording. Having first developed video games before diversifying into the field of music, Belgian tech company Imagine-Line ingeniously translated the playful gaming experience into music production with Fruity Loops. This fostered creativity and empowered a generation of young people across London to spend hours on FL Studio, crafting their own compositions from scratch. From experimentally turning digital dials with no knowledge of synthesis, sometimes in fact not even bothering to change the default 140 bpm tempo of Fruity Loops projects which became characteristic of Grime, these youngsters would proceed to create bona fide hits that would influence music not only in Britain but across the globe.

It's not as though the producers or MCs of the early Grime scene necessarily had conscious intentions to create music that would be revered for decades to follow. Few could have predicted the enduring acclaim their songs would receive or envisioned them as future classics. Armed with rudimentary tools at best, the pioneers of Grime crafted their music spontaneously, often from the confines of their bedrooms or living rooms. The unfinished quality of many early Grime releases owed to their creation in home studios, if they could even be qualified as such. Many Grime vocals were laid in wardrobes, with cheap microphones, often without professional accessories like pop shields.

Many of Grime's young pioneers hadn't actively purposed to become artists in the first place. Instead, they stumbled into music creation organically, spending considerable time experimenting with the increasingly accessible software available to them. Dirty Danger of Grime crew Ruff Sqwad, for example, recalls first beginning to make instrumentals after being bought a Windows computer by his parents for his school work.

Video games had already afforded the youth of Grime some technological capability and helped to prime their aesthetic palates. Similar to how some young people like myself would learn to navigate code through styling our social media accounts like Piczo with bespoke fonts, coordinating colours and lo-fi uploads of our favourite songs. An almost religious indulgence in computer games familiarised us with a wide range of digital interfaces and shaped our sensibilities. Many of us grew as digital natives, habitually using all sorts of computer systems from tender ages, playing for hours on end for instance on consoles sold by leading gaming companies like Nintendo. My Gameboy and N64 were formative gateways into the digital world.

The influence of gaming on Grime is significant, with some of the scene's pioneering producers having first forayed into music production using old games consoles. Artists like JME have reported creating some of their very first compositions on consoles like Nintendo's 1998 Game Boy Camera. Earlier applications like *Mario Paint* on the Super Nintendo Entertainment System (SNES) provided an electronic audio-visual canvas for players to create their own art, animations and music. The fact that the program had very limited features was not only conducive to creativity but necessitated it. Released in 1992, *Mario Paint* was the first game to use a mouse rather than a conventional controller for consoles, introducing players to this concept before it became commonplace on PCs.

Beyond acclimatising users to digital interfaces from early on, vintage games have also influenced Grime's tones, textures and content. The 8-bit sounds of classic series like Mario have been appropriated within the genre, interwoven into its sonic and cultural tapestry. A noteworthy volume of the song titles, vocabulary and symbolism from the Grime catalogue also point to the enduring influence of gaming culture. For all the panic and controversy the genre went on to generate, Grime has always retained a sure sense of youth and playfulness.

The characters and narratives from famous games series like Pokemon and Mario have been incorporated into Grime, serving as inspiration for MCs' similes and metaphors.

'*Skid round the corner like Yoshi and Toad*', spits Skepta on a 2008 song called 'Still Tippin''. Here, Skepta describes his urgent driving style by referencing the fictional dinosaur and mushroom-headed figures that players might select to represent them in the high-octane racing game *Mario Kart*. Skepta is one of the most internationally recognisable names and faces from Grime, and co-founder of the legendary crew Boy Better Know alongside his blood brother, JME.

JME diverged from the hypermasculine image and exaggerated claims of criminality often presumed of Grime or expected from MCs. Instead, JME has valued authenticity, often unapologetically expressing in his verses his appreciation for music, motor vehicles and all kinds of computer devices.

A true tech enthusiast, JME's bars in dense lyrical exhibits like '96 Fuckeries' are nods to everything from the elementary Nokia phones once used for composing ringtones to Apple's ever-developing mobile operating systems. JME challenges stereotypes about Grime's accused ignorance and uncritical violence not only through his quirky personhood and witty punchlines, but also directly through his journalism and activism. In 2014, JME presented an insightful and exposing Noisey music documentary called *The Police vs Grime Music*. The documentary examined the over-policing of events championing the genre.

Yet for all his subversiveness, JME per the essence of Grime has still explored the prospect of confrontation in his music. *'You'll get a punch in the face like BLAM!,'* he raps on the title track of his 2010 album of the same name. As seen before in Lethal Bizzle's smash hit, 'Pow!', the use of onomatopoeia is well established in Grime, as MCs almost comically explore the theme of conflict. The marriage between gaming culture and Grime has certainly contributed to this trend. The much-loved video game series *Street Fighter* for example is often referenced endearingly in Grime. Similar to how Kung Fu culture informed the aliases and motifs of Hip Hop supergroup

Wu-Tang Clan, the sounds, symbols and protagonists of the Japanese gaming franchise have been absorbed into Grime.

'If it's me you're mad at, you'll get a scar on your chest like Sagat,' raps D Double on 'Street Fighter Riddim'. *'It's not a game like Street Fighter 4,'* he states, assuring listeners of the seriousness of his threats.

Yet the animated nature of his vocal delivery and the cartoonish graphics of the accompanying video are disarming. When D Double E raps about desiring a 'big Belly like Rufus,' an obese Kung-fu expert from *Street Fighter*, he is speaking about his ambitions for wealth.

Another classic Grime beat called 'Streetfighter' was produced by Dizzee Rascal. In 2004, he finally responded to popular demand by releasing this infectious instrumental on white label vinyl, years after its initial production. The fragmented production samples the ethereal theme tune associated with the fictional character Chun Li, a female martial artist first introduced to the world with the arrival of *Street Fighter 2* in 1991. Audio snippets from the franchise have featured within many Grime songs and continue to appear in its more recent output. Lord of the Mics clashes are commenced with the 'Fight!' announcement sampled from the game's second version. The game's distinctive 'Hadouken!' and 'Perfect!' sound effects can regularly be heard throughout the Fire in the Booth freestyles as hosted by BBC Radio 1Xtra DJ Charlie Sloth. Developed by gaming company Capcom, which is also responsible for cult classics like *Resident Evil* and *Devil May Cry*, *Street Fighter*'s various instalments have long been available on a wide range of the consoles produced by companies from Nintendo to Sega.

Among my generation, Sony's PlayStation caused the biggest frenzy, eclipsing much of the competition in popularity among young Londoners. Games like *Crash Bandicoot*, for example, per the name of a rather unrelated 2006 freestyle by Grime veteran Wiley, were initially developed exclusively for the PlayStation platform. The influence of PlayStation on broader pop culture, as well as in Grime music in particular, is substantial. Similar to *Mario Paint* before it, the *Music 2000* game available on the PS1 allowed users to program their own beats. Its colorful grid interface simulates channels of sound, enabling players to sift through synthesized audio samples ranging from drum and bass elements to retro leads and warm pads. These selected sounds could be arranged into rhythmic and melodic patterns, with effect units like phasers applied and tailored to taste. *Music 2000* has been cited numerous times among the earliest applications that some of the trailblazers of Grime first used to create instrumentals.

Sony then updated the PlayStation six years after the release of the original. The PS2 arrived in March 2000 and, more than two decades later, it remains the best-selling games console of all time. Many from the Grime generation will affectionately remember afternoons crammed in bedrooms among friends for long stints of PS2 gameplay. Controllers were eagerly passed between players according to established codes. Winner stays on. Being whitewashed 3-0 meant having to pass the pad over to the next person in line. With friendly competition keenly embraced in both worlds, the parallels between gaming and Grime music are clear. From hit points to multiple strike combos, the concepts and imagery of combat oriented games like *StreetFighter*, *Mortal Kombat* and *Tekken* lent itself perfectly to the culture of clashing in Grime. Reloads in Grime sets can be compared to slow motion replays in fighting games in celebration of spectacular KO's. The grunts and exclamations of characters in such games have made for compelling sound effects, as have the squealing tyres of getaway vehicles in games like *Grand Theft Auto*. The scandalous storylines and details from *GTA*, furthermore, have been borrowed by rappers to help tell fantastical tales of alleged criminal exploits.

Both Grime and gaming are enjoyed as shared experiences, fostering camaraderie and facilitating the formation of community. Multiplayer games encourage young people to congregate around screens similar to how MCs and audiences huddle around decks and microphones. Each culture produces its own rituals, aesthetics and vocabularies which have contributed significantly to the identities of many young people in London and beyond.

One of the reasons for the burgeoning popularity of games consoles at this time was their affordability compared to personal computers. As the price of computers became more reasonable and desktops made their way into more homes, they too would begin to shape the sound of Grime music. While many more economically challenged families were still unable to comfortably purchase their own, computers could increasingly be accessed at work, in the classroom, libraries or at youth clubs.

I recall for instance feeling excited in ICT lessons while browsing Grime songs instead of the spreadsheets I was instructed to work on. Warm memories include visiting Hackney Central or Dalston library with friends to mess about on the PCs. Computers served work and learning purposes as well as providing a source of entertainment. Digital word processing for example made completing school work more efficient, while applications like Windows Media Player enabled the enjoyment of music, images and videos. Before the omnipresence of Apple devices like Macs and iPhones, it was Microsoft whose products had utterly captured the attention and fascination of young people.

My generation of Grime was raised on PlayStation and Windows XP. In the same way that Grime songs have interpolated theme tunes and repurposed the blips from video games, the jingles and chimes of early Windows operating systems have also been widely sampled. 'MSN Riddim' was a widely circulated, frantic number, novel because of its use of sound effects from Microsoft's wildly popular instant messaging platform.

From computers to mobile phones, from production, to distribution, it can easily be seen how technology has fundamentally changed music. Its meaning for Grime is particularly profound. The genre's ascent from bedroom experimentalism to commercial success means that Grime MCs have by now performed in venues as esteemed as the Royal Albert Hall with full orchestra ensembles.

The electronic synths of Grime are so unique, though, that live renditions of songs are liable to sound incomplete and less convincing than their original versions if these critical elements are lost. As such, Grime favours PA sets, per the lineage of sound system culture. Even when traditional instruments are recruited for live Grime performances, artists and their music directors often use electronic backing tracks in addition to preserve songs' original impact and texture. This illustrates just how indispensable the digital domain has been for the development of the genre.

Technology catalysed a shift across the creative landscape, not only pushing artistic boundaries, but also paving the way for a more inclusive and participatory arts culture. Facilitating the transfer of power from the physical and financial spheres to the digital and cultural, technology is an important arena of resistance against sociopolitical marginalisation. Technology affords new modes of autonomous self-expression and channels of communication to demographics whose perspectives may otherwise remain overlooked. Employing these transformative tools of cultural production, the Grime generation forged their own paths to create a rich vibrant scene. Through welcoming and harnessing the power of technology, this generation surmounted the attempts of traditional gatekeepers to quash their art. In doing so, they permanently reshaped the British cultural landscape, and started a movement that grew far beyond their wildest dreams.

NO HATS, NO HOODS

NEEDLE DROP: WILEY, 'NO QUALMS' FT. CHIPMUNK, J.M.E & SKEPTA (REVOX RADIO EDIT)

On Kano's 2005 debut studio album *Home Sweet Home*, there's a tune called 'Nobody Don't Dance No More'. The song transitions between contrasting sections, at first upbeat, driven by bouncy drums with a rhythm reminiscent of House music. A pulsing synth plays happy major chords before the song suddenly becomes more cinematic and obscure. The initially chirpy, rolling hi-hats become more spacey and sparse, a rough snare snaps above a rumbling synth bass.

In his bars, Kano fondly recounts his experiences as part of a generation who wore their best clothes and danced freely at UK Garage raves. Only 20 years old himself at the time, Kano laments that a younger generation were more likely to stay stone-faced and stush at the function.

'These kids nowadays, they don't make 'em like they used to,' he observes. *'They don't even dance in the raves like we used to.'*

Kano proceeds to detail the settings of his time, describing scenes so celebratory and wholesome they could be familial. In the early days of the South London Sunday Scene where UK Garage flourished, many of the gatherings took place in the daytime, with some attendees bringing their children along. As the scene evolved, adult UK Garage raves became more prevalent, characterised by sophisticated, indulgent settings, where champagne flowed as the beverage of choice. The nights were soundtracked by smooth records like Ramsey & Fen's 'Lovebug' and M Dubs's 'Over You'. Young men adorned themselves in dapper attire, sporting low, faded haircuts, crisp button-down shirts, and stylish loafers from brands like Patrick Cox. The strict dress codes enforced at UK Garage events mandated hard sole shoes and prohibited items such as hats and hoods. The sporty ensembles worn by Ruff Sqwad in Simon Wheatley's photographs would likely have seen them turned away from popular nights like Twice as Nice, which were marketed toward a more mature audience. Ladies meanwhile wore slinky dresses, mini-skirts, and high heels. Everyone bobbled along to the music, with bubbles in their glasses.

The UK Garage scene epitomized the essence of enjoying oneself while looking impeccably stylish. Delicate silks and luxurious leathers were the fabrics of choice, with denim, despite its widespread popularity in the '90s, notably absent from UK Garage raves. Attendees, heeding the promoters' call to dress to impress, adorned themselves in tailored trousers and sophisticated two-piece ensembles. High-end Italian fashion labels like Gucci and Dolce & Gabbana dominated the era, their prominence documented in striking stills captured by photographers such as Ewen Spencer and Tristan O'Neill. Bold luxury logos, vibrant graphic designs, and daring animal prints adorned the sweaty dancefloors of the city. In this era of Moët and Moschino, ravers often left the tags on their garments as a display of their new acquisitions, with extravagant statement pieces serving as markers of status and style.

As the upbeat melodies of early UK Garage songs like Gabriel by Roy Davis Jr and Peven Everett gradually gave way to the darker sounds of the Pay As U Go Cartel and So Solid Crew, an aesthetic transformation amongst a certain subset of British youth ensued. On the other side of the style spectrum, away from the dressiness required by UK Garage clubs, a surge in streetwear inspired and lifestyle looks proliferated.

While early Garage events had banned trainers, models like Prada's America Cup became cultural staples all the same. As a luxury fashion house, Prada was pioneering in venturing into menswear and sportswear and exploring new materials and silhouettes. Their America's Cup shoe shares its name with the sailing races of the world's oldest international sporting competition. Fusing artisanal fashion with modern functionality, Prada's groundbreaking Linea Rossa range has its roots in the brand's sponsorship of the Italian yachting team who became challengers for The American Cup in the year 2000.

The Linea Roassa range combined technical detailing with new processes of manufacturing, using textiles like nylon. Such synthetic fabrics were previously avoided by the luxury fashion world in favour of traditional natural materials. The breathability of textiles like nylon are more fitting though for physical activity and everyday life. Designed with function, climate and style in mind, items like the backpacks, gilets, and the windbreakers of the early Linea Rossa capsules incorporated technologies like thermal padding, and bore Prada's discreet but distinctive red logo branding. This new marriage of brand prestige and pragmatism made Prada particularly attractive within UK youth culture.

First released in 1997, coinciding with the ascent of UK Garage's into the mainstream, Prada's America's Cup runners epitomise the fusion of luxury fashion's with streetwear and youth culture. In a 2001 feature of So Solid Crew in The Face Magazine, founding member Megaman wears a navy blue pair. With a gently rounded silhouette, patent leather and mesh upper, and Prada's iconic red logo visible vertically down its tongue, this futuristic shoe straddles the line between smart and casual. They can be dressed up with trousers, or worn with jeans or joggers on an off day. Yet, even these classic Pradas were not exempt from the blanket outlawing of trainers at UK Garage nights.

Around this time, something else was also bubbling up in the British underground. At Jungle, Drum 'n' Bass and Ragga raves, the pace of the music was faster, the crowds were more hyper, the dress codes were more liberal. Caps were cool; creps were common. Straight cut jeans covered scuffed pairs of Reebok Classics and Reebok Workouts, both fitting footwear for long hours of intense skanking. Although an element of luxury aspirationalism existed, tastes here were more eclectic. Vintage sportswear was embraced in this scene as much as high-end designers; Versace jeans were worn alongside sportswear brands like Sergio Tachinni, Lacoste and Champion. Some of the outfits from this era looked like updated versions of the Mods styles of the 1960s, with distinctly British brands like Fred Perry and Burberry making regular appearances, and some dancers donning double denim.

With its emphasis on MCs and explosive energy, Grime found its roots more intertwined with these alternative underground scenes of British electronic music compared with the cleaner-cut culture of UK Garage. While Grime's sonic heritage can be traced back to Jungle and UKG, the impact of US Hip Hop culture was also felt strongly in Britain, with groups like The Lox and Dipset serving as stylistic touchstones. Indeed, Grime emerged as a rebellious subculture indigenous to British soil but it could not completely shield itself from American influence, the allure of name-brands, or aspiration for material acquisition which fundamentally characterises advanced capitalist societies.

American brands like Schott and Avirex produced sought-after versions of the MA-2 and leather biker jackets, which became prized possessions among British youth during a period when military and motorcycle apparel enjoyed a season of popularity. The blue Prada runners sported by Megaman in So Solid Crew's 2001 feature in The Face were matched with a classic Avirex jacket. In the video for their 2002 song 'Haters', So Solid Crew members wear similar leather outerwear featuring elaborate iconography as they rap in front of parked motorbikes. In More Fire Crew's 'Oi!' video of the same year, group foreman Lethal Bizzle also wears a black Avirex with contrasting white sleeves. As he performs, the drawstrings of the white hoodie layered beneath flail about. His hands are in black leather gloves as he gesticulates manically towards the camera. More Fire Crew member Ozzie B namedrops Avirex during his verse, as well as Reebok Aztecs trainers.

'Oi!' serves as a time capsule marking a transitional period between the old and new. In one scene in the video, Lethal B walks away from the camera, revealing the revered seagull logo of the Japanese brand Evisu on the back pocket of his jeans. Founded in 1991, deriving its name from the Japanese god of prosperity5, Evisu's designer denim wear line would go on to amass a cult following both in the US and in European countries like Italy and the UK. Much like genesis of Grime, Evisu began as a product of painstaking personal passion rather than a commercial endeavour. The seagull logo that the brand is best known for was initially hand painted in white onto each of the limited number of jeans produced early on. Later releases would be available in a wider range of colourways. Lethal B wears an oversized pair, sagging, and rolled up at the ankles. Evisu's intricate embroidery, cotton and leather labels, and detailed designs featuring everything from handpainted

Japanese calligraphy to graphic prints of dragons and koi fish, became much loved.

The appreciation of brands like Akademiks which were imported from America in the late '90s was a continuation of UK youth culture's turn towards streetwear. The high-end occasionwear prevalent at UK Garage raves, as remembered by Kano, soon gave way to slouchy sportswear, alongside hats and hoods which became integral to Grime's image. Although Grime did not desire the gloss and glamour of UK Garage, its consumers were no less invested in their attire.

Dizzee Rascal's 2002 video for 'Jus A Rascal' sees the young MC perform in evening darkness against the East London skyline. True to his description on 'Cut 'Em Off', which also appears on the tracklist of his debut album, Dizzee's jeans sag drastically beneath his waist, a style which would come to be known as bussin' low batties in Black British youth culture. The statement piece of his first outfit in the video is once again a black leather jacket, adorned with logos of Major League Baseball teams like the Chicago White Sox, Chicago Cubs and the Cincinnati Reds. While Baseball never quite penetrated the British mainstream or Grime culture for that matter, the aesthetics of American sports still influenced the fashion of the genre as it emerged.

Another character in Dizzee's video wears a Boston Celtics basketball jersey, and matching beanie hat. The baseball cap completing Dizzee's outfit is busily decorated in colorblock, its crown is white, the underside of its peak a bold blue, the logo of the Philadelphia Phillies team appears front and centre in red. Throughout the video, Dizzee wears it at different angles—cocked left or right to various degrees; pulled low at some points, covering his eyes; tipped towards the sky at others, revealing more of his face.

As Grime continued to mature into a more cohesive sound

and scene, it cultivated its own distinct culture, growing more self-assured in the process. External influences started to diminish; there were immediate domestic issues to contend with. The optimism around the approach of a new millennium for instance faded as bleaker realities set in, such as the glaring wealth disparity between newly developed districts like Canary Wharf and underdeveloped East End areas such as Stratford, Bow and Bethnal Green. The lingering flamboyance of '80s and '90s fashion morphed into a more muted modern minimalism. Designer suits were traded for tracksuits, which became the quintessential article of clothing in Grime culture.

With brands like Adidas and Kangol endorsing global Hip Hop superstars like Run DMC and LL Cool J to market their products in the '80s and '90s, the cultural relevance of tracksuits catapulted. The tracksuit would translate to a mass audience, becoming staple in fashion and lifestyle as well as sports, where they first gained traction. Tracksuits epitomise cool, comfort, and convenience. Made from lightweight fabrics like nylon and polyester, or plush velour as seen in the designs of labels like Juicy Couture, tracksuits allow fuller freedom of movement which is more appropriate for Grime's active energy than the rigidity of denim.

With the UK's socioeconomic precarity and widening inequality, many younger millennials of the British underground would not have had the means to keep up with the luxury image of the outgoing Garage scene. Sold in matching sets, at more reasonable price points, and in a range of eye-catching colourways, tracksuits offered more durability compared to delicate designers as Grime stars and enthusiasts moshed in crowds at soundclashes or mounted roofs after sundown to conduct their covert pirate radio activities.

Brands like Akademiks and Eckō Unltd. joined Adidas as

popular brands in the UK underground, as did Lot29, whose clothes featured cartoon characters like the Looney Tunes and Donald Duck. Trackies were adopted as loungewear for the everyday activities of youngsters like chilling at home, playing games consoles in bedrooms, making music in basements or youth clubs, or simply running around town. With the advent of the internet, young people like myself could scour sites like eBay to get our hands on special stock, while former generations had no option but to travel to shops in places like Roman Road to access the best fits.

Worn even to school where possible, trainers became the fundamental form of footwear for Grime culture. No company would become more central in Grime fashion than Nike, whose Air Max footwear range has been generational. Designed by Tinker Hatfield, the Air Max 1 marked Nike's breakthrough trainer. Its upper, crafted from mesh and suede; paired with a foam sole featuring the company's distinctive air bubble. The hugely successful shoe was first retailed from March 26 1987, an anniversary still reverently observed by streetwear fans today as Air Max Day.

Many iterations of the Air Max have followed and become iconic in their own right. Marking the final decade before the arrival of the new millennium, the Air Max 90s are memorable for their comfort and stylishness. The Air Max BWs, as worn by Dizzee on the cover of Boy In The Corner, landed in '91. The Air Max 95s are now absolute classics; there have been over 150 colourways released since the first grey pair with neon highlights. Those outside of the culture might be confused to hear the Air Max 95s more regularly referred to as '110s', an unofficial nickname derived from the product's previous recommended retail price of £110 in the UK. At the time of writing, they retail from £174.99. For us long-time footwear aficionados, trainers serve as reliable trackers of inflation.

The brainchild of Sean McDowell, bearing design details inspired by Florida's palm trees, the Air Max TNs were released in 1998. Like many other models, these trainers were originally designed for running but soon repurposed by consumers for everyday use. They quickly became highly desirable and widely trendy. Sporty and sturdy, yet still stream-line and subtle, the all black TNs (aka Tuned 1s) remain my personal favourite runaround trainers. They've proven to me to be all but indestructible, able to withstand daily wear in all kinds of weather, sometimes through treacherous terrain.

Although Nike had long been a forerunner of athletic wear, the 2007 release of their first 'tech pack' was pivotal, further shifting the style of the UK's underground and concretising the company's impact beyond footwear. This range updated Nike's innovative windrunner jacket with new materials and details like advanced heat retention technology to trap body warmth between the garment's lightweight synthetic layers. Later versions would use ultra-light goose-down material for insulation, as well as laser-cut ventilation for breathability. Such consideration of climate is appreciated given London's infamously inconsistent weather. The protection that Nike's tech-fleece tracksuits offer against wind and rain has contrib-uted to their popularity among young people of the inner-city. The so-called 'no-sew' manufacturing processes were also employed in the production of the tech-pack, resulting in streamlined pieces without seams, ensuring maximum comfort, mobility and a distinctly modern look. The sweat-pants that came with the tech-pack gained acclaim for their tidiness and versatility. Their tapered silhouette allow them to be worn in various settings for an assortment of purposes. Much to the dismay of the political class, hooded tracksuit sets became the mainstay of youth attire.

The functional minimalism and formidable brand

presence of Nike eclipsed smaller, niche labels like Lot29 whose tracksuits had dominance for a brief period. Even up until today, Nike tech trackies remain the ubiquitous uniform for the children of Grime, serving as a core component of the aesthetic of urban youth culture. The chevron design of the classic windrunner can be seen across the chests of young people across the country, who are also likely to have Jordan 4s or Air Force 1s on their feet.

Nike products have provided inspiration and proved influential for the Grime generation. This powerful influence, however, has not been one-directional, with the growing stature of Grime and underground UK youth culture also helping to sustain Nike's relevance and contributing to its sizeable market share. Nike itself has honoured Grime's lasting legacy, with artists like Dizzee Rascal being offered official collaborations with the company.

As part of the campaign promoting his fourth studio album, Tongue N' Cheek, Dizzee Rascal teamed up with designer Ben Drury to produce an exclusive pair of Air Max 90s in 2009. Their design features a sandy suede and leather upper, while the trainer's contrasting tongues are bright pink per the human anatomy. There is meticulous attention to detail; the shoelaces bear reflective stitching, the toe box and collar are perforated; the back panel of the trainers which usually feature Nike Air branding have been replaced with the logo of Dizzee's Dirtee Stank record label. The release of this model marked a full circle moment since the artist donned BWs on the cover of his debut album. Produced in extremely limited quantities, the asking price for rare, pre-loved pairs of the Tongue N Cheek 90s on sites like StockX is in the thousands.

Other Grime artists such as Skepta have also been invited to work with Nike on trainer and apparel drops.

'Please don't step on my SK's 'cos I ain't down for scuffing,' the

veteran MC raps warningly on a pensive track called 'Still', which is the intro to his 2017 *Vicious EP*.

With a stern tone, and linguistic sophistication not atypical of Grime, Skepta seems to suggest that his footwear being trod upon could lead to a scuff on his shoe as well as a scuffle of the physical kind. The trainers he refers to are his own 2017 collaboration with Nike; Skepta was enlisted to design a special pair of Air Max 97s to commemorate the shoe's 20th anniversary. Called the 'Ultra 17s', Skepta's 97s arrived in a copper, rose-gold and black colourway, inspired by his trips to the desert lands of Essaouira in Morocco. The success of this first product led to a further Nike x Skepta trainer release the following year. This time, the structure of the Air Max 97s was merged with the silhouette of the classic Air Max BWs to create a striking hybrid.

Having already merchandised his own Boy Better Know clothing range, Skepta's collaborations with apparel companies would venture beyond trainers. In 2018 he introduced the Nike SK H86 hat. Crafted from Nike's signature fleece jersey material, the main feature of this baseball cap were its ear-flaps which could either be folded up against the crown or flipped down to cover the sides of the face. The essential headwear brand New Era had previously released versions of similar dogear caps which were popular among the Grime generation in the early 2000s.

The influence of Grime culture on my community compelled my peers and I to make periodic pilgrimages across town in search of specific items of clothing, whether to JD Sports, one of the boutiques on Roman Road, or even the West End. We would procure caps from the New Era store on Carnaby Street or Dark n' Cold on D'Arblay Street. Our journeys were driven by a shared passion for the distinctive styles associated with the genre. New Era's collection of London

Underground themed hats were an instant hit, allowing us to proudly rep our ends through our attire. The New Era caps bearing the distinguishable eyes logo of the Minor League Baseball team Lake Elsinore Storm also caused a sensation. The design's glaring gaze communicates a sense of seriousness that resonated with the unflinching attitude of Grime.

Growing up, throwing on a cap felt as fundamental for me as wearing underwear. Outfits looked painfully plain and incomplete to me when not accessorised with a matching hat of some sort. I resented having to visit places that prohibited me from wearing one. Without a hat, and/or a big, hooded jacket, I felt more vulnerable to outside forces, not least the unforgiving British wind assaulting my level-one shaved head. Young people like myself nationwide acquired impressive headwear collections over time.

Leaders like Skepta forged ahead. The fur trapper hats that the Meridian MC regularly wore from early on in his career brought a sense of soviet militancy to his streetwear ensembles, which often incorporated his own Boy Better Know merch. A 2006 video sees Skepta freestyling in a bedroom alongside other Boy Better Know crew members, including his younger blood-brother, JME. JME has his hair in braids; remarkably, he's not wearing his signature durag. Grime fans know that this is a rare and unlikely sight. Meanwhile, the polar white fur of Skepta's aviator hat matches the bold lettering of his Boy Better Know T-shirt.

An archival image of Meridian Crew presents the archetypical aesthetic of Grime's embryonic era. Big H is in the back of the photo, wearing a grey windbreaker with contrasting yellow highlights. He has a black baseball cap on under its raised hood; its front zipper can be pulled all the way up to conceal half of the wearer's face. Beside Big H is Bossman, in a classic black Nike hoodie. In the front row is JME, his black hoodie bears no visible branding. It is fashioned from a premium-looking fabric, with intricate, stitched detailing.

Today, Skepta is one of the most celebrated style inspirations in British entertainment, named by British *GQ* as one of the 50 best dressed men of 2020. Since launching in 2017, his clothing label MAINS has appeared on the cover of ES, been featured in Vogue, and debuted at London Fashion Week. Skepta first walked these rarefied runways in 2015 with British streetwear designer Nasir Mazhar, dressed in all black, in a nylon utility tracksuit and Nike Air Forces. He has since modelled for Calvin Klein and Bottega.

Grime's impact on the world of fashion would transcend any one figure. In 2019, Treble Clef's classic 'Ghetto Kyote' instrumental soundtracked the Louis Vuitton show at Paris Fashion Week. An orchestra brings to life the legendary production's memorable stringed melody. It couldn't have been predicted the extent to which the aesthetic of Grime would permeate popular culture.

WHITE LABLE CLASSICS

NEEDLE DROP: DANNY WEED, 'CREEPER'

In the contemporary media landscape, the swift dissemination of digital content to an expansive global audience, contrasts greatly with the world in which Grime was born. A standout moment within Grime's sphere occurred in 2019, it involved Dave, an emerging, then 20-year old rapper from Streatham, whose debut album *Psychodrama* had just been released. The viral video sees Dave taking crowd participation to its extreme during a performance at Glastonbury festival.

'I got this track called "Thiago Silva", *yeah,'* Dave says to the crammed audience, who cheer in response.

'Who is sober enough to sing these lyrics along with me?'

A young volunteer named Alex is ushered to the stage by security. He takes a moment to compose himself, a swig from a can of water, and is raring to go. Once the beat drops, Alex enthusiastically raps almost every word of the song with Dave. He feeds off of Dave's energy to hype up the crowd around particular lines. The audience roaring in support is made up of people from cities across the UK, who would have grown in conditions and had experiences vastly different to the lives led by the young, working-class children who created Grime. Widely reported in outlets like the *BBC* and *The Guardian*, this

Glastonbury moment illustrates how far Grime has travelled from its inception in the shadows of London's enclaves.

Dave and Ladbroke Grove MC AJ Tracey's song 'Thiago Silva' meanwhile represents Grime's intergenerational impact. Though released in 2015, 'Thiago Silva's backing track is sampled from a classic instrumental from Grime's golden era. Produced by Rapid of the iconic Grime crew Ruff Sqwad, 'Pied Piper' originally came out in 2002 in the genre's heyday. It is a certified Grime anthem, driven by a distinctive, classic square lead so common in electronic dance music that programs and plugins often come pre-loaded with such a patch.

Just as Dizzee Rascal had harnessed his production skills using his school's music facilities while expelled from his other lessons, Bow-based Ruff Sqwad were also in secondary when they burst onto the scene. It's not hard to understand why making music and being involved in Grime would be more alluring than the rigidity of formal education. There were even occasions where the pull of the studio led these burgeoning creatives to forego the confines of the classroom altogether. Formed initially in 2001, Ruff Sqwad's impact on Grime remains indelible, solidifying their legacy as one of the most foundational and esteemed crews in Grime. Their unique style of production, spearheaded by the in-house pair Prince Rapid and Dirty Danger, helped to change the land-scape of the genre.

'Pied Piper' is a capture of the spirited energy of the early Grime scene. Although the instrumental has only four elements, it is no less effective for its minimalism. A simple drum and snare pattern lay the rhythmic base of the track, accented by a subtle percussive sample. Anything the instrumental might be considered lacking in musical complexity is compensated for by the irresistible groove of the sparse drum sequence, the variable arrangement of the track's components, and the immediate catchiness of its melody. The fun, memorable melody is composed from notes that form the F#m key, not that Rapid would necessarily have paid particular attention to such theory when creating. Instead, through passionately consuming music and obsessively practising the process, the youth of Grime attuned their ears intuitively. Created within this context of free exploration and uninhibited self-expression, 'Pied Piper' emerged as a reflection of youthful exuberance, embodying the essence of Grime, while captivating a range of audiences and standing the test of time. Even though Grime fans will recall a whole host of MCs from D Double E and Esco to Scratch and Skepta spitting on 'Pied Piper' whether on dubs or as part of Radio sets, the instrumental stands sturdily alone as an unerasable piece of Grime history.

Such instrumentals are cornerstones of Grime culture. Their dark, forceful soundscapes are usually enough to invoke feeling, captivate listeners', and narrate a story. Some Grime beats are ingeniously simple, leaving ample space for MCs energetic, meandering flows. Other productions are more elaborate masterpieces, sublime and complete even without vocals. The Grime generation can be presented as a convincing example of how creative excellence can be achieved even with very limited material resources and no formal training. The equipment that many classic Grime tunes were made on was usually elementary. More often than not, the creation process was spontaneous and organic. It's not as though producers or MCs necessarily sat down with the explicit goal of creating enduring classics, rather they were driven by the camaraderie of shared moments among friends or the solitary inspiration in the comfort of their bedrooms.

XTC (RUFF SQWAD)–'FUNCTIONS ON THE LOW' (2004)

'Functions on the Low' is a sombre, reflective instrumental, produced in 2004 by another young Ruff Sqwad affiliate, XTC. In a YouTube documentary about the business of Grime, XTC tells British *GQ* that the beat was inspired by his introspection about day-to-day life. Many years later, 'Functions on the Low' still retains its magic and has people enquiring about its history and origins. The instrumental has aged like wine fine; it seems to gain appreciation with more time. Just one of the numerous unauthorised uploads of the instrumental on YouTube have amassed over hundreds of thousands of views, highlighting its enduring popularity and value to the culture. 'This tune used to get me gassed back when I was what... 13?! Still does,' reads the most liked comment. The instrumental's longevity transcends mere nostalgia. Even today, 'Functions on the Low' is truly something special. The understated melody of the instrumental invokes a sense of calm that is almost antithetical to the hyperactive, discordant energy common in Grime. Having pushed the envelope in this way, it makes sense then that 'Functions on the Low' has been hailed as a classic from the Grime era and has been vocalled many times by various MCs since its release.

'*Ruff Sqwad's not dead*,' says pivotal Grime figure Jammer as he introduces a 2015 performance for BBC's *Live Lounge*. '*It's emotional*,' he announces dramatically over the subdued melody that will be instantly recognisable to those in the know as being from 'Functions on the Low'. Jammer is accompanied on stage by a bassist, pianist and string orchestra. The fluid, legato articulations of the four violinists who play in unison add a layer of sonic richness that elevates the record and deepens its emotional impact. Of course, XTC had access to no such classical instrumentation when he originally made the tune. Nor clearly did he need any. He'd made the tune without any collaborators, in the isolation of the early hours of one fateful morning. It was these twilight settings that inspired the second part of its title. In Jammer's BBC rendition, the original lead melody of 'Functions on the Low' is digitally interwoven with the live offerings of instrumentalists. The fact that something would be lost if the sound was substituted illustrates the unique, irreplicable sonic aesthetic only achievable through the modern synthesis Grime relied so heavily upon. The genre was shaped by the technological context in which it emerged, illustrating the symbiotic relationship between Grime and technology.

The Grime scene was unpredictable. Anyone even from the privacy of their bedroom could happen to create an instrumental or song that would travel farther than they could ever have imagined. XTC recalls for instance being contacted on Myspace by someone all the way in Canada who had got their hands on a copy of Functions. Steady demand for the record led him to press up another 1000 units of white label vinyls following its initial run. At home in Britain meanwhile, XTC can be cited with the rest of Ruff Sqwad as pioneers who laid the foundations for the next generation of producers and artists. Aside from being similarly titled, the 2010 song 'On the Low' by MC South East London MC Maxsta draws upon the same spirit of cathartic reflection that inspired 'Functions'. Big Shizz's description of his feelings as *freezing cold* in his appearance on the song's chorus is also reminiscent of the wintry metaphors abundant in Wiley's early catalogue.

From the instrumental selection to the content of his bars, Jammer's Live Lounge performance is a loving ode to the glorious if unglamorous history of the Grime scene. *'It was all a dream, I used to read* RWD *magazine*,' he raps, appropriating the words of the late Hip Hop legend Biggie to the UK context. *'From the Jungle like Skibba and Shabba D,'* his verse continues, paying homage to pioneering MCs who were prominent within the Jungle scene which helped give rise to Grime. It was this dark, uptempo music as championed by pirates such as Kool FM that directly inspired Grime veterans like D Double E to write and perform their own lyrics. D Double E in turn would inspire people like Kano towards artistry. Many of the leading Grime MCs pay homage to D Double as being among the first and best.

'Me and D Double been causing trouble since Nasty Crew coming through your hi-fi,' Jammer brags nostalgically. His lyrics offer an insight into Grime culture, from its musical origins, to its inherent competitiveness, to the tendency of MCs to roll deep, that is, move around in full entourages as crews: *'Do it BIG like Notorious,'* Jammer spits, *'25 Gs on tour with us.'*

In May 2015, before the public release of Jammer's Live Lounge performance, a new-school South London MC had released a freestyle video on YouTube entitled 'Shut Up'. He too spat over 'Functions on the Low'. In doing so, he introduced this classic instrumental to a whole new generation of young people. Stormzy's 'Shut Up' freestyle has now been viewed over 100 million times. That Grime could command such large listenership would have been unfathomable to its original creators and participants.

The 'Shut Up' video sees a young Stormzy dressed in a bright red Adidas tracksuit in a park.

'State your name cuz,' he's instructed by an off screen voice at the start of the clip.

'Functions's enchanting melody plays in the background.

'Stormzy init,' he dutifully responds.

'*And what are we doing today?*' the interviewer asks.

'*Repping, init,*' replies Stormzy, grinning with confidence.

His friends who fill the video's background adlib throughout his impressive performance.

'*Got about 25 Gs in my posse*', Stormzy raps; his words are evidenced onscreen as being more than just lyrical hyperbole. In its candidness and focus on bars above aesthetics, Stormzy's video is much like the freestyles as seen on DVDs like *Lord of the Mics*, to which he makes reference to in his verse.

In other songs, Stormzy similarly acknowledges the history of the culture he now represents.

'*Shoutout to my big bro Wiley, that's a badman from early*', he spits on 'Know me From', released a couple months prior.

Stormzy's 'Shut Up' video going viral led to a studio version of the freestyle being made available for digital download in September 2015. This release would go on to peak at number 8 in the UK Singles Chart on 18 December, after Stormzy was tapped to perform it at the O2 Arena by British boxing heavyweight Anthony Joshua during his ringwalk. '*Man try say he's better than AJ, tell my man Shut Up,*' rapped Stormzy, remixing his bars for the huge occasion, jeering at Joshua's opponent, Dillian Whyte. Ruff Sqwad is not dead. Ruff Sqwad cannot die. And through Stormzy's performance, the nation would see that Grime itself was indeed alive and well.

MUSICAL MOB—'PULSE X' (2002)

'Pulse X' is an early Grime instrumental produced by Youngstar of the West London crew Musical Mob. Released in 2002, 'Pulse X' is discordant and aggressive compared to the smooth melodiousness of riddims like 'Functions on the Low' which came after. 'Pulse X' crash-landed on the scene before the term Grime even did. Its production is minimal;

there are no frivolities, not even an introduction before the beat drops. The first note of the instrumental after its immediate start is one of thumping bass. It plays along with a classic, syncopated kick and snare pattern, spruced up by scattered hi-hats which provide a head-bopping bounce. This basic drum arrangement remains unchanged for the whole duration of the instrumental as it alternates between two simple 8 bar loops throughout. The first is loud and full, dominated by an imposing 808 bassline, while the pulsing, less imposing low end of the second segment makes for a slightly sparser arrangement. A vocal sample shouting out the group responsible for the production repeats every 32 bars.

'Pulse X' sounds as though it could have been made on *Music 2000*, a retro 8-bar music sequencing programme first released by Sony as early as 1998. Its lofi frequencies sound like clipped, overblown audio. This distorted sonic aesthetic was achieved deliberately by resampling techniques processing the classic TR-808 sound as emulated by Propellerhead's ReBirth RB-338 software with effects like compression and overdrive. The simplicity of 'Pulse X' was perfect for a scene in which MCs were increasingly the stars of the show. Although the instrumental alone can fetch reloads and mash up a rave, it still almost invites lyrics to be overlaid on top of it. Pirate radio giant DJ Slimzee for instance dropped 'Pulse X' during a 2003 Sidewinder set featuring Wiley and Dizzee, who both destroyed the beat accordingly. Sidewinder was a company known for events and sets platforming musical subcultures like Grime, UK Garage and drum and bass. Regarded as one of the earliest examples of Grime music; 'Pulse X' helped to usher in a period that was definitely distinct from the era of UK Garage which preceded it.

'Ayo, big up the Pay As U Go Cartel,' says Dizzee at the start of the set.

'That's how Slimzee's going on?' he asks, as the DJ seamlessly mixes from one bassline number into another Wiley produced instrumental.

His question is rhetorical, posed to show approval of the DJ's selection. By the time 'Pulse X' drops, both MCs are comfortably in their swing, each taking turns to spit verse after verse with alluring pizzazz.

'Pulse X' first broke in July 2001 when played in Ayia Napa by UK Garage outfit Heartless Crew whose raves still sell out today. With Napa being a top party destination for Brits and other young Europeans, this exposure further stimulated demand for the record. 'Pulse X' continued to circulate in tape packs in the underground. The initial batch of vinyl records independently pressed by Musical Mob proved to be a commercial success, selling at £10 per unit. A small scale distribution deal helped the group move thousands of units within the first couple weeks of the record's official release in March 2002, an impressive feat within a fledgling scene with minimal infrastructure and few formal routes to market.

The impact of 'Pulse X' has since been lasting; it quintessentially represents the darker, more brutalist direction that UK music would travel in as it broke away from the more palatable UK Garage that had previously dominated the charts. The energy of tracks like 'Pulse X' is resolutely more anarchic. Youngstar would be subsequently tapped to produce for artists like Dizzee on his sophomore album, *Showtime*. There was an explosion of similarly bassy, skippy instrumentals to follow as new producers arrived on the scene, at once becoming increasingly experimental while also returning to a no-frills musical foundation of visceral rhythms and booming basslines.

WILEY—'ESKIMO' (2002)

'Eskimo' was officially released by Wiley in the summer of 2002 after being teased on the underground circuit following its creation roughly two or three winters before. Wiley's dedication to music and his vision for nurturing a sustainable environment conducive to the flourishing of underground music fueled his creative journey. Wiley's musical output was a product of him being inspired by a broad range of music, particularly the rapid, clamorous sounds of Hardcore and Jungle in which he'd also participated when MCing alongside the likes of Skibadee and Flowdan.

'We had no one to look up to. So we took bits of jungle. Bits of ragga. Bits of garage. In the end we created something different,' Wiley explains in his autobiography, titled Eskiboy, one of the MC's old school monikers.

'Eskimo' is born of such creative freedom. In oral accounts of the instrumental's origin, Wiley has reported that it was created at a bleak time in his personal life when he (once again) had no money and few musical opportunities. With no regard for commercialism then, and unencumbered by the pressures of catering to an audience, Wiley forged ahead producing music that genuinely reflected his own experiences, tastes and sonic disposition. 'Eskimo's arrangement begins with a scratching sound effect reminiscent of a DJ wheeling a record. The instrumental's drums are more refined and intricate than the skeletal minimalism often associated with the earliest Grime releases. Their rhythm and bounce almost invoke the spirit of Ragga, Dancehall, and the adjacent Caribbean genres Wiley was reared on as a child as he attended sound systems and dances with his musician father.

'Fling ah Ragga Riddim like it's '03,' Wiley would spit over a

decade later on his hit single 'Boasty',which features East End actor and musician Idris Elba alongside Jamaican Dancehall star Sean Paul. This musical fusion reflects Wiley's disparate yet compatible sensibilities. Wiley's famed 'Eskimo' composition, however, is speedier and more aggressive, and its drum breaks and distinguished square wave bassline are unmistakably London.

Wiley's musical journey can be traced back to his formative years, where exposure to his father's band's jam sessions cemented his deep affinity for music. Much before 'Eskimo' was even thought of, Wiley had long been experimenting with acoustic instrumentation, playing rhythmic patterns for instance with drumsticks on random household items. He'd later switch to software like Logic and Fruity Loops for their convenience, delving deeper into the world of sound synthesis. More complex than extremely stripped back numbers like 'Pulse X', 'Eskimo' comprises various segments; several futuristic, synthesised sounds play complementary melodies. Like 'Pulse X', the track is arranged in cyclical loops, with some 8 bar segments becoming more dense and climactic before reverting back to the drums and bassline at the song's core. The gliding square bass heard in 'Eskimo' and many other instrumentals by Wiley was programmed by tweaking synth presets on the Korg Triton. Though this sound is not at all exclusive to Grime, or to 'Eskibeat' as Wiley then labelled his creations, it became common within the Grime context.

'Eskimo' was released by Wiley's own record label, Wiley Kat recordings. He went on to sell over 10,000 copies of the record on vinyl, all from the boot of his vehicle per the hustler ethos necessitated by the lack of alternative distribution outlets. Prolific as ever, Wiley would later release a 2nd version of 'Eskimo' as well as what he would call a 'devil's mix', a bass prominent rendition of the track in which the drums are barely audible, inviting listeners to become immersed in its intense, sinister soundscape. As is common in a genre as inherently collaborative as Grime, other artists would also step up to the plate to put their own spin on Wiley's work. South London collective Nu Brand Flexxx for instance would produce a choppy remix that would be called 'Eskimo 3', while DJ, Producer and MC Skepta would release 'Pulse Eskimo', a mashup of the two classics that are Wiley's 'Eskimo' and Musical Mob's 'Pulse X'. Legend has it that 'Pulse Eskimo's alternative title 'Gunshot Riddem' was given after someone discharged a firearm into the air as a part of a frenzied crowd reaction to the eruptive tune being played during a Roll Deep set at Sidewinder's 2002 Bonfire Bonanza event.

'This was the moment everything changed,' Kano told music outlet the *FADER* of 'Eskimo' as he ranked the production at number 1 in his list of top Grime instrumentals.

'For me, there's like life before "Eskimo" and life after it. Life before was Garage... not like 2-step Garage, like the tail-end of Garage. You know, heavier basslines and becoming a tiny bit more aggressive. But I think when "Eskimo" came that was the moment that Garage turned to Grime. And at the time we had never heard anything like it. It's fresh today, you know what I mean? There's still nothing like it. It's realising who we are. We have a scene now, solidifying a movement.'

DANNY WEED—'CREEPER' (2002)

Like 'Functions on the Low', 'Creeper' was also produced spontaneously during unsociable, bedtime hours. Rather than being a solo endeavour, however, 'Creeper' was the product of collaboration. Danny Weed is most commonly remembered and credited for its creation, but he has detailed receiving behind the scenes assistance from his friend, Cage. The mildly echoed, slightly detuned stabs that form half of 'Creeper's melody give the instrumental an eerie quality which make its name appropriate. This distinctive melody is what drives the record forward, as do its jumpy drums. There is a coarse snare sample and hectic percussion. The main melody between staccato strings and a familiar square lead.

'Creeper' could not have come to exist without community. The story of 'Creeper' is one of long-term, hyperlocal, intergenerational ties. Having also grown up in Bow E3, Danny Weed and his brother were part of the same close-knit friendship group as Wiley, DJ Target and Scratchy, all members of Roll Deep Crew. They'd been born in the same hospitals; their homes were a stone's throw from each other; they'd come of age together, sharing formative adolescent experiences like being fired from their first day-jobs. Their parents and even grandparents had known each other for many years. Cage, whose real name is Nick Denton, was manager to Wiley and Dizzee Rascal. It is perhaps unsurprising that these figureheads are relevant to the story of 'Creeper'. Wiley's status as a Godfather of Grime music for instance is scarcely contested; he is readily recognised as a key driving force of the genre. Wiley's creative and entrepreneurial flair have been celebrated by the Grime community as well as by the British state who in 2018 awarded Wiley an MBE for his services to music. Known for encouraging and investing in the talents of those around him, Wiley's selfless if eccentric disposition motivated and helped enrich the entire scene.

Like Dizzee Rascal, Skepta, and many other producers and artists in Grime, Danny Weed was initially a DJ. Decks have always been critical to Grime. DJing serves as a crucial entry-point into all things related to sound. Mixing for example attunes one's ears to intricate rhythms and such other fine subtleties embedded within music. Being a sound selecta primes one's sonic palate by requiring exposure to a high volume and broad range of music. As the importance of recordings within Grime rose to meet that of performance, however, and the demand for a larger variety of riddims for MCs to spit over increased, more and more people would be compelled to create their own instrumentals. Indeed, Grime seems to encourage the constant acquisition of new skills, as DJs turned their hands to producing beats and writing bars, and some MCs eventually hung up the mic to manage other artists, become music executives, or attend to passions in enterprise.

Danny Weed made his first ever instrumental under the tutelage of Wiley, who had invited him to collaborate on a remix he'd been commissioned to create. Wiley recruited Danny Weed for the task even though he had no track record in production; he'd observed the process enough times from hanging around the likes of Target who was responsible for songs from 'Champagne Dance' to instrumentals like 'Earth Warrior'. 'Creeper' is Danny Weed's most famous creation, released via Roll Deep Recordings in 2002. The format was white label vinyl, lacquer cut in limited quantities at JTS Studios in Hackney. This self-starting, ever-determined nature of the Grime scene is one of the key reasons for its enduring impact. Digital copies of 'Creeper' were sent between friends' devices and uploaded onto the internet to be consumed on demand. 'Creeper' became an instrumental of legend within the Grime scene, and is frequently mentioned as one of the best and most representative of the genre's original soul. 'Creeper' within the Grime catalogue is perhaps comparable to what the Alchemist-produced instrumental for Nas's 'Purple' is within Hip Hop. Released in the same year, both beats are archetypal of their genre, and ignite the instincts of MCs to freestyle along to its 8 bar loops. Danny Weed went on to produce instrumentals like 'Salt Beef' and help put together songs on Roll Deep Crew's albums. 'Creeper' alone, however, etches Danny Weed's name not only into the history of Grime but into the lineage of British electronic music more generally.

In a time of bold creativity yet unhampered by industry expectations or label politics, foundational productions like 'Pulse X', 'Eskimo Riddim' and 'Functions on the Low' fuelled the growth of an unruly, mutant sound that would blossom into a fully-fledged scene of its own. There are countless other instrumentals which would also be mentionable. The synthesised brass on Stimpy and Scruface's 'Nutty Violins' together with the record's catchy, pitched up vocal chops and skippy drums, make the instrumental truly unique. Producer Low Deep would employ similar vocal sampling and pitching techniques to create the emotive instrumental 'Never See Me Fall', which is otherwise composed of an airy melody playing atop synthesised strings. Arriving deeper into the Internet age, the latter two beats never saw official dubplate releases but are nevertheless reflective of the raw, lively essence of Grime. Though Grime would continue in its course, and mainstream interest would eventually culminate, these early instrumentals are still some of the best and most innovative music to come out of the genre and out of Britain.

HOOD ECONOMICS
THE DISTRIBUTION AND
CONSUMPTION OF GRIME

NEEDLE DROP: KANO, 'HUSTLER'

When Grime first emerged from the UK's underground, it wasn't taken seriously as an artistic endeavour or recognised as a legitimate form of creative expression. The staunchly anti-social genre therefore did not benefit from the infrastructure of the mainstream music industry. Grime was actively resisted, blocked from coexisting alongside existing genres like UK Garage. In order to have even a remote chance of being heard by the masses, Grime had to create its own platforms. The marginalised young people behind Grime had to find some way of spreading their sound beyond their cramped bedrooms and immediate urban localities.

Space and place have always been important in Grime, with MCs' proudly representing their local areas in their songs. Through clues in the music, it's almost possible to draw a psychic map of the geographies integral to Grime's incubation. 1999 Grime pirates like Freeze FM on 92.7FM were based in West London, as were innovators like Jon E Cash and Dread D of Black Ops Crew. Together, they pioneered new styles of bass heavy, electronic music in the early 2000s initially known as sub-low. The development of this muddy, anti-industry sound took place well away from the hedonistic congestion of Oxford Street and the wealth of West London Boroughs like Westminster or Kensington and Chelsea. On the other side of the compass, in East London, there was Rinse FM (on 100.3FM), and De Ja Vu FM (on 92.3FM), broadcasting from Bow and Hackney Wick. Rinse FM was launched by DJ Slimzee and Geeneus in 1994, while Deja Vu was acquired in 1997 by the accomplished UK music entrepreneur Sting, who developed it into the third most popular radio station in South East England. Rinse and Deja Vu FM were the respective bases of Roll Deep and N.A.S.T.Y crew. Roll Deep were mainly from Tower Hamlets, while N.A.S.T.Y's core members were from the Plaistow, Greengate and Forest Gate areas of East London.

South London was home to the legendary Choice FM, available on 96.9FM and 107.1FM. Choice FM is warmly remembered as the first licensed Black British radio station, launching in 1990 out of a small studio in Brixton. The station still occupies the same frequency today, but has been operating as Capital XTRA since its acquisition by This is Global Radio in 2013. In its heyday Choice FM was a groundbreaking brand unapologetically championing Black music from Britain and beyond. South West London was also home to several members of So Solid Crew, whose accomplishments in UK Garage elevated them to celebrated urban icons. Meanwhile, North London fostered a plethora of pirate radio stations, such as Mission, Heat, and Axe FM, along with notable MCs like JME, Scorcher, and Skepta. The young people of Grime inherited a claustrophobic physical and sociocultural environment, densely populated and characterised by a stifling lack of access to resources. The relentless privatisation of public services and amenities at the time of the genre's genesis resulted in even fiercer competition over the increasingly scarce physical space in London. Too young to take to the ballot themselves, and perhaps too socially disenfranchised to do so even if given the chance, Grime's youth were confined to informal spaces. They convened in the undesirable crevices of the city, from neglected, local street-corners and beneath vandalised bus shelters to the dizzying heights of the rooftops from which they'd eventually conduct their pirate broadcasting activities.

PIRATE RADIO

Grime music did not have many allies in its formation. From music venues to record labels, politicians, music stores and mainstream media, Grime was not valued for much of its journey. The only place outside itself where the genre found a home on was the radio, specifically pirate radio. It was through the rogue wavelengths that the Grime generation would announce their presence to the world. The history of Grime's relationship with pirate radio is fondly recalled by participants and onlookers alike. Brave and creative as they were, though, the young Londoners of the late '90s who traversed the vast city and scaled its high-rise buildings to broadcast their developing sound were actually not the first to exploit pirate radio technology.

Today, several well-known radio stations have their roots in pirate culture. Kiss FM, for example, began as an unlicensed station in autumn 1985 before transitioning to authorised programming from a location on Holloway Road five years later. Even the BBC's flagship station, Radio 1, was preceded by the highly influential, albeit illegal, operations of Radio Caroline. Radio Caroline, a pirate radio venture, started broadcasting as early as 1964 from ships in international waters. Operating outside the jurisdiction of any one state, the station mostly managed to avoid legal consequences, although international authorities viewed their presence and activities unfavourably.

Despite the controversy, the legacy of pirate radio reigns strong, leaving a lasting mark on British culture and pop music. The government initially cited concerns about the potential interference with frequencies used by official marine vessels as one of the reasons for regulating pirate activities. Additionally, there was a purported need to ensure proper revenue collection for the state and artists. The truth however likely involves the state's need to monitor public sentiment and control discourse and culture.

In the 1980s, Home Secretary Leon Brittan launched an official crackdown on pirates. By that point there had been an uncontrollable proliferation of unlicensed radio stations.

'Pirates, I have no time for', he'd said.

'I think we should crack down on them as hard as we can.'

But the surveillance, raids and array of legal measures directed against pirate radio broadcasters would prove positively futile. By the close of 1987, there were scores of unlicensed stations in London, in spite of consistent interference from the Department of Trade and Industry. Many of the pirate stations which were pivotal for Grime music throughout the '90s could not have come to exist without this heritage.

The struggle encountered by Grime in gaining visibility and recognition had remnants of a battle fought before. During the Conservative governments' reign, there was a focus on economic stimulation, accompanied by a brutal motivation to dismantle Britain's Welfare state. The cultural landscape of 1980s Britain under Prime Minister Margaret Thatcher appeared barren and bleak, particularly concerning radio programming catering to diverse audiences. Mainstream stations like LBC, Capital, and BBC Radio London primarily served the white mainstream, playing almost exclusively the homogenous pop music that had long dominated the charts.

Launched in 1980, the pirate station Dread Broadcasting Corporation played a pivotal role in catalysing a cultural revolution as the first radio station entirely dedicated to broadcasting Black music. Broadcasting from locations in West and Northwest London, including Ladbroke Grove and Neasden, DBC was at its core subversive, challenging the prevailing norms of the era regarding race and culture. Operating without authorization during a time of deepening racial tensions, as exemplified by the 1981 Brixton riots, the impact and significance of Dread Broadcasting Corporation extended far beyond just music. The station's raw representation of young Black Britain offered wider society an unprecedented insight into our tastes, cultures, and concerns. Although preceding pirate radio stations like Radio Invicta had already begun playing Black music genres like Funk, Soul and R&B, these stations did not translate authentically to the young Black audiences of the inner city. Radio Invicta's broadcasts, though enjoyed by many, were too polished to appeal to or capture the essence of Black British culture at the time.

The high-profile white presenters such as Chris Hill, Pete Tong, Froggy, and Steve Walsh of the Soul Mafia collective felt less relatable. Hailing from peripheral towns like Essex and Kent, these DJs gained recognition through their residencies in clubs like the Top Rank in suburban Purley. Whilst white music lovers were able to enjoy the luxury of dancing all day to imported Jazz-funk records at these regularly sold-out events, The reality for many young Black Londoners was far less welcoming. They often faced the likelihood of being turned away from venues due to discriminatory door policies, along with the potential for harassment from police officers in an increasingly hostile environment.

Dread Broadcasting Corporation was by contrast founded, run and staffed by young Black Londoners. The station foregrounded Black British identity in all aspects of its affairs, even down its red, gold and green branding, all significant colours in the Rastafarian tradition. The Caribbean accents which could be heard presenting on the station felt far more familiar to listeners. Many such community led radio stations would follow in DBCs footsteps, all contributing to changing the landscape of British music forever.

No two pirate radio shows were ever the same. Etched into the memories of old-school Grime enthusiasts, many fondly recall hearing classic dubplates played on radio shows for the first time. Missing a broadcast might mean forfeiting your single opportunity to hear an exclusive riddim. To mitigate against this risk, it became common for listeners to record shows onto cassette tapes for replay and redistribution purposes. Yet, despite the efforts to capture the essence of the live experience, something was inevitably lost when playing the recorded version. Pirate radio became a rigorous training ground where spitters refined their craft, put their talents to the test and faced the scrutiny of live audiences. Charismatic DJs, veteran MCs and up-and-coming talent all graced the airwaves each seeking to make a name for themselves. Fans would excitedly tune into shows having heard them previously promoted. Murmurs of which other Grime stars could turn up would spread like wildfire through communities. Dynamism and spontaneity were at the essence of Grime music on pirate radio, so much so that MCs might arrive at radio sets much to the surprise of even the stations' owners, let alone the listening public.

Pirate radio gave Grime music a significant signal boost,

and the genre tore through the UK's cities. The illicit status and covert activities of pirate broadcasts added both to their transience and allure. Fans, enchanted by the broadcasts, may have envisioned sophisticated setups, but the reality was often cramped spaces with makeshift equipment, disrupting neighbours with noisy productions.. In time, these infant, haphazard operations evolved into fully fledged stations and brands, with more considered production and even advertising functions. The influence of the pirates became so colossal that actual record labels or even police departments would engage with stations to promote their messages to the growing numbers of listeners. The revenue generated from such advertising in addition to the monthly subscriptions that MCs had to pay in order to perform on air helped stations not only sustain their activities but to diversify into new endeavours such as event promotion.

CUTTING HOUSES

Following this period, the Grime scene blossomed fast. An increasing number of producers and MCs stepped forth from every corner of the city. A range of businesses soon popped up , offering useful services for Grime artists, or stocking highly sought-after products for dedicated fans. Among these, cutting houses played a crucial role, where Grime's creators would go to duplicate their dubplates, that is, to produce a limited number of their latest music pressed onto 12-inch vinyl records. Establishments like Music House in Tottenham Hale or JTS Studios in Hackney are where many of the legendary songs from Grime's catalogue were first pressed up into physical formats. Such sites are critical to the histories of many seminal Grime records, from the obscure and icy collection of primitive productions that Wiley referred to as Eski-Beat, to the early output of artists like Lady Fury, and Roachee and XTC of Ruff Sqwad. Among the reams of notable titles produced at JTS Studios are Wiley's 'Ice Pole Remix', Ruff Sqwad's 'Xtra' and N.A.S.T.Y. Crew's 'Take You Out'. Those of the dubplate era who are particularly attentive to detail may at some point have noticed the company's name inscribed in capital letters along the circumference of some of their old school Grime vinyls. JTS Studios still exists today, on Digby Road, not far from the Bow back-roads that the likes of DJ Slimzee and Tinchy Stryder once frequented.

The entrepreneurial spirit that has long defined Grime culture is perhaps best demonstrated through this ecosystem of independent record production and distribution. Before Grime music blew up and the ubiquity of the Internet, the foundations of its underground scene lay in the specialised network of record stores selling rare Caribbean and American exports. Beyond adept mixing skills, a DJ's reputation was intricately tied to their access to exclusive records. Unlike the imported vinyl popularly played by DJs throughout the '80s, Grime operated within a more localised supply chain. The records played on pirate radio were produced on home soil. DJs' cultivated relationships with producers and artists, often receiving exclusive dubplates or unreleased white labels to play on air.. This symbiotic exchange proved mutually beneficial for all involved: DJs could take credit for breaking certain songs and artists, while stations expanded their listenership and market share. The young, gifted creators of Grime meanwhile enjoyed a budding infrastructure through which they could proudly present their latest works and communicate with their growing audiences.

The economics of pressing up and shifting white label records could prove to be rather lucrative for artists. This enterprising activity was certainly formative to the long careers of scene forerunners like Wiley who is rumoured to have made at least tens of thousands of pounds through this method alone. Before labels like XL or Relentless would offer early deals to Grime acts, producers and MCs routinely invested their own money into duplicating their instrumentals and dubs. Having a pirate radio DJ play one of your records was priceless marketing that would help generate buzz and stimulate further demand. Public sentiments towards a record would be reflected in the volume and tone of calls and texts from listeners. As more and more Grime events were organised, new underground anthems could also be broken on the live circuit.

EVENTS, VENUES, RECORD STORES & DVDS

Grime has often been misunderstood as being inclined towards violence. From records like 'Pow!' being banned at raves to authorities refusing licences to events intending to feature such Black, underground music, the live music landscape has consistently been hostile towards Grime. Police and other decision-makers often used the provocative names of nights like Stampede to justify shutting down events due to safety concerns. The unfortunate reality, though, is that stereotypes about the inherent criminality of young Black men and the lawlessness of our cultures fed into a disproportionate fear of the music leading to disorder. As a result, physically gathering in congregation around Grime music was discouraged by authorities which meant the Grime generation, once again, had to channel the clandestine energy of pirate radio operations when promoting and organising Grime events. In clever bids to evade police detection, many early Grime events were publicly marketed as being for audiences aged under 18.

Despite such efforts, events like La Cosa Nostra at Hackney's Ocean venue still ended explosively with physical confrontations between police officers and young attendees.

East London venues like Ocean, along with Stratford Rex and Palace Pavillion in Clapton, were havens for the growing Grime scene, very different from the exclusive and over-priced clubs of Central London. Located opposite Hackney Town Hall on Mare Street, Ocean served as an exciting hub for grassroots music and youth culture before its closure. Subsequently, Ocean became home to Rising Tide, an independent arts charity dedicated to increasing music and creativity industry access for young people. At old school Grime events like Sidewinder, or Young Man Standing, fans had the opportunity to see their favourite MCs take to the stage. Such an enchanting live experience was a sure step-up from merely hearing artists' voices through pirate radio airwaves.

Throughout the years. vivid tales have recounted the electrifying atmosphere of crowds listening to never-before-heard music at Grime events. Following a discovery of a new hit at raves like Eskimo Dance, eager partygoers would rush to purchase a copy from local record stores, which were increasingly stocking Grime music at this time. Astute artists would make sale or return deals with stores like Uptown Records in Bow to incentivise them to stock their latest releases. Grime's popularity saw countless units of independently produced vinyl fly off shelves across London as well as much further afield.

As Grime continued its meteoric rise, the once-dominant white label format was updated by the more modern CD, marking an important change in how listeners consumed music. Concurrently stores began carrying merchandise from various Grime crews. Leading the charge were groups like Boy Better Know, who marketed their own branded products to forge stronger connections with fans and broaden revenue streams.

Many young people, myself included, would journey to Grime retailers to purchase coveted Boy Better Know T-shirts, available in a wide array of colours and designs. Situated in prime central London locations, stores like Dark N Cold offered essential representation for young Black Londoners like myself. Operating from a small unit in Soho, Dark N Cold sold Grime artists' music and merchandise alongside other streetwear brands like New Era.

The Grime sound continued to evolve as audiences' appetite for new content grew. Advancements in technology provided new ways to capture and showcase the essence of the culture. With personal computers becoming commonplace and music production equipment more affordable, portable video recording technology allowed Grime youth to conveniently document their experiences. DVD series like *Risky Roadz* emerged as a result. Armed with digital cameras and camcorders bought by their parents and grandparents, impassioned Grime innovators hit the streets to capture MCs' freestyles and offer behind-the-scenes glimpses into events.

These DVDs not only helped fans put faces to the names of Grime's most celebrated artists but it also shaped the visual aesthetic of the genre. For example, the gritty, grainy texture of rare archival footage and graffiti-style fonts featured on DVD title screens became emblematic of Grime. Equally just as important were the fact these visuals gave fans a window into the distinct fashion sensibilities of the scene. From the angled baseball caps to the staple that were baggy tracksuit bottoms wore low on the waist.

In the annals of Grime history, one institution stands out as somewhat of a mecca from the genre's enthusiasts: Rhythm

Division, an independent Grime shop located at 391 Roman Road near Bow until its closure in 2010. A significant portion of the footage for numerous episodes of *Risky Roadz* was captured within the hallowed confines of Rhythm Division. Renowned as one of the main stockists of Grime music and merchandise, Rhythm Division was akin to the hood's version of HMV. While there were other record shops that sold Grime, people would travel long distances to visit Rhythm Division in particular. The vibrant market culture of Roman Road ensured the area was always bustling with activity and commerce, bolstering Rhythm Division's esteemed reputation in the Grime scene as not just a record store, but a pivotal Grime landmark.

For a young Rooney Keefe better known as *Risky Roadz*, his formative years were spent as a devoted patron of the store during his secondary school days, fate soon wove an unexpected offering as he would eventually find himself a part-time role at the store. At Rhythm Division, one could meet various Grime MCs and producers who would visit the store for business or social reasons. Rooney established organic relationships with artists like Ghetto, Lethal Bizzle, and Dizzee Rascal, who frequented Rhythm Division to deliver their new material. Leveraging this familiarity, Rooney eventually proposed their involvement in the *Risky Roadz* DVD series, a concept he and the store's manager, Sparky, had developed.

Rhythm Division's bright blue facade is easily recognisable as the backdrop of many of the freestyles and behind the scenes clips from *Risky Roadz*. The shop also served as the venue for numerous Grime sets over the years before its 2010 closure. Prior to its transformation into the quaint coffee shop it is today, Rhythm Division's walls were adorned with vinyl records, event flyers, and stickers, while turntables and a PlayStation provided background music and entertainment for shoppers. Rather than rushing out after making purchases, visitors were encouraged to linger and soak in the Grimey ambiance. In this way, sites like Rhythm Division were crucial to the development of a community of Grime fans and participants alike. Series like *Risky Roadz* meanwhile were formative to the identities of viewers like myself, and have unsurprisingly been cited as direct influences for the newer generation MCs like Novelist. Other examples of Grime DVD series include *Practice Hours*, *Aim High* and *Conflict*, as well as the actionpacked *Lord of the Mics*. Promoted by Boy Better Know artist Jammer, *Lord of the Mics* series compiles footage of MCs engaging in spirited clashes, showcasing their lyrical prowess on the mic.

Far more exclusive than the publicly accessible Rhythm Division, the Leytonstone basement that the classic *Lord of the Mics* clashes are filmed in is crucial to the story of Grime. These DVDs encapsulated the essence of the culture and contributed to its visual identity. MCs from Sharky Major to JME used marker pens, for example, to scribble their tags across the walls of Jammer's dimly lit lyrical dojo. *Lord of The Mics*'s vandalistic aesthetic is consistent with the defiant spirit of Grime. The vehement energy and competitive intensity of *Lord of the Mics* clashes furthermore can be felt through the screen; the shaky footage often seems to complement MCs' dizzying flows. Kano vs. Wiley and Skepta vs. Devilman are but two examples of particularly memorable matchups. These specific DVDs were at once wildly popular and widely circulated yet rare and challenging to obtain. Series like *Lord of the Mics* provide invaluable archival footage from Grime's golden era and played a pivotal role in its distribution and growth. These early visual offerings laid the groundwork for Grime's representation on television and the digital revolution facilitated by platforms like YouTube.

LIMEWIRE, CHANNEL U AND YOUTUBE

In the early 2000's the internet became an essential gateway into Grime especially for those geographically distant from London's inner city. Platforms like GrimeForum and Rewind Forum (stylised as RWD) provided online hubs for Grime fans to share opinions and discuss the latest releases. Applications such as Limewire meanwhile facilitated the sharing of media files between peers. This radical torrent technology meant that people from all around the world could easily download files including software, videos, and music onto their devices. Once downloads were complete, users became so-called seeders from whom data could be leached for others to access the desired content. The internet posed a challenge to existing infrastructure of distributing hard copies of Grime records to physical stores. Artists swiftly lost a significant pathway to visibility and revenue, forcing them to adapt to the digital landscape in order to remain relevant. It was a new era. Vinyl records took a backseat to MP3s; Grime songs and radio sets were now being shared between friends' phones via Infrared and Bluetooth technology or uploaded to social media profiles.

As the buzz around the music grew, so did the demand for visuals. The significance of video in Grime became evident; the emergence of Channel U in many ways seemed to echo the rise of the DVD. Established in 2003 and available on Sky Digital, Channel U provided a crucial platform for Grime culture, offering urban acts the opportunity to have their work broadcast on primetime TV for the first time in the genre's history. Grassroots acts often pooled resources and invested their own finances into producing music videos. Rather than being a hindrance, the limited budget necessitated innovation.

Where production value may have lacked, engaging concepts, quirky transitions and striking locations certainly compensated for it. The inner-city streets and gritty tower blocks where MCs lived or frequented served as backdrops for early Grime videos. From the raw editing to the styling, Grime videos on Channel U usually forewent glitz and glamour in favour of authenticity.

When YouTube launched in 2005, it took the internet by storm. The video sharing platform gained such immense popularity that Google acquired it within just a few months of its launch. Unlike traditional media outlets controlled by gatekeepers who dictate content, audiences were now able to select and stream their preferred media content on demand. DVD series like *Risky Roadz* capitalised on YouTube, using it to promote new releases and tease fans with unseen clips. The advent of YouTube spurred further innovation; new platforms dedicated to documenting the burgeoning Grime scene emerged, building on the legacy of DVD series like *Risky Roadz*. One especially important platform is SBTV, which began in November 2006 as the YouTube account of a young Jamal Edwards. Little did anyone know at the time how culturally significant the platform would become for my generation.

Edwards named his channel after the pseudonym he occasionally used when rapping: Smokey Barz. This moniker was fitting for the fiery freestyles the platform became renowned for regularly uploading. My friends and I eagerly rushed home from secondary school every day to spend countless hours on *SBTV*, watching music videos, listening to our favourite MCs spit bars, discovering emerging acts. Jamal Edwards served as the streets' A&R long before Sony RCA offered him a platform through which he could sign his own artists. SBTV epitomised Grime's intrinsically DIY approach. The earliest videos uploaded to the channel were shot by Edwards himself using a handycam he received from his mother as a gift. Edwards at the time was only in the tender years of teenagehood, without any kind of formal training or team of staff. Edwards learned both about video production and enterprise on the job. From these humble beginnings, SBTV rapidly grew to execute slick, full-scale productions and become a bonafide brand of its own, amassing traffic which easily rivalled the viewership of conventional television networks.

Where Black music had previously faced systematic exclusion from the mainstream, platforms like SBTV helped democratise access and provided visibility for artists. Today's leading UK artists, including Dave, were introduced to the nation through SBTV's Warm Up Sessions, while even pop megastars like Ed Sheeran benefited early on from appearing on the acoustic version of SBTV's trademark F64 freestyle series. The cultural impact of the company has been truly monumental, not only in the UK and much further afield. SBTV provided a blueprint for companies like GRM Daily, Mixtape Madness, and Link Up TV, which have all played significant roles in platforming and boosting acts in Afro Swing, Drill, Rap and more.

From white label vinyl pressings played on pirate radio to digital audio shared between friends, from candid recordings of freestyles and clashes to professionally produced music videos, the Grime scene has been both prolific and innovative. This creative approach to distribution, necessitated by the lack of alternative options, propelled Grime from obscurity to a national sensation. The medium of video offered unprecedented insight into the underground culture, while the internet's reach extended the culture far beyond its inner-city origins. After long being marginalised or outright ignored, the young people of the Grime scene finally captured the attention of the British public.

WHO'S GOT THE LYRICS

NEEDLE DROP: GHETTO, 'REAL TALK'

Where UK Garage prioritised musicality, Grime foregrounded lyricism. Instrumentals became the backing tracks for MCs' verbal gymnastics. Grime embraced repetition and encouraged crowd participation, but was less concerned with catchy choruses or singing in a traditional sense. The transition from the vibes-centric nature of UK Garage to the lyrical focus of Grime, was a gradual process and one that solidified Grime as a distinct genre.

A legion of MCs stepped forth, beginning to quickly outnumber the DJs and producers. More and more crews cliqued up, configuring themselves into self sufficient units that produced, performed and promoted their own music. Due to their lived experiences of deepening inner-city poverty, new forms of racism, and polarising public policy, MCs' content would become realer and rawer compared to the glitz and glamour of old.

Records like Ms. Dynamite's 'Booo!' served as early indicators of the looming regime change. Just as The Ranking Miss P and DJ Camilla had been significant presences on the old pirate radio station Dread Broadcasting Corporation, Ms. Dynamite began hosting shows on Freek and Raw FM before making her own music. 2001 would be a busy year for the budding South London MC, who took both the underground and charts by storm with the release of 'Booo!' and appearing on So Solid Crew's momentous debut album. In a scene and subculture so dominated by men, the contributions of women are often eclipsed. It was artists like Lisa Maffia though whose sung choruses and bridges on tracks like So Solid's 'No Good 4 Me' propelled them to undeniable hits. Lisa Maffia's verse on '21 seconds' is among the most compelling and memorable, while Ms. Dynamite's entrance on 'Envy' is arguably the song's highlight.

'Booo!' is distinguishable because of Ms. Dynamite's verbose vocal performance. Her pen is ferocious; she flows effortlessly over the monstrous, Sticky-produced instrumental. 'Booo!' might be filed next to the output of other experimental producers of this era such as Wookie, who achieved his darker sound by slowing down Drum 'n Bass. 'Booo!'s arrangement is intricate, its introduction exhibits Ms. Dynamite's melodic abilities. Ms. Dynamite is more than an MC or Garage act; the songstress draws from a broad range of musical influences from Soul to Reggae. After her sweetly sung intro on 'Booo!', Ms. Dynamite switches to straight shelling. Her vocal delivery is dynamic and confident, her writing witty and skilful.

'Let my lyrical tongue be your medicine,' she raps, before launching into a further fiery verse.

With an imposing 808, Ms. Dynamite invites listeners to *'feel the bad gyal bass'* with precision. Her pronunciation and inflection bear the influence of her Jamaican heritage. Throughout the song, the powerful bassline dynamically alternates between octaves, adding depth to the sonic landscape. Aptly named the 'dirty mix', the original version of 'Booo!' predominantly features bass and drums, providing a solid foundation for Ms. Dynamite's lyrical delivery. Subtle pizzicato strings sit atop a bellowing low-end and fractured drums. The sick production and Ms. Dynamite's stunning lyricism cemented 'Booo!' as a timeless classic.It's the combination of stellar production and Ms. Dynamite's captivating lyricism that solidifies 'Booo!' as a timeless classic.

'Booo!' is dominated by bars to an extent previously uncommon in Garage. Ms. Dynamite's performance marries the more traditional hosting style of the UK Garage scene she first came through with the thick lyricism that would be foregrounded in Grime. Her rhyme schemes are complex; she manically switches between flows for the song's duration.

'This one's psychotic, it should be sectioned,' she brags, her mental health metaphor expressing her surety of 'Booo!'s excellence.

Ms. Dynamite's content is also substantive. Her lyrics on 'Booo!' admonish men to be more appropriate and respectful towards women in club settings instead of non-consensually handsy. She encourages good vibes; she disavows weapons.

'Fuck the borers; fuck the guns,' says Ms. Dynamite, her advice no less wise for its profanity.

Instead, the MC brandishes her pen as her sword, spraying bars rather than firearms. She nevertheless adopts militant motifs, describing her bars as lyrical shots. Confounding stereotypes about rap's obsession with drugs, 'Booo!'s mention of cocaine is made only as a simile for how affecting and addicting Ms. Dynamite knew her music would be. Instead of narcotics, Ms. Dynamite offers listeners a *'bass injection'*, a natural high induced by music and movement.

This breakout record would prove to be game-changing. Online footage from a 2009 video sees a diverse crowd whistling, screaming and reaching out towards Ms. Dynamite as she tears up Notting Hill Carnival with a captivating performance of the track. Shot almost a decade after the song's original release, the footage transports viewers to the event, although the pixelated, shaky quality may not fully convey the vibrancy of the moment. Ms. Dynamite fetches multiple reloads; the audience can't get enough of her UK anthem. Enjoyed by old school ravers and younger listeners alike, 'Booo!' is an intergenerational gift, still ringing off whenever it's played or performed up until today.

While narrowly missing out on a Top 10 UK record, 'Booo!' still performed impressively. It peaked at number 12 in the official charts, and was the top UK Dance single for some time after its release. 'Booo!'s success paved the way for Ms. Dynamite to sign to Polydor records as a solo artist. While her debut studio album *A Little Deeper* would transcend the confines of UK Garage or Grime to demonstrate her musical eclecticism, 'Booo!' helped popularise a style of music where lyricism reigned. In September 2002, she made history as the first Black woman to be awarded a Mercury Music Prize as a solo artist, winning over nominees such as The Streets and pop icon David Bowie. Her list of accolades expanded with several BRIT Awards in 2003 and 2006. In 2018, in recognition of her contributions to music, the pioneering artist received an MBE.

Records like 'Booo!' laid the foundation for songs like More Fire Crew's similarly titled 'Oi!' to flourish in 2002, by which point the Garage sound and scene had transformed even more. Produced by Platinum 45, 'Oi!' exudes an unmistakably anti-commercial vibe compared to the mainstream chart hits of its era. Its electrifying instrumental features a jumpy percussive loop accompanied by a vocal chant punctuating each beat. The squelching, electronic bassline feels at least adjacent to Garage, while the rhythm of the drums would not sound out of place in a Dancehall rave or carnival. The dry, racy composition invokes the energy of Jungle. Made up of just a few bass notes, 'Oi!'s melody can barely be qualified as such. Yet the production is all the more effective for its skeletalism. Most importantly, it allows the MCs on the record to shine as the main attractions, perfectly complementing their rapid-fire flows.

The verses of Neeko, Ozzie B, and More Fire Crew frontman, Lethal B, are dense and dexterous. Their bars are full of rudeboy attitude and inner-London slang, per the irresistible influence of the Black diaspora. The competitive essence of what would become the Grime scene is heard on 'Oi!', as Lethal B disses the rhymes of his peers as *'lame'* and Neeko dismisses the *'player hate'* that his crew receive because they're *'nang'* (i.e. excellent, and, in this context, superior). What functions as the song's hook is barely separable from its verses. 'Oi!' was not written with a traditional chorus in mind; its refrain was adapted off the cuff from Lethal B's opening bars.

'Oi! Who's that boy Lethal B?' the record begins, after a dramatic spoken introduction which refers to the legendary Grime venue Stratford Rex and revered clothing brand Avirex. The More Fire Crew members agreed that they'd start their respective verses similarly, each spelling out their own stage names.

'Uh oh, there's that N double E,' Neeko continues.

Ominous exclamations like *'Oi!'* and *'Uh oh'* helped grab listeners' attention. Perhaps the anti-social attitude of the record contributed to the interest that the mainstream music industry would eventually show it. 'Oi!' oozes authenticity and cool, zooming in on the tastes and lifestyles of a demographic otherwise underrepresented in British culture and mostly over-looked by wider society.

'Oi!'s last verse is a highlight as the More Fire Crew go back-to-back, playfulling trading lines in a lyrical relay which has the catchiness of a nursery rhyme. While Grime bars are not usually melodic per se, the best MCs are intentional with their intonation, and great verses often invite listeners to singalong. Officially released in 2002 after being produced independently and pressed initially on a £35 dubplate the year before, 'Oi!' remarkably ascended to number 8 in the UK Singles Charts. It provided onlookers a clear insight into the musical and cultural revolution that was taking place away from the homogeneity of chart music.

The revolution was lyrical, and lyrics also thrived outside of studio recordings. Grime sets were action-packed live performances during which dense line-ups of MCs took turns to spit bars. DJs frantically mixed instrumentals and MCs seamlessly matched their rhythm. Each MC might perform an 8 or 16 bar verse before making way for the next. Mic hogging was bad etiquette.

Sets could be heard either through pirate radio broadcasts or seen live at the limited range of raves that centred this mutating millennial sound. When Garage promoters began struggling to secure London venues to hold their raves in, they ventured further afield, to towns and cities like Swindon and Bristol. One iconic series of events from this time was Sidewinder. A 2002 iteration of Sidewinder was marketed as a Bonfire Bonanza and held at The Sanctuary music arena in Milton Keynes.

East London Grime crew Roll Deep jumped on stage to deliver a live set but their appearance was abruptly cut short due to the uncontrollable excitement of the crowd. Despite the brevity of their appearance, every moment of the roughly 20-minute performance was electrifying. Danny Weed and DJ Karnage manned the decks, seamlessly alternating between spinning instrumentals, while Wiley, Dizzee Rascal, Jamakabi and Flowdan took turns on the microphone. Wiley was the first to grab the mic, commanding attention from the outset and earning an immediate wheel up within seconds, showcasing his prowess just three bars into his verse.

'*Nuff ah dem are my yout; nuff ah dem are minor,*' the Bow E3 MC roars, prompting the wheel.

Roll Deep brought the rich history of Jamaican Sound System culture to Buckinghamshire. Following is Danny Weed's timeless classic, 'Creeper', providing the backdrop for Dizzee's climactic verse filled with references to rifles, uzis, and shotguns. The synchronicity of Roll Deep's performance is striking, almost rehearsed, with Wiley's dynamic adlibs seamlessly filling the spaces left by Dizzee for dramatic effect. This dazzling lyrical exhibition appears spontaneous, a testament to their raw talent and acute musical reflexes rather than meticulous preparation for a specific event.

Dizzee's skill earns him a reload as quickly as Wiley's, prompting excitement among the crowd. In a moment of enthusiasm, someone fires an actual firearm into the air, interpreting Dizzee's '*guns in the air*' bar literally, adding to the commotion. Remarkably, the show continues without interruption.

'*Brap, brap, brap!*' exclaim the MCs, their sharp sound effects simulating bullets.

It's from this landmark event that Skepta's cacophonous instrumental 'Pulse Eskimo' gets its alternative name, 'Gunshot Riddim'. The riddim drops as the rave goes on, continuing the chaos. Danny Weed and DJ Karnage carry on dropping a serious selection of white label classics throughout the set. In-house Roll Deep anthems like Wiley's 'Eskimo' and Dizzee Rascal's 'Go' appear alongside releases like Dom Perignon & Dynamite's 'Hungry Tiger' and a sped up version of Youngstar's 'Bongo Madness'. There are many more wheel-ups as the MCs reel off bars. Jamakabi's deep voice and thick Jamaican accent are captivating; in one verse, he quotes Sister Nancy's classic 'Bam Bam'. Dizzee Rascal meanwhile demonstrates the hybridisation of Caribbean and British culture as he asserts that he *'couldn't give a rasclart or a rat's arse.'* There are other Raskit lyrics which especially stand out; simple lines like *'hit 'em like a lightning bolt,'* impactful because of his forceful delivery and cutting pronunciation of every syllable.

Initially archived in tape packs now listenable online, this succinct 2002 Sidewinder set is an archetypal example of the centrality of lyrics in Grime, and the raw, live-and-direct energy of early raves. Contrasted with this live Roll Deep performance, other sets showcased numerous crews collaborating or engaging in clashes with each other.. Another 2002 moment involved Roll Deep and N.A.S.T.Y. Crew performing back-to-back on Deja Vu FM. DJs Karnage and Mak 10 select the riddims, while Roll Deep MCs like Biggie Pitbull, Scratchy and Tinchy Stryder exchange verses with D Double E, Sharky Major and Stormin' MC (R.I.P.) of N.A.S.T.Y. crew. There are countless big ups and shout outs as the packed roster of MCs take turns passing the mic, spitting lyrics over classic Grime instrumentals.

Deja Vu FM's East London headquarters served as the location of a 2003 set organised in celebration of Jammer's Birthday. Members of various crews including Roll Deep, N.A.S.T.Y., Slew Dem, Boyz In The Hood, Ruff Sqwad and East Connection all showed up for the occasion, gathering around the microphone. MCs from Kano and Crazy Titch to Dirty Danger and Esco (R.I.P.) grace the mic to drop verses. Captured on video and distributed via DVD, the MCs are seen tightly gathered in a small room, fellowshipping around decks and a mic. Such sets show the camaraderie that Grime culture fostered and spotlight the raw talent of the youngsters behind the genre.

Yet as much as there was solidarity and collaboration, competition has always been a crucial element of Grime culture.

'If you're not a top boy in your crew, then what you doing?' Wiley asks as part of one of his verses, referring to the friendly competitiveness that existed even between MCs on the same team.

The dedication of MCs to their craft and their desire to distinguish themselves among their peers not only elevated standards across the board but also propelled the entire culture forward. On rare occasions, artistic competition teetered on the brink of physical confrontation.

A DVD fittingly named *Conflict* contains footage of an infamous 2003 clash between Crazy Titch and Dizzee Rascal, again held at Deja Vu FM3. The clash gets heated as Dizzee challenges Titch for repeatedly failing to adhere to the unwritten rules of Grime, specifically the practice of passing the mic after 8 or 16 bars. At one point, Titch spits more than 32 bars without giving the mic over, deviating from the customary norms. When another Titch verse exceeds 16 bars, Dizzee starts to object. Crazy Titch is dismissive and attempts to carry on spitting. Tensions rise, words are exchanged, some indiscernible, and tempers flare.

'I'm not a mook!' Dizzee Rascal exclaims repeatedly refusing to be intimidated and asserting his right to stand up for himself even though he was younger.

'Don't hold him,' Dizzee says, as Crazy Titch starts towards him and the other MCs in the room intervene to restore order. Titch challenges Dizzee to settle matters outside, and the dispute escalates onto the roof of the building. Fortunately, the situation is defused before any violence erupts.

While most Grime clashes were peaceful, the intensity of rivalries often spilled into spirited music performances. MCs and their crews fiercely competed for the top spot, their reputations hanging in the balance. Such was the visceral energy of Grime and the pivotal role of lyrical prowess in shaping the burgeoning scene.

By the mid-2000s, Grime was a sure sensation, a distinguishable sound of its own with a dedicated cult following. Crews like Ruff Sqwad straddled the old and new school, with Prince Rapid already having produced several white label classics and members like Tinchy Stryder having participated in early Sidewinder sets alongside Grime scene elders. Ruff Sqwad are behind some of the records that best represent Grime as a genre, including a 2006 dub called 'Xtra'. An instrumental version of 'Xtra' was released in 2005. The production is symphonic, the synthesised string melody sounds somewhat sinister. Ruff Sqwad's 2006 vocal mix of 'Xtra' is a masterclass in MCing.

The crew's onomatopoeic bars shout out East London (*where the mandem ah boop!*) Place has long been important in UK underground music; Grime especially helped popularise the tradition of MCs repping their endz on songs.

Young people across the nation throughout the early-mid noughties obsessively consumed and created Grime music. Writing lyrics had become a popular way for young people to express and represent themselves and receive recognition from their peers in the process. Many painstakingly practised their flows and punchlines in preparation for their mainstage moment. One solo artist who achieved success around this time was Chipmunk, whose lyrical ability and savvy exploitation of social media helped him to gain visibility. Chipmunk burst onto the scene around 2006, leveraging MySpace to share his recordings, which users streamed and shared on their profiles. Audaciously dubbing himself the *'Grime scene saviour'* from the very opening line of his breakthrough song, 'Who Are You?', Chipmunk's zeal and advanced lyricism at just 16 years old quickly demanded attention. Impressively, he was already on his third mixtape by the time 'Who Are You?' landed but it was this single that introduced the MC to a wider audience. One unofficial reupload of the slick music video on YouTube has over 300,000 views.

On 'Who Are You?', Chipmunk offers details about his personal and musical background. He describes matching his *'Gladesmore jumper'* with an *'Adidas sneaker,'* adapting his standard secondary school uniform into a sportier ensemble. He calls himself as a *'T High Streeter,'* proudly referring to the North London location he grew up in. In describing himself as a *'Chick King eater,'* Mr Munk gives listeners hyperlocal context about his Tottenham neighbourhood. Their accessibility and presence across communities meant that many young people of the inner-city often congregated in chicken shops at lunch times or after school. Chipmunk's distinctive flow in this verse and two syllable rhyme scheme has also been used by other MCs, from fellow North Londoners and Boy Better Know crew members Skepta and Frisco to UK Garage veteran MC Viper. Even newer MCs like Chipmunk couldn't have come to exist without the fundamental contributions of the old Garage scene. Produced by Skeamz, the instrumental for 'Who Are You?' has a cinematic quality somehow reminiscent of Oxide and Neutrino's 'Bound 4 Da Reload'. Both songs sample dialogue from films, with 'Who Are You?' containing audio from the 1996 horror movie *Scream*.

UK Garage defector and key Grime scene architect Wiley also used this flow. In 2007, Wiley extended an invitation to

Chipmunk, along with a young West London MC named Ice Kid, to freestyle on DJ Tim Westwood's rap show. Broadcast on Radio 1 and Radio 1Xtra, Tim Westwood's rap shows attracted a large listenership and helped bring visibility to the UK underground, although the DJ has since faced allegations of sexual misconduct.

In the video, Wiley can be seen beaming proudly in the background of the video, bopping his head erratically as Chipmunk and Ice Kid drop bars over Flukes's 'Hood Economics' instrumental. Chipmunk steps forward first, delivering a breathtaking lyrical display as he seamlessly switches between verses for the whole length of the beat. Ice Kid's penetrating voice, insightful philosophies, and intelligent metaphors meanwhile make for another engaging performance. Chipmunk would go on to release much more music and achieve commercial success. Both MCs would be fondly remembered as Grime scene prodigies. This 2007 freestyle now has over 3 million views and 3 thousand comments on YouTube.

Another epic freestyle dropped on the same platform the following year, becoming one of the best displays of lyricism in Grime history. A YouTube video of Skepta's 2008 Westwood freestyle has amassed almost 9 million views, which is extraordinary given Grime's hyperlocal origin and the limited reach of the early pirate radio broadcasts. Skepta's style of MCing is distinctive for its simplicity and wit. He seems charged with energy, bobbling and bouncing in front of the microphone before beginning his freestyle over Bless Beats's 'Where's My Brother?' Instrumental.

Skepta's lyrics are unflinching; his bars channel the rough-edged, confrontational energy inherent in Grime.

I heard a tune called "Who's Got Lyrics?",*'* says Skepta early on in his freestyle.

Skepta refers to a 2008 track by Ghetto which calls him out by name, among many other MCs.

'I made a tune called stupid question,' Skepta retorts, never backing down from a lyrical challenge.

His charismatic performance lasts for over 8 minutes, packed with entertaining one-liners and sharp jabs at his detractors. Many of Skepta's bars are amusing and quotable.

'I'm champagne, you're Lambrini to me,' he raps, comparing alcoholic beverages to describe himself as superior to his peers.

Skepta's depiction of his lifestyle in his lyrics is compelling, from his vivid vignettes of street life to his devoted ambassadorship of the Ed Hardy clothing brand. His no-frills approach to MCing is refreshing; part of Skepta's appeal is his candour and direct, punchy lyricism. Brimming with confidence in his landmark Westwood freestyle, Skepta declares himself the microphone champion and king of Grime. He has since gone on to become stunningly successful.

Skepta was ranked number 3 in a list of the 10 best UK MCs published by MTV base in 2010. Chipmunk was jointly placed at number 10 with rapper and activist Lowkey. MCs like D Double E and P Money are also listed, ranked below more commercial acts like Tinie Tempah and Professor Green. Lists like these are always bound to be subjective and end up rattling feathers, but one artist in particular had a big problem with MTV Base's 2010 rankings. Ever outspoken, Greengate MC Ghetto (known today as Ghetts) made his grievance with his omission from the Top 10 MCs list clear. Ghetto was part of Grime crew The Movement alongside spitters like Wretch 32 and Devlin. Devlin had made MTV's list, but Ghetto felt he was not ranked highly enough. In response, Ghetto put out a scathing song called 'Who's on the Panel?' directly addressing the decision makers who'd left him off the list. With his trademark dizzying flows and remarkable rhyme schemes, Ghetto has always taken the art of MCing seriously, treating the form like a competitive sport.

Grime is a fiercely competitive genre that prioritises lyrics. Some MCs come up with their bars spontaneously and instinctively, while others put a great deal of thought into and carefully refine their writing.

10

CAN THE UNDERGROUND GO MAINSTREAM?

NEEDLE DROP: TINCHY STRYDER, 'MAINSTREAM MONEY'

Grime recordings were self-produced, A&R'd by the streets, released without much infrastructure. Grime has always been a DIY genre, operating on the fringes of the fringes of the mainstream and striving relentlessly to penetrate the public consciousness. The genre was not confined to the sluggish release schedules of the formal music industry. Early producers and artists churned out instrumentals and dubs tirelessly, satisfying the voracious appetite of their growing audience. There was no bureaucracy; no external approval was required before music could be released, a departure from the traditional major label setup.

The quintessential hallmark of legitimacy for music artists, perhaps, is the studio album. However, even the inception of Grime's first album signed to a record label wasn't born from commercial aspirations. Working on some of his early material on the computers at secondary school, Dizzee Rascal was fuelled by sheer expressive impulse when he produced and wrote some of the songs on *Boy In Da Corner*. Released in 2003 by pioneering indie record label XL recordings, *Boy In*

Da Corner sold unforeseeably well and earned critical acclaim. The generational record produced 2 top 20 singles; while the third, 'Jus' A Rascal', reached number 30 in the singles charts. *Boy In Da Corner* peaked at 23 in the official albums charts, winning the 2003 Mercury Award for Best British album. After receiving the coveted award and £20,000 cash prize, Dizzee Rascal doubled back to his Bow housing estate. Many young people across the UK's inner-cities would have been inspired to witness such success. The impact of *Boy In Da Corner* was extraordinary; many of the albums which followed from the budding Grime scene wouldn't be as momentous.

Wiley's 2004 'Treddin' on Thin Ice' was culturally significant all the same. The first lead single 'Wot Do U Call It' was literally genre-defining, reaching 31 in the official charts. The second single 'Pies' reached number 45. 'Pies' quirky chorus reflects Wiley's eccentric character while the album's title track exposes the MC's pensive and vulnerable side. Most of the album is produced by Wiley himself. A stripped back version of the landmark 'Eskimo' instrumental appears on the track-list as an interlude. One song is produced by DJ Target and Danny Weed; a couple others feature additional production from Cage. With guest appearances from Wiley's younger comrades Kano and Tinchy Stryder, 'Treddin' on Thin Ice' spotlights the raw talent of the UK's underground.

Another one of the first Grime acts to secure a record deal was Shystie. Hailing from my hometown Hackney, Shystie provided crucial representation for young Black women. She first practised MCing during break times at sixth form then went on to spit verses on pirate radio. Before her hit single 'One Wish', which she is probably best known for, Shystie gained underground traction with her white label response to Dizzee Rascal's 'I Luv U'. Polydor Records released her debut studio album *Diamond in the Dirt* in 2004.

True to Grime's prioritisation of lyrics, *Diamond in the Dirt* starts with Shystie spitting an acapella verse. Next up in the tracklist is the album's standout single, 'One Wish', a true classic from the Grime catalogue. 'One Wish' was our very own homegrown anthem before we would start singing US R&B singer Ray J's ballad of the same title the following year. Shystie's sharp lyrics about *'life on the blocks'* of *'H-Town'* prove impactful. Across *Diamond In The Dirt*, she broaches issues including violence, poverty and misogyny, experimenting with conceptual approaches to songwriting. The album is less convincing, however, in its more popminded moments; it sold modestly and received mixed reviews from critics.

Released by V2 Records in 2005, Lethal Bizzle's *Against All Oddz* would also be transient. Lethal B had made waves in the underground and stormed the charts in 2000 and 2004 with More Fire Crew and the roster of MCs he assembled for 'Forward Riddim'. Unfortunately, his debut solo studio album would fail to cut through to the mainstream or shake even the grassroots Grime scene the way 'Oi!' and 'Pow!' did.

There is one standout song called 'What We Do' which reached number 23 in the UK singles charts. 'What We Do' is by UK production duo the Kray Twinz, featuring Lethal B, Gappy Ranks and US rap star Twista. The orchestral instrumental for this transatlantic collaboration features a high-pitched, chopped vocal sample that makes the song especially memorable. The music video for 'What We Do' was also put into heavy rotation on Channel U, the beloved TV station dedicated to Grime and UK Rap. *Against All Oddz* as an album, however, would not leave a lasting impression on the landscape of British music.

An enduring testament to the cultural impact of the Grime scene is the album *Home Sweet Home*. In June 2005, when I was in year 8, a 20 year old MC called Kano released his debut album on *679 Recordings* (a Warner Music Group subsidiary). This unforgettable album soundtracked a pivotal point of my youth, and remains today my personal favourite from the Grime catalogue.

Kano's musical journey was marked by his early exposure to diverse sonic influences. Initially showing promise as a footballer, he eventually gravitated towards music, drawn in by the rich tapestry of sounds around him. Raised in East London, Kano's sonic education was shaped by the rhythms of reggae and dancehall, instilled in him during his formative years. Trips to Jamaica broadened his musical horizon, introducing him to the likes of Buju Banton.

Yet, it was the vibrant East London scene that truly moulded Kano's artistic identity. Immersed in the sounds of UK Garage, Drum n' Bass, and Jungle, he found inspiration in the animated delivery and agile lyricism of MCs like D Double E. Additionally, the influence of American rap, particularly the works of icons like late Biggie, left its imprint on a young Kano. Through this amalgamation of influences, Kano discovered his own voice and embarked on a path that would cement his place in the annals of Grime history.

Before signing an album deal and rising to mainstream prominence, Kano built up popularity on the underground circuit. He regularly appeared on pirate radio station Deja Vu FM alongside N.A.S.T.Y. crew, and famously clashed Grime scene veteran Wiley on Lord of the Mics. In one classic Risky Roadz clip, Kano is standing near his house, casually dropping a freestyle in an Adidas bathrobe on the roadside. Not only did he routinely shell it down on pirate radio and live in the flesh at raves, he was also active in the studio. Early Kano dubs circulated widely on white label vinyl.

The sentiment of the *Home Sweet Home* album is neatly summarised in the opening couplet of a 2004 Kano freestyle over Treble Clef's legendary 'Ghetto Kyote' instrumental.

'I'm from the hood, but it's just home,' Kano raps after a long, skippy instrumental build up.

'... And ain't no place like home, sweet, home.'

In his music, Kano seems equally as patriotic about East London as he is about Jamaica. *Home Sweet Home* proudly celebrates areas like East Ham, Plaistow and Canning Town, although Kano's vivid vignettes would prove relatable to 'ghetto kids' all over. He hails up his E6 postcode on one track; on others, he mentions key East London spots like Faces, an Ilford club where evenings are liable to become eventful. The influence of Kano's Jamaican heritage, meanwhile, is heard in his diction in certain moments and use of patois phrases and slang, as well as his referencing of classic Reggae riddims.

'DJ, wheel up that rahtid tune,' Kano exclaims on 'Nobody Don't Dance No More', mimicking ravers' excitable roars in response to hearing their favourite songs played at functions.

The first official single from *Home Sweet Home* was 'Ps and Qs', a certified Grime classic and archetypical example of the genre. Kano's verses are dense and dexterous; he could not have known then that they would be recited word-for-word by Grime fans for decades to come. 'Ps and Qs' makes no attempt at a conventional, melodic chorus. Kano was not chasing pop appeal. At the same time, he seems acutely aware of his star quality, predicting his ascent to the mainstream.

'I'm too deep, how can Kano stay underground?', he asks on the tune, his rhetorical question and reference to himself in the third person signalling his steadfast confidence.

Kano's rapid-fire flows glide gracefully over DaVinChe's dynamic production. Several synth sounds play complementary melodies, a booming brass fills the lower frequencies. The drum sequence forms a fragmented rhythm, a skippy shaker is scattered between crunchy snares.

'Typical Me' was *Home Sweet Home*'s second single. The riotous hit was Kano's first to chart, peaking at number 23, preparing an audience for his album. Like several other songs across *Home Sweet Home*, 'Typical Me' is produced by Fraser T. Smith. A distorted electric guitar lead roars as Kano and Ghetto narrate stories of drunk and disorderly nights ending with altercations with ego-tripping bouncers at nightclubs.

Home Sweet Home is absolutely informed by but also transcends Grime. 'I Don't Know Why' samples English band Black Sabbath, marrying Rock and Rap like Rick Rubin and Jay Z on '99 Problems'. 'Typical Me' is exactly 140 beats per minute, the standard tempo of Grime, while the *Home Sweet Home* album spans across a range of speeds and rhythms. 'Mic Check 1-2' races along at 174 bpm, while songs like 'Sometimes' feel Hip Hop adjacent at a steady pace of 100 bpm. The instrumental for '9-5' sounds like one 50 Cent might have picked. Another song starts with chirpy House chords over a percussive 4x4 drum pattern. Across the album, thick, wobbly bass lines invoke the feeling of Hardcore and Drum n' Bass. Reggae music and Jamaican culture are also represented; Kano's sombre 'Signs in Life' interpolates a 1995 song called 'Never Dis Di Man' by Jamaican singer, Sanchez.

For all Kano's versatility and sonic experimentation, *Home Sweet Home* is uncompromisingly, unmistakably Grime. The album highlights how Grime is much more than just a sound, but an identity and an approach. A product of old school raves and radio sets, Kano is Grimey through and through. There is reference on his debut album to key sites like DejaVu FM's roof and raves like Sidewinder. Songs like 'Reload It' point back to the roots and foundations of Grime culture—the rapid pace stemming from Jungle, DJs spinning riddims, MCs spitting mean 16s, trying to earn as many wheel-ups as possible. Per Grime's spirit of camaraderie, Kano is joined on the song by his frequent collaborators D Double E and Demon, who each deliver excellent verses.

'I get the tune jacked like jill,' raps D-Double E, appropriating the popular nursery rhyme to execute his boastful simile. He embellishes his verse with his trademark sound effects.

On the other side of the sonic spectrum of *Home Sweet Home* are softer singles like 'Nite Nite' and 'Brown Eyes'. Both of these songs deal with the topic of romantic relationships and are placed beside each other on the album tracklist. 'Nite Nite' is produced by The Streets' Mike Skinner and features Nigerian British vocalist Leo the Lion. With its bright chord progression and silky chorus, 'Nite Nite's gentleness perhaps defies Grime convention, but its 137 bpm is tempo is as expected. Produced by DaVinChe, 'Brown Eyes' is significantly slower, with a laidback rap rhythm and R&B sensibilities. DaVinChe's serene wind-chime synths form a smooth backdrop for Kano's reluctantly lovestruck lyrics.

Whether contemplating matters of a hesitant heart, bragging about his lyrical abilities, detailing drunken misadventures, or soberly reflecting on the state of society, Kano is impressively eloquent and offers refreshing perspective. The content on *Home Sweet Home* is far from surface level. On 'How We Livin'', the young MC inverts his introspection to consider the condition of his wider community, which contrasts starkly with his growing stardom. Kano sounds painfully aware that his success is anomalous, that society does not meritocratically distribute opportunity to all.

Home Sweet Home is a phenomenal effort, excellent evidence of Grime's promise. The album feels like a journey through the city after dark. Listeners are introduced to various scenarios and characters, guided by Kano's insightful narration. His unique ability to marry witty lyricism with relatability, vulnerability, and reflection wise beyond his years helped Kano stand out from his counterparts. *Home Sweet Home* introduced the young East London MC as one of the UK's most formidable writers. In one of the album's more solemn moments, Kano wonders how his music would be received by the British audience.

'*...can the underground go mainstream?*' he asks himself, pondering his fate.

Time would reveal the answer, in his own case, at least, to be a resounding 'yes.' *Home Sweet Home* received rave reviews and is certified Gold status today. The classic record exhibited Grime's potential for eclecticism, demonstrating its commercial viability while never straying too far from the genre's essence.

2005 may have been the final year of Grime's golden era. The following decade was up and down for the genre. The sound of Grime became uncertain, losing its authenticity as more and more artists aspired towards mainstream money. Meanwhile, the excitement that Grime had started stirring in the music industry dwindled. There were a few albums which held the fort for genre in the interim, like Wiley's 2007 *Playtime Is Over* which produced bangers like 'Gangsters' and 'Bow E3'. Kano's 2008 *140 Grime Street* also represented well for the scene, giving us songs like 'Hunting We Will Go' which was inspired by American TV series *The Wire* and again features Ghetto.

Apart from these more established and recognisable names, though, the mainstream remained shut to many emerging artists from the Grime scene. Per the DIY origins of Grime, many MCs pressed on in any case, recording and distributing their own music directly to their fans. Influenced by the activities of stateside rappers, MCs began independently compiling their dubs into longer form bodies of work, exploring a wider range of sounds and subjects compared with Grime's earliest output. Though nevertheless challenging, being able to reel off lyrics as part of sets or on quick dubs is one thing, while putting together a cohesive body of recorded work is another.

Ghetto's 2008 *Freedom of Speech* is a solid example of a project from this period. Tracks like 'Real Talk' show off the Greengate MC's fluid flows and multisyllabic rhyme schemes. Ghetto sounds like a man on a mission on the mixtape; the tone of much of the music is muted and serious. Ghetto shares his limelight with MCs like Griminal and his fellow The Movement crew members Devlin and Wretch 32 who feature on the mixtape. Production meanwhile is overseen by Lewi White and Smasher.

It was also in 2008 that Ghetto teamed up with *Risky Roadz* to present *Fuck Radio*, put together in protest of the marginalisation Grime faced from the mainstream. The *Fuck Radio* series features phenomenal freestyles from some of the Grime scene's finest. Before mainstream platforms would be interested in interviewing them, MCs documented their own activities, compiling behind the scenes footage into DVDs for fans. Ghetto was bursting with artistic ambition; his frustration with an exclusionary music industry was palpable. He would take matters into his own hands to promote his own work and ensure that his talent was given the platform it deserved.

The youngsters behind Grime deserve props not only for their creativity but their entrepreneurialism. They pushed the envelope from artistry to enterprise. They built brands and businesses from the ground up, using guerilla marketing techniques like street teams to promote their mixtapes and merch. As adult responsibility loomed for the youngsters of Grime, many thought about how they would forge financially stable, legitimate careers from their creative endeavours. On a song called 'Mountain', Ghetto wonders whether making Grime music would eventually afford him a mortgage. 'Unsigned Hype' also articulates the unrealised aspirations of many Grime MCs and laments the creative limitations they face because of lack of investment. Their independent activities could only take them so far. As much as Grime emerged as an anti-industry genre, its young creators would rightfully seek recognition and remuneration for their efforts.

Some MCs managed to make successful crossover tunes, like Wiley with 'Wearing My Rolex' in 2008, which spent 6 weeks in the Top 10 UK singles charts, peaking at number 2. The single can be described as Grime meeting Electro. The following year brought Boy Better Know's 'Too Many Man', a bonafide banger which still shuts down functions over a decade on. The popular party tune spent two weeks in the charts, peaking at number 79 but its cultural significance in the UK underground is even more pronounced. With its bouncy, percussive rhythm, 'Too Many Man' is more Funky House than it is a Grime track. It seemed that artists would have to deviate from the Grime sound for their work to be seen and celebrated.

As more and more artists made cultural compromises in pursuit of prominence, the edge of Grime gradually lost to the pop formulas of the mainstream. There was a painful phase of artists chasing hit singles which diluted the sound of Grime for mass appeal. Much of the music that was being released from a once blossoming Grime scene could no longer be accurately be qualified as such. Even if songs like Tinchy Stryder & Dappy's 'Number 1' (2009) or Roll Deep's 'Good Times' (2010) were commercially successful, they were removed from Grime's roots and not nearly as groundbreaking as the genre's early output. Even Grime flag flyer Kano would release a dubious 2009 single called 'Rock N Roller' that awkwardly adopts autotune and an unlikely, unconvincing pop aesthetic.

Albums like JME's 2010 *BLAM!* helped maintain a balance during this dire time for Grime. Although JME's musical approach is lighthearted compared with his grittier counterparts, *BLAM!* is a Grime album in the truest sense, from its decidedly digital style of production and use of classic, crunchy synths, to its featuring of MCs like Tempa T and Trigga. *BLAM!'s* onomatopoeic title and animated artwork are also typical of the genre. The album's outro 'Mario's Flag' is a manic, electronic instrumental, pointing back to the white label tradition of the late '90s and early 2000s. *BLAM!* reflects the influence of subcultures like gaming and WWE on the Grime generation; JME's lyrics mention consoles like the SNES alongside the elbow drop wrestling move. *BLAM!* was well received by its target audience. The independent release managed to ascend to number 66 in the official charts. Even though this entry lasted but 1 week, and JME especially is known for rejecting measures like chart positions as arbiters of success, such is significant all the same given Grime's obscure origins.

The following years were quiet for Grime. A big moment came in 2014 when Boy Better Know affiliate Meridian Dan dropped 'German Whip'. The breakout record seemingly landed from nowhere, suddenly taking the industry by storm. Featuring fellow crew members JME and Big H, 'German Whip' peaked at number 13 in the charts, reminding the mainstream that Grime was still alive and well in the underground and a force to be reckoned with as ever. 'German Whip' sparked something of a renaissance in Grime, preparing a path for MCs like Stormzy who would go on to drop big tracks like 'Shut Up', recorded over an archival instrumental by Ruff Sqwad affiliate XTC.

In 2016, Skepta's eagerly anticipated fourth studio album was released on Boy Better Know recordings. *Konnichiwa* is a stunning composition just shy of 45 minutes in length. Having been a key player in Grime since its embryonic stages, Skepta traces the genre's history on *Konnichiwa*, illustrates its evolution, and represents its future. Bold, bedazzling are bountiful across the album. As can be reliably expected from the trailblazing MC, Skepta's lyricism is characteristically fierce and entertaining.

'I killed every song that I touched, then I turned into MC Hammer, they can't touch me,' he raps on *Konnichiwa*'s intro and title track.

Skepta is definitely on form, as far as his pen is concerned. His flow and cadence are spellbinding as he borrows from the context of US Hip Hop to form his braggadocious punchline.

The second song on *Konnichiwa* is fittingly entitled 'Lyrics'. It begins with an audio clip from a 2001 clash between Heartless Crew and Pay As You Go.

'Lyrics for lyrics,' says Wiley, reminding participants of the musical confines of the competition as proceedings become eruptive.

'Lyrics' derives its chorus from this classic soundbyte and is featured as the second track on *Konnichiwa*. Skepta's musical style and approach have been shaped by the context of clashes and radio sets. This rich lineage of Grime is ingrained within *Konnichiwa*, interwoven in the album's sonic and conceptual tapestry. The growling bassline and vocal chants in 'Lyrics's choppy production are fondly familiar. There is a guest appearance from young South London Grime ambassador Novelist, signalling Grime's intergenerational continuity.

Despite its unprecedented international appeal, *Konnichiwa* is unabashedly British. Skepta makes no cultural concessions, returning definitively to Grime's rough-edged aesthetic after a season of musical experimentation. The first single from

Konnichiwa was released in June 2014, featuring Skepta's brother, JME. 'That's Not Me' is a striking statement of authenticity. Self-produced by Skepta like most of the rest of the album, the smash single bears Grime's signature sound. Its electronic flute lead is reminiscent of the Korg Triton synthesiser, and of classic songs like Wiley's 'Pies' and 'Morgue'. The Tim and Barry directed music video for 'That's Not Me' also essentialises Grime. The Adenuga siblings are dressed in all black, wearing hoodies and caps, energetically performing their bars behind DJ decks. Edited into the background is footage of Skepta and JME rapping on the roadside in the Meridian area of Tottenham where Boy Better Know crew originated. The video's lo-fi style and cutaways of the walls of Jammer's basement invokes the feeling of old *Lord of the Mics* sets.

Konnichiwa's second single 'Shutdown' has a similarly repetitive hook that invites listeners to sing along. A synthesised string melody and squelching bass line are the canvas for Skepta's punchy verses. Skepta spits about wearing tracksuits at fashion shows, achieving musical success with no label, and about Grime being much more than just a genre or culture but a religion. Apart from producing his own tracks, Skepta is distinguishable as an MC because of his conviction and hyperrealism. Skepta is disarmingly candid and direct in his bars instead of being needlessly convoluted. His lyrics remain relatable even though his achievements are remarkable. He raps about travelling to the BRITS on the train and walking home in wet weather after shutting down Wireless Festival.

Another single from Konnichiwa is called 'Ladies Hit Squad', borrowing its title from the former name of UK Garage crew Pay As U Go. While its hook is performed by American Hip Hop artist, ASAP NA$T, Skepta recruits Grime icon D Double E for a guest verse. D Double's sound effects and dramatic diction are captivating; he effortlessly embodies the art of MCing. That Skepta could independently procure transatlantic collaborations with artists as big as Pharrell Williams, furthermore, is both a testament to Grime's growth from its humble, hyperlocal beginnings, and an indication of his own creative stature.

Konnichiwa performed amazingly commercially, peaking at number 2 in the UK charts. The album also charted in Sweden, Holland, Switzerland, America, New Zealand and Australia, and received deserved critical acclaim. The £80 visuals for 'That's Not Me' won a MOBO award for best video, while Konnichiwa won the 2016 Mercury Prize for best British album. Crowned the best album of 2016 by Apple Music, *Konnichiwa* is a celebration of Grime's maturation and evolution since its improbable millennial conception. It demonstrates how Grime has grown to become globally instructive.

In spite of the initial doubt and detraction from commentators, the Grime scene has produced some excellent albums and bodies of work. Records like *Home Sweet Home* and *Konnichiwa* prove that Grime at its best can not only coexist but compete with the mainstream, not only here in the UK but the world over.

THE FUTURE OF BLACK BRITISH MUSIC

NEEDLE DROP: HEADIE ONE, 'BACK TO BASICS (FT. SKEPTA)'

Few could have predicted the colossal heights that Grime would reach. Today, the list of accolades shared between Grime artists is extensive and legendary. MCs have stormed the charts, won coveted awards, launched lucrative businesses and generated life-changing revenue. Music of Black origin, especially Rap, has become instructive for British youth culture.

Wiley and Dizzee Rascal were each given MBEs for their contributions to the British arts, as was the late Jamal Edwards, whose entrepreneurial genius with SBTV helped Grime penetrate the UK's consciousness. In 2020, some of Wiley's social media posts were assessed by police for antisemitic hate speech, he was consequently stripped of his MBE for 'bringing the honours system into disrepute.' In 2019, Grime descendant Dave joined Dizzee Rascal and Skepta as a fellow Mercury prize winner. The rise of Grime, starting from its grassroots origins, is a testament to its enduring impact as one of the most influential subcultures in British history.

New-generation acts like AJ Tracey and Bugzy Malone who emerged from recording war dubs and spitting in Grime sets have enjoyed commercial success. The popularity of Black British music has created opportunities for young people across the nation. Beyond the UK, Grime and its offspring have garnered global acclaim , with British Rap becoming a valuable cultural export. In 2012, Wretch 32 won the BET Award for Best International Act. A decade later, a young North West London rapper named Knucks would be nominated for the same category at the 2022 BET Awards. Although Knucks's sound isn't technically Grime, his music is informed by its legacy.

Grime was once viewed as an anti-social pastime for working-class kids than a legitimate form of creative expression. The sheer passion and persistence of its pioneers has helped the genre to ascend from being banned in nightclubs to billed at the most esteemed venues. In 2019, Kano performed an epic headline show at the Royal Albert Hall, backed by a full orchestra. The powerful production garnered a glowing five star review from *The Telegraph*, a remarkable achievement in stark contrast to the era when Grime events had to operate covertly to evade shutdowns. MCs who once navigated pirate radio stations through secret entrances to evade the authorities are now merking the mainstages at festivals. Following the successful release of his album *Konnichiwa* in 2017, Skepta headlined Wireless Festival. Stormzy's headline performance at the world famous Glastonbury Festival in 2019 marked a historic moment for Grime music and Black British culture. Today, *Konnichiwa* is now a certified Gold record, while Stormzy's first two studio albums have received Platinum certification from the British Phonographic Industry. Hailing from opposite sides of London and different generations, both artists are shining examples of Grime's growth and the life-changing possibilities it has offered its artists. Representing different generations and hailing from opposite sides of London, both Stormzy and Skepta exemplify Grime's evolution and the transformative opportunities it has offered its artists.

Stormzy's debut album *Gang Signs & Prayer* topped the Official UK Albums Chart and won the Brit Award for British Album of the Year in 2018. In 2019, the cover art for his sophomore album *Heavy Is The Head,* was hung on the walls of the National Portrait Gallery. Photographed by Mark Mattock, the artwork depicts the crowned Croydon rapper Stormzy posing topless against a regal, forest green background. In his hands is the stab proof vest from his Glastonbury performance. Designed by the renowned Bristolian artist Banksy, the vest bears a monochrome reinterpretation of the Union Jack flag, its desaturated tones hinting at the darker historical legacies often overlooked in revisionist narratives on empire.

Stormzy's ascent to headlining the UK's premier festivals and being showcased in prestigious institutions like the National Portrait Gallery was unimaginable from Grime's humble beginnings. The young MC is not only a contemporary ambassador for Grime but one of the most recognisable names in British entertainment. His appearances on major television programs like *The Jonathan Ross Show* and *Later... with Jools Holland* for interviews and performances underscore the genre's journey from struggling for radio airplay to achieving primetime recognition. Stormzy's influence extends far beyond music. His initiatives, such as the Stormzy Scholarship provide financial aid to Black students at Cambridge University, and his Merky Books imprint at Penguin Books, which published the cult-classic *Keisha the Sket*, highlight his commitment to social change and literary representation.

Grime's impact has transcended music and shaped broader aspects of Black British culture. MCs like Big Zuu and Big Narstie have successfully transitioned to television, with each securing their own series commissioned by Dave and Channel 4, respectively. Big Zuu's *Big Eats* focuses on cooking; its 4th season aired in winter 2023. The *Big Narstie Show* was co-presented by comedian Mo Gilligan and renewed for five seasons before it ended in 2022.

Black British music culture has given rise to celebrated drama series. Dushane Hill, the kingpin protagonist of the critically acclaimed crime series *Top Boy*, is portrayed by Ashley Walters, once known as Asher D of So Solid Crew. New-generation Grime descendant Little Simz acts alongside Ashley Walters as Dushane's nail technician girlfriend. Veteran Grime MC Kano delivers a stellar, standout performance as the cynical but complex character, Sully. Dave also makes a brief appearance as a deranged drug dealer freshly released from jail. Aesthetically reminiscent of *Kidulthood* and compellingly soundtracked by Black British artists, *Top Boy* became a sure sensation. The series amassed a sizable international viewership and attracted business investment from stateside megastar, Drake.

In 1999, before Grime was an official, distinguishable phenomenon, British Rap accounted for 3.6% of all singles purchased in the UK. By 2020, this figure rose to 22%. Of course, Grime is not singularly responsible for this significant percentage increase. In the mid-late noughties, artists like Giggs and Blade Brown represented Road Rap, recounting street stories over Hip Hop instrumentals. Their 2007 collaboration *Hollow Meetz Blade* is one example of the UK's golden era of independent mixtapes. Giggs's 'Talkin' da Hardest', an epic freestyle over a 2007 Dr. Dre beat, is often called Britain's unofficial national anthem. Since Grime's heyday, just after the turn of the millennium, a myriad of new musical styles have sprouted. Even if its influence is not especially audible in the sound of subsequent subgenres like the Afroswing of the 2010s, Grime's legacy is nevertheless lasting. The genre brought visibility to the Black British underground and helped lay the foundation for a robust infrastructure that continues to benefit artists to this day. Afroswing in contrast to Grime, adopted a more global outlook and makeup. Although Grime is a product of migration and multiculturalism, it is unmistakably British. Afroswing consciously embraces Black diasporic identity. Its sound is characterised by polished melodies, a departure from Grime's discordance and lyrical focus. With artists like Yxng Bane, Kojo Funds and Not3s sweetly serenading the ladies on songs like 'Fine Wine' and 'Addisson Lee', AfroSwing is lighter in sentiment than the despondence of Grime. Afroswing's percussive elements inspire movement, while Grime's music is known to incite energetic mosh pits.

Despite these stylistic differences, AfroSwing pioneer J Hus still cites Grime and Garage as key influences on his music alongside Afrobeats and Dancehall. Working with producers like JAE5, J Hus dips into and successfully blends these diverse sounds. For instance the song 'Plotting' from J Hus's debut album *Common Sense* incorporates UK Garage's signature bright sound and bouncy rhythms. Platforms such as Link Up TV and Mixtape Madness, inspired by the pioneering work of SBTV, played a crucial role in promoting the early careers of artists like Giggs and J Hus, who have since achieved significant commercial success. The very name of the popular UK music outlet GRM Daily is a nod to the generational importance of Grime.

It was in the mid-2010s that Drill music began its journey to becoming the presiding sound of Black British youth culture. While Grime was preceded by UK Garage and informed by the British sounds of Drum 'n Bass and Jungle, Drill music emerged as an evolution of Hip Hop. Drill music merges melancholic melodies with trap rhythms and Gangsta Rap attitudes. It races along at around 144-150bpm with rolling hi-hats and a bias towards bass. Drill was first popularised by Chicago artists like Chief Keef around 2011, but has gone global since its Illinois inception.

UK Drill music is inevitably influenced by earlier British genres like Grime. With their signature sliding baselines and sparse arrangements, producers like Carns Hill, MKThePlug and M1OntheBeat have been seminal architects of UK Drill's soundscape. Tion Wayne and Russ Millions became the first artists to top the Official UK Charts with a Drill single called 'Body' in 2017.

Before the genre crash-landed at the heights of the music industry, a young East London MC called Unknown T made waves with his Drill hit, 'Homerton B'. The 2018 single derives its name from the Hackney location of Unknown T's upbringing. 'Homerton B' quickly went viral for Unknown T's distinctive, deep voice, crisp delivery, and fluid flows. The music video amassed over 1 million views in just three weeks on GRM Daily, and at the time of writing has been seen on YouTube more than 29 million times. 'Homerton B' spent 17 weeks in the UK Singles Chart, peaking at number 48. The single paved the way for Unknown T to perform at festivals, including Leeds and Reading, as well at the London O2 Arena where he appeared at Drake's 2019 headline show.

Uploaded on a YouTube channel called Cord is a 2022 video of a sit-down conversation between Unknown T and veteran MC D Double E8. The pair had collaborated on a 2020 song called 'Double Trouble' as part of a mixtape released in celebration of GRM Daily's 10 year anniversary. The intergenerational influence of UK Garage is reflected even in the glossy Prada trainers Unknown T wears as the two artists speak on camera a couple years later. Grime and UK Drill could not have blossomed without the fundamental foundations of UK Garage and Jungle.

The MCs discuss various subjects. Unknown T tells a funny story about once practising his bars so passionately that he ended up fainting. He shares how artists like D Double E, Boy Better Know and Chip(munk) encouraged him to take his own lyricism seriously. Unknown T's flows do sound like they could have been influenced by the MCs of old. Like the UK Garage MCs of the late '90s, Unknown T's dynamic intonation on his tracks stops just short of singing. The animated adlibs he has become well-known can be compared to D Double E's signature sound effects. Both Unknown T and D Double E attribute their fan-favourite exclamations to pure 'vibes', agreeing that uninhibited expression is key to their artistry.

D Double E details how his business dealings have evolved since his earlier years of artistry. He celebrates having managed to independently secure brand partnerships with companies like Ikea and Pepsi in 2019 and 2021. It was once unlikely that such a grassroots British genre might soundtrack a Christmas advert for Scandinavian furniture but Grime has matured to newfound global appeal.

Unknown T mentions a time when he faced the prospect of lengthy imprisonment for a 2018 incident of serious violence. He was charged through joint enterprise laws in 2019 and remanded in custody until his 2020 acquittal by a jury following a trial. In such court proceedings, rappers' lyrics are increasingly being posited by prosecutors as evidence of their criminal propensity. In cases across the country, bars written and performed by young people as entertainment have contributed to their criminal convictions.

Presenting themselves as experts on rap and gangs, police officers submit dense witness statements which disproportionately focus on youth culture instead of more material and relevant evidence like forensics or CCTV. Rap verses are routinely inaccurately transcribed by police officers who invoke inflammatory narratives of tit-for-tat, gangland violence. If not effectively challenged by clued up defence teams, these mistranslations may subsequently be presented before judges and juries, potentially affecting judicial outcomes. This dubious practice of prosecuting rap goes even further than mechanisms like Form 696 to criminalise culture.

A legal first came in 2019 when South London Drill duo Skengdo and AM were given suspended prison sentences for breaching a gang injunction by performing one of their records. The Metropolitan Police claimed that Skengdo and AM's 'Attempted 1.0' incites gang violence; the pair were prosecuted for playing the song at a 2018 show at Camden music venue, KOKO. The controversial ASBO measure has been updated by civil injunctions and Criminal Behaviour Orders. Among other restrictions like geographic exclusion zones and curfews, artists who are subject to such state discipline might be required to receive prior authorisation before being able to release new music.

Like UK Garage and Grime before, Drill music found itself implicated in a moral panic about youth violence. In the few years leading up to 2020, the disaffected genre was scapegoated for a spate of stabbings and surge in knife crime. Grime had in a way been prophetic. The teenage angst it encapsulated would only intensify with more austerity and conservative commitment to capital over community. With Drill, the sound of young Britain would become even bleaker in style and substance. Yet while much Drill music does graphically describe crime and violence, these social issues by far predate the Gen Z genre and will persist long beyond it if the root causes remain unaddressed. Those familiar with rap's conventions know, furthermore, that performances are most often hyperbolic rather than literal. It is important therefore that creative expression is not conflated with actual criminality.

Drill's aesthetic and attitudes have transformed significantly since its stateside, street-centred origins. As the subculture assimilates with the mainstream, Drill songs and videos increasingly feature melodic choruses and choreographed dances. In spite of the divisive discourse it has generated, Drill has become increasingly influential in global pop culture. The genre's international outlook is exemplified in a 2022 mixtape called *No Borders* by Tottenham artist Headie One. *No Borders*'s tracklist is full of features from Headie's European counterparts. There are appearances from artists like Luciano from Germany, Shiva from Italy, Frenna from the Netherlands, and Yasin the Don from Sweden. Headie One is one of UK Rap's most innovative and successful artists. His 2020 debut studio album *Edna* landed at number 1 in the UK Charts, while his 2019 mixtape peaked at number 5.

Ladbroke Grove artist Central Cee followed suit in 2021, landing at number 2 in the UK Albums Charts with his debut mixtape *Wild West*. This success proved not to be just luck as his sophomore tape *23* claimed the chart's top spot the following year. Central Cee has since released hits like 'Doja' and 'Sprinter' (featuring Dave). 'Doja's bouncy, percussive rhythm feels like Dancehall, while its melody samples 'Let Me Blow Ya Mind', a 2001 song by US Hip Hop artist Eve (featuring Gwen Stefani). Such is the rich genealogy of Black culture, linked across geography and time. Central Cee is the first British rapper to reach one billion annual Spotify streams and has become one of the best-known UK MCs internationally.

Central Cee's viral freestyle on US radio station Power 106 FM has amassed over 7 million YouTube views. The groundwork laid by rappers like Skepta and Giggs who collaborated with American artists like ASAP Rocky and 2 Chainz helped pave the way for Central Cee's international breakthrough. The young West London MC was recently featured on US

Hip Hop superstar J Cole's mixtape on a song alongside Dreamville artist Bas. In 2023, he was reported to have signed a multimillion dollar two-album deal with Columbia Records.

Although Grime is no longer as prominent as it was in its prime, the genre is inscribed in the DNA of British music. Instead of being transient, one hit wonders, it is heartening to see that Grime veterans like Kano have enjoyed enduring success. The young people I work with today are more likely to know Kano as Sully from *Top Boy* than to know him for his early hit 'Ps and Qs'. This longevity and influence across various mediums stand as a testament to the remarkable talent within Black Britain. The impact of Grime extends beyond music, through fashion, television, and art, showcasing its lasting cultural significance.

ESSENTIAL LISTENING

SCAN HERE TO LISTEN
ON SPOTIFY

1. REBOUND X—RHYTHM N GASH

2. KANO—OVER AND OVER

3. DIZZEE RASCAL—CUT 'EM OFF

4. SIA—LITTLE MAN (EXEMEN WORKS)

5. AMIRA—MY DESIRE (DREEM TEEM REMIX)

6. SWEET FEMALE ATTITUDE—FLOWERS

7. SO SOLID CREW—21 SECONDS

8. D DARK (FT. BECKZ, VORTEX, DARKBOI, CREEPER CRISIS, KRUCIAL, ROYAL & KRAZE)—ON THE BLOCK

9. WRETCH 32 (FT. GHETTS, MERCSTON & SCORCHER)(I.E. THE MOVEMENT)—USED TO BE

10. SO SOLID CREW—OH NO (SENTIMENTAL THINGS)

11. DJ LUCK & MC NEAT—A LITTLE BIT OF LUCK

12. OXIDE & NEUTRINO—BOUND 4 DA RELOAD (CASUALTY)

13. TODD EDWARDS—STEAL U'RE HEART (98 EXTENDO VERSION)

14. TINA MOORE—NEVER GONNA LET YOU GO (ARTFUL DODGER REMIX)

15. GROOVE CHRONICLES—MILLENIUM FUNK

16. MONSTA BOY—SORRY (I DIDN'T KNOW)

17. WOOKIE (FT. LAIN)—BACK UP (TO ME)

18. WOOKIE (FT. LAIN)—BATTLE

19. SO SOLID CREW—ENVY (THEY DON'T KNOW)

20. UK APACHE & SHY FX—ORIGINAL NUTTAH

21. WILEY—WOT DO U CALL IT

22. WILEY—ICE RINK

FRANKLYN ADDO

23. WILEY—IGLOO
24. WILEY—TREDDIN' ON THIN ICE
25. CHIPMUNK—FIRE ALIE
26. CLEPTOMANIACS—ALL I DO (BUMP N FLEX DUB EDIT)
27. DANIEL BEDINGFIELD—GOTTA GET THRU THIS
28. ARTFUL DODGER—RE-REWIND
29. B15—GIRLS LIKE US
30. LETHAL BIZZLE—POW! (FORWARD RIDDIM)
31. MORE FIRE CREW—OI!
32. JME—96 FUCKERIES
33. DIRTY DANGER/RUFF SQWAD—MISTY COLD
34. PLASTICIAN (FT. JME, SKEPTA & TINCHY STRYDER)—STILL TIPPIN'
35. JME—BLAM!
36. D DOUBLE E—STREET FIGHTER RIDDIM
37. DIZZEE RASCAL—STREETFIGHTER
38. WILEY—CRASH BANDICOOT
39. KANO—NOBODY DON'T DANCE NO MORE
40. RAMSEY & FEN (FT. LYNSEY MOORE)—LOVEBUG (ORIGINAL BUMP MIX)
41. M DUBS—OVER YOU (BREAK BEAT MIX)
42. ROY DAVIS JR (FT. PEVEN EVERETT)—GABRIEL
43. SO SOLID CREW—HATERS
44. DIZZEE RASCAL—JUS A RASCAL
45. SKEPTA—STILL
46. DAVE & AJ TRACEY—THIAGO SILVA
47. PRINCE RAPID/RUFF SQWAD—PIED PIPER
48. XTC (RUFF SQWAD)—FUNCTIONS ON THE LOW
49. MAXSTA—ON THE LOW
50. STORMZY—SHUT UP
51. MUSICAL MOB—PULSE X
52. WILEY—ESKIMO
53. WILEY—ESKIMO (DEVIL'S MIX)
54. NU BRAND FLEX—ESKIMO 3

156

55. SKEPTA—PULSE ESKIMO (GUNSHOT RIDDIM)

56. DANNY WEED & CAGE—CREEPER

57. DJ TARGET—EARTH WARRIOR

58. DANNY WEED—SALT BEEF

59. TINIE TEMPAH—HOOD ECONOMICS

60. WILEY—ICE POLE REMIX

61. RUFF SQWAD—XTRA

62. N.A.S.T.Y. CREW—TAKE YOU OUT

63. GHETTS—WHO'S GOT?

64. MS DYNAMITE—BOOO!

65. CHIPMUNK—WHO ARE YOU?

66. ICE KID & CHIPMUNK—WESTWOOD FREESTYLE

67. SKEPTA—WESTWOOD FREESTYLE

68. WILEY—WHERE'S MY BROTHER

69. SHYSTIE—ONE WISH

70. KRAY TWINZ (FT. LETHAL B, GAPPY RANKS, TWISTA)—WHAT WE DO

71. KANO—TYPICAL ME

72. KANO (FT. GHETTO)—HUNTING WE WILL GO

73. WILEY—WEARING MY ROLEX

74. BOY BETTER KNOW—TOO MANY MAN

75. MERIDIAN DAN—GERMAN WHIP

76. SKEPTA (FT. D DOUBLE E, A$AP NAST)—LADIES HIT SQUAD

77. UNKNOWN T & D DOUBLE E—DOUBLE TROUBLE

78. HEADIE ONE (FT. SKEPTA)—BACK TO BASICS

79. CENTRAL CEE—DOJA

80. YXNG BANE & KOJO FUNDS—FINE WINE

81. NOT3S—ADDISSON LEE

82. J HUS—PLOTTING

83. TION WAYNE & RUSS MILLIONZ—BODY

84. UNKNOWN T—HOMERTON B

85. SKENGDO & AM—ATTEMPTED 1.0

86. CENTRAL CEE, DAVE—SPRINTER

REFERENCES

CHAPTER 1: MY PERSONAL RELATIONSHIP WITH GRIME

1. Addo, F. (2022) *Resisting the Criminalization of Rap*. Cambridge University Press.

CHAPTER 2: 277 TO LEAMOUTH

1. Plagenhoef, S. (2003, July 6). *Dizzee Rascal: Boy in Da Corner*. Pitchfork. Available at: https://pitchfork.com/reviews/albums/2345-boy-in-da-corner.

2. Morton, S. (2016, September 15). *Dizzee Rascal to perform at the Copper Box Arena*. Newham Recorder. Available at: https://www.newhamrecorder.co.uk/things-to-do/21438854.dizzee-rascal-perform-copper-box-arena.

3. Hunter, M. (1981). *The Victorian Villas of Hackney*. Hackney Society. Available at: www.hackneysociety.org/documents/Victorian_Villas_1981.pdf.

4. *Hackney's heritage*. (2016). London Borough of Hackney. Available at: https://hackney.gov.uk/hackney-history.

5. Bernard, J. (2020, October 19). *Dizzee Rascal Returns Home*. Vice. Available at: https://www.vice.com/en/article/88a4a4/dizzee-rascal-e3-af-interview-2020.

CHAPTER 3: I DON'T CARE ABOUT GARAGE

1. *Top of the Pops through the decades.* (2004, Nov 29). The Guardian. Available at: https://www.theguardian.com/music/2004/nov/29/popandrock.television.

2. Simpson, D. (2019, January 29). *Oxide & Neutrino: how we made* 'Bound 4 Da Reload' *(Casualty)*. The Guardian. Available at: https://www.theguardian.com/culture/2019/jan/29/oxide-neutrino-how-we-made-bound-4-da-reload-casualty.

3. *Rewind 4Ever: The History of UK Garage.* (2013). [Documentary]. Dir. by Alex Lawton. London: Visual Vybe Productions. Available at: https://vimeo.com/187881802.

4. *The Dreem Teem: Radio Show.* (2018, December 22). [Podcast]. BBC Radio 1 (Vintage). Available at: https://www.bbc.co.uk/programmes/p06w9lwl.

5. Luprdubz (2015, June 9). *Groove Chronicles - Millenium Funk.* [Online video]. Available at: https://www.youtube.com/watch?v=Tkca-tENnjo.

6. *Garage wars.* (2000, December 8). The Guardian. Available at: https://www.theguardian.com/friday_review/story/0,,408024,00.html.

CHAPTER 4: DAVID CAMERON IS A DONUT

1. Anderson, B. (2002, April 29). *The time for sentimentality is over. Let's tame these feral children now.* The Independent. https://www.independent.co.uk/voices/commentators/bruce-anderson/the-time-for-sentimentality-is-over-let-s-tame-these-feral-children-now-9179371.html.

2. *Cameron 'hoodie' speech in full.* (2006, July 10). BBC News. Available at: news.bbc.co.uk/1/hi/5166498.stm.

3. *Mall bans shoppers' hooded tops.* (2005, May 11). BBC News. Available at: http://news.bbc.co.uk/1/hi/england/kent/4534903.stm.

4. Tyler, I. (2013). *Revolting Subjects: Social Abjection and Resistance in Neoliberal Britain.* United Kingdom: Zed Books.

5. Honigsbaum, M. (2005, April 26). *Concern over rise of 'happy slapping' craze.* The Guardian. Available at: https://www.theguardian.com/uk/2005/apr/26/ukcrime.mobilephones.

6. *Margaret Thatcher: a life in quotes.* (2013, April 8). The Guardian. Available at: https://www.theguardian.com/politics/2013/apr/08/margaret-thatcher-quotes.

7. Dean, M. (2013, April 9). *Margaret Thatcher's policies hit the poor hardest – and it's happening again.* The Guardian. Available at: https://www.theguardian.com/society/2013/apr/09/margaret-thatcher-policies-poor-society.

8. Lupton, R.; Vizard, P; Fitzgerald, A.; Fenton, A.; Gambaro, L; Cunliffe, K. (2013). *Prosperity, Poverty and*

Inequality in London 2000/01-2010/11. Centre for Analysis of Social Exclusion, LSE. Available at: https://sticerd.lse.ac.uk/dps/case/spcc/rr03.pdf.

9. Glennerster, H. (2004). *One hundred years of poverty and policy.* York: Joseph Rowntree Foundation.

10. *Full text of Tony Blair's speech.* (2005, September 27). BBC News. Available at: news.bbc.co.uk/1/hi/uk_politics/4287370.stm.

11. Sanchez, M. (2021, April 13). *Asbo bars pirate DJ from the rooftops.* The Standard. Available at: https://www.standard.co.uk/hp/front/asbo-bars-pirate-dj-from-the-rooftops-7173468.html.

12. Hall, S. (1978). *Policing the Crisis: Mugging, the State, and Law and Order.* United Kingdom: Holmes & Meier.

13. *Q&A: Operation Trident.* (2006, September 14). BBC News. Available at: news.bbc.co.uk/1/hi/uk/5342246.stm.

14. *The Business Of Grime.* (2016, July 26). [Documentary]. Dir. by Ewen Spencer. London: British GQ. Available at: https://www.youtube.com/watch?v=3_2AVogIb5c.

15. *Form 696: 'Racist police form' to be scrapped in London.* (2017, November 10). BBC News. Available at: https://www.bbc.co.uk/news/uk-41946915.

16. Hancox, D. (2011, February 3). 'Pow!': *anthem for kettled youth.* The Guardian. Available at: https://www.theguardian.com/music/2011/feb/03/pow-forward-lethal-bizzle-protests.

17. Lethal Bizzle. (2006, June 8). *David Cameron is a donut.* The Guardian. Available at: https://www.theguardian.com/commentisfree/2006/jun/08/davidcameronisadonut.

18. Cameron, D. (2006, June 11). *You're talking rubbish, Lethal Bizzle... lyrics about guns and knives do destroy lives.* Daily Mail. Available at: https://www.dailymail.co.uk/news/article-390139/Youre-talking-rubbish-Lethal-Bizzle--lyrics-guns-knives-destroy-lives.html.

19. *Tales From The Grime Generation: Dexplicit Interviewed.* (2014, April 10). Clash Music. Available at: https://www.clashmusic.com/features/tales-from-the-grime-generation-dexplicit-interviewed.

CHAPTER 5: THE TECHNOLOGY OF GRIME

1. Woods, O. (2018). The digital subversion of urban space: power, performance and grime. *Social & Cultural Geography*, *21*(3), 293–313. https://doi.org/10.1080/14649365.2018.1491617

2. Emery, D. (2009, March 3). *Pirate radio 'puts lives at risk'.* BBC News. Available at: news.bbc.co.uk/1/hi/technology/7919748.stm.

3. Limer, E. (2023, December 22). *This Four-Track Tape Recorder Made Me Fall In Love With Music All Over Again.* Gear Patrol. Available at: https://www.gearpatrol.com/tech/audio/a45461959/tascam-portastudio-414-mkii.

4. Roland, M. (2014, June 30) . *The Early Days Of The Minimoog.* Electronic Sound. Available at: https://www.electronicsound.co.uk/features/time-machine/the-early-days-of-the-minimoog.

5. Raw, S. (2016, Feb 29). *Wot U Call It, Eski? The Stickiness Of Grime's Old-School Sounds.* Complex UK. Available at: https://www.complex.com/music/a/son-raw/the-evolution-of-grime-production.

6. Howell, Steve. (2005, November). *The Lost Art Of Sampling: Part 4.* Sound on Sound. Available at: https://www.soundonsound.com/techniques/lost-art-sampling-part-4.

7. Johnson, Derek. (2007, November). *Propellerhead Reason 4.* Sound on Sound. Available at: https://www.soundonsound.com/reviews/propellerhead-reason-4.

8. Poster, M. (2007). *Internet Piracy as Radical Democracy?.* In: Dahlberg, L., Siapera, E. (eds) *Radical Democracy and the Internet.* London: Palgrave Macmillan.

9. DaMetalMessiah. (2024, February 26). *Ruff Sqwad: The Process Behind Their White Label Classics [Full Interview].* [Online Video]. Available at: https://www.youtube.com/watch?v=RG-gCd3MaAo.

10. *The Police vs Grime Music* (2014). [Documentary]. Dir. by Alex Hoffman. London: Noisey. Available at: https://www.youtube.com/watch?v=eW_iujPQpys.

CHAPTER 6: NO HATS, NO HOODS

1. *Rewind 4Ever: The History of UK Garage.* (2013). Dir. by Alex Lawton. London: Visual Vybe Productions. Available at: https://vimeo.com/187881802.

2. Cooper, L. (2021, November 18). *Remembering the golden days of UK garage.* Evening Standard. Available at: https://www.standard.co.uk/lifestyle/uk-garage-scene-reggie-yates-pirates-film-es-magazine-b966768.html.

3. Spencer, E; Constantine, E, Quick, J. (2022). *While You Were Sleeping: 1998 - 2000.* United Kingdom: Damiani.

4. Gorsler, F. (2023). *Prada's Sneaker Pedigree is Unquestionable: Roundup of the Most Iconic Models.* High Snobiety. Available at: https://www.highsnobiety.com/p/prada-sneaker-history.

5. Salamone, L. (2020, December 2). *Prada's long red thread: Twenty years of sneaker culture told in a single release.* NSS Magazine. Available at: https://www.nssmag.com/en/fashion/24451/adidas-x-prada.

6. Lyle, P. (2001). *The Flash Street Kids.* The Face Magazine. Volume 3. (Number 57, October).

7. Stoute, S. (2011). *The Tanning of America: How Hip Hop Created a Culture That Rewrote the Rules of the New Economy.* United States: Penguin Publishing Group.

8. *Behind the Design: Air Max Plus OG.* (2017). Nike. Available at: https://www.nike.com/gb/launch/t/behind-design-air-max-plus-og.

9. Dahlgren, P. (2018, August 10). *The history of Nike Tech Pack.* NSS Magazine. Available at: https://www.nssmag.com/en/fashion/15826/the-history-of-nike-tech-pack.

CHAPTER 7: WHITE LABEL CLASSICS

10. BBC Music. (2019, 1 July). *Dave (feat. Alex) - Thiago Silva* [Online Video]. Available at: https://www.youtube.com/watch?v=e1vlLJCr9Lo.

11. *The Business Of Grime.* (2016, July 26). [Documentary]. Dir. by Ewen Spencer. London: British GQ. Available at: https://www.youtube.com/watch?v=3_2AVogIb5c.

12. BBC Radio 1Xtra (2016). *Jammer - Functions On The Low (Live From Maida Vale).* [Online Video]. Available at: https://www.youtube.com/watch?v=O5OMsnSfUUw.

13. Stormzy (2015, May 17). *Shut Up.* [Online Video]. Available at: https://www.youtube.com/watch?v=RqQGUJK7Na4&t.

14. Get Darker (2015). *Slimzee, Wiley & Dizzee Rascal – Sidewinder Promo Mix – 2002*. [Online]. Available at: https://soundcloud.com/getdarker/ slimzee-wiley-dizzee-rascal-sidewinder-promo-mix-2002

15. Wiley. (2017). *Eskiboy*. London: William Heinemann

16. Raw, S. (2016, February 29). *Wot U Call It, Eski? The Stickiness Of Grime's Old-School Sounds.* Complex. Available at: https://www.complex.com/music/a/son-raw/ the-evolution-of-grime-production

17. Hancox, D. (2017, January 24). *Wiley: the enigmatic Godfather of Grime.* The Guardian. Available at: https://www.theguardian.com/music/2017/jan/24/ wiley-godfather-grime

18. Get Darker (2015). *Roll Deep - Sidewinder - The Bonfire Bonanza 2002 [Dizzee Rascal, Wiley, Flowdan, Jamakabi].* [Online]. Available at: https://soundcloud.com/getdarker/ roll-deep-sidewinder-bonfire-bonanza-2002-dizzee-rascal- wiley-flowdan

19. The Fader. (2019). *Kano's lists his top five grime instrumentals.* [Online Video]. Available at: https://www.youtube.com/ watch?v=mz88AgR7KH0

20. Rinse FM. (2022). *Grime History Lesson #002 with DJ Argue & Danny Weed.* [Online Video]. Available at: https://www. youtube.com/watch?v=ft9A4WIg49A.

CHAPTER 8: HOOD ECONOMICS

1. Second Home (2016, December 15). *A Psychogeographic Guide to Grime.* Available at: https://medium.com/workan-dlife/a-psychogeographic-guide-to-grime-4151f989ceed.

2. *Freeze FM A London Pirate Radio Story.* (2021, May 28). [Documentary]. Dir. by Ashley J. Available at: https://www.youtube.com/watch?v=z1_Rv45M-P4.

3. Keith, J. (2018, November 14). *20 Reasons to love T Williams.* Trench. Available at: trenchtrenchtrench.com/features/20-reasons-to-love-t-williams.

4. *First black radio station Choice FM awarded Blue Plaque in honour of its contribution to British history.* (2021, April 2). Voice Online. Available at: https://www.voice-online.co.uk/entertainment/2021/04/02/first-black-radio-station-choice-fm-awarded-blue-plaque-in-honour-of-its-contribution-to-british-history.

5. Adams, L. (2024, March 30). *Radio Caroline: The pirate radio station turns 60.* BBC News. Available at: https://www.bbc.co.uk/news/uk-england-essex-68677694.

6. BBC News. (2022). *Dread Broadcasting Corporation: The pirate that changed British radio.* [Podcast]. Available at: https://www.bbc.co.uk/programmes/p0djj3r2.

7. *The Last Pirates: Britain's Rebel DJs* (2017). [Documentary]. Dir. by Jaimie D'Cruz. BBC. Available at: https://www.bbc.

co.uk/programmes/b096k6g1.

8. Robinson, Kane (Kano)(2008). *'Hustler', 140 Grime Street* [CD]. London: Bigger Picture Music

9. *Hackney Ocean waves goodbye to grim past with Ritzy revamp.* (2021, April 12). The Standard. Available at: https://www. standard.co.uk/hp/front/hackney-ocean-waves-goodbye-to-grim-past-with-ritzy-revamp-6552968.html.

10. Lynskey, D. (2015, May 28). *How the compact disc lost its shine.* The Guardian. Available at: https:// www.theguardian.com/music/2015/may/28/ how-the-compact-disc-lost-its-shine.

11. Finamore, E. (2018, November 6). *Risky Roadz: Behind The Videos That Shaped Grime.* Clash Music. Available at: https://www.clashmusic.com/features/ risky-roadz-behind-the-videos-that-shaped-grime/.

12. Alemoru, K. (2022, February 21). *How Jamal Edwards captured the early days of grime.* Dazed. Available at: https:// www.dazeddigital.com/music/article/33567/1/ how-jamal-edwards-captured-the-early-days-of-grime.

13. Odukoya, R. (2022, February 22). *How Jamal Edwards changed the Black British music scene forever.* GQ Magazine. Available at: https://www.gq-magazine.co.uk/culture/ article/jamal-edwards-obituary.

CHAPTER 9: WHO'S GOT LYRICS?

1. *Devotional*. (2007). [Exhibition]. National Portrait Gallery. London. 16 June - 25 November 2007. https://www.npg.org.uk/whatson/exhibitions/2007/devotional/ms-dynamite.

2. Mighty Moe (2009, Sept 1). *Ms Dynamite perf Boo! on the Heartless Crew Stage at Notting Hill Carnival 2009*. [Online Video]. Available at: https://www.youtube.com/watch?v=1Gag1F3M65k

3. Chrisafis, A. (2017, February 15). *Ms Dynamite's victory blasts Mercury norms*. The Guardian. https://www.theguardian.com/uk/2002/sep/18/arts.mercuryprize2002

4. Get Darker (2015). *Roll Deep - Sidewinder - The Bonfire Bonanza 2002 [Dizzee Rascal, Wiley, Flowdan, Jamakabi]*. [Online]. Available at: https://soundcloud.com/getdarker/roll-deep-sidewinder-bonfire-bonanza-2002-dizzee-rascal-wiley-flowdan

5. Get Darker (2016). Deja Vu FM: *Roll Deep B2B Nasty Crew - Deja Vu FM 92.3 - 2002*. [Online]. Available at: https://soundcloud.com/getdarker/roll-deep-b2b-nasty-crew-deja-vu-fm-923-2001

6. Ester (2016, Feb 1). *Jammer's Birthday Bash FULL DVD [2003]*. [Online Video]. Available at: https://www.youtube.com/watch?v=jBT0vhU_6yI

7. Off the Radar. (2023, August 17). *Conflict DVD ft Dizzee, Crazy T, Wiley, Tinchy, D Double E, Demon, God's Gift & More.* [Online Video]. YouTube. Available at: https://www.youtube.com/watch?v=hGo7wj9MO1Y.

CHAPTER 10: CAN THE UNDERGROUND GO MAINSTREAM?

1. Hancox, D. (2016, May 6). *Interview: Dizzee Rascal's Music Teacher.* Red Bull Music Academy. Available at: https://daily.redbullmusicacademy.com/2016/05/dizzee-rascal-music-teacher-interview

2. Hasted, N. (2004, July 1). *Shystie: My life of grime.* The Independent. https://www.independent.co.uk/arts-entertainment/music/features/shystie-my-life-of-grime-45441.html

3. Martin, L. (2016, April 4) *Interview: Kano.* Red Bull Music Academy Daily. https://daily.redbullmusicacademy.com/2016/04/kano-interview

4. *Who's on Kano's list?* (2017, February 14). The Guardian. https://www.theguardian.com/music/2007/aug/20/3

5. DaMetalMessiah. (2024, June 5). *10 essential grime documentaries to watch online now.* DJ Mag. https://djmag.com/features/10-essential-grime-documentaries-watch-online-now

6. Gumble, D. (2016, December 7). *Apple Music and iTunes unveil best of 2016 lists.* Music Week. https://www.musicweek.com/talent/read/apple-music-and-itunes-unveil-best-of-2016-lists/066825

CHAPTER 11: THE FUTURE OF BLACK BRITISH MUSIC

1. Mata, W., Campbell, T. (2024, February 23). *London grime MC Wiley stripped of MBE by Cabinet Office for 'bringing honours system into disrepute.'* Evening Standard. https://www.standard.co.uk/news/london/london-grime-mc-wiley-cabinet-office-mbe-antisemitism-b1141214.html

2. McCormick, N. (2019, October 8). *Kano, Royal Albert Hall, review: when grime conquered Queen Victoria's venerable showpiece.* The Telegraph. https://www.telegraph.co.uk/music/what-to-listen-to/kano-review-royal-albert-hall-grime-conquered-queen-victorias

3. Beaumont-Thomas, B. (2020, March 26). *'Nothing but an honour': new Stormzy portrait hung in National Portrait Gallery.* The Guardian. https://www.theguardian.com/music/2019/dec/04/stormzy-portrait-hung-in-national-portrait-gallery

4. Jones, J. (2023, May 23). *Designed by Banksy, worn by Stormzy: the banner of a divided and frightened nation.* The Guardian. https://www.theguardian.com/music/2019/jul/01/

vest-designed-by-banksy-worn-by-stormzy-glastonbury-the-banner-of-a-divided-nation

5. Carty-Williams, C. (2021, October 9). *'I turned against Keisha the Sket for a long time': Jade LB on returning to her noughties viral story.* The Guardian. https://www.theguardian.com/books/2021/oct/09/i-turned-against-keisha-the-sket-for-a-long-time-jade-lb-on-returning-to-her-noughties-viral-story

6. Davies, S. (2021, 9 August). *How UK rap became a multimillion-pound business.* Financial Times. Available at: https://www.ft.com/content/58ecd23f-e1e7-4932-9d70-c57f1b170851

7. Copsey, R. (2021, May 7). *Tion Wayne & Russ Millions score first UK Number 1 drill single with Body.* Official Charts. https://www.officialcharts.com/chart-news/tion-wayne-russ-millions-score-first-uk-number-1-drill-single-with-body__33093/

8. CORD. (2022, September 25). *When Unknown T and D Double E Meet For The First Time!* [Online Video]. YouTube. https://www.youtube.com/watch?v=GJPSHzxtvPw

9. Rymajdo, K. (2020, December 8). *Prosecuting Rap: how a UK legal project is fighting the use of rap lyrics in court.* DJ Mag. https://djmag.com/longreads/prosecuting-rap-how-uk-legal-project-fighting-use-rap-lyrics-court

10. Hancox, D. (2023, December 7). Skengdo and AM: the drill rappers sentenced for playing their song. *The Guardian.* https://www.theguardian.com/music/2019/jan/31/skeng-do-and-am-the-drill-rappers-sentenced-for-playing-their-song

REFERENCE LIST:

Addo, F. (2022) *Resisting the Criminalization of Rap*. Cambridge University Press.

Alemoru, K. (2022, February 21). *How Jamal Edwards captured the early days of grime*. Dazed. Available at: https://www.dazeddigital.com/music/article/33567/1/how-jamal-edwards-captured-the-early-days-of-grime.

Anderson, B. (2002, April 29). *The time for sentimentality is over. Let's tame these feral children now.* The Independent. https://www.independent.co.uk/voices/commentators/bruce-anderson/the-time-for-sentimentality-is-over-let-s-tame-these-feral-children-now-9179371.html.

Beaumont-Thomas, B. (2020, March 26). *'Nothing but an honour': new Stormzy portrait hung in National Portrait Gallery.* The Guardian. https://www.theguardian.com/music/2019/dec/04/stormzy-portrait-hung-in-national-portrait-gallery

Bernard, J. (2020, October 19). *Dizzee Rascal Returns Home*. Vice. Available at: https://www.vice.com/en/article/88a4a4/dizzee-rascal-e3-af-interview-2020.

BBC Music. (2019, 1 July). *Dave (feat. Alex) - Thiago Silva* [Online Video]. Available at: https://www.youtube.com/watch?v=e1vlLJCr9Lo.

BBC Radio 1Xtra (2016). *Jammer - Functions On The Low (Live From Maida Vale)*. [Online Video]. Available at: https://www.youtube.com/watch?v=O5OMsnSfUUw.

BBC News. (2022). *Dread Broadcasting Corporation: The pirate that changed British radio.* [Podcast]. Available at: https://www.bbc.co.uk/programmes/p0djj3r2.

Cameron 'hoodie' speech in full. (2006, July 10). BBC News. Available at: news.bbc.co.uk/1/hi/5166498.stm.

Cameron, D. (2006, June 11). *You're talking rubbish, Lethal Bizzle... lyrics about guns and knives do destroy lives.* Daily Mail. Available at: https://www.dailymail.co.uk/news/article-390139/Youre-talking-rubbish-Lethal-Bizzle--lyrics-guns-knives-destroy-lives.html.

Cooper, L. (2021, November 18). *Remembering the golden days of UK garage.* Evening Standard. Available at: https://www.standard.co.uk/lifestyle/uk-garage-scene-reggie-yates-pirates-film-es-magazine-b966768.html.

Chrisafis, A. (2017, February 15). *Ms Dynamite's victory blasts Mercury norms.* The Guardian. https://www.theguardian.com/uk/2002/sep/18/arts.mercuryprize2002

Carty-Williams, C. (2021, October 9). *'I turned against Keisha the Sket for a long time': Jade LB on returning to her noughties viral story.* The Guardian. https://www.theguardian.com/books/2021/oct/09/i-turned-against-keisha-the-sket-for-a-long-time-jade-lb-on-returning-to-her-noughties-viral-story

Copsey, R. (2021, May 7). *Tion Wayne & Russ Millions score first UK Number 1 drill single with Body*. Official Charts. https://www.officialcharts.com/chart-news/tion-wayne-russ-millions-score-first-uk-number-1-drill-single-with-body__33093/

CORD. (2022, September 25). *When Unknown T and D Double E Meet For The First Time!* [Online Video]. YouTube. https://www.youtube.com/watch?v=GJPSHzxtvPw

Dahlgren, P. (2018, August 10). *The history of Nike Tech Pack*. NSS Magazine. Available at: https://www.nssmag.com/en/fashion/15826/the-history-of-nike-tech-pack.

Dean, M. (2013, April 9). *Margaret Thatcher's policies hit the poor hardest – and it's happening again*. The Guardian. Available at: https://www.theguardian.com/society/2013/apr/09/margaret-thatcher-policies-poor-society.

DaMetalMessiah. (2024, February 26). *Ruff Sqwad: The Process Behind Their White Label Classics [Full Interview]*. [Online Video]. Available at: https://www.youtube.com/watch?v=RG-gCd3MaAo.

DaMetalMessiah. (2024, June 5). *10 essential grime documentaries to watch online now.* DJ Mag. https://djmag.com/features/10-essential-grime-documentaries-watch-online-now

Davies, S. (2021, 9 August). *How UK rap became a multimillion-pound business.* Financial Times. Available at: https://www.ft.com/content/58ecd23f-e1e7-4932-9d70-c57f1b170851

Devotional. (2007). [Exhibition]. National Portrait Gallery. London. 16 June - 25 November 2007. https://www.npg.org.uk/whatson/exhibitions/2007/devotional/ms-dynamite.

Emery, D. (2009, March 3). *Pirate radio 'puts lives at risk'*.
BBC News. Available at: news.bbc.co.uk/1/hi/tech-
nology/7919748.stm.

Ester (2016, Feb 1). *Jammer's Birthday Bash FULL DVD [2003]*.
[Online Video]. Available at: https://www.youtube.com/
watch?v=jBT0vhU_6yI

Finamore, E. (2018, November 6). *Risky Roadz:
Behind The Videos That Shaped Grime.* Clash Music.
Available at: https://www.clashmusic.com/features/
risky-roadz-behind-the-videos-that-shaped-grime/.

*First black radio station Choice FM awarded Blue Plaque in honour
of its contribution to British history*. (2021, April 2). Voice
Online. Available at: https://www.voice-online.co.uk/
entertainment/2021/04/02/first-black-radio-station-choice-
fm-awarded-blue-plaque-in-honour-of-its-contribution-to-
british-history.

Form 696: 'Racist police form' to be scrapped in London. (2017,
November 10). BBC News. Available at: https://www.bbc.
co.uk/news/uk-41946915.

Freeze FM A London Pirate Radio Story. (2021, May 28).
[Documentary]. Dir. by Ashley J. Available at: https://www.
youtube.com/watch?v=z1_Rv45M-P4.

Full text of Tony Blair's speech. (2005, September 27). BBC
News. Available at: news.bbc.co.uk/1/hi/uk_poli-
tics/4287370.stm.

Gallagher, R. (2017). 'All the Other Players Want to Look at My Pad': Grime, Gaming, and Digital Identity. G | A| M| E Games as Art, Media, Entertainment, 1(6).

Garage wars. (2000, December 8). The Guardian. Available at: https://www.theguardian.com/friday_review/story/0,,408024,00.html.

Get Darker (2015). *Slimzee, Wiley & Dizzee Rascal – Sidewinder Promo Mix – 2002.* [Online]. Available at: https://soundcloud.com/getdarker/slimzee-wiley-dizzee-rascal-sidewinder-promo-mix-2002

Get Darker (2015). *Roll Deep - Sidewinder - The Bonfire Bonanza 2002 [Dizzee Rascal, Wiley, Flowdan, Jamakabi].* [Online]. Available at: https://soundcloud.com/getdarker/roll-deep-sidewinder-bonfire-bonanza-2002-dizzee-rascal-wiley-flowdan

Get Darker (2016). Deja Vu FM: *Roll Deep B2B Nasty Crew - Deja Vu FM 92.3 - 2002.* [Online]. Available at: https://soundcloud.com/getdarker/roll-deep-b2b-nasty-crew-deja-vu-fm-923-2001

Glennerster, H. (2004). *One hundred years of poverty and policy.* York: Joseph Rowntree Foundation.

Gorsler, F. (2023). *Prada's Sneaker Pedigree is Unquestionable: Roundup of the Most Iconic Models.* High Snobiety. Available at: https://www.highsnobiety.com/p/prada-sneaker-history.

Gumble, D. (2016, December 7). *Apple Music and iTunes unveil best of 2016 lists.* Music Week. https://www.musicweek.com/talent/read/

apple-music-and-itunes-unveil-best-of-2016-lists/066825

Hackney's heritage. (2016). London Borough of Hackney. Available at: https://hackney.gov.uk/hackney-history.

Hackney Ocean waves goodbye to grim past with Ritzy revamp. (2021, April 12). The Standard. Available at: https://www.standard.co.uk/hp/front/hackney-ocean-waves-goodbye-to-grim-past-with-ritzy-revamp-6552968.html.

Hall, S. (1978). *Policing the Crisis: Mugging, the State, and Law and Order.* United Kingdom: Holmes & Meier.

Hancox, D. (2011, February 3). 'Pow!'*: anthem for kettled youth.* The Guardian. Available at: https://www.theguardian.com/music/2011/feb/03/pow-forward-lethal-bizzle-protests.

Hancox, D. (2016, May 6). *Interview: Dizzee Rascal's Music Teacher.* Red Bull Music Academy. Available at: https://daily.redbullmusicacademy.com/2016/05/dizzee-rascal-music-teacher-interview

Hancox, D. (2017, January 24). *Wiley: the enigmatic Godfather of Grime.* The Guardian. Available at: https://www.theguardian.com/music/2017/jan/24/wiley-godfather-grime

Hancox, D. (2023, December 7). Skengdo and AM: the drill rappers sentenced for playing their song. *The Guardian.* https://www.theguardian.com/music/2019/jan/31/skeng-do-and-am-the-drill-rappers-sentenced-for-playing-their-song

Harkins, P., & Prior, N. (2021): *(Dis)locating Democratization: Music Technologies* in Practice, Popular Music and Society,

DOI: 10.1080/03007766.2021.1984023

Hasted, N. (2004, July 1). *Shystie: My life of grime.* The Independent. https://www.independent.co.uk/arts-entertainment/music/features/shystie-my-life-of-grime-45441.html

Howell, Steve. (2005, November). *The Lost Art Of Sampling: Part 4.* Sound on Sound. Available at: https://www.soundonsound.com/techniques/lost-art-sampling-part-4.

Hunter, M. (1981). *The Victorian Villas of Hackney.* Hackney Society. Available at: www.hackneysociety.org/documents/Victorian_Villas_1981.pdf.

Johnson, Derek. (2007, November). *Propellerhead Reason 4.* Sound on Sound. Available at: https://www.soundonsound.com/reviews/propellerhead-reason-4.

Jones, J. (2023, May 23). *Designed by Banksy, worn by Stormzy: the banner of a divided and frightened nation.* The Guardian. https://www.theguardian.com/music/2019/jul/01/vest-designed-by-banksy-worn-by-stormzy-glastonbury-the-banner-of-a-divided-nation

Keith, J. (2018, November 14). *20 Reasons to love T Williams.* Trench. Available at: trenchtrenchtrench.com/features/20-reasons-to-love-t-williams.

Lethal Bizzle. (2006, June 8). *David Cameron is a donut.* The Guardian. Available at: https://www.theguardian.com/commentisfree/2006/jun/08/davidcameronisadonut.

Limer, E. (2023, December 22). *This Four-Track Tape Recorder*

Made Me Fall In Love With Music All Over Again. Gear Patrol. Available at: https://www.gearpatrol.com/tech/audio/a45461959/tascam-portastudio-414-mkii.

Luprdubz (2015, June 9). *Groove Chronicles - Millenium Funk.* [Online video]. Available at: https://www.youtube.com/watch?v=Tkca-tENnjo.

Lupton, R.; Vizard, P.; Fitzgerald, A.; Fenton, A.; Gambaro, L; Cunliffe, K. (2013). *Prosperity, Poverty and Inequality in London 2000/01-2010/11.* Centre for Analysis of Social Exclusion, LSE. Available at: https://sticerd.lse.ac.uk/dps/case/spcc/rr03.pdf.

Lyle, P. (2001). *The Flash Street Kids.* The Face Magazine. Volume 3. (Number 57, October).

Lynskey, D. (2015, May 28). *How the compact disc lost its shine.* The Guardian. Available at: https://www.theguardian.com/music/2015/may/28/how-the-compact-disc-lost-its-shine.

Mall bans shoppers' hooded tops. (2005, May 11). BBC News. Available at: http://news.bbc.co.uk/1/hi/england/kent/4534903.stm.

Margaret Thatcher: a life in quotes. (2013, April 8). The Guardian. Available at: https://www.theguardian.com/politics/2013/apr/08/margaret-thatcher-quotes.

Martin, L. (2016, April 4) *Interview: Kano.* Red Bull Music Academy Daily. https://daily.redbullmusicacademy.com/2016/04/kano-interview

Mata, W., Campbell, T. (2024, February 23). *London grime MC Wiley stripped of MBE by Cabinet Office for 'bringing honours system into disrepute.'* Evening Standard. https://www.standard.co.uk/news/london/london-grime-mc-wiley-cabinet-office-mbe-antisemitism-b1141214.html

McCormick, N. (2019, October 8). *Kano, Royal Albert Hall, review: when grime conquered Queen Victoria's venerable showpiece.* The Telegraph. https://www.telegraph.co.uk/music/what-to-listen-to/kano-review-royal-albert-hall-grime-conquered-queen-victorias

Mighty Moe (2009, Sept 1). *Ms Dynamite perf Boo! on the Heartless Crew Stage at Notting Hill Carnival 2009.* [Online Video]. Available at: https://www.youtube.com/watch?v=1Gag1F3M65k

Morton, S. (2016, September 15). *Dizzee Rascal to perform at the Copper Box Arena.* Newham Recorder. Available at: https://www.newhamrecorder.co.uk/things-to-do/21438854.dizzee-rascal-perform-copper-box-arena.

Odukoya, R. (2022, February 22). *How Jamal Edwards changed the Black British music scene forever.* GQ Magazine. Available at: https://www.gq-magazine.co.uk/culture/article/jamal-edwards-obituary.

Off the Radar. (2023, August 17). *Conflict DVD ft Dizzee, Crazy T, Wiley, Tinchy, D Double E, Demon, God's Gift & More.* [Online Video]. YouTube. Available at: https://www.youtube.com/watch?v=hGo7wj9MO1Y.

Plagenhoef, S. (2003, July 6). *Dizzee Rascal: Boy in Da Corner.* Pitchfork. Available at: https://pitchfork.com/reviews/albums/2345-boy-in-da-corner.

Poster, M. (2007). *Internet Piracy as Radical Democracy?.* In: Dahlberg, L., Siapera, E. (eds) *Radical Democracy and the Internet.* London: Palgrave Macmillan.

Q&A: Operation Trident. (2006, September 14). BBC News. Available at: news.bbc.co.uk/1/hi/uk/5342246.stm.

Raw, S. (2016, February 29). *Wot U Call It, Eski? The Stickiness Of Grime's Old-School Sounds.* Complex UK. Available at: https://www.complex.com/music/a/son-raw/the-evolution-of-grime-production.

Rewind 4Ever: The History of UK Garage. (2013). [Documentary]. Dir. by Alex Lawton. London: Visual Vybe Productions. Available at: https://vimeo.com/187881802.

Robinson, Kane (Kano) (2008). *'Hustler', 140 Grime Street* [CD]. London: Bigger Picture Music

Roland, M. (2014, June 30) . *The Early Days Of The Minimoog.* Electronic Sound. Available at: https://www.electronicsound.co.uk/features/time-machine/the-early-days-of-the-minimoog.

Rymajdo, K. (2020, December 8). *Prosecuting Rap: how a UK legal project is fighting the use of rap lyrics in court.* DJ Mag. https://djmag.com/longreads/prosecuting-rap-how-uk-legal-project-fighting-use-rap-lyrics-court

Sanchez, M. (2021, April 13). *Asbo bars pirate DJ from the rooftops.* The Standard. Available at: https://www.standard.co.uk/hp/front/asbo-bars-pirate-dj-from-the-roof-tops-7173468.html.

Salamone, L. (2020, December 2). *Prada's long red thread: Twenty years of sneaker culture told in a single release.* NSS Magazine. Available at: https://www.nssmag.com/en/fashion/24451/adidas-x-prada.

Second Home (2016, December 15). *A Psychogeographic Guide to Grime.* Available at: https://medium.com/workandlife/a-psychogeographic-guide-to-grime-4151f989ceed.

Simpson, D. (2019, January 29). *Oxide & Neutrino: how we made 'Bound 4 Da Reload' (Casualty).* The Guardian. Available at: https://www.theguardian.com/culture/2019/jan/29/oxide-neutrino-how-we-made-bound-4-da-reload-casualty.

Spencer, E; Constantine, E, Quick, J. (2022). *While You Were Sleeping: 1998 - 2000.* United Kingdom: Damiani.

Tales From The Grime Generation: Dexplicit Interviewed. (2014, April 10). Clash Music. Available at: https://www.clashmusic.com/features/tales-from-the-grime-generation-dexplicit-interviewed.

The Business Of Grime. (2016, July 26). [Documentary]. Dir. by Ewen Spencer. London: British GQ. Available at: https://www.youtube.com/watch?v=3_2AVogIb5c.

The Police vs Grime Music (2014). [Documentary]. Dir. by Alex Hoffman. London: Noisey. Available at: https://www.

youtube.com/watch?v=eW_iujPQpys.

The Fader. (2019). *Kano's lists his top five grime instrumentals.* [Online Video]. Available at: https://www.youtube.com/watch?v=mz88AgR7KH0

The Last Pirates: Britain's Rebel DJs (2017). [Documentary]. Dir. by Jaimie D'Cruz. BBC. Available at: https://www.bbc.co.uk/programmes/b096k6g1.

Tyler, I. (2013). *Revolting Subjects: Social Abjection and Resistance in Neoliberal Britain.* United Kingdom: Zed Books.

Wiley. (2017). *Eskiboy.* London: William Heinemann

Woods, O. (2018). *The digital subversion of urban space: power, performance and grime. Social & Cultural Geography, 21(3), 293–313. https://doi.org/10.1080/14649365.2018.1491617.*

ABOUT THE AUTHOR

Franklyn Addo is a writer, multidisciplinary artist, and youth advocate. His work leverages the therapeutic value of art, and sits at the intersection between creativity and community. He uses literature and music to engage with young people in local. neighbourhoods, schools and prisons. His writing has ranged from articles in platforms including *The Guardian* and *Independent* about Black British culture and policing, to a *Cambridge University Press* paper arguing against the criminalisation of rap. He has also co-authored a Manchester University report about racism in UK courts. *A Quick Ting On: Grime* is his first book.